LIVING BEYOND LOSS

Death in the Family

LIVING BEYOND LOSS

Death in the Family

Edited by

Froma Walsh
and
Monica McGoldrick

W. W. Norton & Company • *New York* • *London*

First published as a Norton paperback 1995

Printed in the United States of America.

Library of Congress Cataloging-in-Publication Data

Living beyond loss: death in the family / edited by Froma Walsh and
  Monica McGoldrick.
            p.   cm.
    Includes index.
    ISBN 0-393-70203-0
    1. Loss (Psychology)   2. Death—Psychological aspects.
3. Bereavement—Psychological aspects.   I. Walsh, Froma.
II. McGoldrick, Monica.
BF575.D35L54   1991   306.9—dc20   90-20668

W.W. Norton & Company, Inc., 500 Fifth Avenue, New York, N.Y. 10110
W.W. Norton & Company, Ltd., 10 Coptic Street, London WC1A 1PU

    5 6 7 8 9 0

To the memory of those who taught us most about death

From Monica

Joseph D. McGoldrick
Margaret R. Phiffer Bush
Mary Gertrude Cahalane
John Michael Zamborsky
Don McCook
Hughie McGoldrick

From Froma

Mary Jo Bourassa Weisberg
George L. Weisberg
George B. Walsh

and to a brilliant teacher who led the way

Murray Bowen
1913 — 1990

Foreword

Two years ago a friend of mine died rather abruptly. He passed away in Argentina and, in fact, I didn't even hear of his brief illness until after his death. He was, chronologically speaking, my oldest non-family friend: we were kindergarten buddies. The labyrinths of our respective life paths disconnected for three decades, but some twenty years ago we reestablished our intimacy. We would exchange occasional letters; however, since we lived 6000 miles apart, we would see each other just a couple of times a year, whenever our wandering lives would place us at reasonable reach. Each time it would take a few moments to rekindle the bond, to feel at home once again in the old, comfortable, trusting, warm friendship.

His death deprived me of many valued things: he was a repository of my identity ("Hi, Carlos!"), and of my history ("Do you remember when . . . ?"), and was a valuable source of emotional nourishment ("It's good to see you"), of personal social feedback ("When you did X, I felt . . . "), and of concern about my health ("You look tired. Are you taking good care of your health?"). The relationship was reciprocal, and so it provided me with the soothing experience of also being a repository of *his* identity and history and a resource for his emotional nourishment, feedback, and concern. It was a long-lasting friendship, with a rich fund of shared memories that could be awakened by one or the other of us; some reminiscences — perhaps a trivial scenario shared only by us — will remain dormant in me from his death on, as there is no one else to activate them. He was a friend of many of my friends, and his absence will be compounded by the unavoidable loss of connection with them through him, which was displayed each time we talked about friends, made social plans to see them, and the like. The pain of a loss highlights the blessing of what we had.

I dwell on this complex experience because, irreplaceable as this lost relationship may be, most of its attributes were not unique to it: no one else, to be sure, can share with me those memories of Herr Sultzberger, our terrifying music teacher from kindergarten; but I can list a number of intimate, long-lasting, rewarding friendships beyond this one, each unique, each cherished, each intrinsically and individually not essential for my survival. The storm stirred up by the death of my friend is paradigmatic of the effect of some of the many losses that we go through during our lives, and from which we generally emerge in one piece, although somewhat changed.

The vacuum — of identity, of history and continuity, of emotional nourishment, of social feedback, of concern over health, of validation, of responsibility — produced by a loss of one of those links that constitute our self-in-context is a universal experience. For some it is the loss of a relationship close to our heart — the death of our parent, of an old friend, of a faithful pet; for some it may be a physical attribute or a part of our body — a taut, youthful skin beginning to wrinkle or a limb lost in an accident; it can be the vanishing of a projection into our future — the sudden awareness that a dream will never be realized — or into our past — we discover that an idealized figure of our childhood was corrupt. Others are bereft of a treasured object or valued property — our first car has been stolen, a fire burned all our cherished photographs; or they see closely held values vanish — our country's army invades a foreign land, or Kennedy is assassinated. And so many of us live through a shift in context — we migrated, leaving behind icons, markers and friends. Losses are the shadow of all possessions, material or immaterial.

What is the process by which we become healed of this wrenching experience, by which this intolerable absence becomes tolerable, by which this existential emptiness is filled? And even if we rob these questions of all their drama, and we ponder the fate of a minor loss, the question is still puzzling. What is the role of introjects, and of other people — family, friends, acquaintances — in the process of grieving? And where does the healing take place? In the intimate territory of the private imaginary? In the consensually validated arena of the way things are told and reality is built? In the complex gallery of mirrors of the interpersonal world? And within that world, is the process in the intimate, intense, interactive fabric of our immediate family, or the broader tapestry of our social network?

It occurs in *all* those places or, more precisely, the experience proper is totally unique for each individual-in-context, and the conceptualization of the process is a function of the constructs of the describer/observer: models are the ideological nets that catch, organize, and provide meaning to whatever is out there. Experiences, however hot they may be when felt, are cooled by the mediating effect of language, which in turn is organized by explicit or implicit conceptual models.

The hot and the cool exalt each other in this book. While immersed in its pages, I found myself experiencing intense emotions evoked by the themes and characters that populate the chapters, and a rich aesthetic pleasure when visiting the multiple models through which processes are discussed by the editors, Froma Walsh and Monica McGoldrick, and the different authors. Sometimes I would gravitate toward a cozy armchair where, nestled in a quilt almost too heavy, and with Mahler providing a fitting background, I read parts of this book as a novel. At other times, I would discover myself sitting at my desk, furiously taking notes for future reference. There were chapters, I had no doubt about it, that had ME as the main character—at least that was my strong impression—while others alluded to one or another of my patients—probably puzzled by now about why so many tears lately, why so many rituals.

This book has been for me as much an adventure of self-discovery as an enriching, challenging professional experience. It has expanded my capacity to think and therefore to talk and therefore to observe and therefore to do and therefore to think about one of the universal themes of human experiences. I couldn't wish a better journey for the reader.

—Carlos E. Sluzki, M.D.
Chairman, Department of Psychiatry
Berkshire Medical Center
October, 1990

Contents

Some Personal Reflections on Loss

THIS PAST YEAR was the 20th anniversary of my mother's death. Her death, of course, did not end our relationship, and I have never stopped missing her. I wanted to find a meaningful way to commemorate her loss. Her gifts as a pianist and organist and the love of music we shared brought to mind the carillon bells of the Rockefeller Chapel on my campus at the University of Chicago. I arranged a simple concert of bells on the evening of the anniversary. My husband, John, my daughter, Claire, and I climbed to the top of the bell tower to the carillon organ and looked out over the city as the bells peeled harmoniously into the crisp night air.

I had not been at all prepared for my mother's protracted terminal illness that struck in my mid-twenties. Fitting Erikson's portrayal of normal young adulthood, I had successfully launched and was pursuing my own career development and on the brink of commitment to marriage. Like many of my peers, I was in an intensive program of graduate studies 2,000 miles from my parents' home. Only later did my training in human development provide a helpful normative perspective on the inherently incompatible life cycle imperatives (which I have described in my chapter on later life in Carter and McGoldrick's *The Changing Family Life Cycle*). At the time, my conflict was heightened by my awareness—and my mother's comment—that I was busy as a professional helping families in my clinical setting while I was not there for my own family in their time of need, a conflict intensified by my position as an only child. Before and after my mother's death, I was praised by my mental health colleagues and supervisors for my "strength," "resiliency," and high functioning in not missing a beat in full training demands. My new in-laws, unable to attend the funeral and wishing to spare us all a painful interaction, never mentioned my mother's death on our next visit (or thereafter). Our culture's denial of the impact of loss, coupled with the myth that young adults are detached from parents, contributed to minimization of the importance of my connection and loss. Unattended issues went underground, surfacing in my other relationships, until I pursued my own valuable family-of-origin work, in part facilitated by Jeanette Kramer and by many conversations with Monica about our families. I learned from this experience to counsel my own students and others to take time out from their fast-paced lives and overflowing commitments for what may be their last opportunity to spend time with the dying or, following a death, to make time and space for mutual family support and attention to their own loss issues.

My experience with my mother's death taught me to do it differently with my father. With the added impetus of the film *I Never Sang for My Father*, shown at a Georgetown Family Institute Symposium, I stopped postponing efforts I always intended to make to improve our relationship and to know him better. Valuable coaching by Murray Bowen and a cross-country drive with Monica paved the way. My relationship with him had deepened profoundly when, several years later, he was diagnosed with cancer and given only a few months to live. I was no less committed elsewhere, then 1,000 miles away, with a new deanship, marriage, and a ten-month-old baby. Ironically, I faced the very situation of concurrent grandparent death and birth of a child that both Monica and I had investigated in clinical research projects. We had noted that inherent stress of conflicting life cycle tasks: caring for a dying parent and attending to bereavement juxtaposed with parenting demands and attachment to a child born around that time. In contrast to well-functioning families who experienced the concurrent loss and birth, the more dysfunctional families had failed to mourn. When I was suddenly caught in the same dilemma, my research reinforced my sense of the crucial importance of attending to loss issues while balancing both sets of demands. I put work aside and mobilized resources at home to be with my father, arrange hospitalizations, clear out his apartment and belongings, settle him into a partial-care residence, and handle funeral arrangements— an exhausting set of challenges as an only child with no nearby relatives. Assurance that my child was well cared for in my absence and preoccupation eased the inherent difficulties. While I grieved my father's loss, I was at peace with our relationship and grateful for those long days sitting quietly with him at his bedside.

I was saddened, and even angry for a time, that my father's brother was not there for my father in his dying, or for my support. But I came to realize that the sudden heart palpitations that made him cancel his travel plans (and subsided shortly after the funeral) must have expressed the ache in his heart at the impending loss of his only surviving brother, the third brother having been shot and killed, a few years earlier, in an inner-city robbery of the business they had operated together. Even more unbearable had been the recent illness and death of his young daughter-in-law, with a devastating impact on his son (a Vietnam veteran) and three small grandchildren, whom he loved dearly. We have moved beyond that time to a renewed closeness.

My daughter, Claire, first learned about death and loss in the marvelous story *Charlotte's Web*, on a videotape she received for her fourth birthday from Monica, who is her godmother. The story, which we watched many, many times, sparked wonderful conversations about the special relationship between the spider and the pig, the normality of death in the life cycle, the sadness of loss, and the importance of carrying on memories and forming new attachments.

I have also learned immeasurably from the times that I myself have had a close brush with death, forcing me to confront the terror of my own mortality and jolting me with a greater (and, at times, uncomfortable) clarity of vision. Those experiences, along with the loss of loved ones, have made me realize how precious time is, sharpened my sense of priorities, lowered my tolerance for bullshit, and catalyzed shifts in my life course, to affirm deeper values and human connectedness.

—Froma Walsh

Although we were Irish, my family grew up trying to become WASP, and perhaps for that reason, seemed to have a "no mess, no fuss," avoidant attitude toward death. When I was in high school my favorite teacher died of melanoma. His family and mine were close personal friends, but we had moved away shortly before, and so we did not attend the funeral. I had no chance to put the experience together—with his family, his friends, and my friends. In 1961, just after I returned from my first year in college, my nanny died, shortly after having a stroke. I had not been told that she was dying and did not get to see her before her death. She had raised me from birth, braided my hair every day, knew the secrets of my childhood, taught me everything she knew for 17 years, but I was protected from seeing her before she died. At the funeral, she was eulogized by a funeral director who had never met her, and we did not attend the burial. For months I kept imagining I saw her on the street. I did not visit her grave until 27 years later, when I asked her niece to take me and learned for the first time her middle name.

In April of 1964 my college boyfriend was killed in a car accident. His best friend and I, who were both devastated by the experience, decided not to go to the funeral—it was far away, we did not know the family, and no one encouraged us to go. It took me two years to get to his home town of Allentown, Pennsylvania, to go to the grave. My fantasy was that I would find a small country cemetery and wander through the stones until I found his. No such luck, as I realized when I got there and saw the thick phone book with numerous churches listed. I called his mother, who acted as if she had been waiting for me the whole time and who knew exactly what I needed. She met me immediately, drove me past the scene of the accident and to the cemetery. She told me the story of the death and then gave me time alone at the grave before taking me to her home, where I met other family members. She even apologized afterwards for not having prepared me for the shock of meeting my dead boyfriend's brother, who looked so like him. The experience put something together that had been an obsession for two years. I realized what a critical difference it makes to be able to mourn and share the mourning.

When my grandmother died in 1966 I was not informed that she had died for two weeks, so I did not attend her funeral, though I lived nearby. In March 1971 my favorite Aunt Mamie died of old age in a nursing home on Staten Island. She had been our Santa Claus from my earliest childhood, coming to visit loaded down with shopping bags of books and goodies. She, more than anyone, was the family storyteller of who had come before us. She told us of her brothers Din, and Tim, and Tom, and Dan, and Jack, and most of all of my grandfather Neil. And she told us of our many cousins, whom she also loved as her children, and what they were doing. She also spoke often of her own death, saying always, "Make sure they carry me out from Casey's, and make sure I have my glasses on. I want to see who's there." I was the first to arrive at Casey's funeral home for her wake. She did not have her glasses on, and I asked the funeral director to get them, which he did. She knew how important it was for people to come—to share and be part of the mourning. It was an essential request to honor.

My family seems to have changed a good deal since the early years in dealing with death. When my father died in 1978, I shared the death with my mother. I was alone with him for hours before he died, and at the moment he died I felt reassured that the window was open, "just in case," to let the spirit out, according to the old Irish superstition. My mother, sisters, and family friends were all involved in planning a memorial service that reflected who he was for all of us.

The ideas in this book have been developing in me for thirty years from these formative experiences.

—Monica McGoldrick

Introduction

THE SUBJECT OF death is the last taboo in the field of family therapy. Our theory, research, and practice have confronted such daunting problems as schizophrenia, substance abuse, family violence, and incest, and yet we have scarcely approached the topic of loss. Of all life experiences, death poses the most painful adaptational challenges for the family as a system and for every surviving member, with reverberations for all other relationships. Our society's denial of death compounds the difficulty. American society deals poorly with death, denying its impact, removing the dying from their homes and communities, and failing to provide cultural supports to assist families in the process of adaptation to loss. At the same time, medical advances increasingly pose families with unprecedented life and death decisions. Yet the field of family therapy, like the field of mental health and the larger society in which both are embedded, has given scant attention to loss.

Curiously, until this volume, there has not been a single book on the family impact of death in the entire family therapy literature or, even more broadly, in the field of mental health.* The few systems-oriented articles that contribute to our understanding of loss are scattered in journals and multi-topic texts, unseen and unintegrated by most family therapy trainees and practitioners. In mental health and social science disciplines, attention

---

*As this book went to press, Elliott Rosen's excellent text on families facing terminal illness, *Families Facing Death: Family Dynamics of Terminal Illness*, was published.

to death and mourning has lacked a systemic perspective, with the family seen as a backdrop in supporting or impeding individual recovery from loss. Because of this narrow focus on the bereaved individual and his or her direct relationship with the family member who died, the *family impact* of loss has gone unexamined, including the immediate and long-term effects on parents, children, siblings, extended family, and others who may not even have known the deceased but are touched by their relationships with survivors.

Moreover, theory and practice have been grounded in untested assumptions and myths about "normal" vs. "abnormal" bereavement. These have pathologized experiences not fitting the standard deemed "normal." Recognition is needed of the importance of family processes in mediating the impact of loss, promoting mastery and growth, or contributing to dysfunction. This understanding requires appreciation of the diversity in individual, family, and cultural responses to loss.

Furthermore, developmental theory and research have focused predominantly on the consequences of parent loss in childhood (primarily mother loss, with father loss tending to be ignored). Losses of a parent or sibling in a young adult life are particularly unexplored. We need to examine the differential impact of loss at various stages in the family life cycle, for members in various roles and relationships, and for the family as a functional unit.

While family systems theory introduced a new paradigm for understanding the network of relationships in families, in the development of the family therapy field the systemic impact of loss has remained largely unexplored. With the ascendancy of structural and strategic models of family therapy, attention has focused on "here and now" transactional processes and "co-constructions of reality." The inescapable fact of death, relationships with dying or deceased members, and reverberations throughout the system have often remained outside the frame of inquiry and observation. Jay Haley once put it succinctly: "I don't believe in ghosts." Even when the importance of a particular death has been noted, our theory has lacked a framework for understanding the devastating impact certain losses can have on family processes and has made little sense of the ongoing problems that may follow from a family's inability to mourn its losses.

Only a few family therapy pioneers have addressed the family impact of loss. Twenty-five years ago Norman Paul first described the effects of unresolved mourning on other relationships, especially on marital dysfunction. Murray Bowen, around the same time, called attention to the disruptive impact of death or threatened loss on a family's functional equilibrium, describing the emotional shockwave that reverberates through an entire family system long after the loss of an important member.

Our own interest in the subject of loss and the development of this book parallel the growth of our relationship as treasured friends and colleagues over more than 20 years. In the early 1970s, involved in separate family research projects in different parts of the country, we shared our insights and hypotheses concerning intergenerational patterns of unresolved mourning we observed in work with families of schizophrenic patients, those with other serous disturbances, and families of normal offspring. Over the years, influenced by the seminal ideas on loss of Bowen and Paul, and by the work of many contributors to this volume, we have continued to discuss our research and clinical cases and to advance our own systemic formulations and interventions with loss.

Recently, a number of interesting developments in theory, research, and clinical practice dealing with loss in families have been occurring, but with little contact among innovators. To bring these leaders of our field together for a fruitful exchange, we, along with Norman Paul, organized an International Colloquium on Loss and the Family in July 1988 at Ballymaloe in Ireland. It was an exceptionally stimulating gathering. In the midst of many expert presentations, we (Monica and Froma) decided to bring our dialogue to a more personal level. Instead of presenting our own papers, we decided to use our time block to explore our own mortality. We asked participants in small groups to address the following: Explore your fantasies and fears about your own death. Consider the following questions: how long do you expect to live? how do you imagine your death? what sort of funeral rites would you want at your death? what legacies would you leave? The experience was extraordinarily meaningful. In confronting universal issues of mortality and loss, the hierarchy and boundaries commonly constructed between "expert" and client/patient/family were erased. Moreover, we were all struck by the power of legacies of loss in our own families and cultural surround, and by the saliency of different issues depending on our stages in the family life cycle.

The International Loss Conference galvanized our long shared interest in developing a book on loss from a family systems perspective. Like the conference, the idea for this book was generated by an impetus to gather together the best work in the area of loss and families, including classic articles by Paul and Bowen published long ago, and new papers presenting the cutting edge of theory development, research, and clinical practice. Although almost all of the authors of this volume did present their work at the International Conference in Ireland, this book is not a collection of conference papers or proceedings, which would have made a weighty tome. We have tried to select the most important systemic ideas and research efforts relevant to clinical practice.

This volume is the first to examine the impact of loss on the entire family system and to consider both normative and dysfunctional processes in relation to each family's life cycle passage and cultural context. While much has been written about loss from an individual or dyadic focus, the papers in this volume examine loss as a multifaceted family phenomenon—rippling

out into the extended reaches of a family and down into the next generations.

The chapters in this book, while addressing different aspects of loss, share
a systems perspective, with a number of basic premises. The family approaches and reacts to loss as a relationship system, with all members partic-
ipating in mutually reinforcing interactions. Loss has implications for how
the family adapts to later experiences and for individuals not directly related
to the member who has died. Patterns set in motion around the death of a
family member have both immediate impact and long-term ramifications in
family development over the course of the life cycle and across many generations.

Our concern with the family impact of loss reflects a multigenerational,
developmental perspective. Rather than regarding events surrounding a family death as pathological causes of disorder, we view them as normative
transitions in the family life cycle that carry the potential for growth and
development, as well as for immediate distress or long-term dysfunction. We
realize that the family response to loss is as critical in adaptation as the
death. Families influence how the event is experienced and the long-term
legacies of loss. By attending to family processes, clinicians can promote
healthy adaptation to loss and strengthen the family unit in meeting other
life challenges. Sharing a multigenerational perspective on loss, we are careful to attend to the legacies of past losses in the family system in all clinical
assessment and intervention. Equally important, our consideration of loss
takes into account the cultural diversity in mourning processes.

The authors in this volume bring special areas of expertise and a variety of
intervention approaches to address a number of issues relevant to practitioners, such as adolescent suicide, intergenerational legacies, and death in the
therapist's own family. Loss of a child, a parent, a spouse, and a sibling are
explored. Useful clinical guidelines and techniques are offered for assessment and intervention with families anticipating loss, for those recently
bereaved, and for family members experiencing long-term complications.

In Chapters 1 and 2, Froma Walsh and Monica McGoldrick present a
systemic orientation and a family life cycle perspective on loss. In Chapter 3,
Monica McGoldrick elaborates clinical assessment and intervention guidelines that flow from this framework in her work with loss. Chapters 4 and 5
present the groundbreaking ideas of Murray Bowen and Norman Paul in
their now classic early articles. In the following paper, Monica McGoldrick
offers a fascinating account of the multigenerational legacies of loss in
several prominent families. Next, John Byng-Hall, whose longstanding
work on intergenerational transmission processes has been of great interest
to us both, provides a rich example of his clinical work on family scripts and
loss. Also influenced by the concept of scripts in his work on family belief
systems, John Rolland contributes a paper on the neglected topic of antici-

patory loss, based on his family systems developmental model with chronic and lifethreatening illness. Closely related is the situation of ambiguous loss, described in the next article by Pauline Boss, whose landmark research has delineated the detrimental effects of ambiguity surrounding loss on family functioning and mastery of loss experiences.

The important subject of cultural diversity in mourning requires many perspectives. Monica and her colleagues, Nydia Garcia-Preto, Paulette Moore Hines, Evelyn Lee, Rhea Almeida, and Elliott Rosen summarize their work on cultural differences in beliefs about loss and mourning practices. Following this, Evan Imber-Black applies her fruitful ideas on the importance of rituals in marking family transitions to the specific problems of loss. Next, David Epston, a close collaborator with Michael White, stimulates us with his innovative interventions with loss from their shared perspective of recreating family narratives.

Steven Gutstein offers a creative and effective family network approach with adolescent suicide, a subject that he has been working on for many years. The chapter by Sandra Coleman presents an overview of her important research, with various colleagues over many years, investigating intergenerational traumatic loss patterns in families of substance abusers and their link to the self-destructive behavior in addiction. Finally, we've saved for last a marvelous paper by Betty Carter, delivered at a Georgetown Symposium many years ago, on her own efforts to deal with family of origin issues around the impending death of her father.

This book is intended to provide a useful text for professionals working with family members dealing with threatened loss, the immediate aftermath of a death, and the long-term effects of past loss. The systemic perspective and family interventions with loss should prove valuable in the training and practice of a range of professionals, including (1) family therapists, social workers, psychologists, and psychiatrists; (2) family practitioners, nurses and other health care providers in hospitals, hospices and outpatient health care facilities; (3) clergy, pastoral counselors, and funeral personnel. It will also appropriately serve as a basic text for college and graduate courses addressing death and dying and the impact of loss.

There are signs that our society and our field are beginning to confront crucial family issues concerning death and loss. This volume is not only timely; examination of these issues is long overdue. The fear of death is our deepest terror and the loss of a loved one our most profound sorrow. We must challenge the taboo that has silenced the field of family therapy and other professionals on the subject of death, obscuring our recognition of loss issues and blocking our communication with families and our ability to help them. We hope that this book will serve to break this last taboo.

— Monica McGoldrick and Froma Walsh

Acknowledgments

MANY PEOPLE DESERVE thanks for their input, direct and indirect, into this book: Peter Sterling Mueller, a generous, if not always easy mentor and colleague for many years, whose profound understanding of the impact of death on families deeply influenced my own work; Norman Paul, whose courageous willingness to face loss with families and whose original thinking and generosity as a teacher were extremely helpful to me over many years; Murray Bowen, whose brilliant ideas will light the way long into our future, and whose personal generosity with his time and thoughts whenever I have sought him out over the past 17 years is deeply appreciated. He has influenced my work immeasurably. His death, just as this book was going to press, pains me. I hope my efforts in this book reflect well the debt I owe to him (though he would undoubtedly never have wanted the acknowledgment.)

I thank my mother, Helen McGoldrick, my sisters, Neale and Morna, my aunt, Mildred McGoldrick Cook, along with my friends, Betty Carter, Joyce Richardson, Carol Anderson, Meyer Rothberg, Michael Rohrbaugh, Rich Simon, Imelda McCarthy, Nollaig Byrne, Sandy Leiblum, Jane Sufian, Charlotte Fremon Danielson, Nydia Preto, Paulette Hines, and Evan Imber-Black, for their support in so many ways over so many years, and specifically for helping me understand the meaning of life and the meaning of death. I thank also Jeannine Stone and Gary Lamson of the UMDNJ-CMHC at Piscataway; Henry Murphree, M.D., Chairman of the Department of Psychiatry, Robert Wood Johnson Medical School—UMDNJ; and Mary Scanlon, Library Director of UMDNJ—RWJ Library of the Health Sciences for their generous help. My sister Neale was not only an enormous emotional support, but an untiring help with the technical aspects of this book—genograms and computer.

I thank also my husband, Sophocles, and my son, John, for the hours this book took away from them. Vicki Zarra and the staff at Yellow Brick Road have provided my son two loving and enriching homes away from home, which have been a great source of reassurance for me in my work, while Cherie Allen, Aimee Copp, and Halia Yevtushenko provided support at home.

— *Monica McGoldrick*

It is difficult to single out but a few of the many colleagues, friends, and family members who have contributed in so many ways to my thinking about death and loss and to the development of this book. I would especially like to thank several University of Chicago colleagues. Margaret Waller, my teaching assistant, offered insightful feedback, and Young Chang, my research assistant, gave very capable editorial assistance. I owe much to Bertram Cohler, long a mentor, colleague, and friend, who recently lost his wife, Ann. Jeanne Marsh, Dean of the School of Social Service Administration, and Bennett Leventhal, Chief of Child and Adolescent Psychiatry, have enthusiastically supported the creation of a Center for Family Health, which John Rolland and I co-direct, for research and clinical training to address family life challenges. John, my husband as well as my colleague, has greatly enriched my perspective on loss through our many discussions, sharing his own work and reflections on his critical life experiences.

I will never forget those friends who have been there for me in my times of loss and life-threatening situations. Elza Bergeron Gross, my former Peace Corps roommate, stood by my side through the illnesses and funerals of both my parents. George Walsh put his work aside to care for me after a near-fatal auto accident, reading to me the entire Tolkien trilogy. Mary Zaglifa, generously sharing her own experience, taught me more than any physician about recovery from meningitis and gave me courage and humor through hard times. Carol Anderson, Celia Falicov, Michele Scheinkman, Janet Murphy, Karen Countryman, and Katherine Goldberg have always been there for me, as I hope I will be for them.

— *Froma Walsh*

This book reflects for both of us our shared interest and collaboration over more than two decades. We have each been enriched by our extraordinary friendship, which continues to grow and deepen with our life cycle passage. Together, we want to thank Susan Barrows for her support and efficiency in every aspect of the production of this book. She has been superb to work with. Finally, we want to express our appreciation to the clinical families, colleagues, friends, and our own families whose life experiences we have drawn from in our case illustrations of family adaptation to loss.

—Froma Walsh and Monica McGoldrick

Contributors

Rhea Almeida, M.S.W.
Director
Institute for Family Services
Somerset, New Jersey and
Adjunct Instructor
Rutgers Graduate School of
    Social Work
New Brunswick, New Jersey

Pauline Boss, Ph.D.
Professor
Family Social Science
University of Minnesota
St. Paul, Minnesota

Murray Bowen, M.D.
Clinical Professor
Georgetown University Medical
    Center and
Director
Georgetown University Family
    Center

John Byng-Hall, F.R.C. Psych.
Tavistock Clinic
London, England

Betty Carter, M.S.W.
Director
Family Institute of Westchester
Mount Vernon, New York

Sandra B. Coleman, Ph.D.
Director, Behavioral Medicine
Family Practice Residency
    Program
Eastern Maine Medical Center
Bangor, Maine

David Epston
Co-Director
Family Therapy Centre
Auckland, New Zealand

George H. Grosser, Ph.D.
Former Instructor
Department of Psychiatry
Harvard Medical School
Cambridge, Massachusetts

Steven E. Gutstein, Ph.D.
Private Practice
Houston, Texas

Paulette Moore Hines, Ph.D.
Director, Prevention Services
University of Medicine & Dentistry of
    New Jersey
University of Mental Health Services
Piscataway, New Jersey
Faculty
Family Institute of New Jersey
Metuchen, New Jersey

Evan Imber-Black, Ph.D.
Director, Family & Group Studies and
Professor, Department of Psychiatry
Albert Einstein College of Medicine
Bronx, New York

Evelyn Lee, Ed.D.
Associate Clinical Professor
Department of Psychiatry
University of California
San Francisco, California

Monica McGoldrick, A.C.S.W., Ph.D.
Director
Family Institute of New Jersey
Metuchen, New Jersey
Associate Professor of Clinical
    Psychiatry
Robert Wood Johnson Medical School
New Brunswick, New Jersey

Norman Paul, M.D.
Lecturer
Department of Psychiatry
Harvard Medical School
Cambridge, Massachusetts

Nydia Garcia-Preto, A.C.S.W.
Clinical Director
Faculty
Family Institute of New Jersey
Metuchen, New Jersey

John S. Rolland, M.D.
Associate Professor of Clinical
    Psychiatry
Pritzker School of Medicine and
Co-Director
Center for Family Health
University of Chicago
Chicago, Illinois

Elliott Rosen, Ed.D.
Faculty
Family Institute of Westchester
Mount Vernon, New York and
Consulting Psychologist
Jansen Memorial Hospice
Tuckahoe, New York

Froma Walsh, Ph.D.
Professor
School of Social Service
    Administration &
Department of Psychiatry and
Co-Director
Center for Family Health
University of Chicago
Chicago, Illinois

LIVING
BEYOND
LOSS

Death in the Family

1

Loss and the Family:
A Systemic Perspective

FROMA WALSH   MONICA MCGOLDRICK

THROUGHOUT HISTORY AND in every culture, mourning rituals have facilitated not only the integration of death but also the transformations of survivors. Each culture, in its on ways, offers assistance to the community of survivors in moving forward with life. In Hong Kong, mourners leaving a Chinese funeral are each given an envelope containing three items: a white wash-cloth, intended to wipe away the tears; candy, to remind the bereaved of the sweetness of life and to be shared with other survivors; and a coin, as a symbolic token of the ancient custom of reimbursing mourners for travel to the funeral so that they wouldn't suffer further loss.

From a family systems perspective, loss can be viewed as a transactional process involving the deceased and the survivors in a shared life cycle that acknowledges both the finality of death and the continuity of life. Coming to terms with this process is the most difficult task a family must confront in life. This chapter will present a systemic view of loss, considering the impact of the death of a family member on the family as a functional unit, with immediate and long-term reverberations for every member and all other relationships. While recognizing the diversity in individual, family, and cul-tural responses to loss (see McGoldrick, Almeida, Hines, Preto, Rosen, & Lee, Chapter 10), we regard family processes as crucial determinants of the healthy or dysfunctional adaptation to loss. We will identify major family tasks that, in our clinical experience, promote the process of coming to terms with loss and moving forward with life. We will examine crucial variables that can either facilitate adaptation or complicate the process and contribute to immediate or long-term dysfunction. Such factors concern the manner of death, the family and social network, the timing of loss in the family life cycle, and the sociocultural context of loss.

In Western societies before the present century, people died at home and even children were not protected from the sights or smells of death. As is still prevalent in poor communities throughout the world, families had to cope with the precariousness of life, with death striking young and old alike. With high rates of mortality for infants, children, and women in childbirth, along with the much shorter life span (averaging 47 years in 1900 in the U.S.), it was rare to grow up without experiencing a death in the immediate family. Parental death often disrupted nuclear families and shifted them into other forms, producing complex networks of full, half, and step relationships, and vast extended kinship systems (Scott & Wishy, 1982).

Thus, the nostalgic American image of the traditional normal family as intact is a myth (Walsh, 1983a); our denial of death contributes to the maintenance of that myth. In our times we have come to hide death, making the process of adapting to loss all the more difficult. In contrast to traditional cultures, our society lacks cultural supports to assist families in integrating the fact of death with ongoing life (Aries, 1974, 1982; Becker, 1973; Mitford, 1978). Geographical distances separate family members at times of death and dying. Medical practice and technology have complicated the process by removing death from everyday reality, while at the same time confronting families with unprecedented decisions to prolong or terminate life. Most recently, families have begun to organize in efforts to reclaim the dying process.

Death, of course, is not the only loss. Marital separation or divorce, displacement from a job or a home, diminished functioning in chronic illness, or having a disabled child also involve losses, including loss of our dreams and expectations. All change in life, including desired change such as marriage or retirement, requires loss. We must give up or alter certain relationships, roles, plans, and possibilities in order to have others. And all losses require mourning, which acknowledges the giving up and transforms the experience, so that we can take into ourselves what is essential and move on.

In whatever different forms and circumstances, mourning must be experienced. Recent investigations by Wortman and Silver (1989) and their analysis of a wide body of research confirm that mourning responses vary widely. At the same time, epidemiologic studies have found that the death of a family member increases vulnerability to premature illness and death for surviving family members (Osterweis, Solomon, & Green, 1984), especially for a widowed spouse and for parents who have recently lost a child (Huygen, van den Hoogen, van Eijk, & Smits, 1989). Furthermore, family developmental crises have been linked to the appearance of symptoms in a family member (Hadley, Jacob, Miliones, Caplan, & Spitz, 1974). In view of the profound connections among members of a family, it is not surprising that adjustment to loss by death is considered more difficult than any other life change (Holmes & Rahe, 1967).

Yet in our review of the vast clinical and research literature on loss, we were astonished by the neglect of a family focus. There have been important contributions to our understanding of the dying process (Kübler-Ross, 1969; Worden, 1982) and efforts to distinguish "normal" from pathological bereavement in individual survivors, from Freud's (1917) treatise on mourning and melancholia, to groundbreaking studies by Becker (1973), Bowlby (1961, 1980), Engel (1961, 1975), Glick, Weiss, and Parkes (1974), Lindemann (1944), Parkes (1972, 1975), and Pollock (1961). However, particularly in the contributions from a psychoanalytic perspective, consideration of the family has been restricted narrowly to the dyadic relationship between a symptomatic individual and the deceased relative (e.g., Pinkus, 1974; Schiff, 1977; Viorst, 1986). At most, note is taken of the reactions of others, supportive or not, to this bereaved person's experience (e.g., Wortman & Silver, 1989). Asymptomatic family members are presumed to be adjusting normally without assessment of their part in the interactional system. Moreover, developmental theory and research, focused predominantly on the effects of parent loss in childhood for individual development (e.g., Furman, 1974), have neglected the impact of loss at different stages in the family life cycle, for various members and for the family as a functional unit (see McGoldrick & Walsh, Chapter 2).

By and large, the mental health field has failed to appreciate the impact of loss on the family as an interactional system. An individual coping response that may be functional—or dysfunctional—for that person has consequences for other family members and relationships that can only be appreciated through an examination of the system. Insufficient attention has been given to the immediate and long-term effects for siblings, parents, children, and extended family. Legacies of loss find expression in continuing patterns of interaction and mutual influence among the survivors and across the generations (see McGoldrick, Chapter 6). The pain of death touches all survivors' relationships with others, some of whom may never have even known the person who died.

A SYSTEMS PERSPECTIVE ON LOSS

It is remarkable that in all the literature in the field of family therapy, there is not a single book on loss. While family systems theory introduced a new paradigm for understanding family relationships, the particular significance of loss has been addressed by only a few systems theorists, most notably Murray Bowen and Norman Paul. In his classic 1976 paper (Chapter 4 in this volume), Bowen boldly stated his position on the role of death in families, a subject he had then been thinking about for 30 years:

> Direct thinking about death, or indirect thinking about staying alive and avoiding death, occupies more of man's time than any other subject. . . . Chief among all taboo subjects is death. A high percentage of people die alone, locked into their own thoughts, which they cannot communicate to others. There are at least two processes in operation. One is the intrapsychic process in self which always involves some denial of death. The other is the closed relationship system: People cannot communicate the thoughts they do have, lest they upset the family or others.

Bowen described the disruptive impact of death or threatened loss on a family's functional equilibrium, viewing the intensity of the emotional reaction as governed by the level of emotional integration in the family at the time of the loss and by the functional importance of the member lost. A well integrated family may show more overt reaction at the moment but adapt quickly, in contrast to a less integrated family, which may show little immediate reaction but respond later with physical or emotional problems. Bowen described the emotional shock wave that may reverberate throughout an entire family system long after the loss of an important family member:

> [A] network of underground "aftershocks" . . . can occur anywhere in the extended family system in the months or years following serious emotional events in a family. It occurs most often after the death or threatened death of a significant family member, but it can occur following losses of other types. It is not directly related to the usual grief or mourning reactions of people close to the one who died. It operates on an underground network of emotional dependence of family members on each other. The emotional dependence is denied, the serious events appear to be unrelated, the family attempts to camouflage any connectedness between the events, and there is a vigorous emotional denial reaction, when anyone attempts to relate the events to each other.

Bowen maintained that knowledge of the shock wave provides vital information for therapy, without which the sequence of events may be treated as unrelated. Accordingly, he considered it essential to assess the total family configuration, the functioning position in the family of the dying or deceased member, and the family's overall level of life adaptation, in order to help family members before or after a death.

Norman Paul has been the other family therapy pioneer to recognize the profound impact of loss in families (Paul, 1967, 1980; Paul & Grosser, 1965;

see Chapter 5). Paul has found that however intense the aversion to death and grief, their force will be expressed nonetheless. Grief at the loss of a parent, sibling, or other important family member, when unrecognized and unattended, may precipitate rejection of a spouse or child. This may occur shortly after the loss or much later, as when a child reaches the same age as that of the parent at bereavement. In some cases, grief trauma may block intimacy or intrude into sexual behavior, in the form of sexual withdrawal or dysfunction, extramarital affairs, or even incestuous involvement (Paul & Paul, 1982, 1989). He views the therapeutic task as bringing the aborted grief out into the open so that it can be dealt with as part of a family's normal life experience. With Betty Paul, his insightful collaborator, Norman Paul has devoted his clinical career to developing ways to confront unrecognized mourning and deal with its effects on subsequent relationships. He has been most innovative in audiotape and videotape confrontations and replay, and in split-screen imaging of a client with a photo of a deceased parent. In cross-confrontation, stressor tapes of other families' emotionally charged therapy experiences with delayed grief provide sanctions for families to consider and share their own inaccessible or unacceptable feelings of loss. Other stressor stimuli, such as poems, letters, film clips, or literature, may be used to bring painful feelings to the surface (Paul, 1976; Paul & Paul, 1982, 1989). Both Bowen and Paul, in different therapeutic approaches, have emphasized the importance of coming to terms with loss and changing relationship patterns associated with it.

Despite these groundbreaking advances, there have been few contributions to the family literature with a systemic view of loss. Herz (1980, 1989) expanded on Bowen's ideas, discussing key factors in family adaptation. We ourselves have articulated a systemic perspective on history and loss (McGoldrick & Walsh, 1983), as well as the normative patterns and complications of death at different life cycle phases (Walsh & McGoldrick, 1987; see Chapter 2). However, only a few researchers have brought a systemic perspective to the study of death and loss, notably Coleman and Stanton on unresolved mourning in families of addicts (Coleman & Stanton, 1978; Stanton, 1977; see Coleman, Chapter 14). Only a handful of clinical papers in family journals have addressed the systemic ramifications of loss, notably articles by Welldon (1971), Howe and Robinson (1975), Williamson (1978), Reilly (1978), Hare-Mustin (1979), and Kuhn (1981). A useful book for families facing impending loss has just been published by Rosen (1990).

In our view, family therapy's inattention to loss goes hand in hand with our culture's denial of death (Becker, 1973; McGoldrick & Walsh, 1983). Both are problematic for families in dealing with loss. Because our society treats grief as a private matter, clinicians, like others outside a family, tend to avoid inquiry about the impact of loss, reinforcing the "invisible commu-

nity of the bereaved" (Rosaldo, 1989). Paul has commented on the reluctance of therapists, as well as clients, to confront the topic of death:

> Of all the different topics considered representative of normal family processes,
> the one experienced as least normal and most abnormal is the mourning process.
> The problem here is that it is generally regarded as normal in the literature, only
> to be resisted consciously and unconsciously with great force when it actually
> occurs in oneself. The main paradox is that while there exists a constant shadow
> of death in everybody's life, everybody is entertaining notions of his or her own
> immortality. (Paul & Paul, 1982, p. 229)

Paul cautions that a clinician's aversion to death and grief may hamper the
ability to diagnose and treat a family systemic problem correctly as grief-
related, resulting in unhelpful focusing on secondary symptoms.

The neglect of loss in family therapy was furthered by the split that
occurred in the development of the field regarding the relative importance of
the individual vs. the family system, of "content" vs. "process," and of
history vs. the here-and-now, for the understanding and treatment of family
dysfunction (Madanes & Haley, 1977). With the paradigmatic shift to a
systems orientation, focus on the individual, on content issues, and on past
influences was regarded by many as unsystemic, associated with more reduc-
tionistic traditional models of psychotherapy (Fisch, Weakland, & Segel,
1982). As structural and strategic family therapists shifted focus to family
organizational patterns and communication processes that could be observed in current interaction, loss issues were deemed insignificant in understanding problem maintenance and irrelevant to system change. Loss was
dismissed as "merely" a content issue, involving intrapersonal feelings and
reactions to events, particularly in the past; accordingly, it was relegated to
the domain of psychoanalysis. More recently, constructivist theorists further
devalued the significance of life events (presumably including death) by
arguing that reality can never be known, that all experience is subjectively
co-constructed, and, therefore, that any attempt to "discover" factual occurrences is misguided and irrelevant to changing current views (see Hoffman,
1990).

Unfortunately, such false polarizations have prevented many from appre-
ciating the critical importance of loss for families and family therapy. When
clinical assessment and intervention are limited to ongoing transactional
patterns among members present in an interview or currently sharing a
household, relationships that have been lost (past) or threatened losses (future) remain out of view, though they may bear directly on the family's
current distress. Loss is not simply a discrete event; rather, it involves a
transactional process over time, with the approach of death and in its after-

math. Individual distress following loss is not only due to grief, but is also a consequence of changes in the realignment of the family emotional field (Kuhn, 1981). Loss modifies family structure, generally requiring reorganization of the entire family system. Perhaps most important, the meaning of a particular death and individual responses to it are shaped by the family belief system, which in turn is modified by all loss experiences (Reiss & Oliveri, 1980). If we are to appreciate the diversity and complexity of loss processes, we need to attend to the interplay of individuals in their family and social context; to process *and* content; to history as well as the here-and-now; and to the factual circumstances of a death as well as its meaning for a particular family.

In order to help families with loss, family therapists must reappraise family history, replacing deterministic assumptions of causality with an evolutionary perspective. Like the social context, the temporal context provides a matrix of meanings in which all behavior is embedded. Although a family cannot change its past, changes in the present and future occur in relation to that past. Systemic change involves a transformation of that relationship. Indeed, as Hoffman (1981) has commented,

> A problem may remain frozen until patterns connected with the original laying down of the problem are changed. . . . Bowen's use of history suggests strongly that it is not the revisiting of the past, but the redoing of the present, that counts. (p. 249)

We propose that families need to be in balance or harmony with their past, not in a struggle to recapture it, escape from it, or forget it. We view therapy as helping families regain a sense of continuity and motion from the past toward the future. They may do this by changing the beliefs embedded in their views of the past that are preventing them from moving on. Helping them reconstruct their history and place their losses in a more functional perspective is an essential part of helping them change their relationship to their past and their future.

FAMILY ADAPTATION TO LOSS

The family life cycle model of Carter and McGoldrick (1989) offers a framework for taking into account the reciprocal influences of several generations as they move forward over time and as they approach and react to loss (see McGoldrick & Walsh, Chapter 2). Death poses shared adaptational challenges, requiring both immediate and long-term family reorganization and changes in a family's definitions of its identity and purpose. The ability to accept loss is at the heart of all skills in healthy family systems, in contrast to severely dysfunctional families, who show the most maladaptive patterns in dealing with inevitable losses, clinging together in fantasy and denial to blur reality and to insist on timelessness and the perpetuation of never-broken bonds (Lewis, Beavers, Gossett, & Phillips, 1976).

Adaptation does not mean resolution, in the sense of some complete "once and for all" coming to terms with the loss. Rather, it involves finding ways to put the loss in perspective and to move on with life. The cherished psychoanalytic notion of working through loss to accomplish a complete resolution does not fit the experience of most individuals and their families (Wortman & Silver, 1989). Adaptation has no fixed timetable or sequence, and significant or traumatic losses may never be fully resolved. The multiple meanings of any death are transformed throughout the life cycle, as they are experienced and integrated with life experiences, including, of course, other losses.

Family Adaptational Tasks

While it would be a mistake to impose expectations of fixed stages, sequences, or schedules on such a complex process as grief, given the diversity of family and individual coping styles, we believe there are crucial family adaptational tasks which, if not dealt with, leave family members vulnerable to dysfunction. Based on research and clinical experience, we can identify two major family tasks that tend to promote immediate and long-term adaptation for family members and to strengthen the family as a functional unit.

   1. **Shared acknowledgment of the reality of death and shared experience of loss.** All family members, in their own ways, must confront the reality of a death in the family. Bowen (Chapter 4) draws our attention to the importance of contact with the reality of death and, in particular, to the inclusion of children:

> I urge family members to visit dying family members whenever possible and to find some way to include children if the situation permits. I have never seen a child hurt by exposure to death. They are "hurt" only by the anxiety of survivors. Well intentioned attempts to protect children or "vulnerable" members from the potential upset of attending such events isolates them from the shared experience and risks impeding their grief process.

Acknowledgment of the loss is facilitated by clear information and open communication about the facts and circumstances of the death. Inability to accept the reality of death can lead a family member to avoid contact with the rest of the family or to become angry with others who are moving forward in the grief process. Longstanding sibling conflicts and cutoffs can often be traced back to the bedside of a dying parent, or to the graveside.

Funeral rituals (Imber-Black, Chapter 11) and visits to the grave (Williamson, 1978) serve a vital function in providing direct confrontation with the reality of death and the opportunity to pay last respects, to share grief, and to receive comfort in the supportive network of survivors. Sharing the experience of loss, in whatever ways a family can, is crucial to successful adaptation. The following example underscores the value to all of including a vulnerable family member in the mourning process:

> Sam Marcus, aged 74, had been confined to a nursing home for five years after suffering severe brain damage when hit by a car. His wife and daughters had adjusted over time to the loss of the husband and father they had known and managed gradually to cope with profound personality changes, sporadic violent outbursts, and, most painful for them, his recent failure to recognize them. Anticipating his further decline and death, the daughters were caught by surprise when their mother, though in apparently good health, died suddenly. The sisters strongly wanted their father to take part in the funeral, even though the doctors refused to release him, fearing disruptive behavior, and insisted that he did not understand that his wife had died and would only be confused by the experience. To include him, the sisters decided to hold the service in the nursing home (to the dismay of the funeral director, who doubled their bill for the inconvenience). When their father was wheeled in they sat on either side of him, although he gave no sign of recognition. As the sisters each rose and spoke of their mother's life and death, tears flowed down the father's cheeks. Afterwards, they sat silently together, holding hands.

Family communication is vital over the course of the loss process. While keeping in mind that individuals, families, and cultures vary in the degree to which open expression of feelings is valued or functional, there is strong evidence from research on well-functioning families that clear, direct communication facilitates family adaptation and strengthens the family as a supportive network for its members (Walsh, 1982). A climate of trust, empathic response, and tolerance for diverse reactions is crucial. The mourning process also involves sharing attempts to put the loss into some meaningful perspective that fits coherently into the rest of a family's life experience and belief system. This requires dealing with the ongoing negative implications of the loss, including the loss of dreams for the future.

Families are likely to experience a range of feelings depending on the unique meaning of the relationship and its loss for each member and the implications of the death for the family unit. Strong emotions may surface at different moments, including complicated and mixed feelings of anger, disappointment, helplessness, relief, guilt, and abandonment, which are present to some extent in most family relationships. Anthropologist Rosaldo (1989) writes of his reactions to the sudden, accidental death of his wife, also a prominent anthropologist, when she lost her footing as they walked along a mountain trail and fell down a sheer precipice:

> Immediately upon finding her body I became enraged. How could she abandon me? How could she have been so stupid as to fall? I tried to cry. I sobbed, but rage blocked the tears. Later, powerful visceral emotional states swept over me. . . . I experienced the deep cutting pain of sorrow almost beyond endurance, the cadaverous cold of realizing the finality of death, the trembling beginning in my abdomen and spreading through my body, the mournful keening that started without my willing, and frequent tearful sobbing.

Rarely are such emotions expressed so directly in our culture, where sharing intense negative feeling tends to produce discomfort and distancing in others. Furthermore, the loss of control in experiencing such overwhelming feelings can frighten family members and others who may block communication of the experience.

When we take into account the multiple, fluctuating, and often conflicting, responses of all members in a family system, we can appreciate the overwhelming complexity of any family mourning process. Tolerance is needed for different responses within families and for the likelihood that some members may be out of phase with others, given the differences in the meaning of relationships and in individual coping styles. When a bereaved spouse is also a parent of small children, emotional expression may be blocked by the responsibilities of single parenthood, with children and well-intentioned relatives colluding to keep the sole surviving parent strong and functioning. When parental grieving is blocked, a child is more likely to become symptomatic.

In families where certain feelings, thoughts or memories are disallowed by family loyalties or social taboos, communication blockage may contribute to symptomatic behavior or feelings may go underground to surface in other contexts, disconnected from their source. When feelings are unbearable or unacceptable, they may be delegated and expressed in a piecemeal fashion by different members (Reilly, 1978). One member may express all the anger for the family while another is in touch with only sadness; one shows only relief, another is numb. When a family is unable to tolerate feelings, a member who expresses the unspeakable may be scapegoated or extruded. In addition, the shock and pain of a traumatic loss can shatter family cohesion, leaving members isolated and unsupported in their grief, risking dysfunctional consequences, as in the following case:

Mrs. Campbell called the child psychiatric clinic for help with her 11-year-old daughter's school problems. The therapist found that the problems had been identified by the school a year earlier, but had worsened in the past month, just after the oldest son, age 18, had been the innocent victim of a gang-related shooting. The father began drinking heavily, withdrawing from the family. The next eldest son, age 17, carried the family rage into the streets, seeking revenge for the killing. Two other middle sons showed no reaction, keeping out of the way and behaving "as good as gold." The mother, in her pain, turned her attention to her daughter's preexisting problems. Family therapy provided a context for family griefwork, while repairing the family fragmentation and promoting a more cohesive network for mutual support and healing. It was especially important to involve the "well" siblings, who had been holding in their own pain and confusion so as not to further burden or upset their parents. On follow-up six months later, the daughter was doing well in school and the family reported that the experience of pulling together in the sharing of grief had strengthened their capacity to deal with other problems.

2. **Reorganization of the family system and reinvestment in other relationships and life pursuits.** The death of a family member disrupts the family equilibrium and established patterns of interaction. The process of recovery involves a realignment of relationships and redistribution of role functions needed to compensate for the loss and carry on with family life. Promoting cohesion and flexibility in the family system is crucial to restabilization. The upheaval and disorganization experienced in the immediate aftermath of a loss may lead families to make precipitous moves into new homes or marriages. The further dislocation may make matters worse. Some families may try to hold on rigidly to old patterns that are no longer functional to minimize the sense of loss and disruption in family life.

Mrs. Robbins sought help for "communication problems" with her 16-year-old daughter, Donna, who was sullen and withdrawn. The household consisted of the mother and three daughters. Mr. Robbins, killed in an auto accident six years earlier, had been beloved by his family. The loss was compounded when the 16-year-old daughter Pam (who had been closest to her father) had run away with her boyfriend only weeks later, severing all contact with the family. Shortly after, Nick, an old family friend, had persuaded Mrs. Robbins to move to his city to start a new life. He helped her find a job and an apartment next door to his own. The eldest daughter, then 18, became her helpmate and got a job to help support the family, putting aside her own plans for college.

Despite the move, Mrs. Robbins vowed to carry on family life as if her husband were still "at the head of the table," and to raise "his" daughters as he would have done himself. Together they maintained the unrealistic expectation that she should carry on as if she were both parents and that they should continue everyday life just as before father's death. Although mother now worked full-time to support the family, she painstakingly prepared dinners that had been the father's favorites, serving them each night at the dinner hour that had fit his schedule. Nick joined them for dinner like an awkward guest. Family picnics and holidays were celebrated exactly as they had been with Mr. Robbins. With the therapist's exploration, the girls admitted that they had outgrown many of the activities and only pretended to enjoy them. Now teenagers, they wanted to spend more time with friends, but felt it would be disloyal to both parents to voice discontent. The mother acknowledged her strain in trying to maintain the family as if it were still intact. Therapy then focused on helping them to mourn their loss and to modify traditions to better fit their changing developmental needs and their structure as a single-parent household.

The process of mourning is quite variable, often lasting much longer than people themselves expect (Wortman & Silver, 1989). Each new season, holiday, and anniversary is likely to reevoke the loss. Overidealization of the deceased, a sense of disloyalty, or the catastrophic fear of another loss may block the formation of other attachments and commitments. Family members may refuse to accept a new member who is seen as replacing the deceased when the loss has not been integrated, as in the Robbins case:

As family therapy progressed, the girls began to voice complaints about Nick: "That man next door spends too much time hanging around our apartment." "He's a creep." "He's nowhere near the man our father was." "We don't want him to be our father." After having moved too quickly into a new relationship, its status remained ambiguous nearly six years later. While they kept separate apartments, Nick slept in mother's bedroom, each night setting up a cot next to her single bed, and each morning putting it away. This clandestine ritual expressed the persisting ambivalence in their relationship. In the aftermath of her husband's death, Mrs. Robbins had found support and consolation from Nick, and the move brought a welcome escape from her daily surroundings that reminded her constantly of the loss. Yet she never felt "quite right" about full commitment to him and was depressed, overweight, and unhappy in her job. Therapy shifted to a phase of couple sessions, which revealed Nick's reluctance to ever fully commit himself to her and her daughters, due to a past bitter divorce and cutoff from his own children. Realizing their relationship was "deadlocked," she decided to end it.

With this loss, Mrs. Robbins found herself dreaming nightly of her former husband and was flooded with feelings of missing him. A series of individual sessions reviewed her marriage and the meaning of its loss for her. Utilizing photographs and an empty chair, she had two "conversations" that she wished she had had with her husband: the first to say goodbye before his death, and the second, in the present, to update him on their daughters and herself since his death, and their need now to move on with their lives while cherishing his memory. She asked the therapist if she could keep tapes of those sessions and later said she felt a tremendous weight off her mind: "I won't have to carry all those feelings around in my head anymore because I have them all on tape."

Family therapy with loss requires the same ingenuity and flexibility that families need to respond to various members and subsystems as their issues come to the fore. As changes occur in one part of a system, changes for others will be generated. Decisions to meet with an individual, couple, or family unit are guided by a systemic view of the loss process.

With the Robbins family, the final phase of therapy involved a reconvening of the mother and daughters. They sorted through old boxes in the attic, deciding to hold onto certain keepsakes, while letting go of others. For the anniversary of the death, Mrs. Robbins wrote an obituary that she had been asked, but unable, to write at the time of his loss. This stimulated the daughters to write poems and make drawings in memory of their father. With great enthusiasm, they gathered these into a booklet, which they sent to relatives and friends. The therapist coached the mother in her efforts to reconnect with her estranged daughter, Pam, who finally came home for a visit. Over the next few years, the family kept the therapist updated on important life passages, the mother getting a new apartment and a more satisfying job and the daughters going on to college.

Factors Influencing Family Adaptation to Loss

A number of factors influence the impact of a death and the nature and length of a family's response. Building on the work of Bowen (1976) and Herz (1980, 1989) and research on family functioning (Walsh, 1982, in press), we can identify several patterns that tend to complicate family adaptation to loss and pose higher risk for dysfunction. If we are to understand why some losses can be devastating for certain individuals and their families, clinicians and researchers must carefully evaluate these variables and address them in any intervention plan.

THE MANNER OF DEATH. *Sudden or lingering death.* Sudden deaths or deaths following protracted illness are especially stressful for families and require different coping mechanisms (see Rolland, Chapter 8). When a person dies unexpectedly, family members lack time to anticipate and prepare for the loss, to deal with unfinished business, or in many cases even to say their goodbyes.

When the dying process has been prolonged, family caregiving and financial resources are likely to be depleted, with needs of other members put on hold. Relief at ending patient suffering and family strain is likely to be guilt-laden. Moreover, families are increasingly confronted with the excruciating dilemma over whether, and how long, to maintain life support efforts, at enormous expense, to sustain a family member indefinitely in a vegetative state or in chronic pain, with virtually no hope of recovery. Controversy over medical ethics, religious beliefs, patient/family rights, and criminal prosecution extend to the most fundamental questions of when life ends and who should determine that end. Such questions can be anguishing for families caught between patient wishes for the right to die with dignity and the medical ethos to save lives at all cost (and above all, do no harm). Families can be torn apart by opposing positions of different members or coalitions. Clinicians can help family members to prepare and discuss living wills, to share feelings openly about such complicated situations, and to come to terms with any decision taken.

Ambiguous loss. Ambiguity surrounding a loss interferes with its mastery, often producing depression in family members (see Boss, Chapter 9). A loved one may be physically absent but psychologically present, as in hostage situations, "disappearances" of political dissidents, or soldiers missing-in-action. The uncertainty about whether a missing family member is dead or alive can be agonizing for a family. For instance, in the case of a missing child, a family may become consumed by efforts to maintain hope while fearing the worst, and by desperate searches and attempts to get information to confirm the fate of their child. The inability to recover a body is likely to complicate grieving, as families of the Challenger crew reported in their difficulty grieving over empty coffins and their agony until the recovery of body parts of their loved ones.

In other situations of ambiguous loss, a family member may be physically present but psychologically "dead," as in the case of deteriorated Alzheimer's patients (see Boss, Chapter 9). It is important to help family members to deal with the loss of important aspects of their relationship without extruding the person as if already dead.

Violent death. The devastating impact of violent deaths reverberates throughout a family system. Body deformity or dismemberment may be a recurrent image in memories or nightmares for years to come, especially for those who witnessed the death. The taking and loss of lives in war may haunt survivors years later, in post-traumatic stress disorders that affect their family relationships, leading to distress and even life-threatening reactions of other members (Figley, 1986, 1989). In the case of one Vietnam veteran, the death years later of an old war buddy triggered a terrifying flashback episode, threat of marital separation, and a suicide attempt by the teenage daughter, signaling the need for family therapy.

The senseless tragedy in the loss of innocent lives is especially hard to bear, particularly when it is the result of violence or negligence, as in drunk driving. For the family of a homicide victim, bereavement may be interminable when members believe that justice has not been served. An entire community can be traumatized by violent crime, which disproportionately strikes poor inner-city families. A major disaster, such as a tornado or hurricane, destroys homes and neighborhoods as well as lives. A sense of security and invulnerability is shattered for all families in such stricken communities. When survivors must live with an ever present threat of recurrence, such as earthquakes, the anticipation of further trauma and loss complicates recovery. Emergency and disaster workers and their families must also cope with their own vulnerability and the life-threatening nature of their work. Firemen report that the hardest part of their job is witnessing the death of a child they were unable to rescue or the loss of a coworker.

Easy access to lethal weapons has contributed to an alarming increase in homicide in the United States, as well as to accidental shootings. Shockingly, homicides are most frequently committed by relatives—sometimes in accidental shootings but more often in the heat of conflict. Husbands' threats to kill their wives if they ever leave them are too often carried out, particularly if they become involved with another man. Increasingly, battered women, seeing no other recourse, are killing their spouses in self-defense or retaliation for longstanding abuse.

Suicides are the most anguishing deaths for families to come to terms with (Cain, 1972; Dunne, McIntosh, & Dunne-Maxim, 1988; Gutstein, Chapter 13). The recent rise in adolescent death symbolism and suicide demands more attention to larger social forces as well as family influences. Clinicians also need to become more alert to family patterns that may pose heightened risk of suicide. Current life-threatening family situations can trigger catastrophic fears of loss and self-destructive behavior. One teenage girl was seen in the emergency room with a gunshot wound in her chest after a gun she had been carrying in her bra accidentally fired. In family crisis intervention, she revealed that she had become frightened by recent late night conflicts between her parents so she removed the gun kept under their mattress and hid it on her to protect them from harm.

Clinicians should routinely note family histories of suicide or other traumatic loss that may predict suicide risk. In one tragic therapy outcome a husband killed himself after the therapist mobilized his wife to threaten divorce unless he agreed to immediate inpatient treatment for an alcohol problem he denied. A family history had not been taken. Subsequently it was learned that, at age 10, his parents had undergone a bitter divorce; caught in a vicious custody battle, he had tried to hang himself. This information would have alerted the therapist to the potential for suicide in the face of threatened divorce.

It must be added that such a threat of suicide should not bind a spouse to remain in a destructive relationship, nor should it imply the spouse's responsibility if a suicide occurs. But while even the most caring therapist may not be able to prevent a suicide from occurring, the risk can be diminished by making covert linkages to past trauma overt, encouraging vulnerable persons to take responsibility for their own actions, mobilizing family support, and promoting visions for a more promising life course (see Epston, Chapter 12). Often, a suicide can be prevented by pressing a despondent person to carefully consider the long-term destructive consequences for loved ones, especially children.

When a suicide occurs, anger and guilt can pervade family relationships, particularly when members are blamed or blame themselves for the death. The social stigma of suicide also contributes to family shame and cover-up of the circumstances. Such secrecy distorts family communication and can isolate a family from social support, generating its own destructive legacy.

FAMILY AND SOCIAL NETWORK.   Consistent with leading research on family functioning (Walsh, 1982, in press), we observe that patterns of family organization, communication, and belief systems are among the most crucial mediating variables in adaptation to loss. The general level of family functioning and the state of family relationships prior to and following the loss should be carefully evaluated with attention to the extended family and social network. Particular note should be taken of the variables discussed below.

Family cohesion and differentiation of members. Adaptation to loss is facilitated by cohesiveness of the family unit for mutual support, balanced with tolerance of and respect for different responses to loss by various family members. Extreme family patterns of enmeshment or disengagement are likely to complicate adaptation to loss. At one extreme, enmeshed families may demand a united front and regard as disloyal and threatening any individual differences, which then must be submerged or distorted. They may seek an undifferentiated replacement for the loss and have difficulty with subsequent separations, holding on to other family members at normal developmental transitions. At the other extreme, disengaged families are likely to avoid the pain of loss with distancing and emotional cutoffs. In family fragmentation, members are left isolated in their grief, each left to fend for him or herself.

Flexibility of the family system. Family structure, in particular family rules, roles, and boundaries, need to be flexible, yet clear, for reorganization after loss. At the extreme, a chaotic, disorganized family will have difficulty maintaining enough leadership, stability, and continuity necessary to manage the transitional upheaval. An overly rigid family is likely to have difficulty modifying set patterns to make the necessary accommodations to loss.

Open communication vs. secrecy. When a family confronts a loss, open communication facilitates the recovery process, as described above in our discussion of family adaptational tasks. It is important for clinicians to promote a family climate of mutual trust, support, and tolerance for a range of responses to loss. Secrecy, myths, and taboos surrounding the loss interfere with mastery. When communication is blocked, the unspeakable is more likely to be expressed in dysfunctional symptoms or destructive behavior.

Availability of extended family, social, and economic resources. The availability of other resources for the family to draw upon can buffer the loss (Anderson, 1982; Kessler, Price, & Wortman, 1985). The extended family can play a vital role in this process, as in the following healthy family:

> Mrs. Lang, the mother of three small children, aged six, four, and 18 months, developed leukemia. Over the next year, through many hospitalizations and lengthy trips across the country for bone marrow replacement, the extended family rallied to support the couple and their children. The two sets of grandparents took turns staying in the home, managing household and childcare responsibilities. This buffered the turmoil, allowed Mr. Lang to accompany his wife, and minimized dislocation for the children, who were able to remain at home, with daily routines and peer contact. Mr. Lang's sister also pitched in, spelling the grandparents' shifts and taking the children for outings. In the year following the mother's death, the family support was sustained, with gradual reallocation of many responsibilities to a live-in housekeeper.

When longstanding conflicts, cutoffs, or social stigma (as in AIDS) have left families disengaged and isolated, clinicians working with loss can be helpful by mobilizing a potentially supportive network and promoting a healing reconciliation (see Gutstein, Chapter 13).

Prior role and functioning of the deceased member in the family system. The more important the person was in family life and the more central his or her role in family functioning, the greater the loss. The death of a parent with small children is generally far more devastating than the loss of an elderly grandparent who has become more peripheral to the functioning of the family. The loss of a leader or caretaker will be sorely felt, whereas the death of a quarrelsome troublemaker may bring a sigh of relief. The death of an only child, or the only son or daughter, leaves a particular void, especially for parents who are unable to conceive another child. Families run the risk of dysfunction if, at one extreme, they seek to avoid the pain of loss by denying the significance of an important family member or by instant replacement. At the other extreme, they can become immobilized if they are unable to reallocate role functions or form new attachments.

Conflicted or estranged relationships at the time of death. Family relationships are bound to have occasional conflict, mixed feelings, or shifting alliances. When conflict has been intense and persistent, where ambivalence is strong, or when relationships have been cut-off altogether, the mourning process is more likely to be complicated, with fallout for other relationships. In therapy, the coaching process (McGoldrick, Chapter 3) can be useful in addressing immediate or long-term complications of a loss. When death is anticipated, as in life-threatening illnesses, clinicians should make every effort to help patients and their families to reconnect and to repair strained relationships before the opportunity is lost. Often there is hesitance to stir up painful emotions or dredge up old conflicts for fear that negative confrontations would increase the risk of death. Family therapists need to be sensitive to these fears and actively interrupt destructive interactional spirals, helping patient and family members to share feelings constructively with the aim of healing pained relationships, forging new connections, and building mutual support. A conjoint family life review (Walsh, 1989) can foster transformation by helping members to share different perspectives, to place hurts and disappointments in the context of the family's life cycle challenges, to recover caring aspects of relationships, and to update and renew relationships that have been frozen in past conflict.

LIFE CYCLE TIMING OF LOSS. The particular timing of a loss in the multi-generational family life cycle may place a family at higher risk for dysfunctional consequences (see McGoldrick & Walsh, Chapter 2). Complications are more likely in cases of (1) untimely loss, (2) concurrence of multiple losses or of loss with other major family stresses, and (3) past traumatic, unresolved loss, and, in particular, transgenerational anniversary replications.

Untimely loss. Every culture has a saying to express the belief that the best death comes at the end of a long and productive life, especially when there are children and grandchildren to live on into the future. Untimely loss is harder to bear: It seems unjust to die "before one's time," just as it seems a cruel misfortune for the surviving family. Family life cycle timing and social expectations, as well as chronological years, contribute to the untimeliness of a death and the impact of loss on survivors (see McGoldrick & Walsh, Chapter 2). For instance, widowhood in early marriage is much more difficult than in later life because of unfulfilled hopes and dreams, the lack of fit with other couples at the same life phase, and the lack of models of the same cohort for adjustment to widowhood (Neugarten, 1970; Parkes & Weiss, 1983). Multiple roles and relationships in families complicate the loss experience further, as in the death of a spouse/parent at the family stage of rearing young children.

The death of a child is the most tragic of all off-time losses, reversing generational expectations. As expressed by the Chinese saying, "White hair should never follow black," the life course is experienced as out of order if a child dies before parents.

Other family stresses concurrent with loss. The temporal concurrence of *multiple losses* or of *loss with other developmental milestones and stressors* produces a pileup of stress that is likely to overwhelm families, complicating tasks of mourning. The concurrence of stress events may be coincidental. In other cases, significant loss or a near-death experience may trigger other relationship changes, such as divorce, precipitous marriage, or conception of a child. A careful family evaluation and sketching of a time line can alert clinicians to the confluence of multiple losses or of loss with other developmental milestones, as in the following consultation on a case of marital violence:

> Mike was in a group for men who batter, while Mary, his wife, was in a group for battered women. They now sought marital counseling, as Mary was on the verge of leaving the marriage. The husband's physical abuse had become a problem over the past three years. The therapist's attention to their repetitive cycles of interaction seemed unhelpful. A consultant was called in who tracked family history, which had not previously been explored, and learned that during that time the couple had been reeling under the shock and pain of a sequence of losses. First, Mike's father, from whom he had been estranged, had died of a sudden heart attack; next, his brother had died of lung cancer; then his business had gone bankrupt just before the birth of their fourth child. Mary's mother, who had been her mainstay, had died; and most recently, Mike, had lost control while driving and totaled his car, the whole family barely escaping serious injury. Mike had never disclosed these losses in his men's group, since the group focused on his current behavior, and couldn't recall ever sharing his feelings about them with anybody, including Mary, who had turned to her close friends for support. She noted that this was the first time someone had connected his violent outbursts to their loss experiences. The couple agreed that the marital strain of the cumulative losses, on top of parenting demands for their new baby and three other children, was more than they could bear, triggering heated arguments that escalated into violence. It would be difficult to help this couple without attending to their recovery from these multiple losses.

The concurrence of loss with other developmental milestones may pose incompatible tasks and demands, particularly with a new marriage or the birth of a child. While such events may bring special joy and a sense of renewal in a family, the processes of mourning and those for establishing a marriage, or for parenting an infant, are inherently conflictual. Becoming absorbed with one is likely to interfere with the other; trying to manage both simultaneously is overwhelming. Moreover, the relationship with a new partner or with a child born at a time of loss may be confounded with the lost relationship. In our clinical and research experience, families confronting such conflicting life cycle challenges may be at risk for later problems if mourning is blocked by other demands or attachments (see McGoldrick & Walsh, Chapter 2). The special position of a child serving a replacement function may stimulate extraordinary creativity or life achievement or it may contribute to severe dysfunction (see McGoldrick, Chapter 6). While patho-

genic consequences are by no means inevitable, our experience does suggest
the value of preventive intervention for families confronting the simultaneous challenges of loss and birth. Such intervention should promote spousal
and kin support so that the grief process can be attended to while the needs
of the child are met.

Multigenerational family legacy of loss. Some families and individuals
with prior traumatic loss seem to have been made hardier by the experience,
whereas others are left more vulnerable to subsequent losses. Where separation issues are prominent in problems presented clinically, the relevance of
past losses should be carefully assessed. Where families have difficulty with
normative transitions such as launching, we pay particular attention to indi-
cations of unresolved mourning of past losses where recall is blocked or
distorted and where feelings are cut off or extremely intense (see McGoldrick, Chapters 3 & 6).

Past losses can intersect with current life cycle passage in many ways. One
woman, who married a man she had met just as her mother was dying, had
little grief reaction until her marriage ended in divorce several years later and
she found herself preoccupied with thoughts and dreams of her mother. In
other cases, a family may experience a transitional crisis when a child who
has been serving a replacement function attempts to leave home or commit
to a new relationship. Research on families of substance abusers has found
connections between self-destructive behavior of the addict, family separation, and unresolved mourning of previous traumatic family losses (see
Coleman, Chapter 14).

Transgenerational anniversary patterns are important to note (Walsh,
1983b; McGoldrick & Walsh, Chapter 2), where the age or family transition
at symptom onset coincides with the point in the life cycle a generation
earlier when a parent either died or was bereaved. When individuals reach
the same age at which a parent died, particularly the premature death of the
same-sex parent, it is not uncommon for them to suddenly become concerned with their own mortality. Some start new fitness regimens and feel
they must "get through the year," while others anticipate replicating their
parent's fate, and may even behave self-destructively (Engel, 1975). Concern
about a spouse's mortality may arise when he or she reaches the age of death
of one's own parent of the opposite sex.

The occurrence of symptoms is often found to coincide with losses in past
generations at the same point in the life cycle, as in the following case:

> Joanne and Ralph were seen in family therapy after their 22-year-old son Joey
> barely survived a drug overdose on the eve of his wedding. Joanne acknowledged
> that it was harder for her to have Joey (her namesake) leave home to marry than it
> had been with their other children, but she didn't know why. The therapist in-

quired about the parents' own experiences leaving home. Joanne told of running off to marry her husband against her father's wishes. She had been furious at her father's opposition and he, in turn, refused to speak to her. He died suddenly of a heart attack six months later, without the opportunity for reconciliation. At this point in her story, Joanne burst into tears, saying, "Somehow it feels the same now."

It was crucial to inquire beyond the obvious dyadic linkages of Joanne with her father and with her son and explore other system patterns connected to current problems.

Joanne had been very close to her mother, who, widowed, spent the rest of her life depressed and lonely. When asked if she ever worried that history might repeat itself, Joanne admitted that she worried often about her husband's health, and his disregard of his overweight condition. In recent months he had complained of chest pains but refused to see a doctor. With Joey leaving, she worried that something terrible might happen and she would end up like her mother. In fact, given her catastrophic expectations and lack of a model for couples in later life, she and her husband had never discussed any dreams or plans for their future together after the launching of their children. As the couple was helped to focus on their future, Ralph had a medical workup and started taking better care of himself, and they celebrated their son's marriage.

When systems patterns are replicated across the generations, it is important to make covert linkages overt, to differentiate the present from the past, and to help the family to move forward at this life cycle transition. An appreciation of the power of covert family scripts (see Byng-Hall, Chapter 5) and of family legacies (Boszormenyi-Nagy & Spark, 1974) is important to an understanding of the transmission of such patterns in loss (see McGoldrick, Chapter 6 for further discussion). Anniversary reactions are most likely to occur when there has been a physical and emotional cutoff from the past and when family rules, often covert, prohibit open communication about past traumatic events, as in the following case:

An 18-year-old boy was hospitalized for an acute psychotic reaction that occurred on his summer vacation in Europe. In a family evaluation, members were constrained together, reluctant to talk about the son's breakdown. In a following individual session with mother, she told the following story. The father, a Jewish refugee from Poland, had, at the age of 18, witnessed the shooting of his brother, lost contact with his entire family, and was interred in a concentration camp. Surviving the war, he came to the U.S. where he became a physician and met his wife, who was his patient. On their first date, she had asked about the numbers on his arm, but, seeing him so shaken, had decided never to mention it again. As the children grew up, there was an implicit rule never to discuss the father's past, although the numbers on his arm were a constant reminder. For the son's 18th birthday, the father gave him a summer trip to Europe. While there, the son became profoundly depressed and broke the rule of silence, writing home that he could not enjoy his holiday knowing what had happened to his father at the same age and in the same place. His parents did not reply. His subsequent breakdown brought him home.

In family therapy, communication was opened on the linkage of past and present. Family members were commended for their longstanding consideration of their father and their wish to spare him further pain by discussing what might be unbearable for him. However, it was agreed that this "ban" was no longer necessary, as the father was no longer as vulnerable as he once might have been. The son's "birthday present" could be taken as an opportunity to reconnect with the past. On case follow-up a year later the son was doing well in college and, interestingly, majoring in Communications. The parents had made a trip to the father's home in Poland, which had proved immensely valuable for him and deepened the marital relationship.

An individual's dissociation, denial, and repression may be important coping skills in surviving and mastering catastrophic trauma and loss, as occurred in the attempted genocide of the Nazi holocaust. But over time, the maintenance of such patterns may have dysfunctional consequences for other members of a family system. The persistence of communication blockage and emotional and physical cutoffs from the past is likely to constrict marital relationships and risk serious fallout for the next generation.

SOCIOCULTURAL CONTEXT OF DEATH. *Ethnic, religious, and philosophical beliefs*. A family's belief system is a critical influence on adaptation to loss. Beliefs about death and the meanings surrounding a particular loss are rooted in multigenerational family legacies, in ethnic and religious beliefs, and in the dominant societal values and practices (McGoldrick, Pearce, & Giordano, 1982; see McGoldrick, Chapters 6 & 10). Clinicians need to appreciate the power of belief systems for healing the pain of loss as well as the destructive impact of blame, shame, and guilt surrounding a death (Rolland, Chapter 8). Such causal attributions are especially strong in situations of traumatic death where the cause is uncertain and questions of responsibility or negligence arise. Family members may hold secret beliefs that they — or others — should have done something to prevent a death. It is important to help families share such concerns, view them as normal, and come to terms with the extent and limits of their control in the situation.

Sociopolitical and historical context of loss. During times of war, the impact for families of combat deaths is heavily influenced by social attitudes about the war involvement. In the United States, highly charged, conflicting positions on the Vietnam War seriously complicated family adaptation to loss. In contrast, loss in World War II was assuaged by a common sense of patriotism and heroism for a noble cause and victory. We are only beginning to recognize the effect of the threat of nuclear destruction on families, particularly on children growing up with the uncertainty that their generation will have a full life ahead and the very real risk that all life will end.

Cancer and AIDS have become the epidemics of our times, each generating tremendous stigma and fear of contagion (Sontag, 1988). The AIDS epidemic has led many, including clinicians, to distance from patients, impairing family and social support, as well as the delivery of critical health care. Distinctions are too often made between "innocent victims," such as children born with AIDS or individuals who have contracted the disease through blood transfusions, in contrast to those who are condemned for having "brought it on themselves" through homosexuality or drug use. Clinicians can help to reduce social stigma and unfounded fears of contagion so that death by AIDS is not made all the more painful and isolating for all.

More generally, societal attitudes toward homosexuality complicate all losses in gay and lesbian relationships. Lacking the legal standing of marriage, a partner may be denied death benefits when a relationship is ended by death. The death of a partner may be grieved in isolation when the relationship has been a secret or has been disapproved of by the family or the community. The epidemic of AIDS is all the more devastating in the gay community—and increasingly for men, women, and children in poor inner city neighborhoods—because of the multiple losses and anticipated losses experienced in relationship networks (Klein & Fletcher, 1986). As one man lamented: "Death and dying are all around us and any of us could be next."

Gender role constraints. Although our society has been changing rapidly, normative expectations for men and women in families have lagged behind emerging realities of family life (McGoldrick, 1989; McGoldrick, Anderson, & Walsh, 1989). Mothers are particularly vulnerable to blame and guilt because of societal expectations that they bear primary caretaking responsibility for the well-being of their husbands, children, and aging parents. Women have been socialized to assume the major role in handling the social and emotional tasks of bereavement, from the expression of grief to caregiving for the terminally ill and surviving family members. Daughters and daughters-in-law carry those responsibilities for their own and their husbands' extended families. Now that most women are combining job and family responsibilities, they are increasingly overburdened. Men, who are socialized to manage instrumental tasks, tend to take charge of funeral, burial, financial, and property arrangements, but tend to remain more emotionally constrained and physically peripheral in the aftermath of loss. Society's denial of male vulnerability and dependency needs and the sanctions against men's emotional expressiveness undoubtedly contribute to marital distress after the loss of a family member and to the high rate of serious illness and suicide for men following the death of a spouse.

The different coping strategies of men and women can increase marital strain, even for couples with previously strong and stable relationships (Videka-Sherman, 1982). For example, in a study of parents' reactions to sudden infant death syndrome (SIDS), fathers reported anger, fear, and a loss of control, along with a desire to keep their grieving private, whereas mothers responded more with sorrow and depression (DeFrain, Taylor, & Ernst, 1982). Fathers are more likely to withdraw, to take refuge in their work, and to be uncomfortable with their wives' expressions of grief, not knowing how to respond and fearful of losing control of their own feelings. Mothers may perceive their husbands' emotional unavailability as abandonment when they need comfort most, thereby experiencing a double loss. When husbands are expressive and actively involved in a child's illness and death and in the family bereavement process, the quality of the marriage improves markedly.

These findings have important clinical application. Self-help groups and individual psychotherapy, while potentially valuable interventions, appear to have limited impact on recovery when marital relationship dynamics are not addressed as well (Videka-Sherman & Lieberman, 1985). Most commonly it is women who present themselves — or are sent by their husbands — for depression or other symptoms of distress concerning loss, while their husbands appear to be well-functioning and see no need of help for themselves. Interventions need to be aimed at decreasing the sex-role split so that all family members can experience their own grief and be supportive to one another in adapting to loss. It is important to facilitate fuller involvement for men in the socioemotional tasks of the loss process, which will enrich their experience of family life as it lessens the disproportionate burden for women. A greater flexibility of allowable roles for both men and women will permit the full range of human experiences in bereavement as in other areas of family life.

The full participation of male and female family members in mourning rituals should be encouraged. One woman, at the death of her 100-year-old grandmother, expressed her desire to be a pallbearer at the funeral. One cousin replied that only males could do that; another added that they already had picked six pallbearers (all happening to be male grandchildren). She persisted, suggesting that they simply have more than six. In the end, all twelve grandchildren, including five women, shared that important experience.

CONCLUSION

Of all human experiences, death poses the most painful adaptational challenges for families. In this overview chapter, we have presented a systemic perspective on loss, examining the far-reaching ramifications of a death in the family throughout the relationship system. We have identified key family adaptational tasks with loss that clinicians can actively promote for families blocked in moving on with life. These tasks involve (1) shared acknowledgment of the reality of death and shared experience of loss, and (2) reorganization of the family system and reinvestment in other relationships and life pursuits.

We have also delineated a number of crucial variables that can either facilitate or adversely affect family mourning processes. To better understand the healthy or dysfunctional consequences of any loss, clinicians and researchers should give close attention to the manner of death, the functioning of the family and social network, the life cycle timing of loss, and the sociocultural context. More specifically, losses involving the following complications should be examined more carefully:

(a) sudden or lingering death
(b) ambiguous loss
(c) violent death, especially suicide
(d) enmeshed or disengaged family patterns, lacking tolerance for different responses or cohesion for mutual support
(e) lack of flexibility of system
(f) blocked communication and secrecy, myths, taboos surrounding death
(g) lack of kin, social, and economic resources
(h) important role functioning of the member lost, with precipitous replacement or inability to reinvest
(i) conflicted or estranged relationship at death
(j) untimely loss
(k) multiple losses or other family stressors concurrent with loss
(l) multigenerational legacy of unresolved loss, particularly transgeneration anniversary replications
(m) family belief system invoking blame, shame, or guilt surrounding death
(n) sociopolitical and historical context of death, fostering denial, stigma, or catastrophic fears

In order to understand how some individuals are deeply scarred by loss while others show resilience and are even strengthened by the experience, we strongly recommend that future research and clinical inquiry examine more fully the family context of loss, with attention to these family adaptational tasks and critical variables. Mastery or dysfunction associated with loss is not simply an indication of individual bereavement but is also a product of family mourning processes.

As will be discussed in Chapter 2, knowledge of the normative developmental tasks at each stage in the family life cycle can help clinicians be aware of and respond to the particular ways in which loss is likely to intersect with salient family life cycle issues. Early intervention that is sensitive to such complications can have important preventive value. In many cases, movement forward in the life cycle may be blocked by unresolved mourning issues from the past. Most families have experienced numerous losses; extensive family histories are not required, nor is it necessary to delve into every past loss. Attention to the family adaptational tasks and variables discussed in this chapter can usefully guide inquiry and intervention (see McGoldrick, Chapter 3). It is most important to normalize the process of mourning, in a wide range of responses, and to promote continuity in the face of loss.

It should be kept in mind that loss can also lead to growth. Families that have experienced many traumatic, untimely deaths (see McGoldrick, Chapter 6) may develop either a feeling of being "cursed" and unable to rise above the experience, or they may come to see themselves as survivors, who can be struck down but never beaten. Loss can be a catalyst for remarkable creativity and achievement (Eisenstadt, 1978; see Coleman, Chapter 14). Yet, when families are unable to master the challenges posed by death, the fallout may be damaging, in terms of personal well-being and the capacity to experience life and love fully.

When families can come together and share the grief experience, quite positive changes are likely to accompany the distress, strengthening the family unit and all members. The finality of death brings awareness that time is limited and precious, and can be the impetus for reconnection and repair of longstanding conflicts, before it is too late (see Carter, Chapter 15). Families can develop a clearer sense of life priorities, an increased valuing of relationships, and a heightened capacity for intimacy and empathy. Often, a sense of resilience emerges, as family members recognize formerly unrealized potential and a shared conviction that they can survive any adversity. It is this sense of empowerment and human connectedness that we strive to foster in our clinical interventions as families approach loss, in the immediate aftermath of a death, or in long-term complications of past loss. In hearing their pain, we validate their courage, their struggle, and their strength.

Death and loss blur the boundaries between "us" and "them" — clinical experts and distressed families — since we are all vulnerable. In order to help families with loss, we as clinicians and family therapy as a field must face the inescapable fact of death, the inevitability of loss in life, and the terror of our own mortality. "To be close to death 'powerfully concentrates' [you]. . . . The piquancy is that you are spurred even more to rethink life, to reinvent yourself, to ask the embracing question: What shall I do with the rest of my life" (Lerner, 1990). We need to come to terms with our own fears of death and the limits of our control in order to detoxify issues of loss so that we do not continue to deny their significance or neglect them in our theory and practice. By coming to accept death as part of life, and loss as a transforming experience, we—and our field—will discover new possibilities for growth.

REFERENCES

Anderson, C. (1982). The community connection: The impact of social networks on family and individual functioning. In F. Walsh (Ed.), *Normal family processes*. New York: Guilford.

Aries, P. (1974). *Western attitudes toward death: From the middle ages to the present*. Baltimore: Johns Hopkins University Press.

Aries, P. (1982). *The hour of our death*. New York: Vintage.

Becker, E. (1973). *The denial of death*. New York: The Free Press.

Boszormenyi-Nagy, I., & Spark, G. (1984). *Invisible loyalties*. New York: Brunner/Mazel.

Bowen, M. (1976). Family reaction to death. In P. Guerin (Ed.), *Family therapy*. New York: Gardner.

Bowlby, J. (1961). Processes of mourning. *International Journal of Psychoanalysis, 42*, 317–340.

Bowlby, J. (1980). *Attachment and loss: Vol. 3. Loss: Sadness and depression*. London: Hogarth.

Cain, A. (Ed.). (1972). *Survivors of suicide*. Springfield, IL: Thomas.

Carter, B., & McGoldrick, M. (Eds.). (1989). *The changing family life cycle: Framework for family therapy* (2nd ed.). Boston: Allyn & Bacon.

Coleman, S. B. (1981). Incomplete mourning in substance-abusing families: Theory, research and practice. In M. Aronson (Ed.), *Group and family therapy*. New York: Brunner/Mazel.

Coleman, S. B., & Stanton, D. M. (1978). The role of death in the addict family. *Journal of Marriage and Family Counseling, 4*, 79–91.

DeFrain, J., Taylor, J., & Ernst, L. (1982). *Coping with sudden infant death*. Lexington, MA: D. C. Heath.

Dunne, E., McIntosh, J., & Dunne-Maxim, K. (1988). *Suicide and its aftermath*. New York: Norton.

Eisenstadt, J. M. (1978). Parental loss and genius. *American Psychologist, 33*, 211–223.

Engel, G. (1961). Is grief a disease? A challenge for medical research. *Psychosomatic Medicine, 23*, 18–22.

Engel, G. (1975). The death of a twin: Mourning and anniversary reactions. Fragments of 10 years of self-analysis. *International Journal of Psychoanalysis, 56*, 23–40.

Figley, C. (1986). Traumatic stress: The role of the family and social support systems. In C. Figley (Ed.), *Trauma and its wake. Vol. 2: Post-traumatic stress disorder: Theory, research, and treatment*. New York: Brunner-Mazel.

Figley, C. (1989). *Helping traumatized families*. San Francisco: Jossey-Bass.

Fisch, R., Weakland, J. H., & Segal, L. (1982). *The tactics of change*. San Francisco: Jossey-Bass.

Freud, S. (1917 [1915]). Mourning and melancholia. In J. Strachey (Ed. & Trans.), *The standard edition of the complete psychological works of Sigmund Freud* (Vol. 14). New York: Norton.

Furman, E. (1974). *A child's parent dies: Studies in childhood bereavement.* New Haven: Yale University Press.

Glick, I., Weiss, R., & Parkes, C. (1974). *The first year of bereavement.* New York: Wiley.

Hadley, T., Jacob, T., Miliones, J., Caplan, J., & Spitz, D. (1974). The relationship between family developmental crises and the appearance of symptoms in a family member. *Family Process, 13,* 207-214.

Hare-Mustin, R. (1979). Family therapy following the death of a child. *Journal of Marital and Family Therapy, 5,* 51-60.

Herz, F. (1980). The impact of death and serious illness on the family life cycle. In E. A. Carter & M. McGoldrick (Eds.), *The family life cycle: A framework for family therapy.* New York: Gardner.

Herz, F. (1989). The impact of death and serious illness on the family life cycle. In B. Carter & M. McGoldrick (Eds.), *The changing family life cycle: A framework for family therapy* (2nd ed.). Boston: Allyn & Bacon.

Hoffman, L. (1981). *Foundations of family therapy.* New York: Basic Books.

Hoffman, L. (1990). Constructing realities: An art of lenses. *Family Process, 29,* 1-12.

Holmes, T., & Rahe, R. H. (1967). The social adjustment rating scale. *Journal of Psychosomatic Research, 11,* 213-218.

Howe, B. J., & Robinson, S. (1975). The "family tombstone" syndrome: An interpersonal suicide process. *Family Therapy, 8,* 393-398.

Huygen, F. J. A., van den Hoogen, H. J. M., van Eijk, J. T. M., & Smits, A. J. A. (1989). Death and dying: A longitudinal study of their medical impact on the family. *Family Systems Medicine, 7,* 374-384.

Kessler, R. C., Price, R. H., & Wortman, C. B. (1985). Social factors in psychopathology: Stress, social support, and coping processes. *Annual Review of Psychology, 36,* 533-572.

Klein, S., & Fletcher, W. (1986). Gay grief: An examination of the uniqueness brought to light by the AIDS crisis. *Journal of Psychosocial Oncology, 4,* 15-25.

Kübler-Ross, E. (1969). *On death and dying.* New York: Macmillan.

Kuhn, J. (1981). Realignment of emotional forces following loss. *The Family, 5,* 19-24.

Lerner, M. (1990). *Wrestling with the angel.* New York: Norton.

Lewis, J., Beavers, W. R., Gossett, J., & Phillips, V. (1976). *No single thread: Psychological health in family systems.* New York: Brunner/Mazel.

Lindemann, E. (1944). Symptomatology and management of acute grief. *American Journal of Psychiatry, 101,* 141-148.

Madanes, C., & Haley, J. (1977). Dimensions of family therapy. *Journal of Nervous and Mental Disease, 165,* 88-98.

McGoldrick, M. (1989). Women and the family life cycle. In M. McGoldrick, C. Anderson, & F. Walsh (Eds.), *Women in families: A framework for family therapy.* New York: Norton.

McGoldrick, M., Anderson, C., & Walsh, F. (Eds.). (1989). *Women in families.* New York: Norton.

McGoldrick, M., Pearce, J., & Giordano, J. (1982). *Ethnicity and family therapy.* New York: Norton.

McGoldrick, M., & Walsh, F. (1983). A systemic view of family history and loss. In M. Aronson & L. Wolberg (Eds.), *Group and family therapy.* New York: Brunner/Mazel.

Mitford, J. (1978). *The American way of death.* New York: Touchstone.

Neugarten, B. (1970). Dynamics of transition of middle age to old age: Adaptation and the life cycle. *Journal of Geriatric Psychiatry, 4,* 71-87.

Osterweis, M., Solomon, F., & Green, M. (Eds.). (1984). *Bereavement: Reactions, consequences, and care.* Washington, DC: National Academy Press.

Parkes, C. M. (1972). *Bereavement: Studies of grief in adult life.* New York: International Universities Press.

Parkes, C. M. (1975). Determinants of outcome following bereavement. *Omega, 6,* 303-323.

Parkes, C. M., & Weiss, R. (1983). *Recovery from bereavement.* New York: Basic.

Paul, N. (1967). The use of empathy in the resolution of grief. *Perspectives in Biology and Medicine, 11,* 153-169.

Paul, N. (1976). Cross-confrontation. In P. Guerin (Ed.), *Family therapy*. New York: Gardner.

Paul, N. (1980). Now and the past: Transgenerational analysis. *International Journal of Family Psychiatry, 1*, 235–248.

Paul, N., & Grosser, G. (1965). Operational mourning and its role in conjoint family therapy. *Community Mental Health Journal, 1*, 339–345.

Paul, N., & Paul, B. (1982). Death and changes in sexual behavior. In F. Walsh (Ed.), *Normal family processes*. New York: Guilford.

Paul, N., & Paul, B. (1989). *A Marital Puzzle*. Boston: Allyn & Bacon.

Pinkus, L. (1974). *Death and the family: The importance of mourning*. New York: Pantheon.

Pollock, G. (1961). Mourning and adaptation. *International Journal of Psychoanalysis, 42*, 341–361.

Reilly, D. (1978). Death propensity, dying, and bereavement: A family system's perspective. *Family Therapy, 5*, 35–55.

Reiss, D., & Oliveri, M. (1980). Family paradigm and family coping: A proposal for linking the family's intrinsic adaptive capacities to its responses to stress. *Family Relations, 29*, 431–444.

Rosaldo, R. (1989). *Culture and truth: The remaking of social analysis*. New York: Beacon.

Rosen, E. (1990). *Families facing death: Family dynamics of terminal illness*. Lexington, MA: D.C. Heath.

Schiff, H. S. (1977). *The bereaved parent*. New York: Penguin.

Scott, D., & Wishy, B. (Eds.). (1982). *America's families: A documentary history*. New York: Harper & Row.

Sontag, S. (1988). *AIDS and its metaphors*. New York: Farrar, Straus, & Giroux.

Stanton, M. D. (1977). The addict as savior: Heroin, death and the family. *Family Process, 16*, 191–197.

Videka-Sherman, L. (1982). Coping with the death of a child: A study over time. *American Journal of Orthopsychiatry, 52*, 688–698.

Videka-Sherman, L., & Lieberman, M. (1985). Effects of self-help groups and psychotherapy after a child dies: The limits of recovery. *American Journal of Orthopsychiatry, 55*, 70–82.

Viorst, J. (1986). *Necessary losses*. New York: Simon & Schuster.

Walsh, F. (Ed.). (1982). *Normal family processes*. New York: Guilford.

Walsh, F. (1983a). Normal family ideologies: Myths and realities. In C. Falicov (Ed.), *Cultural dimensions in family therapy*. Rockville, MD: Aspen.

Walsh, F. (1983b). The timing of symptoms and critical events in the family life cycle. In H. Liddle (Ed.), *Clinical implications of the family life cycle*. Rockville, MD: Aspen.

Walsh, F. (1989). The family in later life. In B. Carter & M. McGoldrick (Eds.), *The changing family life cycle* (2nd ed.). Boston: Allyn & Bacon.

Walsh, F. (in press). *Promoting health in dysfunctional families*. New York: Guilford.

Walsh, F., & McGoldrick, M. (1987). Loss and the family life cycle. In C. Falicov (Ed.), *Family transitions*. New York: Guilford.

Welldon, R. (1971). The "shadow of death" and its implications in four families, each with a hospitalized schizophrenic member. *Family Process, 10(3)*, 281–302.

Williamson, D. S. (1978). New life at the graveyard: A method of therapy for individuation from a dead former parent. *Journal of Marriage and Family Counseling, 4*, 93–101.

Worden, W. (1982). *Grief counseling and grief therapy*. New York: Springer.

Wortman, C., & Silver, R. (1989). The myths of coping with loss. *Journal of Consulting and Clinical Psychology, 57*, 349–357.

2

A Time to Mourn: Death and the Family Life Cycle

MONICA MCGOLDRICK   FROMA WALSH

> There is no love without loss. And there is no moving beyond loss without some experience of mourning. To be unable to mourn is to be unable to enter into the great human life cycle of death and rebirth—to be unable, that is, to live again.

> —Lifton, 1975, p. vii.

A LIFE CYCLE PERSPECTIVE on loss, joining a developmental framework with a family systems orientation, views loss as a transactional process involving the dead with the survivors in a shared life cycle that acknowledges both the finality of death and the continuity of life. Coming to terms with this experience is the most difficult challenge we confront in life.

From a family perspective the same death may involve the loss of a spouse, a child, a sibling, a parent, a cousin, or an aunt at the same time. In each family the unique constellation of these relationships affects the impact of loss on each member, each generation, and the family as a whole (Walsh & McGoldrick, Chapter 1). The meaning and consequences of loss vary depending on the particular phase of life cycle development the family is negotiating at the time of the loss. We are mindful of the variability in family life cycle patterns, given the diversity of family forms and ethnic norms (Carter & McGoldrick, 1989; McGoldrick et al., Chapter 10). At the same time we find it useful to view loss in the context of family tasks at each phase of the life cycle (Herz, 1980, 1989). We do not mean to reify the punctuation of the stream of family interaction over time into life cycle stages; nor do we wish to imply that life courses that deviate from this path are abnormal or pathological. Rather, the framework enables us to identify expectable family challenges around loss at different points over the course of the life cycle. Whatever our therapeutic approach with loss, a family life cycle perspective can facilitate the strengthening of the whole family in its future course.

TIMING OF LOSS IN THE FAMILY LIFE CYCLE

The timing of a loss in the three-generational family life cycle poses different complications that will affect the family's risk for dysfunction (McGoldrick, in press; McGoldrick & Gerson, 1985; Walsh, 1983; Walsh & McGoldrick, Chapter 1). Of special significance in regard to timing are (1) untimely losses; (2) symptom onset coinciding with loss; (3) concurrence of multiple losses or loss with other major life cycle changes; and (4) traumatic loss and unresolved mourning.

Untimely losses. Premature deaths that are "off-time" in terms of chronological or social expectations, such as early widowhood, early parent loss, or death of a child, tend to be more difficult for families to come to terms with than "timely" deaths. Prolonged mourning, often lasting many years, is common. Families struggle to find some justification for the loss. Long-term survival guilt for spouses, siblings, and parents can block achievement of other life pursuits and satisfaction. The death of a child, upsetting generational expectations, is perhaps the most painful loss of all for a family, since it reverses the natural order.

Symptom onset coinciding with recent or threatened loss. A wide range of mental and physical disorders has been found to be associated with recent loss; these may be seen in the individual symptom bearer (Osterweis, Solomon, & Green, 1984) or in the family system (Hadley, Jacob, Miliones, Caplan, & Spitz, 1974). Child behavior problems or marital distress may be linked to the recent or threatened loss of a significant family member. Often, family members do not connect the symptoms with loss and may not even mention a recent or impending death. Clinicians need to be alert to the impact of anticipated losses (see Rolland, Chapter 8), as well as those that have occurred in the past one or two years.

Concurrence of multiple losses or of loss and other major life cycle changes. The temporal coincidence of loss with other major stress events may overload a family and pose incompatible tasks and demands. We pay particular attention to the concurrence of death with the birth of a child, since the processes of mourning and parenting an infant are inherently incompatible. The child born at the time of a significant loss may assume a special replacement function, which can be the impetus for high achievement or dysfunction. Similarly, marrying in the wake of loss is likely to confound the two relationships, interfering either with bereavement or with investment in the new relationship. When stressful events do pile up, family support can be a crucial buffer that facilitates adaptation.

Past traumatic loss and unresolved mourning. In family assessment, genograms and family chronologies are particularly useful in tracking sequences and the concurrence of nodal events over time in the multigenerational family (McGoldrick & Gerson, 1985). In cases of marital breakdown, we are especially careful to inquire about losses that occurred at the start of the relationship, as well as losses coinciding with the onset of marital problems. When a child in a family is the identified patient, we pay particular attention to unresolved losses that coincided with the birth of the symptom bearer. Studies by Walsh (1978) and Mueller and McGoldrick Orfanidis (1976) suggest that the death of a grandparent within two years of the birth of a child may contribute to later emotional disorder of the child, particularly around separation and launching attempts in young adulthood, which disrupt the family balance.

We also pay special attention to transgenerational anniversary patterns, where the age or life cycle stage of the identified patient at symptom onset coincides with the age or stage of a parent at death or bereavement a generation earlier. In such situations, family patterns or scenarios are replicated when a child in the next generation reaches the same age or stage as the parent at the time of death or traumatic loss. It is crucial to assess a risk of suicide or self-destructive behavior when a child reaches the same age as the untimely, traumatic death of a parent, especially the same-sex parent with whom the child had been strongly identified. The more seriously dysfunctional a family, the more likely it is that such linkages are covert and unconnected by family members. In one chilling case, a 15-year-old boy stabbed a man in the street in an apparently dissociated episode that the family ignored. Upon psychiatric hospitalization after a second similar stabbing, family assessment revealed that the father, at the age of 15, had witnessed the stabbing death of his own father in the street. We need family research directed at such transgenerational anniversary patterns in order more fully to understand the transmission processes. In our clinical work, interventions should be aimed at making covert patterns overt and helping family members to differentiate present relationships from the past so that history need not repeat itself.

LOSS AT DIFFERENT FAMILY LIFE CYCLE STAGES

Between Families: Unattached Young Adults

In the vast literature on loss, it is remarkable that so little attention has been given to the impact of loss on young adults. Clinical theory has been strongly influenced by a prevailing myth in our culture that once children have grown up and left home, their relationships with their families are no longer significant. In fact, there is ample research (e.g., Cohler & Geyer, 1982) that normal parent-child relationships remain intimate and interdependent throughout adulthood.

At launching, the family must reorganize as a system and renegotiate intergenerational relationships, from the dependency and hierarchical authority of childhood and adolescence to a more equal balance as adults to adults. Young adults are commonly concerned—as are their parents—that they could slide back into a previous dependency. In families where relationships have been especially close or characterized by intense conflict, young adults may cut off entirely in order to gain physical or emotional distance. Such cutoffs generally produce only a pseudo-autonomy, which disintegrates in contact with the family. However, because this stance fits our society's normative stereotype of independence, the significance of loss may not be recognized, which complicates mourning.

Child loss. The death of a young adult child is a tragedy for the entire family and may produce highly distressing and long-lasting grief (Gorer, 1965). When an untimely death occurs in young adulthood, the family may experience a sense of cruel injustice in the ending of a life before its prime. The young adult was full of potential, on the brink of life commitments and achievements, which he is now prevented by death from realizing. Pain and survivor guilt may block parents and siblings from continuing their own pursuits. Where the young adult has been distant or in conflict with the family, or where he or she dies by suicide or drug-involved accident, mourning is likely to be complicated by the unresolved state of the relationship. Combat-related death in war, even when regarded as heroic or as a sacrifice in the patriotic defense of national or ideological values, is nevertheless heartbreaking for parents, whose grief may persist for years to come (Rubin, 1989). Siblings may be expected to carry the torch and yet be blocked from their own potential by prior sibling rivalry, survivor guilt, and conflicting family injunctions to attempt to replace, but not replace the lost child.

Brian, age 29, sought therapy for a repeated cycle of setting rather grandiose career goals that he pursued at a fevered pitch, only to undermine himself each time on the brink of success. He initially resisted doing family of origin work because he felt extreme discomfort about returning to his parents' home, where in the front hallway was a "shrine" to his older brother, who had been killed in Vietnam at the age of 21. Pictures, medals, and plaques covered the walls. Although only 17 at his brother's death, he felt a strong expectation from his parents to fulfill their dreams for their firstborn son. However, this role induction was coupled with a counterinjunction that it would be disloyal to surpass him. He gradually came to the further realization, given the family idealization of his brother, that try as hard as he could, he would never be able to measure up. Therapy focused on shifting his triangulated position, helping him to unknot this tangle in his ongoing relations with his family.

Parent loss. Given the developmental tasks of young adulthood and the culturally sanctioned tendency to deny the importance of family ties at this time, the impact of loss of a parent for young adults may be seriously underestimated by them and by their families, friends, and even therapists. The terminal illness of a parent may be particularly difficult for young adult children who have moved away and are invested in launching a career and new relationship commitments (Walsh, 1989). They are likely to be torn between their own immediate pursuits and filial caretaking obligations. The developmental imperatives of young adulthood may conflict with the priorities of aging parents who, in order to accept impending death, are attempting to come to terms with their lives as they have been lived (Erikson, 1959). Especially for women whose identities have been bound up with their roles as mothers, this life review centers largely on parenting accomplishments and relationships with their children. Parents may experience heightened physical dependency, as well as a need to draw children in both to affirm that they have been successful in parenting and to enjoy a final closeness with them. Young adult children who are turning—or even pushing—away from their parents, but are not yet secure on their own, may be threatened by closeness and parental dependence. Coping with a dying parent may stir fears of a loss of self. The impact of the parental loss itself may not be acknowledged, and the young adult may distance still further from the family.

Another source of distancing is the fear that newly initiated adult life pursuits will have to be abandoned or put on hold to care for a dying parent or, after the parent's death, for the surviving parent and other family members. This expectation tends to weigh most heavily on the eldest or most parentified child. The eldest son may be expected to become the head of the family with the death of his father, whereas daughters are typically expected to assume major caretaking functions for the surviving parent, younger siblings, and aged grandparents. It is not uncommon for an adult child to move back home to assist in the immediate adjustment of a widowed parent.

Where such caregiving responsibility becomes prolonged, forward movement in the life cycle may be blocked for the young adult.

Grandparent loss. The loss of grandparents at this phase may be easier,
because young adults have had the advantage of having known them
throughout childhood and into adulthood. If the grandparent was cherished, the loss will naturally be upsetting, but emotional ramifications are
more likely to flow down the system if the parent and grandparent had a
troubled relationship that remained unresolved at the time of death.

Young Couples: The Joining of Families Through Marriage

Loss of a spouse. Widowhood in early marriage is relatively uncommon,
and its untimeliness makes bereavement for the surviving spouse extraordinarily difficult (Parkes & Weiss, 1983). Early widowhood tends to be a
shocking and isolating experience, lacking emotional preparation or essential social supports. Not surprisingly, sudden death is more traumatic at this
phase (Parkes, 1972, 1975) than in later life, when lingering deaths tend to
produce greater strain (Gerber, Rusalem, Hannon, Battin, & Arkin, 1975).
Not only do young widow(er)s have to cope with the loss itself, but they are
often shunned by siblings and peers, who need to avoid confronting their
own mortality or possibility of widowhood. There is also a tendency for the
family to expect the widowed spouse to move on quickly to a new relationship, denying the significance of the experience because of the pain it creates. Relationships between the surviving spouse and in-laws, which are
commonly strained at this phase of the life cycle, often become more complicated without the mellowing that comes with years and with grandchildren. If the surviving spouse accedes to pressure not to grieve too publicly or
too long, or runs to a new relationship to avoid the pain of loss, unattended
mourning will most likely be carried along, to surface later. Not surprisingly,
women have greater difficulty than men in moving into a new relationship,
especially when guilt and disloyalty are implied by in-laws. Men tend to
move on more rapidly, expecting a new partner to be sympathetic toward
their continued mourning (Glick, Parkes, & Weiss, 1975).

Loss of an unborn child. Infertility, often a hidden loss, represents the loss
of one's dreams for the future. It currently affects an unprecedented number
of couples, due, in many cases, to the use of certain methods of birth
control and postponement of childbearing, as well as the rise in sexually
transmitted diseases. The impact of loss may be gradual over time, becoming more painful as each monthly cycle passes and as menopause approaches, especially when medical interventions repeatedly fail to result in conception. Distress is likely to be heightened by being out of phase with siblings
and friends who are excited over their own pregnancies or involvement with

newborns. Couples may shun contact with others and avoid discussion of their own situation. It is crucial for clinicians to assuage their feelings that they have not progressed "normally" in the family life cycle without children and to help them find meaningful ways to express their generativity.

Other significant hidden losses include stillbirths, miscarriages, and abortions. These losses are often unknown to others or unacknowledged and regarded as nonevents, making the loss more painful (Lewis, 1976). Women commonly feel the attachment and loss more deeply than their spouses, especially when the child has grown in their bodies during pregnancy. In cases of miscarriage or stillbirth, women are also more likely to blame themselves, fearing that the loss resulted from their own deficiency or harmful actions. Disappointment and sorrow may include the loss of future children and the fear of future pregnancy complications. One couple's grief at a stillbirth was compounded when they were told by a funeral director that memorial services were not held "in such circumstances," but that he would be glad "to dispose of the remains" for them. The husband wanted to put the event quickly behind them and try to conceive another child. The wife persuaded her husband to name the baby and to bury him in a marked grave, which helped the couple to grieve and move on with their lives. Since the loss of a child places couples at risk for marital breakdown, a focused couples group can be especially helpful to facilitate the mourning process and promote the spouses' mutual support.

The impact of such loss experiences will depend greatly on religious or cultural beliefs about the meaning of infertility, stillbirth, miscarriage, or abortion. The trauma challenges the equilibrium of a new couple. Where there is social stigma or a lack of support from family and friends, the couple may turn in on itself, risking either fusion in a "two against the world" stance or mutual blame for the inability to fill each other's sense of loss and emptiness.

Parent loss. When the death of a parent occurs as young couples are focusing on their own lives, it may not be mourned as directly as at other life phases. In fact, parental illness or death may propel an individual into marriage, without realization by either partner of the emotional issues behind the decision to marry (McGoldrick, 1989). When marriage has improved intergenerational relationships, parental loss may not be as difficult as it might have been during the unattached young adult phase. On the other hand, the death of one parent may leave a child (especially an only child, or the only one living in the area) anxious about the dependence and neediness of the remaining parent, as much as grieving for the one who is lost.

An issue that receives scant clinical attention is the change in adult sibling relationships brought on by the death of a parent. Sisters are more likely to be stressed in this process than brothers, because of the expectation in our culture that daughters will be parental caretakers. Brothers tend to share the financial but not the caregiving responsibilities. Old sibling rivalries may erupt into conflict over who was more favored at the end, more burdened by caregiving, or more to blame for the death.

The death of a parent at this phase, when couples are shifting their primary allegiance to the marital relationship, may push them back to family-of-origin obligations, complicating their adaptation to the new system. If it is the second parent who dies, the young adult prematurely becomes the last surviving generation, which may also generate pressure to have children. The sense of responsibility for one's parents may produce conflicts of loyalty between the family of origin and the marriage. Increased attention, physical or financial caretaking of the dying or surviving parent, or absorption in the grief process may stress the marital relationship, especially if the spouse feels neglected over an extended period of time. The lack of support makes mourning more difficult and can lead to mutual disappointment, with fallout for the marital and sexual relationship (Paul & Paul, 1982). The support of one's partner not only facilitates mourning, but also strengthens the marriage and should be promoted in any clinical intervention.

Families With Young Children

Loss of a spouse. For the surviving spouse the loss of a mate at this life phase is complicated by financial and caretaking obligations for the children, which can interfere with the tasks of mourning. Children are likely to distract the bereaved parent from grieving in order to maintain the functioning of their only surviving parent (Fulmer, 1983). Symptoms in a child may serve such a function of distraction. Other siblings may cover over their own grief in order not to further burden the surviving parent. It is important for other adult family members and friends to contribute caretaking, meals, and other concrete supports, to permit the surviving parent to grieve. Generally, widowers receive such support more than do widows in this situation. However, men are less likely to have intimate friendships to facilitate emotional griefwork.

Child loss. The death of a young child is likely to be profoundly distressing for the entire family. Grief tends to persist for years and may even intensify with the passage of time (Rando, 1985). The effect can be devastating on the parents' health and marriage. A number of studies have documented the high distress of bereaved parents on such indicators as depression, anxiety, somatic symptoms, self-esteem, and sense of control in life. The marital relationship is particularly vulnerable after a child dies, with risk of further deterioration of marital satisfaction over time (Videka-Sherman & Lieberman, 1985). Divorce rates as high as 80% have been reported for bereaved parents (Bluebond-Langner, 1978; Kaplan, Grobstein, & Smith, 1976; Schiff, 1977; Strauss, 1975).

It is often said, "When your parent dies, you have lost your past. When your child dies, you have lost your future." The death of a child involves the loss of parents' hopes and dreams. Moreover, the untimeliness and injustice in the death of a child can lead family members to the most profound questioning of the meaning of life. Of all losses, it is hardest not to idealize a deceased child.

Factors regarding the child who dies will have differential effects on the family response. Particularly difficult may be the death of the firstborn, an only child, the only child of one sex, a gifted child, a difficult child for whom parents' feelings have been particularly ambivalent, or a child who dies in an accident for which the parents blame themselves. Because small children are so utterly dependent on parents for their safety and survival, parental guilt tends to be especially strong in accidental or ambiguously caused deaths, such as sudden infant death syndrome (SIDS) (DeFrain, Taylor, & Ernst, 1982). Blame is particularly likely to fall on mothers, who are expected to carry the primary responsibility for child well-being, even where paternal abuse or neglect are implicated. Unattended parental difficulties with the loss of a child may be presented through symptomatic behavior of a sibling, as in the following case.

> The Lamb family was referred for therapy for a "school refusal" problem, when their four-year-old son Danny refused to go to nursery school, despite his good adjustment there the previous year. When asked who was in the family, no one mentioned an older brother, Michael, who had died at the age of four, three years earlier. In taking a family history, the therapist learned that Michael had died suddenly after developing a high fever. The parents attributed the death to a virus he had picked up at nursery school. Mr. Lamb (and his own mother) secretly blamed Mrs. Lamb for letting Michael go to nursery school when the flu was going around. The parents still kept Michael's room the way it had been and the mother continued to celebrate his birthdays with Danny, each year making a birthday cake with candles for the age he would have been if still alive.

Bereavement in the loss of a child has been found to be facilitated when both parents can participate in taking care of a sick child prior to death (Mulhern, Laurer, & Hoffman, 1983) and when they have a consistent philosophy of life (Spinetta, Swarner, & Sheposh, 1981) or strong religious beliefs (Martinson, Moldow, & Henry, 1980). Self-help groups are extremely valuable for bereaved parents, providing a supportive network to facilitate dealing with the pain of the experience (Videka-Sherman & Lieberman, 1985).

Sibling loss. In the death of a child, too often siblings are neglected, along with other family members for whom the loss will also be devastating. The death of a sibling can be followed by prolonged grieving in some children, who may experience anniversary reactions for years afterward (Cain, Fast, & Erickson, 1964). Normal sibling rivalry may contribute to intense survival guilt, which can block developmental strivings well into adulthood. For children, a sibling's death is likely to be accompanied by an experienced loss of the parents, who are preoccupied with caretaking or grieving or may even withdraw from their children out of fear of ever being so vulnerable to loss again. In cases of protracted illness and prolonged caregiving, siblings also must cope with diminished attention to their needs. In many cases, parents become overly vigilant and protective of surviving children and later have difficulty with normative transitions involving separation in adolescence and at launching.

A sibling may also be inducted into a replacement role for the family. In fact, it is quite common for bereaved parents, and parents of a dying child, to conceive another child as soon as possible. Studies suggest that such replacement response is not necessarily pathogenic, since investing energy in surviving children has been found to facilitate positive adjustment over time for parents (Videka-Sherman, 1982). However, the long-term consequences for the replacement child have not yet been well investigated (Cain & Cain, 1964; Legg & Sherick, 1976). Our own clinical experience suggests that this response becomes dysfunctional *if* the child's own needs and unique qualities cannot be acknowledged or valued. In such cases, normative attempts at separation and individuation are likely to become problematic for the child, to disrupt the family equilibrium, and to precipitate delayed grief responses in other family members.

Parental loss. Children who lose a parent may suffer profound short- and long-term consequences (Furman, 1974; Osterweis et al., 1984), including illness, depression, and other emotional disturbances in subsequent adult life. They may later experience difficulty in forming intimate attachments and may carry catastrophic fears of separation and abandonment. Our clinical experience suggests that marital commitments are more likely to be problematic when the opposite-sexed parent has been lost during childhood. Later difficulty in parenting is also common, especially if the same-sexed parent was lost in childhood. A parent may function normally until a child reaches the same age at which the parent had been bereaved. At that point, the relationship may become blocked, the parent may distance, and/or the child may become symptomatic.

Children's reactions to death will depend on their stage of cognitive development, on the way adults deal with them around death, and on the degree of caretaking they have lost. First, it is important for adults to recognize the limitations of a child's ability to understand what is happening and not to be alarmed by seemingly unemotional or "inappropriate" responses. For instance, a small child may approach strangers saying "My mother died" as a way of seeking support and understanding through observing the reactions of others (Osterweis et al., 1984). Second, it is crucial for parents and other adults not to exclude children from the experience of loss, hoping thus to spare them pain (see Bowen, Chapter 4). Third, it is important that the role functions of the lost parent and of the bereaved spouse be recognized and carried out by other family members. If, in addition to the loss of a parent, the child must cope with a vacuum in caretaking while the surviving parent is depressed or preoccupied, there may be serious lasting consequences. A child's handling of parent loss does depend largely on the emotional state of the surviving parent (Rutter, 1966; Van Eerdewegh, Bieri, Parilla, & Clayton, 1982). The supportive role of the extended family should be encouraged.

Grandparent loss. The loss of a grandparent at this phase is likely to be the first experience for a child in learning how to deal with death. Children will probably be most helped if included in their parents' experience of mourning and will be reassured by seeing that the parents can cope with the loss. If the grandparent has suffered a prolonged illness for which a parent assumed major caretaking responsibility, the parent will be stressed by pulls in two directions: toward the heavy responsibilities of caring for young children and toward filial obligations for the dying and surviving parent. As in dealing with any death, the fewer the family resources in terms of available extended family, friends, and financial supports, the more the system will be stressed.

Families With Adolescents

Death at this phase in the life cycle may be particularly traumatic because the primary developmental task of adolescent separation conflicts with the experience of loss, which requires the family to move closer in support of its members.

Child loss. The most common adolescent deaths are from accidents (often complicated by risky or self-destructive behavior, such as drug and alcohol abuse and careless driving), suicide, homicide, and cancer. Where the death is associated with risk-taking behavior, parents and siblings may have angry feelings toward the dead child, frustration about the impulsive behavior, and sadness at the senseless loss. Any number of problems in living, fueled by peer pressure, may have contributed to an adolescent's self-destructive behavior or actual decision to commit suicide. When a suicide attempt occurs, the whole family should be convened, helped to understand and reconstruct meanings surrounding the experience, and helped to repair family fragmentation resulting from earlier adversities (see Gutstein, Chapter 13). It is crucial to explore possible connections to other traumatic losses in the family system (Coleman & Stanton, 1978; Landau-Stanton & Stanton, 1985), especially other suicides, as in the following case.

A 13-year-old boy was hospitalized following an attempted suicide. The boy and his family were at a loss to explain the episode and made no mention of an older deceased brother. Family assessment revealed that the boy was born shortly before the death of an elder son at the age of 13. He grew up attempting to take the place of the brother he had never known in order to relieve his parents' sadness. The father, who could not recall the date or events surrounding the death, wished to remember his first son "as if he were still alive." The boy cultivated his appearance to resemble photos of his brother. Only when asked about his brother did he reply that he had attempted suicide "to join my 13-year-old brother in heaven." The timing corresponded to his reaching and surviving the age of his brother's death and to his concern, with his growth spurt at puberty, that he was changing from the way he was "supposed" to look. Family therapy focused on enabling the boy and his parents to relinquish this surrogate position and to move forward in their development.

In the case of cancer, younger children usually comply with treatment and remain close to their parent, but for adolescents the trauma of the disease and its treatment can become interwoven with rebelliousness, compounding the difficulty for parents. Children may resist medications or required treatments as attempts to control them by parents or medical authorities, thereby taking severe risks with their health. While parents, more conscious of the long-term consequences, struggle with the present-focused adolescent, helping agencies are often caught in between.

Sibling loss. Siblings frequently retreat from family and friends following an adolescent's death. They may talk to no one about the experience, never even clarifying the nature of the death. The differences in coping styles of different family members may compound problems following loss: Typically in our culture, adolescents may rebuff their mothers' attempts to share feelings, as their fathers withdraw or bury themselves in work. Such reactions will, of course, be modified by cultural background and the particular experience of the families of origin in dealing with loss. Unfortunately, if the response styles of family members are very different, this is likely to make grieving even more difficult.

Parent loss. For the adolescent, whose developmental tasks involve a pushing away from parental influence and control, the death of a parent is likely to be complicated by negative and conflictual feelings toward the parent. If other family members idealize the deceased parent, the adolescent's experience of disqualification may lead to an increased sense of being cut off and isolated from family members and of not being understood.

If adolescents have earlier wished to be rid of parental control, they may

develop considerable guilt. The death of a parent at this phase is also complicated by peer models of acting-out behavior to escape pain. Boys who
lose a parent often turn to stealing, drugs, or fighting, or they withdraw
socially, whereas girls are likely to band together with sisters or to sexualize
peer relationships, seeking closeness in order to comfort themselves and
replace their loss (Osterweis et al., 1984). Adolescent acting-out behavior is,
in turn, stressful for the family, and the experience of parental loss at the
same time may overtax the adaptability of the system. Outside agencies may
become involved, particularly school or juvenile authorities. Such larger
systems tend to focus narrowly on the child's problem behavior, which may
only exacerbate the problem. It is crucial to assess the context of behavior
problems routinely and, where recent losses have occurred, to assist the
family, not only the symptomatic child, in resolution.

Grandparent loss. In our experience, the death of a grandparent is often
an underlying precipitant when parents seek treatment for their adolescent's
problem behavior. An adolescent is often the barometer of family feelings,
the one who expresses the unexpressible and who draws needed attention to
family problems. It is crucial to asses recent changes in the extended family.
If the parents cannot deal with their own emotional loss issues, an adolescent often will pick up parental feelings and, lacking a better way to help the
parents, draw fire by misbehavior, as in the following case.

Mrs. Wolff requested psychiatric treatment for her 15-year-old son, Paul, stating
that she feared that he "needed to be institutionalized" because his behavior was
"out of control." He had become unmanageable in recent months and she felt
increasingly helpless in dealing with him. The family assessment interview revealed that eight months earlier the maternal grandmother, with a deteriorating
Alzheimer's condition, had moved in with the family. Mrs. Wolff tearfully described her mounting difficulty in caring for her mother at home. She was
alarmed by her mother's increasing loss of control of functioning and felt helpless
to prevent a potentially fatal accident.

When asked if the family had considered institutionalization of the grandmother, Mrs. Wolff replied that it was "out of the question" and had not been discussed, since she had promised her father on his deathbed, a year earlier, that she
would always take care of her mother. Feeling alone in her burdensome and
conflictual dilemma, Mrs. Wolff became increasingly focused on struggles with
her son over his behavior. In a vicious cycle, the harder she tried to control him,
the more reckless and defiant of her authority he became. Her husband had
increasingly withdrawn from her since her father had died and her mother had
moved in with them, and seemed uncomfortable with the death, with his deteriorating mother-in-law, and with his wife's grieving. Mrs. Wolff felt she was left
totally alone with her dilemma.

Exploration of the husband's genogram and family history revealed that when his own mother had become terminally ill, 5 years earlier, he had left all care-taking responsibilities to his sister. The current situation stirred up lingering guilt and his belief that his failure to assume more responsibility for his own mother's care had contributed to her early death.

Therapy involved reengaging the father in his son's development and his wife's life, while helping her separate out the conflicts and issues she had with her mother from those with her son. The husband's involvement was framed as an opportunity for him to share more fully in caregiving arrangements, as he wished he had done for his own mother. Both parents were encouraged to structure a more clear role for their son in the grandmother's care and also to use some savings to provide extra care for the grandmother so the mother would not burn herself out. While initially resistant to the changes, once it was clear to the son that there were new rules and he had to abide by them, he actually became better than the others at dealing with the grandmother and the one most able to articulate the pain of her increasing deterioration. With more support and specific responsibilities, his acting-out behavior ceased.

A systemic view of the problem situation requires inquiry into the functioning of the marital relationship and possible contributions to the dilemma from the other spouse's family-of-origin experience, as this case indicates. Furthermore, like Paul, adolescents are often less ambivalent and more openly expressive of sadness about the loss of a grandparent than their parents. Naturally, a parent can feel conflicted when having to cope simultaneously with the grandparent's death and the adolescent's separation. This experience will be intensified if the parent's own adolescence was troublesome. Mourning is likely to be complicated by longstanding intergenerational triangles, in which problems between parent and grandparent a generation earlier have led to a coalition between grandparent and grandchild, with the parent (viewed as the common enemy) in the outside position. Without repair, such triangles can be repeated in the next generation.

Launching Children and Moving On

The family at launching experiences a major transitional upheaval as children leave and the two-generational household unit reorganizes as a marital dyad. The impact of the death of a young adult child on parents and of the death of a parent on the young adult have already been discussed. The death of a spouse and a grandparent will be considered here.

Loss of a spouse. At launching, the spouses must renegotiate their relationship, which no longer centers on child-rearing. Concurrently, at midlife, as men typically begin to confront their own mortality, concerns about widowhood start to become prominent for women, who expect to outlive their husbands. Women, who are usually younger than their husbands, are four times more likely to outlive their spouses than men are. Women are likely to be widowed at an earlier age than men and to remain widows for many years. With this anticipation, women who have been financially dependent and emotionally centered on their husbands may be more concerned about the health of their husbands than about their own well-being (Neugarten, 1970). We encourage women to put their own lives in perspective—to consider how they will manage on their own and to build a supportive social network for the years they are likely to spend alone. Men, who are less likely to anticipate widowhood, may lack preparedness and experience greater shock at the loss of their wives. It should be noted that the suicide rate for men widowed at midlife is exceptionally high (Butler & Lewis, 1983).

Widowhood at midlife is much more difficult than in later life because it is off-time from social expectations and not commonly experienced by peers. At launching, couples hopefully reinvest energy in the marriage and make plans for their future together, with the anticipation of sharing activities that have been postponed while child-rearing consumed attention and financial resources. With the death of a partner, these plans and dreams of a shared future are lost. Friends and other couples who are not yet ready to confront their own mortality and survivorship may distance from the survivor. The widow(er) may also be reluctant to burden recently launched children, who are not yet established, or aging parents, who have diminished resources and increased needs for caretaking.

(Grand)parent loss. Couples at launching are typically confronting losses on both sides: As their children are leaving home, their aging parents are declining in health and dying. Research with well-functioning families indicates that most adults in their middle years are prepared to assume increased caretaking responsibilities for aging parents and to accept their deaths as a natural, inevitable occurrence in the life cycle (Lewis, 1976; Neugarten, 1970). Nevertheless, adjustment to loss is frequently complicated by concerns about caretaker burden, neglect, or abandonment; caregiving children may feel that their efforts were unappreciated by the dying parent or by less involved siblings, who themselves may feel guilty that they didn't do more.

Caretaking and mourning processes are likely to be more complicated for the entire family in cases where intergenerational tensions or cutoffs have been longstanding. Clinically we move, wherever possible, to bridge cutoffs and promote intergenerational connectedness, to strengthen the family in coping with its loss. A conjoint family life review (Walsh, 1989) can be valuable in structuring the sharing of memories over the course of the family life cycle in order to gain a more balanced, evolutionary perspective on family relationships. Because growth and change take place continually, members may find that issues that were painful at an earlier stage in the life cycle are currently viewed differently, with new opportunity for resolution of at least more empathic understanding of differences and disappointments.

With the death of aging parents, adult children typically begin to confront their own mortality and to think increasingly about the time that remains ahead of them. The death of the last surviving member of the older generation makes them especially aware that *they* are now the oldest generation and the next to die. Because the existence of grandchildren commonly eases the acceptance of mortality, there may be pressure on the recently launched generation to marry and start a family.

Families in Later Life

With increasing life expectancy, four- and five-generation families are becoming more common, and post-retirement couples with declining resources are increasingly called upon to care for their very elderly parents. The central life cycle task of old age, that of accepting one's own mortality, becomes quite real as siblings, spouses, and peers die around one. Surviving the death of an adult child can be especially painful. Multiple concurrent losses, though common at this time, are nevertheless a shock. In reaction, some older people withdraw from closeness and dependency on other elders so as not to have to experience yet another painful loss. Intergenerational family conflicts may erupt over issues of caretaking, dependency, and loss of functioning and control as health declines and death approaches (Walsh, 1989).

Loss of a spouse. It is inevitable in a marriage that one partner will die before the other. As noted above, women are more likely to outlive their husbands, by seven years on the average. More than three-fourths of men over 65 are married, in contrast to only one-third of women of this age (Butler & Lewis, 1983). This gender imbalance is one of the most poignant problems of the elderly. Older men, who tend to select younger partners, have more marital options; the odds are against women remarrying since there are fewer men in their age group and because relationships with younger men are less socially acceptable. In addition, if the prior marriage was deeply valued or, conversely, burdensome, some older widow(er)s simply prefer never to remarry.

Widowers are at especially high risk of death and suicide in the first year of bereavement because of the initial sense of loss, disorientation, and loneliness, and because of the loss of a wife's caretaking functions. Husbands' vulnerability to loss may also be greater, because men are socialized to minimize their awareness of dependency on their spouses. Furthermore, because men are less likely to be widowed, they are less prepared for the adjustment. Deaths of widowers during the first six months of bereavement have been found to be 40% above the expected rate for married men of the same age.

The process of adjustment to widowhood in later life has been well studied (Lopata, 1973). The psychosocial tasks for this transition are twofold: to grieve the loss of the spouse and to reinvest in future functioning. Lopata has identified three phases in this adjustment process for women, which correspond closely to the family adaptation tasks we have outlined in Chapter 1. The first is to loosen bonds to the spouse and to acknowledge the fact of the death, transforming shared daily experiences into memories; the encouragement of open expression of grief and loss is important at this time. Second, typically within a year, attention turns to the tasks of being physically as well as emotionally alone—the demands of daily functioning, self-support, household management. Next, women typically begin the third phase of adjustment, which involves a shift to new activities and interest in others. Loss in widowhood is often compounded by other dislocations, particularly when the family home and social community are given up or when financial loss or illness reduces independent functioning. It is interesting that widows are the one class of mourners given a specific title defining their status. Yet, that identity is also a constant reminder of the loss and may impede the process of reentry. And, unlike divorce, a deceased spouse is not referred to as an ex-husband or ex-wife.

Death in Divorced and Remarried Families

With current high rates of divorce, remarriage, and redivorce likely to continue, family members are likely to experience a variety of losses. Clinical inquiry must extend beyond the immediate household to the broader network of family relationships and not overlook deaths in prior marriages and stepfamilies. The death of a former spouse may bring a surprisingly strong grief reaction, even though the marriage may have ended years earlier, as in the following case.

Sarah only learned of the death of her former husband, Paul, from a neighbor. Her grief, the intensity of which surprised her, was made more painful by her exclusion from the other mourners, due to everyone's efforts to protect Paul's widow and their children from the potential upset of her presence in the midst of their sorrow. Although Sarah had been very close to Paul's parents and friends for many years, she had never met his second wife and children and was not invited to sit shiva at the family home. She attended the memorial service alone, where, as other mourners avoided contact with her, she felt like a ghost in the shadows.

It was extremely important to her that her current husband and an old friend accompanied her to the gravesite the next day and were comforting to her in her grief.

Just as children's connections throughout the family network should be facilitated, so too their losses should be attended to in the event of the death of kin or steprelations who have been important to them at some phase in their development. It is also important to understand difficulties in the formation of stepparent relations connected to the death of a child in the former marriage. Furthermore, when stepparents do form a strong attachment to stepchildren and assume financial and other responsibilities, the death of their spouse, the biological parent, leaves them with no legal rights to continue their relationship with the children. In other cases, where loyalty conflicts are strong at the death of a parent, children may vehemently contest a will that favors a stepparent over the biological parent. Finally, with the rising prevalence of remarriage, couples are increasingly confronting a dilemma they are uncomfortable discussing: With which spouse should they be buried? For children from the divorced family, old wishes may be rekindled to reunite their parents, for all time, in their graves.

DISCUSSION

An appreciation of the varying complexities of loss over the course of the family life cycle and the predictable challenges commonly associated with adaptation at each developmental stage is extremely valuable for family assessment and intervention. At the same time, given the diversity of family forms, values, and life courses in our society, we must be careful not to confuse common patterns with normative standards (Walsh, 1982) or to imply that alternate life pathways or timetables are pathological where they differ. Many lives and relationships do not fit neatly into the categories and succession of stages described above, and significant losses may be unrecognized. For example, loss issues concerning infertility and miscarriage are not confined to early, childless marriage. Single individuals or couples who have chosen to be childfree may be assumed erroneously to be suffering or compensating for loss, as implied by our language, which labels them as unmarried and childless. The death of a partner is complicated for gay and lesbian couples because of social stigma and legal constraints that fail to legitimize their "marriage." Where the relationship has been kept secret, the very loss must be hidden. The uniqueness of each life course in its context needs to be appreciated in every assessment of the multigenerational family life cycle and in our understanding of the meaning of loss.

REFERENCES

Bluebond-Langner, M. (1978). *The private worlds of the dying child*. Princeton, NJ: Princeton University Press.

Butler, R., & Lewis, M. (1983). *Aging and mental health*. St. Louis: C. V. Mosby.

Cain, A., & Cain, B. (1964). On replacing a child. *Journal of the American Academy of Child Psychiatry, 3*, 443–456.

Cain, A., Fast, I., & Erickson, M. (1964). Children's disturbed reactions to the death of a sibling. *American Journal of Orthopsychiatry, 34(4)*, 741–752.

Carter, B., & McGoldrick, M. (1989). *The changing family life cycle: A framework for family therapy* (2nd ed.). Boston: Allyn & Bacon.

Cohler, B. J., & Geyer, S. (1982). Autonomy and interdependence within the family. In F. Walsh (Ed.), *Normal family processes*. New York: Guilford.

Coleman, S. B., & Stanton, D. M. (1978). The role of death in the addict family. *Journal of Marriage and Family Counseling, 4*, 79–91.

DeFrain, J., Taylor, J., & Ernst, L. (1982). *Coping with sudden infant death*. Lexington, MA: D. C. Heath.

Erikson, E. H. (1959). *Identity and the life cycle*. New York: International Universities Press.

Fulmer, R. (1983). A structural approach to unresolved mourning in single parent family systems. *Journal of Marital and Family Therapy, 9(3)*, 259–270.

Furman, E. (1974). *A child's parent dies*. New Haven, CT: Yale University Press.

Gerber, I., Rusalem, R., Hannon, N., Battin, D., & Arkin, A. (1975). Anticipatory grief and aged widows and widowers. *Journal of Gerontology, 30*, 225–229.

Glick, I. O., Parkes, C. M., & Weiss, R. (1975). *The first year of bereavement*. New York: Basic Books.

Gorer, G. (1965). *Death, grief and mourning*. New York: Doubleday.

Hadley, T., Jacob, T., Miliones, J., Caplan, J., & Spitz, D. (1974). The relationship between family developmental crises and the appearance of symptoms in a family member. *Family Process, 13*, 207–214.

Herz, F. (1980). The impact of death and serious illness on the family life cycle. In E. A. Carter & M. McGoldrick (Eds.), *The family life cycle: A framework for family therapy*. New York: Gardner.

Herz, F. (1989). The impact of death and serious illness on the family life cycle. In B. Carter & M. McGoldrick (Eds.), *The changing family life cycle: A framework for family therapy* (2nd ed.). Boston: Allyn & Bacon.

Kaplan, D., Grobstein, R., & Smith, A. (1976). Predicting the impact of severe illness in families. *Health and Social Work, 1*, 71–82.

Legg, C., & Sherick, I. (1976). The replacement child: A developmental tragedy: Some preliminary comments. *Child Psychiatry and Human Development, 7*, 113–126.

Landau-Stanton, J., & Stanton, M. D. (1985). Treating suicidal adolescents and their families. In M. Mirkin & S. Koman (Eds.), *Handbook of adolescents and family therapy*. New York: Gardner.

Lewis, E. (1976). The management of stillbirth: Coping with an unreality. *Lancet, 2*, 619–620.

Lifton, R. J. (1975). Preface. In A. Mitscherlich & M. Mitscherlich (Eds.), *The inability to mourn*. New York: Grove.

Lopata, H. (1973). *Widowhood in an American city*. Cambridge, MA: Schenckman Books.

Martinson, I., Moldow, D., & Henry, W. (1980). *Home care for the child with cancer* (Final report of Grant No. CA 19490). Washington, DC: National Cancer Institute.

McGoldrick, M. (in press). *You can go home again*. New York: Norton.

McGoldrick, M. (1989). Women and the family life cycle. In M. McGoldrick, C. Anderson, & F. Walsh (Eds.), *Women in families*. New York: Norton.

McGoldrick, M. (1989). The young couple: The joining of families in marriage. In E. A. Carter & M. McGoldrick (Eds.), *The family life cycle: A framework for family therapy*. Boston: Allyn & Bacon.

McGoldrick, M., & Gerson, R. (1985). *Genograms in family assessment*. New York: Norton.

Mueller, P. S., & McGoldrick Orfanidis, M. (1976). A method of co-therapy for schizophrenic families. *Family Process, 15*, 179–192.

Mulhern, R., Laurer, M., & Hoffman, R. (1983). Death of a child at home or in the hospital: Subsequent psychological adjustment of the family. *Pediatrics, 71*, 743–747.

Neugarten, B. (1970). Dynamics of transition of middle age to old age: Adaptation and the life cycle. *Journal of Geriatric Psychiatry, 4*, 71–87.

Osterweis, M., Solomon, F., & Green, M. (Eds.). (1984). *Bereavement: Reactions, consequences, and care*. Washington, DC: National Academy Press.

Parkes, C. M. (1972). *Bereavement: Studies of grief in adult life*. New York: International Universities Press.

Parkes, C. M. (1975). Determinants of outcome following bereavement. *Omega, 6*, 303–323.

Parkes, C. M., & Weiss, R. S. (1983). *Recovery from bereavement*. New York: Basic Books.

Paul, N., & Paul, B. B. (1982). Death and changes in sexual behavior. In F. Walsh (Ed.), *Normal family processes*. New York: Guilford.

Rando, T. (1985). Bereaved parents: particular difficulties, unique factors, and treatment issues. *Social Work, 30*, 20.

Rubin, S. (1989). Death of the future? An outcome study of bereaved parents in Israel. *Omega, 20(4)*, 323–339.

Rutter, M. (1966). *Children of sick parents*. London: Oxford University Press.

Schiff, H. S. (1977). *The bereaved parent*. New York: Penguin Books.

Spinetta, J., Swarner, J., & Sheposh, J. (1981). Effective parental coping following the death of a child from cancer. *Journal of Pediatric Psychology, 6*, 251–263.

Strauss, A. (1975). *Chronic illness and the quality of life*. St. Louis: C. V. Mosby.

Van Eerdewegh, M., Bieri, M., Parilla, R., & Clayton, P. (1982). The bereaved child. *British Journal of Psychiatry, 140*, 23–29.

Videka-Sherman, L. (1982). Coping with the death of a child: A study over time. *American Journal of Orthopsychiatry, 52*, 688–698.

Videka-Sherman, L., & Lieberman, M. (1985). Effects of self-help groups and psychotherapy after a child dies: The limits of recovery. *American Journal of Orthopsychiatry, 55*, 70–82.

Walsh, F. (1978). Concurrent grandparent death and birth of schizophrenic offspring: An intriguing finding. *Family Process, 17*, 457–463.

Walsh, F. (1982). Conceptualization of normal family functioning. In F. Walsh (Ed.), *Normal family processes*. New York: Guilford.

Walsh, F. (1983). The timing of symptoms and critical events in the family life cycle. In H. Liddle (Ed.), *Clinical implications of the family life cycle*. Rockville, MD: Aspen.

Walsh, F. (1989). The family in later life. In B. Carter & M. McGoldrick (Eds.), *The changing family life cycle: A framework for family therapy* (2nd ed.). Boston: Allyn & Bacon.

Walsh, F., & McGoldrick, M. (1988). Loss and the family life cycle. In C. Falicov (Ed.), *Family transitions: Continuity and change*. New York: Guilford.

3

Echoes From the Past: Helping Families Mourn Their Losses

MONICA MCGOLDRICK

The old, unhealed grief does not dissipate, but lingers, burning its way into my adult experience and relationships.

— Pamela York Klainer, *Good Daughter; Good Mother*

Death ends a life, but not relationships, which struggle on in the survivor's mind toward some resolution which they may never find.

— Robert Anderson, *I Never Sang For My Father*

The single most important thing to know about Americans . . . is that . . . [they] think that death is optional.

— Jane Walmsley, *Brit-Think; Ameri-Think*, 1986

DEATH IS THE fundamental issue with which we must wrestle in life. It is at the heart of human experience. It forces us to confront our ultimate priorities — reminding us more powerfully than anything else how much family relationships matter.

Since the denial of death is such a prominent feature of our society (Becker, 1973; Walsh & McGoldrick, Chapter 1), it is not surprising that so many cases revolve around loss, even when it is not the presenting problem. Helping families deal with death is a central aspect of family therapy. I do not believe that purely interactional methods of family therapy are adequate to respond to family experience of loss that has been blocked, and I disagree with those family therapists, such as Haley, who maintain that they don't believe in ghosts and therefore focus their therapy exclusively on the interactions of the living.

To be an effective systems therapist in dealing with death one needs to be committed to the importance of human connectedness and to the continuity of family relationships. Surprisingly often, symptoms reflect a family's difficulty in adapting to loss and moving on, whether the problem is addiction, disturbed behavior of a child or adolescent, anxiety, phobias or compulsions, marital conflicts, depression, or the inability of family members to leave home or commit themselves in relationships.

When family members communicate openly about a death (no matter what the circumstances) and participate together in culturally meaningful rituals (e.g., funeral rites and visits to the grave), death becomes easier to integrate. Attempts to protect children or "vulnerable" members from the experience are likely to make mourning more difficult. Tolerating differences in reaction to death, including the inevitable ambivalent feelings toward the dead, is essential. When family loyalty demands a certain response that does not fit with true feelings, the mourning process is delayed or, in some cases, avoided completely. Until family members can mourn, they remain—to a greater or lesser degree—stuck.

The process of mourning can last for years, with each new season, holiday, and anniversary reevoking the old sense of loss. Even as this process continues, the family must adjust itself to the absence of the dead family member. Roles and tasks are reassigned, new attachments formed, and old alliances shifted. Eventually, there comes a time when most families have in a general way come to terms with their loss, although mourning is never totally over. There will always be events that set off our memories of the lost person, but with time and healing the pain usually becomes less raw and intense, releasing energy for other attachments.

After a loss, families must be restructured without the dead person, whose roles and functions must be taken over by others. The more important the deceased was to the ongoing emotional or practical functioning of the family, the more difficult it is for those remaining to adjust. When a child dies, family restructuring requires finding another focus for the love and care that previously went to that child. If families do not make this readjustment, they may overburden the remaining children or distort their relationships, making someone into a replacement for the dead child.

The loss of a parent or primary caretaker presents the most difficult challenge. Central caretaking functions must be assumed by someone else.

Filling the emotional loss of the parent is still another matter. Sometimes an uncle, aunt, or grandparent can fill in the gap. If resources are unavailable, the loss will be greatly compounded.

When families do not adequately mourn their losses, they cannot move on with the business of living. Instead the feelings go underground. Family members may blame themselves or each other for the death; they may try to mold others into replacements for the lost person or keep themselves from experiencing closeness again. It is not death itself, but avoidance of the experience through mystification and myth, that becomes problematic. Even a traumatic loss can be endured, as long as family members can accept the loss and restructure their relationships so they can move on with life. Families can adapt to the worst of circumstances. Only when they cannot acknowledge the loss and the need to reorganize and reorient the family and their lives do they become stuck (Kuhn, 1981).

ASSESSING DEATH IN THE FAMILY

It is important to track patterns of adaptation to loss as a routine part of family assessment, even when it is not initially presented as relevant to chief complaints. It is most useful to construct a three-generational genogram and a family chronology or timeline of major stress events as part of each family evaluation (McGoldrick & Gerson, 1985, 1989). These tools allow you to organize information gathered in an interview quickly and easily, without taking an elaborate family history. You can note all losses and track their timing, circumstances, and impact. It is then easier to scan for patterns relevant to presenting problems, as well as for coping strategies and resources that will influence the family members' adaptation to their presenting problem.

In assessing a family's response to death, the therapist must take account of the general factors outlined in Chapters 1 and 2.

DYSFUNCTIONAL ADAPTATION TO LOSS

When the process of mourning and moving on becomes blocked, several processes may occur: Relationships rigidify; the family closes itself off; time stops; feelings are blocked by various forms of denial. These patterns must be assessed as part of any clinical evaluation.

(1) *Time stops.* When families cannot mourn, they become locked in time — either in dreams of the past, in the emotions of the present, or in dread of the future. They may become so concerned about potential future losses that they are unable to engage in the relationships they do have,

fearing that to love again will mean further loss. Others focus exclusively on their dreams of the future, trying to fill in the gap left by the loss with new relationships formed on fantasy and escape from the pain. Usually those who cut short their mourning by rushing toward other relationships find that, when the dreams give way to the realities of the new relationship, their pain comes back to haunt them. Problems that families have in other developmental transitions, such as marriage, the transition to parenthood, or launching their children, often reflect this stoppage of time.

(2) *Relationships rigidify.* Sometimes the family closes down entirely, with an inability to attach to anyone. If survivors draw in other family members to replace the dead, their relationships may appear stable though rigid. This may work until the replacement person expresses any individuality, which makes apparent that he or she is not the dead person. This may then trigger a delayed reaction, even long after the original loss experience.

When families are unable to accept a death, they tend to develop fixed ways of relating to handle their fears of future loss. Another indication of denial is a family's unwillingness to make any changes following the death. They may make the dead person's room into a memorial or a mausoleum.

(3) *The family uses denial or escape into frenetic activity, drugs, alcohol, fantasy, myth.* The myths, secrets, and expectations that develop around a critical loss may be incorporated into the rules of the family and be passed down from parents to children. Some families stop all mention of the deceased, as if they could thus banish all the pain. It is as if they attempt to blot the person out of existence.

Many of the patterns we routinely observe in families — drivenness about one's activities, affairs, continuous unresolved conflict, alienation, isolation and fear of outsiders, frequent divorce, depression, workaholism, escaping into TV sports or soap operas — may reflect the inability to deal with loss, which has finally become the inability to connect with anyone else out of fear of further loss.

Myth-making to avoid the realities of a loss entails delusional responses that bind family members to each other in pathological ways and at the same time create great psychological rifts among them, since these responses relate only to the delusion, not to the real person. Such myths naturally affect children who become replacements for family members who have died, even though they may be totally unaware of the connection. People develop serious emotional problems when they have been raised as stand-ins for the unburied ghosts of the past. To become free to be themselves, they must discover the mystery behind their identity and find a way of "exorcising" the ghost or dybbuk (Paul, 1976; Paul & Grosser, 1965; Paul & Paul, 1989).

CLINICAL INTERVENTION

Primary Clinical Goal

The primary goal of therapeutic intervention around death is to empower and strengthen families to mourn their losses and move on. This involves:

(1) *Shared acknowledgment of the reality of the death.* In order to normalize the loss and diminish any sense of mystification, family members are encouraged to learn about the death and face their own and each other's reactions to it. If facts about the death have not been admitted, a therapist can facilitate their learning the facts and accepting the realities.

(2) *Shared experience of the loss and putting it in context.* This usually involves funeral rituals and other experiences through which families can share the emotional legacy of the loss — mourning, anger, pain, regret, lost dreams, guilt, sadness, and missing the dead person. A part of this sharing is joint storytelling about the life and death of the dead person. Such sharing helps families integrate the loss experience into their lives by promoting their sense of familial, cultural, and human continuity and connectedness and empowering them to regain a sense of themselves as moving in time from the past, through the present, and into the future. To develop a sense of control, mastery, and the ability to survive in the face of loss, family members, especially men, may need encouragement to open up relationships with the living and learn more about their family overall — its history, its culture, and the perspectives and stories of different family members.

The movie, *Steel Magnolias,* has a touching example of a typical gender difference in this aspect of dealing with death, when the mother, at her daughter's funeral, tells the story of her daughter's death to her women friends, after the men have left.

> They turned off the machines. Drum [her husband] left. He couldn't take it. Jackson [the son-in-law] left. It's amusing. Men are supposed to be made out of steel or something. I just sat there. I just held Shelby's hand. There was no noise. No tremble. Just peace. I realize as a woman how lucky I am. I was there when that wonderful creature drifted into my life and I was there when she drifted out. It was the most precious moment of my life.

This powerful story of the death helps the mother and all the women in her network to put the death in the context of the life cycle and of life's most important experiences. The mother's sense of privilege at being part of the experience of her daughter's death, as agonizing as it was for her, gives meaning to her life. In therapy, one would want to help the men in the family share in the richness of these nodal life experiences.

When families have become stuck in moving beyond loss it is helpful to expand the context within which the loss is viewed. Sharing memories and stories of the dead can help family members develop more benign, less traumatic perspectives on the role of loss in their lives. Such sharing helps them tolerate their own and each others' differing emotional reactions to the loss, patterns of mourning, and pathways for moving on. It seems important for families to be free to remember as well as to let go of memories. Clarifying and elaborating family stories and narratives about their history are ways to promote this resolution. One of the most difficult aspects of denied or unresolved mourning is that it leaves families with no narratives with which to make sense of their experience. If events cannot be mentioned or if the family "party line" cannot be expanded upon, it is almost impossible for family members to make sense out of their history altogether and gives the next generation no models or guidelines for integrating later losses. Therapy can aid families to create narratives that facilitate and enhance their integration of loss (Laird, 1989).

(3) *Reorganizing the family system.* Where the system has been unable to complete the adaptive tasks of reorganizing without the dead person, therapy can help them accomplish this complex and often painful task. This may entail a shift in caretaking roles or organizational and leadership functions, a reorientation of the social network, a shift in family focus (as when an only child dies), or an emotional reorganization of the generational hierarchy (as when the last grandparent dies).

(4) *Reinvestment in other relationships and life pursuits.* Death can be an important spur to life. Families can be strengthened by the shared experience of loss to focus more clearly on what they want to do in life and on how they want to relate to others. The experience of death can release creative energies, and therapists should foster this development. Clinicians can help family members to redefine their commitments and life priorities and redirect their relationships and activities toward the dying.

Ritualizing Loss (see Imber-Black, Chapter 11)

Through the use of familiarity, repetition and transformation, rituals are important family experiences for marking life cycle transitions. They incorporate symbolic meanings referring to a family or a culture's shared history and shared future. As Roberts says, in rituals, "changes in the present are grounded in past traditions, while future relationships are defined" (1988, p. 11). Often they involve intentional repetition of words, music, food, drink, smells, sights, ceremony, and behavior that suggests continuity and places the experience in context, while marking the changes in roles and status brought on by life cycle transitions. Most funeral rituals incorporate traditions that refer to the experience of previous generations in coming to terms with the experience of death, thus providing family members with a cushion of belonging at the same time that they are experiencing the pain of loss. They provide a special time out of time, that is, an encapsulated time frame, which offers an opportunity for experiencing the overwhelming emotions that death evokes, while also containing such expression.

One of the most important interventions a therapist can make with a family is to help them stay in control of their own mourning rituals. This is not always easy and families themselves may not agree on which traditions to maintain, since family members often have different religious beliefs and different attitudes toward death. For many reasons, including the dramatically rapid shifting values and norms of our culture and its mobility, which tends to cut people off from their roots, family members often are uncomfortable with the traditional mourning rituals of their family and alienated by the technocratic, death-denying, materialistic practices of the health care and funeral industries, which have such a dominant influence on death rituals and customs in the United States. Unfortunately, over the past 50 years, death has become increasingly orchestrated by the medical establishment, which has been oriented toward "overcoming" or preventing death. Physicians are given virtually no training in helping people die or deal with death as a natural process. Other health care personnel, such as nurses, have better training and more experience in helping the dying and their families through the experience of death, but the increasing emphasis of the culture on technology as the primary relationship of the dying generally does nothing but increase a family's sense of loss of control over their relationships and over the experience of death. The recent hospice movement is a tremendously welcome development, helping the dying and their families and friends to experience death as a natural part of life, but it still has little impact on the overall experience of death for most families.

Our culture's denial of death often means that we do not discuss before our death how we want to die and how we want to be memorialized. A great many people make no will at all, in spite of the extreme hardship this omission can have on their survivors. Death is a very private experience. It is very easy for personal aspects to get lost in rituals and customs determined by the medical establishment, religious institutions, or funeral homes. Very often family members' primary memory of a funeral will be of the sense of alienation they felt at the "eulogy" or comments of clergyman who did not know the dead person, or whose values were totally at odds with those of the family. Anything a clinician can do to help the family reclaim their own mourning rituals will have lasting benefit for the family.

Families can be encouraged to deal with these issues by specifying (a) a living will regarding whether they want to have extreme measures taken to keep them alive; (b) a last will and testament, specifying their wishes for their legacy; and (c) a statement of their wishes for their funeral. Particularly if the death is sudden and traumatic, it is extremely difficult in the crisis of the moment for family members to find the emotional energy to think about mourning rituals that will be meaningful for them. There is a great tendency to give up control to anyone else who will take over responsibility for decisions. Thus the clergy and funeral directors are frequently in the position of determining these most important family experiences for total strangers. And they are often the only members of the culture who deal with death and its aftermath on a regular basis.

Clinicians can validate families' experience with institutions in dealing with death so they don't end up feeling it is their own craziness that is creating the problems they experience. They can also be helped to channel their efforts to create the situation they want for the dying person.

Ritualizing loss involves three parts: (1) a ritual to acknowledge and mourn the loss; (2) a ritual to symbolize what the family members incorporate or take with them from the lost person; (3) a ritual to symbolize moving on in life. Helping families construct personally meaningful rituals is an important part of promoting the emotional and structural transformation of the family that loss requires. A toast made at a wedding or an anniversary party or even a eulogy at another family member's death may recall the dead person, and help to put him or her back into the context of family relationships. One young man offered to make the family toast at Thanksgiving and gave thanks for the happy memories they all had of his brother's wife, who had died two years before in an automobile accident. Such evocations to integrate loss even long after the death can have profoundly healing reverberations for the family. One woman held a memorial service 25 years later for her brother who had committed suicide on his birthday, beginning a process of reconciliation that had been aborted a quarter of a century earlier.

Structuring Therapy: Meeting Together or Separately

The question arises about how to structure therapy in dealing with loss — when to give tasks, when to meet with the whole family to help its members deal with a death, and when to coach family members to deal with their losses in private. The therapist must weigh carefully the level of stigma the family may attach to seeing a therapist against the potential value of having an outsider participate in a family discussion of loss. A single long session with family members around a serious crisis may have profound value in changing longstanding patterns by detoxifying buried losses and opening up family relationships. It may become a marker event for the family. Having a therapist present may provide a safety net for some families who do not otherwise dare to discuss painful losses with each other.

On the other hand, there are families for whom the exposure of having a stranger witness their most private discussion adds to the toxicity or humiliation they experience in dealing with their pain. Where family members are at different stages in confronting a loss or have very different coping styles regarding their handling of emotion, as when there has been a recent suicide and some feel the need to talk while for others the pain is too raw, it may make more sense to work alone with those who are ready and to encourage a gradual healing process for the family as a whole. Those who are so motivated can be coached to make use of the various family, religious, holidays, and life cycle rituals that occur over time to integrate the loss (see Imber-Black, Chapter 11). Family members can also be coached to detoxify the loss in a more private context, such as by writing letters, by making visits to the grave, the family home, or to other places of special meaning, or by talking with relatives who have family significance in relation to the loss. Sometimes, of course, it helps to have the family members together, even though they are at different points in their mourning, to create a context of trust within which they can each deal with their mourning in a safe way and bear witness to each other's experience, even if they cannot share it exactly.

Genograms

Genograms are a basic tool for exploring loss in a family (McGoldrick & Gerson, 1985). I routinely do a three-generational genogram in the first session, which lets me know immediately who all the members of the family are, when and how they have died, and what cutoffs, conflicts, strengths, and problems there are throughout the system. Genograms provide a context for asking detailed questions about the family's response to loss, which, more than the loss itself, is the key factor in family dysfunction related to loss.

> Joy Hitchcock initially sought individual therapy for headaches and marital problems, although over time it became evident that she was a longtime polydrug abuser. When her third individual therapist referred the Hitchcocks to me for couple therapy, I wondered immediately about her place in her family and began by doing a genogram (Figure 3.1). She was the fifth of six children, the second child, Martha, having drowned at age 4, three years before Joy was born. Joy knew nothing about this sister and said the family never mentioned her. It seemed clear that the five surviving children each had clearly defined roles in the family. The oldest daughter, Catherine, was the "parent," the superachiever and organizer of the siblings. The third child and oldest son, Robert Jr., was the male standard bearer, the strong, silent type, and the only one with whom the father talked "man-to-man." The fourth child, Jane, born shortly after Martha died, was "the loser," into drugs in a flamboyant manner and always being bailed out by the

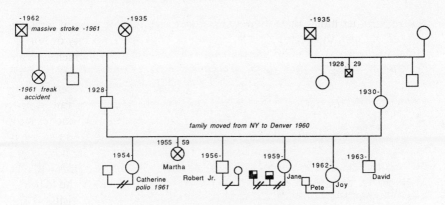

Figure 3.1 Hitchcock Family

parents. The youngest, a son, David, was "the caboose." He was seen as an underachiever, to whom not too much attention was paid. In adolescence he had attached himself to Joy's husband Pete, who became father, brother, and friend to him. Joy's role was to make no waves. When she did by openly living with Pete while in college, the parents cut off her allowance and refused to talk to her, even while they were bailing Jane out of repeated troubles with a drug dealing husband.

Because of the serious nature of Joy's drug problem, I decided to call a family session. Everyone except Jane attended. During this meeting the shadow of Martha over the whole family became apparent. It was clear that her death had become tied up with many concurrent stresses and that all of the children so feared breaking the family's rule of silence that they never even learned the facts about her life and death. Catherine, the oldest, said she had always thought of Martha as her twin. Robert thought for sure he remembered her, although she had died when he was only three. David, the youngest, had thought Martha was the oldest. Joy thought she had lived to be seven. The father knew exactly how old Martha would be now, though he could not remember the ages of his other children, and the mother kept confusing how many children she did have, although she knew to the month and day how old Martha would be now.

Martha's death echoed for each parent losses in their own childhoods, and left a legacy of guilt and blame they could not face. Following her death the family had moved 2,000 miles away, in part to escape memories of her. The next three years were plagued by compounding tragedies: The paternal grandfather suffered a massive stroke while with them and died four months later; the father had a series of business reversals and was forced to move twice in a short period; an aunt was killed in a freak accident; and the oldest daughter developed polio and had to be placed in an iron lung for two years.

My hypothesis about the family process as related to the genogram was that Jane, born early in this period, became the focus for negative energy, and Joy, whose name even suggested the burden she bore, was to embody happiness. As the family members discussed their history and went over the genogram details, the myths and distortions each had carried for years and years became evident and open to clarification for the first time. With much effort and detailed examination of family patterns, the Hitchcocks began to see how they had all been caught in a web of protection, intended to prevent themselves and each other from experiencing loss. Joy's drug addiction was a way of numbing her feelings in order to play the part of happy daughter and not make waves in a family that could not deal with losses.

Exploration of the genogram often clarifies, as it did with the Hitchcocks, the ways in which certain family members become bound up in the legacy of unresolved mourning because of the timing of their birth, their personal characteristics, their sibling position, and so forth (McGoldrick, in press; McGoldrick & Gerson, 1985).

All living relatives are potential sources for unblocking the loss experience, their relevance being determined by their relationship to the dead person and to the survivors and by their potential access to family history in general. Older relatives are especially valuable sources of information. The family history they know will be lost to the next generation if it is not shared.

Asking Questions

Questions are the most powerful tool for gaining a new understanding of a family. Are dates of death barely remembered or honored as holy rites? How comfortable are family members in talking about the deceased and the circumstances of the death? Are both positive and negative memories available? The more information family members have, the more perspective they will gain on themselves and their lives and the better chance they will have to face the future with openness. There are questions we can ask about loss in the family in order to understand the adaptation of previous generations that sets the stage for current family relationships:

1. How did various family members show their reactions to the death? Tears? Withdrawal? Depression? Frantic activity? Did they talk to each other about the loss?
2. Who was there at the moment of death? Who was not present who "should" have been? Who saw the dead body and who didn't?
3. What was the state of family relationships at the time of death? Were there unresolved issues with the person who died?
4. Who arranged the funeral? Who attended? Who didn't? Who gave the eulogy?

5. Was the body cremated or buried? If cremated, what happened to the ashes? Is there a tombstone?
6. Did conflicts or cutoffs occur around the time of death?
7. Was there a will? Who received what legacy? Were there rifts over the will?
8. Who goes to the grave and how often? Who mentions the dead and how often? What happened to the belongings of the dead person?
9. Was there any secrecy regarding the cause or circumstances of the death? Were facts kept from anyone inside or outside the family?
10. What mystification or mythology has been created in the family regarding the dead person since the death? Has s/he been made into a saint?
11. What difference do they think there would have been if the dead person had survived longer? What dreams were cut short by the death?
12. Do family members feel stigmatized by the death? (e.g., a suicide, a death from AIDS)
13. How have the survivors' lives been influenced by their relationships with the dead person? What do they carry with them from this person?
14. What are their cultural and religious beliefs about afterlife and how have their beliefs influenced their understanding of the meaning of their loss?
15. What other beliefs do family members have that may help sustain them in the face of loss, e.g., a sense of family or cultural mission, a sense of survivorship?

These questions cannot, of course, be asked in isolation. I offer them to suggest important areas to think about in a journey with a family toward an expanded understanding of the loss experience.

Other Methods of Opening Families to Buried Loss

Anything that helps to put family members in a frame of mind to reconnect with pieces of a dissociated loss experience can be helpful in this process. This may involve:

1. visits to the cemetery;
2. writing letters to the dead or to the living about the dead;
3. looking at old pictures, framing some to have in the home or making an album;

4. reading old diaries or letters, sorting through memorabilia and possessions and deciding what to keep and what to pass on to others as a
   keepsake, and how to dispose of the rest;
5. keeping a journal of dreams and memories and reflections;
6. having discussions with relatives about the loss;
7. watching movies — *I Never Sang For My Father*, *Cria*, *Dad*, *Steel Magnolias*;
8. reading stories — *A Death in the Family*, *The Death of Ivan Ilych*, *A
   Very Easy Death*, *A Grief Observed*;
9. music — perhaps the favorite music of the client, the family, or the
   deceased.

Once the blocks to the loss have been overcome, we may help family
members: (a) reritualize the loss by a memorial or rite, no matter how many
years it has been since the loss; (b) revise stories of their history to include
the once submerged experience of loss, and reclaim and incorporate hidden
aspects of the lost person's part in the family narrative; (c) revise their
current relationships in light of the now shifting meaning of their history.

Where the family has been unable to mourn for years and years, and the
loss has been covered over, so that family members are not even aware that it
has shaped current family relationships, considerable work in therapy may
be necessary to open family members up to their blocked experience. The
goal here is to get the system moving again when the family operates as if
time has stopped. The first stage often involves helping family members
open up emotionally to the blocked experience of loss.

Norman Paul's creative methods of intervention relate especially to opening families to their buried losses. He searches aggressively in the family
history for the ghost whose shadow blocks the living, and then works to
"exorcize" it. He homes in on the denied emotional experience of loss,
breaking through the walls people have built up, often over a lifetime, as a
result of their inability to mourn. He makes extensive use of videotape to
dramatize and bring into view the hidden aspects of family members'
blocked experience. The experiences recaptured on videotape are then
placed back in the context of the natural system of the family, rather than
remaining between the therapist and client, in contrast to traditional psycho-
dynamic therapy, which focuses on the individual's experience of loss. Paul
also uses the dramatic technique of superimposing a blown-up image of the
family "ghost" on a video screen over the image of the survivor, whose life
the ghost appears to have been dominating. Through this vivid imaging of
the phenomenon of replacement, Paul dramatizes the emotional distortion
that occurs in families where losses go unmourned. He may send clients to

the hospital where a parent died or to a concentration camp where family members were killed to get them in touch with buried feelings. Clients are asked to make audio recordings while going through the experience. The aim of these techniques is to differentiate the living from the dead and free them from "obligations" to the dead or to a family's mythology that has developed to avoid the pain of loss (Boszormenyi-Nagy, 1962; McGoldrick, 1977; Mueller & McGoldrick Orfanidis, 1976; Paul, 1980; Paul & Grosser, 1965; Paul & Paul, 1989).

Underritualized and Overritualized Mourning

Such families have often underritualized their loss. They may have had no funeral service at all, or only a minimal one, with the family perhaps playing no part in designing the ritual. Often important family members have not taken part in the mourning rituals, whether for emotional reasons or because of distance or illness. Families of cultures that minimize the emotional experience of loss may be particularly vulnerable to this sort of underritualization, which can leave the family in a state of emotional limbo for years. The family in the film *Ordinary People* is a typical example of tragic loss, the son's drowning in a boating accident, which has for the most part gone underritualized and from which the family cannot recover. The younger son's eventual suicide attempt, as I see it, reflects his experience that there is no exit for him from the experience that time has stopped. The story is not only about the mother's inability to mourn, but also equally about the father's inability to relate to his own or his wife's grief.

In the following case, the father, who presented his son Michael for therapy, appeared to have no awareness that the presenting problem, Michael's withdrawal and inattention at school, related in any way to unresolved mourning. Zeroing in on the relevant aspects of the family's history and encouraging family members to ritualize their loss allowed the child to become part of the restructured family and move on with them toward a shared future.

Michael Johnson, age 9, had lost his mother when he was 4 from kidney disease, which had led to her deterioration over a two-year period. Eric, Michael's father, had not included Michael in the funeral, hoping to spare him pain. Almost immediately he remarried a woman who had two latency-age sons, but within six months they separated. One year later he remarried again, this time to a woman who had two children by her own previous marriage. Together they had a daughter, now two years old, and a son, now six months old. Eric said therapy was the school's idea; he had no clue why he was there himself. The first session was devoted to laying out the family's genogram, which made immediately apparent the multiple changes family members had experienced and led to the hypothesis that Michael had somehow been "left behind in time" by the death of his mother and had been unable to become a part of this new family.

It was a surprise when the father brought to the second session, for the therapist's information, a letter written by his dead wife. The therapist urged him to read the letter in front of his family, so that the information became theirs, not just his. The letter was a touching review of the first wife's relationships with all her family, thanking them for the love and support she had gotten from everyone — her husband, her parents, his parents, and even his grandparents. She expressed hope that her husband would remarry, urging him to be sure his second wife would love Michael as much as she loved Eric, and told of her dreams for Michael's future and that of the whole family. The reading of the letter made a deep impression on Michael, who proceeded, at the therapist's prompting, to ask his father for the first time many questions about his dead mother. At the end of this session the therapist suggested that the father and son share a private ritual at home of sorting through other memorabilia of the dead mother. By the next session Michael seemed much more lively. The father talked about how Michael was a living reminder of his first wife, since he looked exactly like her. Both became freed up in their relationship with each other, and Michael soon reported that he was getting along better with his stepmother and new siblings.

At times brief interventions can release from within the family hidden strengths, enabling family members to face their loss and find ways of integrating it.

In other families overritualization of loss may inhibit their moving on. Families may make a child's room into a memorial and refuse to change things or dispose of the dead person's clothes even after months or years. They may insist on repeated visits to the grave in ways that become compulsive repetitions, tying up family energy, so that family members are never free to make new commitments.

Rose Gelinas, a Greek woman in her mid-thirties who had lost a six-month-old infant to SIDS after four previous miscarriages, was still obsessed with the loss three years later. She spent hours each day looking at pictures of her dead child and visited the grave several times a week. She talked about the baby constantly and was upset when her husband and other family members told her it was time to move on. Therapy involved expanding the context in which she performed her rituals, exploring the way her husband's withdrawal fed her obsession with the loss, and inviting extended family members to participate with her in dealing with the loss. They were given tasks to learn more about their family, especially about others who had lost children and how they handled their losses.

It turned out that Rose, who was the youngest of six children, had been given to an aunt to raise, because her family was poor. This aunt had had several miscarriages, a stillbirth, and no other biological children. She had doted on Rose until

Rose "abandoned" her to marry George. After this she became extremely threatening, saying at one point when Rose was pregnant that because Rose was so ungrateful she hoped the baby would die. By a strange coincidence, this aunt died on the same day as Rose's baby. Once Rose began learning about her family and unraveling the aunt's story, she could see her aunt's malediction in a different light — as a reflection of her hurt and insecurity, not of her dooming Rose to unhappiness. Rose was freed from her compulsive rituals. She visited her parents in Greece and talked about the family history with her uncle (the aunt's husband). All this helped her develop a more benign perspective on her loss. George, for his part, was helped to see the ways in which his avoidance of his own and his wife's feelings related to his cutoff from his daughter by his first wife, whom he had not seen for 10 years. He was helped to make contact with this daughter, in an effort not to compound his real loss — or hers — further. In doing this he became freer to respond to his wife's experience of pain and support her, rather than stifling her attempts to mourn their mutual loss.

Rose's obsession with her dead baby reflected her sense of invalidation by those around her, as well as the self-blame she had absorbed from her family and undoubtedly from the wider culture, which generally gives women responsibility for whatever goes wrong, especially when it comes to their children. They may also feel guilt and shame over miscarriages, as if somehow the failure of motherhood were their fault.

While women are generally free to weep openly, men, like George, often deny, withdraw, and avoid their grief, fearing a loss of control. The prescribed gender reactions of the culture exaggerate the distress of both men and women. Men generally take refuge in their work and distance from their wives' open mourning, seeing it as a threat to their desperate need to remain in control. Women experience their husbands' pulling away as a double loss. One woman, the mother of three sons, said when we met two years after the death of the oldest son, "Through my eyes flow the tears for our whole family." She had come to think of herself as crazy, was treated by her husband and sons as pathologically depressed and hyperemotional, and had been referred to individual therapy for her "problem." The inability of the father and brothers to cry, talk about their experience, or share their suffering with each other was never labeled a problem, by them or anyone else, until finally the wife's frustration with her husband's insensitivity brought him to my office.

This kind of skewed pattern of grieving is the norm in our culture and breeds isolation. Family members who cannot share their experience of loss are kept from one of the most important healing resources: each other. Clinically it is important to address this imbalance and encourage families to question these responses in themselves and in their culture. When one family member must grieve alone, the pain is that much worse for the one who mourns. Interpreting these reactions as understandable, given the indoctrination of our culture that "real" men don't cry and women are the emotional caretakers, is an important part of helping families come to view their own and each other's reactions with more tolerance and to take responsibility for modifying their dysfunctional responses.

Of course, we must be careful about imposing our definitions of "normal mourning" on our clients. While it is not possible to avoid making personal value judgments about what we consider healthy and adaptive responses to death, we must never be too sure that our values are the best. As Wortman and Silver (1989) have pointed out, we know much less than we think we do about what constitutes healthy mourning and how much grieving is "necessary" or "appropriate" to resolve a loss. It does seem clear that the healing process must include mourning the loss, incorporation of the dead person in the lives of survivors, and restructuring of the family so that they can move on with their lives. Grief is a very personal matter. We should not be too quick to judge how others mourn — whether they should be more expressive or less so. Every family and every person must find their own ways.

Uncovering Buried Loss

Often the first problem clinically is to demonstrate the family history's relevance to the presenting problem and overcome the resistance a client may have to "opening up old wounds." While occasional magical moments do occur in therapy when the "right" question brings about a transformation, more often it is through careful and patient questions and careful listening that one helps clients see the connections between their problems and their underlying family relationships, as the following case illustrates.

> Duncan Forbes (see Figure 3.2), aged 59, a highly successful WASP business executive, sought therapy when his wife, Catherine, requested that they stop stalling on divorce after two years of separation. Duncan had left Catherine because he felt their relationship was dead. Both he and his wife had one goal — to have their marriage magically repaired, making Duncan want to be married again. He claimed that his family of origin was of no relevance and found discussion of his genogram boring. It was only through repeated and detailed discussion of the gaps in his understanding of himself and of events and relationships in his family, made evident in individual meetings and in sessions with his sister and with his three grown sons, that he gradually became willing to take the moves that unblocked the loss experiences in his family. His parents had died many years earlier. His sister was devoted to her image of him as the "golden boy." She was not enthusiastic about his "rummaging around in the family for ghosts," but meeting with her helped him realize how powerful the "no talk" rule had been in

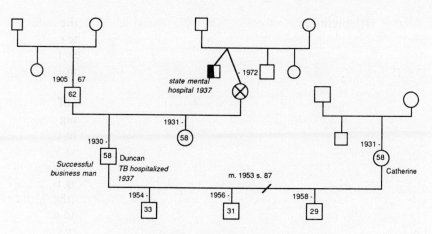

Figure 3.2 Forbes Family

their family. Meeting with his sons, who found him frustratingly unemotional, helped him realize, at least in a general way, that he wanted to get in touch with his feelings.

After eight months of therapy, he finally took a trip to his hometown in West Virginia and visited the only two surviving aunts of his parents' generation, whom he had not visited for many years. He appeared at the next session elated and loaded down with photograph albums, letters, and diaries his mother had kept for most of the years of his childhood. Through the emotional process triggered off for him, he was able to get in touch with his mother's painful life and his own childhood for the first time. As he talked, he also brought up the subject of his father's death and began to cry about it for the first time 20 years after it had occurred. He remembered how he had walked his grandmother up to the casket and how she had moaned repeatedly, "my baby, my baby," as she saw her son, Duncan's 65-year-old father, lying in the casket. His only feeling when his father died had been anger at the physicians for their medical errors.

As Duncan went back to his blocked losses, he began to connect with his feelings for the first time. His past had been locked up by losses his parents themselves had undergone. He was able to read between the lines of his mother's diary about the torment she experienced when her twin brother was sent into a state mental hospital at the same time that Duncan, at age seven, had nearly died of TB and had to be sent to a sanitorium for nearly a year. This uncle was virtually never mentioned again. Duncan could see from the diary how intensely close his mother had been to him, and what a tragedy his loss was for her. He could see, too, how devastated she was by the near loss of her son, in whom she seemed to tie up many of her own dreams and those unfulfilled by her husband and her brother.

Getting in touch with these memories, dreams and reflections freed him to mourn for his parents and then reconnect with his family, who now began to really interest him. He uncovered several "secrets" about his father's affairs and his mother's drinking, both of which had been unacknowledged parts of his family history. For the first time he began to relate to his wife as more than an instrument of his fulfillment or deprivation. He could now begin negotiating their marital problems with her.

Recent Losses

In a sense all families are marked by the shared losses they have endured. At times of loss family members are often forced to deal with each other in intimate ways, which can be particularly difficult if they have grown apart over time. Siblings who have had little to do with each other for years are suddenly forced, under stress, to share wrenching experiences. This has the potential to bring family members together, as they share the hospital watch in the last days and redefine for themselves and each other what family ties have meant to them. But it can also bring to the surface old conflicts. While a death in the family provides an opportunity to rework old relationships — to risk saying what has until now been left unsaid, to reopen relationships that have closed down — it may instead intensify old hurts. Work with family members in the period following a loss can offer opportunities for helping them reverse this process and change even longstanding dysfunctional patterns.

Johanna Imperi (see Figure 3.3) had been seen for therapy over several stressful periods while in medical school. She had become pregnant by her boyfriend while still in high school, married him, and had over the next 10 years been cut off from contact with her father, Joe.

Johanna's mother, who had been chronically ill for years and addicted to prescribed drugs, had died of an overdose (possibly unintentional) when Johanna was eight and her brother John was six. The death intensified conflicts that had already existed between Joe and his wife's family, who blamed him for her death. Joe had felt impotent toward his wife's family and their money. He became resentful when his in-laws gave the children lavish presents and told them not to trust their father. Both children began rebelling against him at a very early age.

Though her father cut her off for her rebelliousness, Johanna managed, with the help of an inheritance from her maternal grandfather and support from her husband's family, to put herself through college and to begin medical school. At this point her husband left her for another woman. She entered therapy for this loss and problems with her son, Alex, who was now a preadolescent. She had made her husband and his family into a replacement family, and now she felt not only the loss of this support but an added sense of betrayal.

During the course of therapy I helped her repair the cutoff with her father and

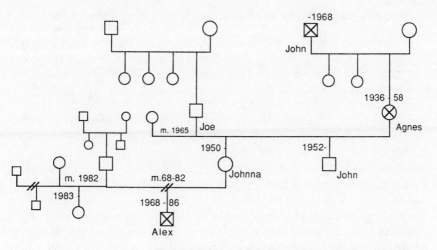

Figure 3.3 Imperi Family

strengthen the relationships with her mother's sisters and her maternal grand-mother, who was still alive. She made efforts to have a working coparental relationship with her ex-husband and to stay connected with his family.

Unfortunately, just at the point when she finished her medical training, her son, who was about to begin college, was run over by a car, after both he and a friend had been drinking. Because I knew her well, I was in a position to coach her through one of the most difficult experiences a person can endure, the death of a child. She had to deal not only with her own overwhelming grief, but also with the conflicts and cutoffs between her father and her mother's family and with sharing the funeral experience with her ex-husband and his second wife and children, who also viewed themselves as Alex's family.

She was even able to deal with her son's friend, who had not been hurt in the accident, and with his family. This was particularly difficult because, given the ambiguity of the death (reminiscent of the ambiguity of her mother's death years before), she was inclined to blame the friend.

Because of the reconnection that had taken place between Johanna and her father during her earlier therapy, he was now able to be the father to her that he had not been when her mother had died. When Johanna told him how painful it was for her to love both him and her mother's family and have them not speaking to each other, he took responsibility for his relationships with his in-laws. He made a point of speaking to them all at the funeral, sympathizing with their distress, and mentioning his dead wife in the conversation. This was part of an important healing process, not only for him but for the whole family, and was the most important thing he could do for his daughter — enabling her to get support without having to struggle with loyalty conflicts toward her family.

In the months after the funeral Johanna was able to go to each relative and talk, not only about the loss of Alex but also about her mother, in a way she had never been able to before. She learned that it had been her mother's dream to go to medical school. This gave her a sense of continuity in fulfilling something for her mother, a connection that had particular meaning as she struggled to make some sense of her son's life being cut short. In this process, she managed to take control of her experience in ways that were very important for her.

This most painful and tragic loss of her son enabled Johanna and her family to focus on and intensify a healing process that had been short-circuited years before. Just as one loss can compound another, one healing experience can come to include or incorporate another.

Dealing with this loss also involved helping Johanna develop a sense of survivorship and some context within which to integrate the loss. Families that have experienced many untimely or traumatic losses may have a sense of doom or even of being cursed (see McGoldrick, Chapter 6), and the therapist will need to help them review their genogram so they can find other ways to put their family history together to remove this sense of powerlessness against forces of doom.

Facing Ambivalence

Loss in situations where the relationships have been ambivalent may be particularly difficult to resolve. Interventions aimed at validating the ambivalence and encouraging the survivors to face the full range of their responses may help to prevent years of coverup around the realities of the loss.

Virginia McCabe sought help shortly after the sudden death of her 61-year-old husband, Ted, of a heart attack. Initially she described her husband as a strong and sensitive man, beloved by everyone. She portrayed herself as the sidekick, who could not figure out how to continue now that her husband, the center of the family, was gone. It was some time before she mentioned that her husband had "perhaps" been an alcoholic. This did not fit at all with her previous descriptions of their life together. She was clearly struggling with divergent images of him.

Reminding her of the cost to a family of idealizing their ghosts, I suggested that for the next session she write an objective biography of him — with all the warts. Her response to this exercise was a dramatic 15-page history, frankly describing his drinking, his changes over the years, the many things they never talked about, their misunderstandings, his avoidance, his humor, their intimacies — the whole complex relationship. It was a touching and profound document. Her private ritual helped her clarify the meaning of their marriage within their family. She reported that one of her sons had asked her what she was working on, when he saw her writing, and asked if he could read it. She calmly said she would prefer not, that it was a private document she was writing about her husband for herself. He respected her boundaries and did not pursue the matter; it was as if clarifying the marriage somehow helped clarify family boundaries as well. She later said it helped her decide what changes she needed to make in her other relationships — with her children and with her siblings. It did not take away the loss, the pain of missing Ted or of the missed opportunities of their relationship. But owning the truth of it strengthened her to look forward and consider what changes she needed to make in her other relationships.

For example, one of her sons had long planned to get married on the father's birthday, which was one month after the death. The family had agreed to this arrangement, but Virginia had found herself resenting and scapegoating her new daughter-in-law as "superficial" and not "fitting into" the family. Virginia had found herself gossiping with her daughters about this new in-law's insensitivity to their family's mourning and intentionally making her entry into the family difficult. Once she had confronted her own marriage honestly, she was able to make a conscious decision to change her behavior toward her new daughter-in-law, who, with this new perspective, turned out to be a pleasant addition to the family.

Validating the Need for Healing Rituals

Where families have not been able to complete their rituals because of the cultural disruption of migration or family problems, therapeutic suggestions can validate their need to mourn and free them to use their own creativity to invent healing rituals to restructure and strengthen their families.

Charles Smith, a 42-year-old African-American, had sought therapy with his wife for their middle daughter, who at age 14 had become pregnant. Therapy focused on various family conflicts and cutoffs, as well as on Charles' deep attachment to certain members of his extended family, which were preventing him from setting appropriate limits on their taking advantage of him. He had experienced multiple losses while growing up in an inner-city ghetto, from which he had struggled hard to escape. During therapy he learned that his stepfather had died suddenly and his half-sister arranged the funeral before he could get there to attend. Charles came to the next session in considerable distress, not only because he had missed the funeral, but because one of his brothers was angry with him for not telling him immediately that their father had died. As we went over his history, we discussed the disruption of family relationships following other losses. I encouraged Charles to think about what he might do to "right the wrong," to mourn the loss and repair the relationship with his brother. Validated to think about this, he immediately came up with a plan to take a trip with his brother to visit the town where his stepfather had lived, to see the home, and to visit the grave. We also discussed how he could prevent his anger at his half-sister from festering into another cutoff, of which his family already had far too many. He readily agreed that going to visit her and her family to "discuss old times" would probably be all that they needed to keep the lines of communication open between them.

Impending or Threatened Loss

The time of impending death may be an excellent opportunity to mobilize families to resolve longstanding issues they may otherwise resist. Death may help them reorder their priorities and complete their unfinished business. Clinicians can facilitate this process by urging family members, through past- and future-oriented questions, to explore family patterns and by empowering them with regard to their current relationships. They can be helped to think through carefully what they want to communicate to other family members to heal past hurts and put their emotional house in order, how they want to spend the rest of their lives, and how they want to arrange their wills and their funerals.

An impending death is likely to intensify whatever relationship patterns are already operating in the family. Our interventions reframe this escalation of conflicts and alliances as natural, while urging family members to use the stress of impending loss to focus their attention and reorder their priorities, in order to take control of their lives and relationships, as the following case illustrates. The therapeutic task is to help family members sit still long enough with their experience to get past the surface distractions, confront the core relationships in their lives, and decide how they want to handle them.

> Peter Mintz, a competent internist, sought help when he suddenly became preoccupied with the possibility of a malpractice suit by one of his patients. He could not concentrate on his work, was spending sleepless nights ruminating about his patients and the mistakes he might have made with them. In taking a genogram of his family I learned that he was the youngest of three brothers. His middle brother, Steve, a lawyer, had been diagnosed three years earlier with lymphatic cancer and was not doing well. Steve was simultaneously going through a stormy divorce involving bitter conflicts with his wife over the children. He had recently been forced out of his law firm because of the time lost from work for his treatments. He was refusing to talk to his parents; he felt they did not understand him and that he had nothing in common with them. Both Peter and Steve viewed their oldest brother, Larry, a wealthy plastic surgeon, as an "obnoxious braggart" and felt totally alienated from him. The only person in the family Steve was in touch with was Peter, whom he called almost daily for advice and consolation. The two brothers were extremely close. Peter told Steve that if the time came when he could not get around and needed care, he could come to live with Peter's family and would not have to be alone.
>
> Now, however, Peter was feeling pulled between his parents and his brother. His parents were becoming more and more distraught about Steve's refusal to communicate with them and were constantly pressuring Peter for information about his brother. Neither brother kept in contact with Larry. As I saw it, Peter's worry

about his patients was a displacement of his anxiety about Steve's anticipated death. He felt he could not handle his family's distress over the cutoff and anticipated death. With this in mind I suggested inviting Steve in for a session.

In the session Steve, the dying brother, repeatedly moved the discussion away from his relationship with his parents by referring to his wife's resentment of them. As he said, his parents were not even on his list of priorities. He spent a good deal of time in the session talking about his ex-wife and her relationship to his parents, before he could focus on the much more relevant issues of his own relationships with them.

In this interview Steve and Peter said that, long before Steve's illness, Peter, though the youngest of the three brothers, had been the caretaker of Steve. They could not explain why Larry had not had this role and described him as a spoiled bully since childhood. Steve, they agreed, had been sickly as a child; he said his parents always treated him as if he weren't smart. As Peter said, "I can even remember as children when we went to the movies, I would be given the money to pay for our tickets." Steve became irate at these memories. I then confronted him about his current behavior:

MM   It sounds like having been treated as weak would leave you never wanting to be vulnerable to your parents, so now in your ultimate vulnerability I could see it would be very hard to admit anything to them. It's curious that things are so cut off with your parents and Larry, but you're extremely in touch with what you feel about Peter. The two of you are so connected. Do you think that when you die they will feel like they failed?

STEVE   I can't imagine why.

MM   I think that must be what they feel already. They try to love you and they don't know how to get through to you.

PETER   They're real angry at him for treating them so shabbily. They don't tell him, but they tell me that. Because you don't tell a guy who has a terminal disease that you are angry at him. I think there is a lot of feeling that they failed. They have a son who they think doesn't love them, and I think they feel that it's a real failure on their part — especially mom, who really is the typical mother. She never had anything other than her children. Whether she did it right or wrong, a lot of heart went into it.

MM   Well, I would guess they must feel they have failed already, but then for you to have a terminal illness and not let them do anything, it's like saying, "Not only did you fail me as a kid, but I'll make you pay now. I won't let you make up for what you didn't do then."

PETER   You mean he's getting back at them?

STEVE   I just never really looked at it like that.

PETER   You think you're getting even, Steve?

STEVE   I must be angry at them. I guess I would have to be. But really, I think it's all my ex-wife's fault because she never liked them and she used to criticize the way they treated me, and for some reason I always believe everything that bitch says, I could never get mad at her.

MM   Maybe your wife has a point. Maybe she was just feeling your feelings for you. You must be absolutely furious with your parents if you won't let them make up now for whatever they didn't do before.

STEVE   I can't get in touch with that. The thing that bothers me is that you said my wife might be right about something.

MM   Well, maybe she's not . . .

STEVE   I feel better already. I have a big hangup on that. I think deep down I'd like to be able to talk to my parents and I don't think they . . . I don't know what I think. It's all really confusing. I haven't really spent a lot of time working on this. It's not even in the list of my priorities right now. It's way on the bottom.

MM   Well, it seems to me that at some level it might be pretty important to you, but we're really here about your brother . . .

STEVE   Yeah, he's footing the bill. How can I help Peter by doing things with the rest of my family?

MM   Well, I think you won't let your parents make up for any wrong they may have done you. And because you won't let them in, and then Peter is aware of that and also aware that you have a lot of needs that they could share with . . .

STEVE   You mean it would take some of the burden off Peter?

MM   Yeah, so in some ways maybe you're also taking it out on him.

STEVE   I guess it would be nice to do something if it would make Peter's life easier.

PETER   Well, that's real easy—just straighten your relationship with mom and dad and then start working on Larry. It's really simple.

STEVE   Larry! He's not even on the sheet of paper!

PETER   Oh yes he is, absolutely.

STEVE   Well, maybe I'm just selfish, but I just can't get concerned about the family's concerns now. I don't know . . .

PETER   But the way it's being put to you is not to get concerned about their concerns but just to get me off the brink of a nervous breakdown. . . . I think I really have been on the verge of being a basket case, when any other time I would have been able to handle a case like this.

STEVE   But when I get panicky it never occurs to me to call my parents. I think I would call a stranger first—it's so foreign to me.

PETER   Is it so foreign that you can't do it?

STEVE   I'm going to obviously have to do it. I'll have to put signs all over the house.

MM   Well, I think the issue is just exaggerated by your illness. That brings things into focus—it's like in your eyes they failed you and now that you're dying that focuses the unresolved feelings in the family. If they think you may die soon and that they failed and can't get to you to make up for it, they must feel terrible and instead of pressuring you they pressure Peter.

PETER   It's like it's all happening at high speed. That's a lot of it.

STEVE   Well, any formulas, I love formulas—give me a formula I can plug into it.

PETER   Steve wants an answer.

MM   Well, one thought I have is that we could meet with all your family.

STEVE   Oh geez!

Following this session Steve called his parents and began talking to them. It seems that, having been forced to confront his part in his family relationships and to sort through his life priorities in the presence of his brother, he knew it mattered to him to reconnect with his parents. The parents were enormously relieved. He even began agitating for a family reunion the following summer. Later we did have a family session in which the parents reviewed the early family history, reminding Steve about the seriousness of his childhood asthma and learning disabilities. His perception of them as the villains of his childhood was shifted into a realization that they had indeed had great faith in his abilities, even when he was having little objective success in school.

This example is typical of the distortions that occur when families cannot talk openly about their experiences. Childhood hurts and misunderstandings about parents become fixed and may fester for years, breeding further distortion in family relationships until the air is cleared by open discussion.

The next step in therapy involved exploring Larry's exclusion from the family, since he seemed a prime candidate for a further cutoff if Steve died. The parents said that Larry had been born shortly after the maternal grandfather died and the grandmother moved into their household. Larry, who was named for his paternal grandfather, became his grandmother's child, with all the special protection and extrusion that entailed. She took him everywhere and showed obvious preference for him, probably as a replacement for her husband. The couple allowed her to do this to accommodate her in her grief over her widowhood. I reframed Larry's role from bully to sacrificial lamb. A relabeling process began, in which over time his exclusion was modified and he and Peter became closer, so that they could be a support system for each other when Steve died.

Wills and Legacies of Loss

Unresolved family issues often become focused on conflicts over wills, which reflect two primary issues: who did more for the deceased and who was more loved by the deceased. Most often it is with the death of the last parent, who is usually the mother, that such conflicts arise, since this death restructures the basic family around the sibling relationships themselves rather than around the parent as center of the family. Cultural relationships will influence how overt this disruptive process will be. For example, Chestang (1990) has suggested that in Black families the conflicts among siblings erupt directly and immediately, particularly between the oldest sister and younger siblings, over who did more for mother and whom she loved the most. While this is often very upsetting for those involved, the good news is that in time they generally move beyond these rifts and hurt feelings. In other cultures, such as the Irish, for example, such conflicts are just as real but are almost never articulated directly. Cutoffs may go on for years or even generations, which can often be traced back to these original, unresolved struggles.

If family members can be coached to explore the implications of wills ahead of time, the damage they may create can sometimes be avoided, as in the following case.

Myra Stein sought help for issues around her father, who had been "ornery his whole life," but who was now in a nursing home and becoming increasingly difficult. She felt in some conflict with her two brothers over responsibility for the father and was troubled by what she feared would happen when the father died and the will was read, since she knew her older half-brother, Paul, was cut out of the will. The father had early divorced his first wife and had had little contact with Paul, the son from this marriage, until Paul sought him out as an adult and for a short time went into business with the father. This endeavor had ended in conflict and the father had, for the past five years, refused to talk to him, in spite of the son's many attempts to reconnect.

Myra had not even known of her older brother's existence until she was 15 but had felt her connection with him very important in later years. She felt Paul's pain that the father had been there for his other two children, but not for him. I coached her to think out for herself what her relationship with her father meant and what her relationship with Paul meant, since she could not control their relationship with each other. She had tried many times over the years with no success to get her father to realize how unfair it was to cut Paul out of his will. Sorting through the meaning of her family relationships now, she was able to make a decision, which she shared with her younger brother that when the father died, she wanted to share the legacy equally with Paul. The younger brother agreed that he wanted to share his half as well. This decision made her more peaceful in dealing with her dying father and freed her up to be more responsive to him. She realized now that while she could not control him, he could no longer control her either.

When the father died, Paul, who had tried one last time, unsuccessfully, to talk with his father on his death bed, was outspoken about his anger at the funeral, which embarrassed the family, but probably expressed feelings others felt toward the father as well. Myra and her younger brother were able to remain calm, clear in their minds that they would now define their sibling relationships, in spite of the influence the father's will might have had over their future. She was able to appreciate her father for what he had given her that was good and take her own action regarding behavior she felt jeopardized other family relationships.

CONCLUSION

We must not as therapists think that we are the only resources for families. Friends, self-help groups, funeral directors, the clergy, nature, books, music, movies can be important sources of inspiration, healing, and connection following a loss. Given the anomie and disconnection of our society, we owe it to our clients to learn about and validate other resources of consolation and meaning.

The examples offered here are simplified sketches of a therapy which is complex and for which there are rarely magical formulas — just as there are rarely magical formulas in life. It is important to maintain flexibility about meeting with family members individually and in different combinations as well as about the timing of therapy. We must respect a family's pace and timing in dealing with these issues. It is also essential to maintain a systemic framework that allows you to move with the client among the past, the present, and the future, as one moves among the internal emotional issues, the immediate family relationships, and the larger contextual issues in which the family is embedded.

Max Lerner (1990) has described that facing death can be a profoundly life-changing experience.

To be close to death "powerfully concentrates a man," as Dr. Johnson put it . . . [it] spurs us to fall back and reinvent ourselves, to savor more fully the life that remains. This means to reimagine who and where we are, what we want of the rest of our lives, what we can whittle away as inessential, what becomes central. (p. 10)

We must help our clients to overcome their own and our culture's denial of death. The main point of this approach to intervention is to empower families to expand the context in which they see themselves and their loss — to see the continuity in their experience from the past and into the future and to see their connection to each other, to their culture, and to all other human beings. This puts not just the death, but their whole lives, in better perspective, strengthening them for the future.

REFERENCES

Becker, E. (1973). *The denial of death*. New York: The Free Press.
Boszormenyi-Nagy, I. (1962). Concept of schizophrenia from the perspective of family treatment. *Family Process, 1*, 103–113.
Chestang, L. (1990). Personal communication.
Kuhn, J. (1981). Realignment of emotional forces following loss. *The Family, 5(1)*, 19–24.
Laird, J. (1989). Women and stories: Restorying women's self-constructions. In M. McGoldrick, C. M. Anderson, & F. Walsh (Eds.), *Women in families*. New York: Norton.
Lerner, M. (1990). *Wrestling with the angel*. New York: Norton.
McGoldrick, M. (1977). Some data on death and cancer in schizophrenic families. Paper presented at Pre-Symposium Meeting of Georgetown Symposium, Washington, DC.
McGoldrick, M. (in press). *You can go home again*. New York: Norton.
McGoldrick, M., & Gerson, R. (1985). *Genograms in family assessment*. New York: Norton.
McGoldrick, M., & Gerson, R. (1989). Genograms and the family life cycle. In B. Carter & M. McGoldrick (Eds.), *The changing family life cycle* (2nd ed.). Boston: Allyn & Bacon.
Mueller, P. S., & McGoldrick Orfanidis, M. (1976). A method of co-therapy for schizophrenic families. *Family Process, 15*, 179–192.
Paul, N. (1976). Cross-confrontation. In P. J. Guerin (Ed.), *Family therapy*. New York: Gardner.
Paul, N. (1980). Now and the past: Transgenerational analysis. *International Journal of Family Psychiatry, 1*, 235–248.
Paul, N., & Grosser, G. (1965). Operational mourning and its role in conjoint family therapy. *Community Mental Health Journal, 1*, 339–345.
Paul, N., & Paul, B. B. (1989). *A marital puzzle*. Boston: Allyn & Bacon.
Paul, N., & Paul, B. B. (1982). Death and changes in sexual behavior. In F. Walsh (Ed.), *Normal family processes*. New York: Guilford.
Roberts, J. (1988). Setting the frame: Definition, functions, and typology of rituals. In E. Imber-Black, J. Roberts, & R. Whiting (Eds.), *Rituals in families and family therapy*. New York: Guilford.
Walmsley, J. (1986). *Brit-think; Ameri-think*. New York: Viking Penguin.
Wortman, C. B., & Silver, R. C. (1989). The myths of coping with loss. *Journal of Counseling and Clinical Psychology, Vol. 37*, No. 3, 349–357.

4

Family Reaction to Death

MURRAY BOWEN

DIRECT THINKING ABOUT death, or indirect thinking about staying alive and avoiding death, occupies more of man's time than any other subject. Man is an instinctual animal with the same instinctual awareness of death as the lower forms of life. He follows the same predictable instinctual life pattern of all living things. He is born, he grows to maturity, he reproduces, his life force runs out, and he dies. In addition, he is a thinking animal with a brain that enables him to reason, reflect, and think abstractly. With his intellect he has devised philosophies and beliefs about the meaning of life and death that tend to deny his place in nature's plan. Each individual has to define his own place in the total scheme and accept the fact that he will die and be replaced by succeeding generations. His difficulty in finding a life plan for himself is complicated by the fact that his life is intimately interwoven with the lives about him. This presentation is directed to death as a part of the total family in which he lives.

There is no simple ways to describe man as part of the relationship around him. Elsewhere (Bowen, 1978) I have presented my own way of conceiving of the human as an individual and, also, as part of the emotional-social amalgam in which he lives. According to my theory, a high percentage of human relationship behavior is directed more by automatic instinctual emo-

---

Reprinted with permission from *Family Therapy*, edited by P. Guerin, New York: Gardner Press, 1976.

tional forces than by intellect. Much intellectual activity goes to explain away and justify behavior being directed by the instinctual-emotion-feeling complex. Death is a biological event that terminates a life. No life event can stir more emotionally directed thinking in the individual and more emotional reactiveness in those about him. I have chosen the concept of "open" and "closed" relationship systems as an effective way to describe death as a family phenomenon.

An "open" relationship system is one in which an individual is free to communicate a high percentage of inner thoughts, feelings, and fantasies to another who can reciprocate. No one ever has a completely open relationship with another, but it is a healthy state when a person can have one relationship in which a reasonable degree of openness is possible. A fair percentage of children have a reasonable version of this with a parent. The most open relationship most people have in their adult lives is in a courtship. After marriage, in the emotional interdependence of living together, each spouse becomes sensitive to subjects that upset the other. They instinctively avoid the sensitive subjects and the relationship shifts toward a more "closed" system. The closed communication system is an automatic emotional reflex to protect self from the anxiety in the other person, though most people say they avoid the taboo subjects to keep from upsetting the other person. If people could follow intellectual knowledge instead of the automatic reflex and gain some control over their own reactiveness to anxiety in the other, they would be able to talk about taboo subjects in spite of the anxiety, and the relationship would move toward a more healthy openness. But people are human, the emotional reactiveness operates like a reflex, and by the time the average person recognizes the problem it can be impossible for two spouses to reverse the process themselves. This is the point at which a trained professional can function as a third person to work the magic of family therapy toward opening a closed relationship.

Chief among all taboo subjects is death. A high percentage of people die alone, locked into their own thoughts, which they cannot communicate to others. There are at least two processes in operation. One is the intrapsychic process in self which always involves some denial of death. The other is the closed relationship system: People cannot communicate the thoughts they do have, lest they upset the family or others. There are usually at least three closed systems operating around the terminally ill person. One operates with the patient. From experience, every terminally ill patient has some awareness of impending death and a high percentage have an extensive amount of private knowledge they do not communicate to anyone. Another closed system is the family. The family gets its basic information from the physician, which is supplemented by bits of information from other sources and is then amplified, distorted, and reinterpreted in conversations at home. The family has its own carefully planned and edited medical communique for the patient. It is based on the family interpretation of the reports and modified to avoid the patient's reactiveness to anxiety. Other versions of the communique are whispered within the hearing of the patient when the family thinks the patient is sleeping or unconscious. Patients are often alert to whispered communications. The physician and the medical staff have another closed system of communication, supposedly based on medical facts, which is influenced by emotional reactivity to the family and within the staff. Physicians attempt to do factual reports to the family which are distorted by the medical emotionality and the effort to put the correct emphasis on the "bad news" or "good news." The more reactive the physician, the more likely he is to put in medical jargon the family does not hear or to become too simplistic in his efforts to communicate in lay language. The more anxious the physician, the more likely he is to do too much speechmaking and too little listening, and to end up with a vague and distorted message and little awareness of the family misperception of his message. The more anxious the physician, the more the family asks for specific details the physician cannot answer. Physicians commonly reply to specific questions with overgeneralizations that miss the point. The physician has another level of communication to the patient. Even the physician who agrees with the principle of telling the patient "facts" can communicate them with so much anxiety that the patient is responding to the physician instead of the content of what is being said. Problems occur when the closed communication system of medicine meets the age-old closed system between the patient and the family, and anxiety is heightened by the threat of terminal illness.

My clinical experience with death goes back some 30 years to detailed discussions about death with suicidal patients. They were eager to talk to an unbiased listener who did not have to correct their way of thinking. Then I discovered that all seriously ill people, and even those who are not sick, are grateful for an opportunity to talk about death. Over the years I have tried to do such discussions with seriously ill people in my practice, with friends and people I have known socially, and with members of my extended families. I have never seen a terminally ill person who was not strengthened by such a talk. This contradicts former beliefs about the ego being too fragile for this in certain situations. I have even done this with a spectrum of comatose patients. Terminally ill people often permit themselves to slip into coma. A fair percentage can pull themselves out of the coma for important communications. I have had such people come out long enough to talk and express their thanks for the help and immediately slip back.

Until the mid 1960s, a majority of physicians were opposed to telling patients they had a terminal illness. In the past decade the prevailing medical dictum about this has changed a great deal, but medical practice has not kept pace with the changed attitude. The poor communications between the physician and the patient, between the physician and the family, and between the family and the patient are still very much as they were before. The basic problem is an emotional one, and a change in rules does not automatically change the emotional reactivity. The physician can believe he gave factual information to the patient, but in the emotion of the moment, the abruptness and vagueness in the communication, and the emotional process in the patient, the patient failed to "hear." The patient and the family can pretend they have dealt clearly with each other without either being heard through the emotionality. In my family therapy practice within a medical center, I am frequently in contact with both the patient and the family, and to a lesser extent with the physicians. The closed system between the patient and the family is great enough, at best. I believe the poor communication between the physician and the family and between the physician and the patient is the greatest problem. There have been repeated situations in which the physicians thought they were communicating clearly, but the family either misperceived or distorted the messages, and the family thinking would be working itself toward malpractice anger at the physician. In all of these, the surgical and medical procedures were adequate, and the family was reacting to terse, brief speeches by the physician who thought he was communicating adequately. In these, it is fairly easy to do simple interpretations of the physician's statements and avert the malpractice thinking.

I believe the trend toward telling patients about incurable illness is one of the healthy changes in medicine, but closed systems do not become open when the surgeon hurriedly blurts out tense speeches about the situation. Experience indicates that physicians and surgeons have either to learn the fundamentals of closed system emotionality in the physician-family-patient triangle, or they might avail themselves of professional expertise in family therapy if they lack the time and motivation to master this for themselves. A clinical example of closed system emotionality will be presented later.

FAMILY EMOTIONAL EQUILIBRIUM AND THE EMOTIONAL SHOCK WAVE

This section will deal with an order of events within the family that is not directly related to open and closed system communications. Death, or threatened death, is only one of many events that can disturb a family. A family unit is in functional equilibrium when it is calm and each member is functioning at reasonable efficiency for that period. The equilibrium of the unit is disturbed by either the addition of a new member or the loss of a member. The intensity of the emotional reaction is governed by the functioning level of emotional integration in the family at the time or by the functional importance of the one who is added to the family or lost to the family. For instance, the birth of a child can disturb the emotional balance until family members can realign themselves around the child. A grandparent who comes for a visit may shift family emotional forces briefly, but a grandparent who come to live in a home can change the family emotional balance for a long period. Losses that can disturb the family equilibrium are physical losses, such as a child who goes away to college or an adult child who marries and leaves home. There are functional losses, such as a key family member who becomes incapacitated with a long-term illness or injury which prevents his doing the work on which the family depends. There are emotional losses, such as the absence of a lighthearted person who can lighten the mood in a family. A group that changes from lighthearted laughter to seriousness becomes a different kind of organism. The length of time required for the family to establish a new emotional equilibrium depends on the emotional integration in the family and the intensity of the disturbance. A well integrated family may show more overt reactiveness at the moment of change but adapt to it rather quickly. A less integrated family may show little reaction at the time and respond later with symptoms of physical illness, emotional illness, or social misbehavior. An attempt to get the family to express feelings at the moment of change does not necessarily increase the level of emotional integration.

The "emotional shock wave" is a network of underground "aftershocks" of serious life events that can occur anywhere in the extended family system in the months or years following serious emotional events in a family. It occurs most often after the death or the threatened death of a significant family member, but it can occur following losses of other types. It is not directly related to the usual grief or mourning reactions of people close to the one who died. It operates on an underground network of emotional dependence of family members on each other. The emotional dependence is denied, the serious life events appear to be unrelated, the family attempts to camouflage any connectedness between the events, and there is a vigorous emotional denial reaction, when anyone attempts to relate the events to each other. It occurs most often in families with a significant degree of denied emotional "fusion" in which the families have been able to maintain a fair degree of asymptomatic emotional balance in the family system. The basic family process has been described elsewhere (Bowen, 1978).

The "emotional shock wave" was first encountered in the author's family research in the late 1950s. It has been mentioned in papers and lectures, but it has not been adequately described in the literature. It was first noticed in the course of multigenerational family research with the discovery that a series of major life events occurred in multiple, separate members of the extended family in the time interval after the serious illness and death of a significant family member. At first, this appeared to be coincidence. Then it was discovered that some version of this phenomenon appeared in a sufficiently high percentage of all families, and now a check for the "shock wave" is done routinely in all family histories. The symptoms in a shock wave can be any human problem. Symptoms can include the entire spectrum of physical illness from an increased incidence of colds and respiratory infections to the first appearance of chronic conditions, such as diabetes or allergies to acute medical and surgical illnesses. It is as if the shock wave is the stimulus that can trigger the physical process into activity. The symptoms can also include the full range of emotional symptoms from mild depression, to phobias, to psychotic episodes. The social dysfunctions can include drinking, failures in school or business, abortions and illegitimate births. An increase in presence of the shock wave provides the physician or therapist with vital knowledge in treatment. Without such knowledge, the sequence of events is treated as separate, unrelated events.

Some examples of the shock wave will illustrate the process. It occurs most often after the death of a significant family member, but it can be almost as severe after a threatened death. An example was a grandmother in her early sixties who had a radical mastectomy for cancer. Within the following two years, there was a chain of serious reactions in her children and their families. One son began drinking for the first time in his life, the wife of another son had a serious depression, a daughter's husband failed in business, and another daughter's children became involved in automobile accidents and delinquency. Some symptoms were continuing five years later when the grandmother's cancer was pronounced cured. A more common example of the shock wave follows the death of an important grandparent, with symptoms appearing in a spectrum of children and grandchildren. The grandchild is often one who had little direct emotional attachment to the grandparents. An example: After the death of a grandmother, a daughter appeared to have no more than the usual grief reaction to the death but reacted in some deep way, transmitting her disturbance to a son who had never been close to the grandmother but who reacted to the mother with delinquent behavior. The family so camouflages the connectedness of these events that family members will further camouflage the sequence of events if they become aware the therapist is seeking some connectedness. Families are extremely reactive to any effort to approach the denial directly. There was a son in his mid-thirties who made a plane trip to see his mother who had had a stroke and who was aphasic. Before that time, his wife and children were leading an orderly life, and his business was going well. His effort to communicate with his mother, who could not speak, was a trying experience. En route home on the plane, he met a young woman with whom he began the first extramarital affair in his life. During the subsequent two years, he began living a double life, his business was failing, and his children began doing poorly in school. He made a good start in family therapy, which continued for six sessions; then I made a premature connection between his mother's stroke and the affair. He cancelled the subsequent appointment and never returned. The nature of the human phenomenon is such that it reacts vigorously to any such implications of the dependence of one life on another.

Other families are less reactive and they can be more interested in the phenomenon than reactive to it. I have seen only one family who had made an automatic connection between such events before seeking therapy. This was a father who said, "My family was calm and healthy until two years ago when my daughter was married. Since then it has been one trouble after another, and the doctor bills have become exorbitant. My wife had a gall bladder operation. After that, she found something wrong with each house where we lived. We have broken three leases and moved four times. Then she developed a back problem and had a spinal fusion. My son had been a good student before my daughter married. Last year, his school work went down and this year he dropped out of college. In the midst of this, I had a heart attack." I would see this as a family with tenuously balanced emotional equilibrium in which the mother's functioning was dependent on her relationship with the daughter. Most of the subsequent dysfunction was in the mother, but the son and father were sufficiently dependent on the mother that they too developed symptoms. The incidence of the emotional shock wave is sufficiently prevalent that the Georgetown Family Section does a routine historical check for it in every family history.

Knowledge of the emotional shock wave is important in dealing with families on death issues. Not all deaths have the same importance to a family. There are some in which there is a fair chance the death will be followed by a shock wave. Other deaths are more neutral and are usually followed by no more than the usual grief and mourning reactions. Other deaths are a relief to the family and are usually followed by a period of better functioning. If the therapist can know ahead of time about the possibility of an emotional shock wave, he can take some steps toward its prevention. Among the deaths most likely to be followed by a serious and prolonged shock wave are the deaths of either parent when the family is young. This not only disturbs the emotional equilibrium, but also removes the function of the breadwinner or the mother at a time when these functions are most important. The death of an important child can shake the family equilibrium for years. The death of the "head of the clan" is another that can be followed by a long-term underground disturbance. It can be a grandfather who may have been partially disabled but who continued some kind of decision-making function in family affairs. The grandmothers in these families usually lived in the shadow of their husbands, and their deaths were less important. The family reaction can be intense following the death of a grandmother who was a central figure in the emotional life and stability of the family. The "head of the clan" can also be the most important sibling in the present generation.

There is another group of family members whose deaths may result in no more than the usual period of grief and mourning. They may have been well liked, but they played peripheral roles in family affairs. They are the neutral ones who were neither "famous nor infamous." Their deaths are not likely to influence future family functioning. Finally, there are the family members whose deaths are a relief to the family. This includes the people whose functioning was never critical to the family, and who may have been a burden in their final illness. Their deaths may be followed by a brief period of grief and mourning, which is then followed by improved family functioning. A shock wave rarely follows the death of a dysfunctional family member unless that dysfunction played a critical role in maintaining family emotional equilibrium. Suicides are commonly followed by prolonged grief and mourning reactions, but the shock wave is usually minor unless the suicide was an abdication of an essential functional role.

THERAPY AT THE TIME OF DEATH

Knowledge of the total family configuration, the functioning position of the dying person in the family, and the overall level of life adaptation is important for anyone who attempts to help a family before, during, or after a death. To attempt to treat all deaths as the same can miss the mark. Some well-functioning families are able to adapt to approaching death before it occurs. To assume that such families need help can be an inept intrusion. Physicians and hospitals have left much of the problems about death to chaplains and ministers with the expectation they know what to do. There are exceptional clergymen who intuitively know what to do. However, many young chaplains or clergymen tend to treat all death as the same. They operate with their theology, a theory about death that does not go beyond the familiar concepts of grief and mourning, and they tend to aim their help at the overt expression of grief. This may provide superficial help to a majority of people, but it misses the deeper process. The popular notion that expression of grief through crying may be helpful to most complicates the situation for others. It is important for the physician or therapist to know the situation, to have his own emotional life under reasonable control without the use of too much denial or other extreme mechanisms, and to respect the denial that operates in the family. In my work with families, I carefully use direct words, such as *death*, *die*, and *bury*, and I carefully avoid the use of less direct works, such as *passed on*, *deceased*, and *expired*.

A direct word signals to the other that I am comfortable with the subject, and it enables others to also be comfortable. A tangential word may appear to soften the fact of death; but it invites the family to respond with tangential words, and the conversation soon reaches the point that one wonders if we are talking about death at all. The use of direct words helps to open a closed emotional system. I believe it provides a different dimension in helping the family to be comfortable within themselves.

The following is a clinical example that illustrates an effort to open the communication with a terminally ill patient, her family, and the medical staff. As a visiting professor in another medical center, I was scheduled to do a demonstration interview with the parents of an emotionally disturbed daughter. En route to the interview room, I learned the mother had a terminal cancer, that the surgeon had told the father, and the father had told the family therapist, but that the mother did not know about it. In my own practice, it would have been automatic to discuss this issue with the family, but I was reluctant to take this course when follow-up interviews would not be possible. A large group of profession people and trainees observed the interview. I elected to avoid the critical issue. The beginning of the interview was awkward, difficult, and sticky. I decided the cancer issue had to be discussed. About ten minutes out, I asked the mother why she thought her surgeon, her family, and the others had not told her about her cancer. Without the slightest hesitation, she said she thought they were afraid to tell her. She calmly said, "I know I have cancer. I have known it for some time. Before that, I was afraid of it, but they told me it was not cancer. I believed them for a time, thinking it was my imagination. Now I know it is cancer. When I ask them and they say 'No,' what does it mean? It either means they are liars or I am crazy, and I know I am not crazy."

Then she went into detail about her feelings, with some moderate tears, but with full control of herself. She said that she was not afraid to die for herself, but she would like to live long enough to see the daughter have a life for herself. She hated the responsibility of leaving the daughter the responsibility of the father. She spoke with deep feeling but few tears. She and I were the calmest people in the room. Her therapist wiped away tears. The father reacted by joking and kidding about the mother's vivid imagination. To prevent his reaction from silencing her, I made a few comments to suggest he not interfere with his wife's serious thoughts. She was able to continue, "This is the loneliest life in the world. Here I am, knowing I am going to die, and not knowing how much time I have left. I can't talk to anyone. When I talk to my surgeon, he says it is not a cancer. When I try to talk to my husband, he makes jokes about it. I came here to talk about my daughter and not about myself. I am cut off from everyone. When I get up in the morning, I feel terrible. I look at my eyes in the mirror to see if they are jaundiced and the cancer has spread to my liver. I try to act cheerful until my husband goes to work, because I don't want to upset him. Then I am alone all day with my thoughts, just crying and thinking. Before my husband returns from work, I try to pull myself together for his sake. I wish I could die soon and not have to pretend any longer." Then she went into some background thoughts about death. As a little girl she felt hurt when people walked on graves. She had always wished she could be buried above ground in a mausoleum, so people would not walk on her grave. "But," she said, "We are poor people. We can't afford a mausoleum. When I die, I will be buried in a grave just like everyone else."

The technical problem in this single interview was to permit the mother to talk, to keep the father's anxiety from silencing her, and to hope the regular therapist could continue the process later. It is impossible to do much toward opening an emotionally closed relationship of this intensity in a single session, although the father said he would try to listen and understand. The patient was relieved to be partially out of the closed system in which she had lived. The therapist said she had known about the cancer but had been waiting for the mother to bring it up. This is a common posture for mental health professionals. The therapist's own emotionality had prevented the wife from talking. At the end of the interview, the mother said, smiling through her tears, "We have sure spent an hour walking around on my grave, haven't we?" As I said goodbye to them in the hall, the mother said, "When you go home tonight, thank Washington for sending you here today." The less expressive father said, "We are both grateful."

There were a few minutes with the audience who had observed the interview. Part of the group had been moved to tears, most were silent and serious, and a few were critical. The criticism was expressed by a young physician who spoke of hurting the wife and having taken away her hope. I was pleased at having decided to take up this issue in this single demonstration interview. En route home, my thoughts went to the differences in audience response and the problems of training young professional people to contain their own emotionality sufficiently to become more objective about death. I guessed it would be easier to train those who cried than those who intellectualized their feelings. This is an example of a good result in a single session. It illustrates the intensity of a closed relationship system between the patient, the family, and the medical staff.

THE FUNCTION OF FUNERALS

Some 25 years ago, I had a clinical experience that illustrates the central point of the next section of this chapter. A young woman began psychoanalysis with, "Let me bury my mother before we go on to other things." Her mother had been dead six years. She cried for weeks. At the time, I was practicing within the framework of transference and intrapsychic dynamics. The patient's statement was used later as a way of describing systems theory about the unresolved emotional attachments between people that remain viable for life, that attach to significant future relationships, and that continue to direct the course of a life. There is a way to utilize the funeral to more completely "bury the dead at the time of death." Few human events provide as much emotional impact as serious illness and death in resolving unresolved emotional attachments.

The funeral ritual has existed in some form since man became a civilized being. I believe it serves a common function of bringing survivors into intimate contact with the dead and with important friends, and it helps survivors and friends to terminate their relationship with the dead and to move forward with life. I think the best function of a funeral is served when it brings relatives and friends into the best possible functional contact with the harsh fact of death and with each other at this time of high emotionality. I believe funerals were probably more effective when people died at home with the family present, and when family and friends made the coffin and did the burial themselves. Society no longer permits this, but there are ways to bring about a reasonable level of personal contact with the dead body and the survivors.

There are numerous present-day funeral customs that function to deny death and to perpetuate the unresolved emotional attachments between the dead and the living. It is most intense in people who are anxious about death and who use the present form and content of funerals to avoid the anxiety. There are those who refuse to look at a dead body because, "I want to remember them as I knew them." There is the anxious segment of society that refers to funerals as pagan rituals. Funeral custom makes it possible for the body to be disposed of from the hospital without the family ever having personal contact with it. Children are commonly excluded from funerals to avoid upsetting them. This can result in a lifetime of unrealistic and distorted fantasies and images that may never be corrected. The private funeral is another custom that avoids the emotionality of death. It is motivated by family anxiety to avoid contact with emotionality in others. It denies the friendship system an opportunity to terminate their relationship with the dead, and it deprives the family of the supportive relationships from friends.

I believe that professional support to a family at the time of death can help the family members toward a more helpful funeral than would be possible if they listened to advice from anxious relatives and friends. In 20 years of family practice, I have had contact with several thousand families, and I have been in the background "coaching" families through hundreds of deaths and funerals. I urge family members to visit dying family members whenever possible and to find some way to include children if the situation permits. I have never seen a child hurt by exposure to death. They are "hurt" only by the anxiety of survivors. I encourage involvement of the largest possible group of extended family members, an open casket, and the most personal contact that is possible between the dead and the living, prompt obituary notices, and the notification of relatives and friends, a public funeral with the body present, and the most personal funeral service that is possible. Some funeral services are highly ritualized but it is possible to personalize even the most ritualized service. The goal is to bring the entire family system into the closest possible contact with death in the presence of the total friendship system and to lend a helping hand to the anxious people who would rather run than face a funeral.

The following is an example of coaching friends from the background. It involved neighbors rather than people in my professional practice. The young parents in their early thirties and their three children ages ten, eight, and five, had come to live with her widowed mother in preparation for the husband's going overseas on a prolonged assignment. On a Sunday one month before his scheduled departure, the young mother died suddenly of a heart attack. The entire community was shocked. That evening, I spent some three hours with the father. He and his wife had been very close. He had dozens of questions about how to handle the present emergency, the funeral, the future of the children, and his own life. He wondered if the children should go to school the next day, what he should tell the teachers, and if he should seek release from his overseas work. In the afternoon, he had tried to tell the children about their mother's death, but he started to cry and the children responded, "Please don't cry, Daddy." He said he simply had to have another mother for the children, but he felt guilty saying this only eight hours after his wife had died.

During the visit, I outlined what I would consider to be the ideal course of action for him. I suggested he take as many of the ideas as were consistent with himself, and if they made sense to him, to use them as far as he could go. I suggested that the ability of children to deal with death depends on the adults, and the future would be best served if the death could be presented in terms the children could understand and they could be realistically involved in the funeral. I warned him of adverse emotional reactions of friends and to be prepared for criticism if he decided to involve the children. In the first hours after the death, the children had been responding to his emotionality rather than to the fact of the mother's death. In this kind of situation, it is common for the children to stop talking and deny the death. I suggested that he get through this block by mentioning the death at frequent intervals during the coming days, and, if he started to cry, to reassure the children that he was all right and not to worry about him. I wanted to keep the channel open for any and all questions they might have. I suggested that the children decide whether or not they wished to go to school the next day. On the issue of involving the children with the dead mother, I suggested that he arrange a time before the funeral to take the children to the funeral home, to remove all other people from the room, and for him and the children to have a private session with their dead mother. I reasoned that this would help the children adapt to the reality of the mother's death, and that it could work if anxious members of the extended family were excluded.

On Tuesday evening, I spent an hour in the bedroom with the father in a chair and the three children in his lap. He could cry, and they could cry and the children were free to ask questions. He told them about the plan to go to the funeral home the following afternoon. The five-year-old son asked if he could kiss Mommy. The father looked to me for an answer. I suggested that would be between the son and his mother. Later, in the living room, I announced to the relatives and friends that the father would take the children to the funeral home the next afternoon, that it was to be private, and that no one else could be present. Privately, I considered it unwise to expose the children to the emotionality in that family. The father's mother said, "Son, that will be too hard on you." The father replied, "Mother, shut up. I can do it."

On Wednesday evening, I visited the funeral home. The entire family–friendship system was present. The maternal grandmother, who had been calm through these days, said, "Thank you very much for your help." The father did a detailed account of the children's visit in the afternoon. The children went up to the casket and felt their mother. The five-year-old son said, "If I kissed her, she could not kiss back." All three spent some time inspecting everything, even looking under the casket. The eight-year-old son got under the casket and prayed that his mother could hold him in her arms again in heaven. Some family friends came while the father and children were in the room. The father and children withdrew to the lobby while the friends went into the room. In the lobby, the youngest son found some polished pebbles in a planter. He was the one who found objects to give his mother as "presents." He took a small pebble into the room and placed it in his mother's hand. The other children also got pebbles and put them into their mother's hand. They then announced, "We can go now Daddy." The father was much relieved at the outcome of the visit. He said, "A thousand tons were lifted from this family today." The following day I attended the funeral. The children did well. The ten-year-old daughter and eight-year-old son were calm. During the service, the eight-year-old whispered to the father, "Daddy, I sure am going to miss Mommy." The five-year-old clung to the father with some tearfulness.

There was some criticism about the father involving the children in the funeral, but he did well with it and the criticism turned to admiration after the funeral home visit. I was in close contact with the family the following year. The father continued to mention the mother's death. Within a week the children were talking about the mother in the past tense. The children stayed with their grandmother. There was none of the usual complications usually seen after a death of this kind. The father took an assignment closer to home, so he could return if he was needed. The following year, the father remarried and took the children with him and his new wife to another city. It has now been 12 years since the death and the family adjustment has been perfect. I am still in periodic contact with the family, which now includes three grown children from the first marriage and younger children from the second marriage. Some years after the death, the father wrote his version of the experience when the first wife died, entitled, "My God, My Wife is Dead." He described his initial shock, his efforts to get beyond self-pity, his resolution to make his own decisions when anxiety was high, and the emotional courage that went into his plan in the critical days before the funeral and burial. This illustrates what I would consider an optimum result from a traumatic death that could have had lifelong sequelae; but this father had more inner strength than any other relative I have seen under stress of this intensity.

Summary

Family systems theory provides a broader perspective of death than is possible with conventional psychiatric theory, which focuses on death as a process within the individual. The first part of this chapter deals with the closed relationship system between the patient, the family, and physicians, and family therapy methods that have been helpful in overcoming some of the anxiety that creates the closed system communication. The second section deals with the "emotional shock wave" that is present to some degree in a significant percentage of families. Knowledge of this, which is the direct result of family research, provides the professional person with a different dimension for understanding emotional interdependence and the long-term complications of death in a family. The final section deals with the emotional impact of funerals and ways the professional person can help surviving relatives to achieve a better level of emotional functioning by calmly facing the anxiety of death.

Reference

Bowen, M. (1978). *Family therapy in clinical practice.* New York: Jason Aronson.

5

Operational Mourning and Its Role in Conjoint Family Therapy

NORMAN L. PAUL   GEORGE H. GROSSER

LOSS OF LOVED ones through death is a common heritage. Man's philosophy, his religion, and his art are in part a response to death. They are an attempt to fix the world into the final form which will be the stay against disintegration.

> Man is in love
> And loves what vanishes;
> What more is there to say?
> —W. B. Yeats

Psychologists seem to have little to say if we must judge from the dearth of psychological literature on the phenomenon of shared grief and its resolution as experienced by a family when a loved one dies. There is, furthermore, very little firsthand observation and description of the process of mourning in individuals in both its natural and pathological forms. The clinical studies that have been published have included summarized accounts and generalizations with few empirical observations.

We are a society materially prepared for death; witness the expansion and diversity of life insurance companies and the steady growth of national social security programs. We open a magazine and are confronted with the

Reprinted with permission from *Community Mental Health Journal*, I, 4, winter 1965.

question: "If you should not be here?" The widespread presence of and interest in plans to prepare for economic security contrast sharply with the lack of knowledge in preparing survivors psychologically for coping with death. We know very little about how and in what ways family survivors of death respond psychologically.

While it is true that such information is absent not only in our culture but in other societies as well, there is one vital difference. In most other areas of the world, children and adults are prepared for death through elaborate forms of ceremony and ritual with accompanying lore and explanations of the meaning of life and death. Such ceremony and ritual have been lost to us through secularization, urbanization, and our comfortable, but deceptive, emphasis on rationality. Nothing in the modern era has supplanted the traditional forms of grieving. Our abbreviated mourning ceremonies, often carefully hidden from children, neither impart empathic understanding nor provide catharsis for this experience. This raises the question of what might happen if a child does not or cannot come to terms with death.

Though anthropologists have shown considerable interest, there have been but few psychiatrists who have pursued death as a theme. Among these have been Freud, Bowlby, Engel, Lindemann, Rochlin, and Parkes. Freud's *Mourning and Melancholia* (1917 [1915]) provided the major stimulus for subsequent dynamic investigations on grief and mourning. His (Freud, 1926) formulation of the importance of separation anxiety as a critical factor in the development of the human being was later elaborated upon by Bowlby. Bowlby's (1961a, 1961b) excellent description of the processes of mourning paralleled his delineation of the sequence of responses observed in children when separated from the care of their mothers. Rochlin's (1961) concept of the dread of abandonment furnished further impetus for understanding some of the enduring effects of the experience of loss in man. More recently, Bowlby (1961c) indicated that separation anxiety, grief and mourning are phases of a single process, adding that, when they are viewed as such, each clarifies the others.

We have been confronted again and again with hospitalized schizophrenic patients who improve during the course of intensive individual psychotherapy but fail to maintain their gains upon the loss or projected loss of the therapist through termination. Such patients tend to decompensate, exhibiting patterns of regression similar to those which were observed prior to initial hospitalization. These observations suggest that the inability to cope with loss might be characteristic of a family pattern acquired in a milieu where other family members shared a similar failing. Our preliminary studies revealed this failing to be present. The structure of the families studied included a set of family relationships highly resistant to change, especially observable in attitudes toward the patient. These attitudes and behaviors, including the patient's reactions to his family, were seen as manifestations of a "fixed family equilibrium." This term refers to a relatively unchanging dynamic state to which there is a tendency to return when disturbed, and which can also be viewed as a pathological homeostasis. A "fixed family equilibrium" was also found in families with neurotic patients, the principal difference being the lesser rigidity with which this state was maintained. Family systems, like all other social systems, tend to maintain an equilibrium which, in the case of the normal family, gradually evolves and alters in accordance with aging and the differential role demands of the life cycle of its members.

A STUDY OF FAMILIES

A clinical study of 50 families with schizophrenic members and 25 families with at least one psychoneurotic member was undertaken. Patterns of inflexible interaction, revealed through amnestic material, were found to have existed for many years prior to commencement of treatment. Most significantly, despite obvious differences in family composition, ethnic origin, religion, and socioeconomic status, these families had one striking feature in common. That feature was the variable patterns of maladaptive response to object loss. This inability to cope with loss was usually expressed through denial of its significance on an affective level. The tendency to maintain this pattern was present in families with varying degrees of psychopathology.

Although the original losses may have occurred as long as 50 years ago, the response to them exercised a lingering effect on the present. Such losses were usually suffered by one or the other parent, often before the birth of the patient. Affects and attitudes toward the lost persons had remained essentially unchanged and recent losses evoked similar reaction patterns. The current style of family life appeared permeated with varying degrees of denial or "warding off" of losses and disappointments. Major changes in family homeostasis, such as those which might result in separation or independence of its members, were often resisted.

This observed pattern was most severe in families with schizophrenic patients. Most of these members were fixated in what Bowlby (1961a) has called the first phase of mourning, "the urge to recover the lost object." In addition, two reactions were observed to be directly related to the family's senior member.

First, the patient becomes endowed through projection with a number of characteristics of the lost object, thus becoming both a target and a carrier of ambivalent feelings. The authors have elsewhere described the mechanisms which tend to maintain the patient in his pathological role, reinforce his symptomatology, and interfere with the development of his identity. The schizophrenic patient often expresses in affective terms an identification with dead persons through references to his own lifelessness.

Secondly, the family tries to prevent both the patient's and to some extent other family members' emancipation, which is often viewed as a potential loss to the unit. This is accomplished by reinforcing those symbiotic ties which normally disappear with further growth of the ego and the development of a personal identity.

These observations helped formulate the hypothesis of a direct relationship between the maladaptive response to object loss and the fixity in symbiotic relationships in the family. One possible key to dislodging this fixation would be to mobilize those affects which might aid in disrupting this peculiar kind of equilibrium.

OPERATIONAL MOURNING

Since abortive mourning or denial of loss seemed to be at the core of this fixation, it appeared that a "corrective mourning experience," even though belated, might be effective in neutralizing the existent symbiotic fixations.

To test this hypothesis in a treatment oriented program, a therapeutic technique was developed that involved the deliberate introduction of a belated mourning experience. The term *operational mourning* was selected to describe this technique because it emphasizes the experiential elements involved in the mourning process. Such experiences come closest to what has been described as mourning reactions and grief work. It consists of a mourning response induced by directed inquiry about the reactions to actual losses sustained by specific family members. The therapist, through repeated review of recollected details surrounding these losses, invites the expression of feelings of the member directly involved. The other family members are then invited to review such feelings as are stimulated through witnessing the grief reaction. This technique is designed to permit children, often for the first time, to observe the expression of these intense feelings by their parents. This can provide a powerful empathic experience. The patient and other family members can kaleidoscopically obtain a sense of affective continuity; the therapist can assure them that the revealed feelings are normal. Displacement of hostility from the original lost object to family members present (usually the schizophrenic patient) can be clarified, and revelation of previously unknown "family secrets" can be achieved. A concomitant feature of *operational mourning* is the open review of episodic threats of abandonment by a parent or other family member which has plagued the family unit with ominous foreboding. Such threats and the resulting anxieties lessen as the original sources of such separation anxieties are worked through.

During these periods of activated mourning, family members acquire an ability to share affective experiences with each other. This increases their familiarity with the experience of grief and its derivatives. Concurrently, they are encouraged by the therapist to react empathically to affects revealed by others. This process contributes to the development of an observing ego in each family member. While family members exhibit variable degrees of resistance to many themes, mourning and the review of lost objects stand out as being the most difficult to pursue.

Our studies to date suggest that avoidance of *operational mourning* is strongest in families with a schizophrenic member. Families with neurotic patients usually are able to pursue this topic spontaneously after the therapist discusses it a few times. It seems that the family's response itself may be a diagnostic criterion.

As the patient begins to exhibit more appropriate behavior, the fixed family equilibrium shows gradual signs of breakdown manifested by symptoms of individual disorganization and heightened intrafamilial friction. Some members with strong symbiotic ties report a variety of psychic and psychosomatic disturbances including insomnia, tension, digestive tract symptoms, depression, and free-floating anxiety. At the same time, some defenses are set in motion. They may take the form of a frantic search for expert advice from physicians or clergymen, or an immersion in a host of "busy-work" activities. Such disorganization is temporary, lasting until emerging individuation becomes apparent. As this occurs, relationships change and conflict tends to subside.

These phenomena are typical of the second phase of the mourning process as described by Bowlby (1961a) and are reminiscent of the temporary personal disorganization that ensues when a patient in individual psychotherapy or psychoanalysis is in the process of relinquishing a deeply entrenched defense mechanism.

Planning for termination begins with the emergence of new interests on the part of each family member. It is associated with a review of the history of the family group and its reaction to the impending separation from the therapist. Ambivalent feelings concerning loss are emphasized with regard to the importance of the ability to bear and accept the affects attending termination of treatment.

A CASE ILLUSTRATION

The following report focuses on the initial phase of conjoint family therapy after denial of the patient's illness and associated family problems have been reviewed. Though the family members have had some prior acquaintance with the history of the loss in question, they had never been exposed to the affective impact of these events. Included is a tape recorded excerpt from the first conjoint family therapy meeting held eight-and-a-half years after the onset of a chronic relapsing schizoaffective schizophrenic reaction in Turner D., Jr., a married 34-year-old father of three children.

The patient's first schizophrenic episode occurred at age 26 when, after several miscarriages, his pregnant wife informed him that she felt life. Within a few days, he exhibited an acute turmoil state manifested by delusions, hallucinations, bizarre posturing behavior, paranoid ideation, and inappropriate affect. He was hospitalized with a diagnosis of acute undifferentiated schizophrenic reaction, severe. He recovered in six months, and obtained a job as a research engineer which he kept for 10 years. His symptoms recurred during the second trimesters of his wife's next two pregnancies in 1955 and again in February, 1960. Since 1960, he has had three periods of hospitalization, averaging six months each. He was treated in individual psychotherapy with concurrent medication from February, 1960. In the late summer of 1962, it was decided to commence a concurrent course of conjoint family therapy once weekly in which his parents, siblings, and wife participated. His wife had been seen in casework therapy from February, 1960.

The D. family, attractive in appearance and vigorous and enthusiastic in attitude, consists of two living parents and five children of which the patient is the oldest. Mr. Turner D., Sr., the father, is a 58-year-old business executive. He was the only surviving child of three sons in his own nuclear family and was reared by his maternal grandparents after his father died in a tannery explosion when Mr. D., Sr., was seven years old. His general passive role as a father has been highlighted by a standing family joke in which he is regarded as the sixth child. His attitude toward the patient has always been distant and uninvolved. Mrs. D., Sr., is a 57-year-old graduate nurse, appearing deceptively feminine and helpless despite her controlling role. In terms of dealing with feelings, this family has been conspicuous for the absence of direct hostile expression with a tendency toward excessive childish gaiety, frantic humor, and giggling when dealing with uncomfortable tension levels.

Operational mourning began with a review of the father's reaction to the death of his own father after the patient had discussed his own personal problems for the first time in the presence of his family. He had characterized himself as being unable to achieve a level of functioning beyond early adolescence. The therapist then inquired about the source of the patient's name.

THERAPIST (NP)   One of the things I wanted to find out here is in terms of, let's go back into time, the way you decided how to name Turner, because this was the beginning of Turner.

MR. D. (blandly)   It was John, first; John.

MRS. D. (very softly)   No.

MR. D.   No?

MRS. D.   No, that was Corky (second son).

MR. D. (with surprise)   Oh, was that Corky?

MRS. D. (with conviction)   I don't think there was ever any question about that a first son would carry his father's name. I mean, I don't, there's anything, we never even thought of anything else, and so we never thought about anything except that he was going to be a boy.

THERAPIST   He really would have had problems if he were a girl. (Everyone laughs.)

MRS. D.   Well, since we had problems over him being . . . to which may, may basically — you don't know how much of this carried over . . . because I don't think it's been a secret. We've talked about it rather openly in the family; Turner (Sr.) always said he'd, you know, be perfectly happy if he didn't have any children; he didn't know what to do with them because he's an only child, basically an only child of only children.

THERAPIST (to Mr. D.)   Your parents were only children, too?

MRS. D. (answering for Mr. D.)   Well, not really. His (referring to her husband) father had two brothers, but they died very early so he had no experience with youngsters and as I just told you a while ago, I wanted eight boys. We had a conflict right in the beginning (laughing nervously).

THERAPIST (to Mr. D.)   Well, what were your ideas about naming him?

MR. D. (with some hesitation)   I can't recall that I had any. I think it was just assumed that, that he would carry on the name of D. because the whole family, uh, the only thing I can remember, uh, about carrying my name is the fact that the whole family of D. were all dying off and he was, he was the one to carry on again if the name, this branch of the family was to continue.

MRS. D.   Turner is a family name.

MR. D.   And my grandfather was Turner.

THERAPIST   And your father?

MR. D.   No. His name was Ebenezer. And so we went back to his father who was Turner.

THERAPIST (to Mr. D.)   Did you know his father?

MR. D.   No, no.

THERAPIST   He died before you were born?

MRS. D. (slightly saddened)   He didn't even know his own father, hardly.

THERAPIST   Do you remember your experience when he died?

MR. D. (blinking back tears)   Yeah. I remember that.

THERAPIST   What do you remember of that?

MR. D.   Well, it was pretty rugged.

THERAPIST   In what sense?

MR. D.   Well you see, (speaking very quickly) he was burned to death. It was an accident, an explosion. My grandfather drove me up to the uh, the fire.

THERAPIST   Your grandfather whom?

MR. D.   Johnson.

THERAPIST   I see.

MR. D.   You see, on my mother's side, and uh, I remember that experience very well, and, uh . . .

THERAPIST   Do you remember what you felt then?

MR. D. (regaining composure)   Well, I thought that I took it in my stride pretty well as I remember it. I went and told everybody in the neighborhood about it and by talking about it, it seemed to help me grasp the situation, and uh, then of course, we were already living with my grandparents so it was just the transfer from my father to my grandfather from then on, and uh . . .

In spite of defensive distracting maneuvers from his wife, the father reluctantly responded to direct inquiry about his father's death. He supplied graphic details with much feeling while the others were listening with rapt attention:

THERAPIST   Did you see your father when he was burned?

MR. D. (increasingly sad)   No. No, I did not. I was not allowed to get out of the car. My grandfather said, "You sit in the car!" and I sat in the car. (His father died September 12, 1912.)

THERAPIST   How do you feel as you recall this experience now? How do you feel here?

MR. D. (begins quiet weeping)   Kind of bad about it.

THERAPIST   Bad in what way?

MR. D.   Uh, (deep sigh) Well, I think it was, things would have been a lot different if he hadn't been killed (continued weeping).

THERAPIST   But I want to know what you feel, I mean . . .

MR. D. (trying to recover composure as he speaks quickly)   Well grief, sorrow.

THERAPIST   Inside, do you feel a sense of sadness?

MR. D. (with renewed weeping)   Yeah, yeah.

THERAPIST   And old hurts come back as you sort of review that?

MR. D.   Yeah I think so.

MRS. D. (sadly)   I always felt sorry, sorrier for his mother than I did for him 'cause I felt he had his life ahead of him and her life stopped. In fact, I don't guess her life ever began.

MR. D.   No, she . . .

THERAPIST   Yes, but in a certain sense I think your life must have stopped too when he died — no father.

MR. D.   That's right (quiet weeping).

He then described some good times he had with his grandfather. Mary, the patient's sister, resonated to this by pointed out that Mr. D., Sr., was a "terrific grandfather." The therapist asked whether this was the way Mr. D., Sr., had viewed his own grandfather; he said "yes" quite readily with some surprise. Somewhat later in this same session, Mr. D., Sr., expressed his annoyance at the therapist for focusing on his feelings about his own father's death, questioning the value of this procedure:

MR. D. (face flushed; angry)   But what effect does it have by talking about it? What . . .

THERAPIST   Ask the other people. Ask them.

MRS. D. (thoughtfully)   This is the question that we have been asking for years. Every time I tried, every time we try to bring up something like this, my dearly beloved goes into his little clamshell and says, "What's the good to talk about it?"

THERAPIST   Well, then, ask the others here and find out.

MRS. D. (with some surprise)   Well, haven't we already told him?

MARY   No, not really.

THERAPIST   Well, he wants to know. I think in all fairness to him, he wants to know, "Is this important?" (To father): This is the question you're asking.

MR. D.   That's right.

MRS. D.   It's terrifically important to me.

MR. D. (demandingly)   Why?

MRS. D.   Because maybe if he can talk about how he feels about his father, he can talk about how he feels about me.

Both Mary and the patient's wife indicated the importance of Mr. D.'s affective review of his early loss. Turner, Jr., the patient, then responded (with hesitation): "Well, well, all during the time that he was talking, I had a well, uh, a sense of, of hurt for him that I never really experienced before, uh, so it was a, a new feeling for me and uh, well, I never heard the story before. My first experience with somebody close to me dying was when Nick Jones (my best friend) died."

The meeting concluded on a positive note. They agreed to pursue conjoint family therapy with a full understanding of its innovative nature. The patient returned to work the following week. Later that same week in individual psychotherapy with the same therapist, he spontaneously reported that, after empathizing with what his father had lived through, he felt "like a man" for the first time on his job. He then revealed he felt strangely depressed, which he related to the absence of his previous high level of anxiety.

DISCUSSION

The above case illustrates the technique of *operational mourning*. In spite of superficial appearances to the contrary, it is apparent that the patient was raised in a family which never shared critical emotions related to the experience of object loss. The mother, in giving the patient his father's name, had expressed the wish that the patient would identify with his father. However, the father's distance and remoteness precluded his being an adequate model for this son except in the area of occupational achievement, an area in which father and patient shared compulsive patterns. As was revealed in this session, the father's own traumatic loss was never worked through during the 50 intervening years. The father's fixation rendered him incapable of expressing the critical affects of sadness and helplessness. He was also impaired in the more important realm of not being able to experience such affects. Crucial in the patient's lack of emotional development was an impairment similar to that of his father.

One difference between this case and families with neurotic patients is that, in the latter, significant losses are usually experienced directly by the patients. In the D. family, the loss was experienced by the father and not directly by the patient. This case illustrates the transgenerational influences of the experience of loss on the schizophrenic process. Hill (1955) and Bowen (1960), among others, without naming any specific influences, have commented on this phenomenon.

This example also highlights how *operational mourning* in conjoint family sessions can activate an empathic potential where other therapeutic settings could not. Although it has been shown that grief reactions can be induced in individual psychotherapy (Lindemann, 1944; Wetmore, 1963), such material would never have led to the interactional consequences of improved relationships within the family that the family setting provided. Turner D., Jr., had the opportunity of personally witnessing and empathizing with the affects his father revealed in recalling a critical event. This seemed to catalyze similar affects in the patient.

The nurturance and appearance of empathy has eluded adequate definition (Paul, 1966). Except as used by the poet, language tends to filter out the essence of the empathic experience. Hostility, anxiety, or joy is commonly expressed and shared but the experience of grief, sadness, or anguish is generally hidden. However, when the latter states are shared, they have a singular poignancy. Man's recognition of the tragic qualities of life has been focused on by the existentialists in terms of aloneness. *Operational mourning*, with its observable empathic responses, lends itself as a technique for therapy and research in one of the most difficult areas of human experience.

Finally, a crucial feature faced directly in the course of *operational mourning* in conjoint family therapy is the issue of termination (Edelson, 1963). Since many therapeutic successes have suffered shipwreck in the final stages of the patient-therapist relationship, this feature of the therapeutic process is emphasized here. Through the reactivation of the experience of prior object loss in conjoint family therapy, the therapist can begin to prepare the family for the reality of the eventual loss of the therapist. Stimulated by therapist-directed inquiry, anticipatory responses to this projected separation are shared. Thus once again, an opportunity is afforded for working through the ambivalences related to loss (Greenson, 1964), and recent gains can be consolidated.

REFERENCES

Bowen, M. (1960). A family concept of schizophrenia. In D. D. Jackson (Ed.), *The etiology of schizophrenia*. New York, Basic Books.

Bowlby, J. (1961a). Processes of mourning. *International Journal of Psychoanalysis, 42*, 317–340.

Bowlby, J. (1961b). The Adolph Meyer lecture: Childhood mourning and its implications for psychiatry. *American Journal of Psychiatry, 118*, 481–498.

Bowlby, J. (1961c). Separation anxiety: A critical review of the literature. *Journal of Child Psychology and Psychiatry*, 251–269.

Edelson, M. (1963). *The termination of intensive psychotherapy*. Springfield, IL: Charles C. Thomas.

Freud, S. (1917 [1915]). Mourning and melancholia. In J. Strachey (Ed. and Trans.), *The standard edition of the complete psychological works of Sigmund Freud* (Vol. 14, pp. 239–258). New York: Norton.

Freud, S. (1926). Inhibitions, symptoms and anxiety. In J. Strachey (Ed. and Trans.), *The standard edition of the complete psychological works of Sigmund Freud* (Vol. 20, pp. 77–156). New York: Norton.

Greenson, R. R. (1964, May). *The problem of working through*. Read at Annual Meeting of the American Psychoanalytic Association.

Hill, L. B. (1955). *Psychotherapeutic intervention in schizophrenia*. Chicago: University of Chicago Press.

Lindemann, E. (1944). Symptomatology and management of acute grief. *American Journal of Psychiatry, 101*, 141–148.

Paul, N. L. (1966). The role of mourning and empathy in conjoint marital therapy. In *Pathogenic social systems and family therapy*. Palo Alto: Science & Behavior Books.

Rochlin, G. (1961). The dread of abandonment: A contribution to the etiology of the loss complex and to depression. In *Psychoanalytical study of the child* (pp. 451–470). New York: International University Press.

Wetmore, R. J. (1963). The role of grief in psychoanalysis. *The International Journal of Psychoanalysis, 44*, 97–103.

6

The Legacy of Loss

MONICA MCGOLDRICK

The idea of death, the fear of it, haunts the human animal like nothing else; it is a mainspring of human activity. . . . Of all things that move man, one of the principal ones is the terror of death.

—Ernest Becker, *The Denial of Death*

You yourself are the embodied continuance
of those who did not live into your time
and others will be (and are) your immortality on earth . . .

—Jorge Luis Borges

BY EXAMINING THE multigenerational ripple effects of loss, we can learn a great deal about how families operate, what happens when they get stuck, and how we can change these patterns. Loss may strengthen survivors, bringing out creativity, spurring them on to accomplishment, or it may leave behind a destructive legacy, all the more powerful if it is not dealt with. The playwright A. R. Gurney has described the legacy of his great-grandfather's suicide, never mentioned in his own lifetime, on his entire family.

My great-grandfather hung up his clothes one day and walked into the Niagara River and no one understood why. He was a distinguished man in Buffalo. My father could never mention it, and it affected the family well into the fourth generation as a dark and unexplainable gesture. It made my father and his father desperate to be accepted, to be conventional, and comfortable. It made them commit themselves to an ostensibly easy bourgeois world. They saw it so precariously, but the reason was never mentioned. (Witchel, 1989)

Four generations later the patterns set in motion by this death were still operating. Gurney was 48 when he first learned of the suicide from his father-in-law, who was a genealogist. This was at the time when Gurney's own father died; in an interesting continuation of the pattern, Gurney himself refuses to talk about his father's death. We may go for generations following patterns set up by the losses in earlier generations we know nothing about. This chapter will use the examples of several well-known families to illustrate the legacy of loss across the generations of a family.

QUEEN VICTORIA

Queen Victoria, who ruled England for two-thirds of a century, dominated the 19th century and in many ways has had continued influence through the 20th. Victoria suffered, as many of us suffer, from the deep-seated effects of the problems of loss on her family relationships. For 40 years she wore mourning dress in the style of the year her husband, Albert, died. Years before Victoria had written, "How one loves to cling to grief" (Benson, 1987, p. 96), and now she certainly did. She developed an obsession with cataloging everything, so that nothing would be changed. She surrounded herself with mementos of the past and gave orders that nothing would ever be thrown away—there were to be no further changes or losses. As long as she lived these orders were obeyed (Strachey, 1921). Victoria's reactions, however constricted and rigid they may appear, are understandable—when they are overwhelmed by a death, people may become rigid, cling desperately to whatever remains, and resist all further change that might mean another loss.

Queen Victoria's adoring father died when she was only eight months old. From that time on she slept with her mother every night until she was 18, sharing everything with her. Victoria was almost completely isolated from other close relationships, since her German mother had immigrated alone to England to marry and the British relatives felt little connection to the mother after the death of her husband.

As Victoria matured, she began to feel smothered by the emotional demands of her exiled mother. When, at 18, she acceded to the throne, she banished her mother emotionally, keeping her at a great distance for the rest of her life. The earlier intense bond between them was replaced almost immediately with a passionate and turbulent relationship with her first cousin and husband, Prince Albert.

Twenty-four years later, when Victoria was 42, her mother died, which sent her into paroxysms of grief, largely due to guilt and remorse over their estrangement. When she began sorting her mother's papers after the funeral, her emotions gave way entirely. Her mother had saved every scrap of Victoria's childhood memorabilia. She felt intense regret for having rejected her (Weintraub, 1987, p. 289).

> Her love for me. It is too touching: I have found little books with the accounts of my babyhood, and they show such unbounded tenderness! To miss a Mother's friendship, not to be able to have her to confide in when a girl (sic) most needs it . . . drives me wild now. (Cited in Woodham-Smith, 1972, p. 412)

Victoria though already a woman in middle age, described herself here as a "girl," elsewhere calling herself a "poor orphan child," no longer cared for after her mother's death (Weintraub, 1987). She seemed, as biographer Weintraub noted, "determined to cherish her grief and not be consoled" (p. 290). For weeks she took all her meals alone, considering her children "a disturbance" and leaving all the business of government to her husband, who was himself already terminally ill.

The death of Albert a few months after that of her mother overwhelmed Victoria completely. She had made Albert into the centerpiece of her life, so that every other relationship was secondary. She did not attend his funeral, but for years she slept with his nightshirt in her arms. She made his room into a "sacred room" to be kept exactly as it had been when he was alive. Every day for the rest of her long life she had the linens changed, his clothes laid out fresh, and water prepared for his shaving. To every bed in which Victoria slept she attached a photograph of Albert as he lay dead.

One can only speculate, with the benefit of our current psychological wisdom, how Victoria's children must have been affected by the distortions loss created in their family patterns. Victoria herself says that, having grown up so isolated with her mother, she never felt at ease with her children (Auchincloss, 1979, p. 151). We know that she refused to make any accommodation to her oldest son's need to learn the experience of ruling—treating him like a child until her last breath, when he was 50.

THE BRONTË FAMILY

Loss may create myths and superstitions that flow down the generations in a family about the dangers of the outside world, influencing descendants who have no conscious awareness of the origins of the beliefs and assumptions on which they operate. The Brontë family (Figure 6.1) seems to have developed the belief that leaving home was dangerous, and in the end no one

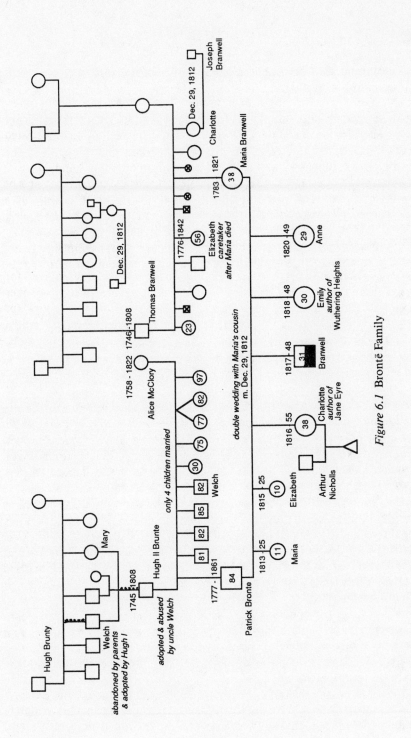

Figure 6.1 Brontë Family

could leave at all. Charlotte, the oldest to survive to adulthood, once wrote as an epitaph for one of her heroines: "The orb of your life is not to be so rounded; for you the crescent-phase must suffice" (Fraser, 1988, p. 483). Such an epitaph might apply to the whole generation of her family. There was something eccentric in the beliefs, behavior, and lives of the Brontës that seems to have been a family legacy they inherited. Charlotte, even in her youth looked somehow like a little old woman; on the other hand, she wore children's chemises all her life. She described herself as "undeveloped." All the Brontës came to be preoccupied with death. For the brother, Branwell, it was a primary preoccupation of his writings and eventually for Emily as well. The idea that she would die young preyed on Charlotte's mind from her youth (Fraser, p. 383), though she, in fact, outlived all her siblings by several years. Explaining to a friend why she could not leave home to start a school with her, Charlotte wrote:

> When I am free to leave home . . . perhaps too I shall be quite past the prime of life — my faculties will be rusted — and my few acquirements in a great measure forgotten. These ideas sting me keenly sometimes — but whenever I consult my Conscience it affirms that I am doing right in staying home — and bitter are its upbraidings when I yield to an eager desire for release. (Fraser, p. 183)

We don't have much information about the earlier generations of this extraordinary family, which produced two of the greatest novelists the world has known: Emily Brontë, the author of *Wuthering Heights*, and Charlotte Brontë, the author of *Jane Eyre*. We may suspect that there were emotional conflicts stemming from loss in the family of the Brontë father, Patrick, since his father and grandfather were both adopted and then mistreated in their adoptive families. The Brontë mother, Maria Branwell Brontë, came from a family in which four children died in infancy or childhood, including the three closest to her in age. We also know that Patrick and Maria were married in a double wedding with Maria's first cousin and Patrick's best friend, and that on the same day Maria's younger sister, Charlotte, married a cousin of theirs in a different town in England. Taking a systemic view of the "coincidence" of events, concurrent events in a family are not viewed simply as random happenings, but as reflecting some deeper systemic connections. This fact, that four members of the same family were married on the same day, may suggest some fusion in the Brontë family, which often results from loss, although we do not know the specific circumstances that led to this multiple marriage.

There followed in the family of Patrick and Maria Brontë a series of tragic losses, which seems to have deeply influenced the future behavior of family members, limiting their ability to leave and turning them inward on themselves and each other. Patrick came to see himself as "a stranger in a strange land," and seems to have conveyed to his children this sense of alienation and need to protect themselves from the outside world. The six children were born in quick succession, and shortly after the birth of the last the mother apparently developed a serious blood disorder, which finally took her life. During the last period of Maria's illness, and coincidental with it, all six of the children developed scarlet fever, which must have intensified the tragedy the family was already experiencing. Maria died an excruciatingly painful death a year later, having rarely seen her children in the last year because of her suffering. Her oldest daughter was only nine and the youngest was not even two. Patrick seems to have found his children's presence a painful reminder of his wife rather than a comfort:

> Oppressive grief sometimes lay heavy on me . . . when I missed her at every corner, and when her memory was hourly revived by the innocent, yet distressing prattle of my children. (Fraser, p. 28)

Patrick withdrew into himself and began dining alone, which he continued to do for the rest of his life. His daughter later said, "He did not like children . . . and the noise made him shut himself up and want no companionship — nay, to be positively annoyed by it" (Fraser, p. 28). From the time of Maria's death onward nothing in the Brontë home was changed — no furniture was moved, added or eliminated — and very few people ever visited. The rigidity about other changes, similar to Queen Victoria's attempt to control her world after her overwhelming losses, is a common response in families that have experienced serious loss. It is as if time stops. Families may close down, attempting to control those aspects of their world over which they still have some power, since in the one area that really matters — human relationships — they have lost the sense of control.

The mother's unmarried sister, Elizabeth, moved in and remained for the rest of her life. When, four years later, the two oldest daughters died, a family caretaker was added, who also remained for the rest of her life. She died within a week of the death of the last surviving Brontë child, Charlotte. Throughout their childhood the six children were left very much on their own and, while the externals in their lives did not change, they developed a remarkable inner life. From childhood they began to write stories together in a microscopic handwriting in tiny books, no bigger than two inches square, more than 400 of which have survived. The writing of those stories is in an almost private script, as if, while cut off from the outside world, they were fusing with each other in their minds and in their imaginations; their minds roamed free in fantasy, creating historical sagas with imaginary characters, combined with historical personages they heard about.

When the oldest daughter was 12, she and her sisters were sent to a local boarding school for ministers' children, but unfortunately further tragedy followed this attempted expansion of the family's horizons. Both she and the second sister developed tuberculosis at the school and died within a few months. The death of the oldest, Maria, named for her mother, was especially tragic, because the school authorities were very abusive to the dying child in her last days and the others had to observe the tormenting of their favorite sister, who had for so long been their mother's replacement. The morbidity of it all must have been exaggerated by the fact that the cemetery where mother and sisters lay buried surrounded the family house on two sides and there could be no getting away from the eerie sense of death in those gravestones.

The tragedy of these young losses must have reinforced for the Brontës the developing idea that life in the outside world was dangerous. The children were withdrawn from school, and from then on when any of the remaining four children tried to leave home, they were forced to return, whether because they became ill or dysfunctional away home or because someone at home became ill or needy. The only son, Branwell, on whom the greatest hopes were placed, was accepted at the Royal College of Art in London and left home to attend, but never arrived, returning home soon afterwards addicted to drugs and alcohol. From then on he periodically left home for jobs, which he never managed to keep. Of the three surviving sisters, Charlotte was the most successful at leaving home, managing at one point to stay away at a school for two years, and she was the only one able to develop friendships outside the family. She too, however, always returned home.

The real deterioration of Branwell coincided with his three sisters publishing their first works, which they did under male pseudonyms, telling no one, neither their father nor their brother, what they were doing. By the time Branwell died, three years later, the sisters were highly renowned by their own names. Unfortunately, Emily became ill just when Branwell died and never left the house again. She died three months later. Anne became ill at this time as well and died five months after Emily, leaving only Charlotte of the six siblings. Regarding her dead siblings, Charlotte feared that "the shadow of their last days must now, I think, linger forever" (Fraser, p. 325). Her description of her reactions at the time are an excellent expression of the legacy of trauma on a family:

> I must not look forwards, nor must I look backwards. Too often I feel like one crossing an abyss on a narrow plank—a glance round might quite unnerve. (Fraser, p. 320)

Charlotte returned to her work:

The loss of what we possess nearest and dearest to us in this world produces an effect on the character: we search out what we have yet left that can support, and, when found, we cling to it with a hold of new-strung tenacity. The faculty of imagination lifted me when I was sinking. . . . Its active exercise has kept my head above water ever since. (Fraser, p. 340)

Charlotte had various suitors, the most persistent of whom was her father's curate, Arthur Nicholls. When, a few years later, she finally agreed to marry him, her father went into a rage and fired Nicholls; however, a year later, unable to put up with Nicholls replacement, Patrick Brontë relented and agreed that Nicholls could marry Charlotte, if they would both agree never to leave him. They agreed. Charlotte was not really in love with Nicholls, as we know from her letters to her two close friends, but shortly after the marriage she accompanied her husband to his home in Ireland. There she began to see him in a different light — she saw his humor and found him more interesting in the context of his family. She began to fall in love with him. She returned from her honeymoon, however, out of anxiety about her father's health, which soon improved. Hers, however, began to deteriorate. She had become pregnant and when she died a few months later, she lost the baby as well. The cause of her death is unclear. It seems generally that her pregnancy symptoms of vomiting exacerbated a tubercular condition and she died of exhaustion and dehydration. Her beloved caretaker, Tabby, died shortly before. At the time of her death Charlotte was 38, the same age as her mother, Maria Branwell Brontë, had been when she died. Only Patrick now survived, and he lived on another six years, dying at the ripe age of 86.

Thus came the end of a most creative family. One might almost feel they were "doomed" psychologically by the impact of previous deaths on their mythology about loss. The legacy of loss on a family may go a long way beyond those who were affected by it at the time. Clinically, our job is to empower families to free themselves from dysfunctional mythology and review their history so that they can open new possibilities for their future.

PATTERN REPETITION IN FAMILIES

Families tend to repeat themselves. Though the actual behavior may take a variety of forms, the same issues tend to be played out from generation to generation. Bowen (1978) terms this the multigenerational transmission of family patterns, hypothesizing that relationship patterns in previous generations provide implicit models for family functioning in the next generation. The juxtaposition of nodal events intensifies family process and increases the likelihood of emotional transmission of patterns to the next generation.

Whether death in a family leads parents to neglect or overfocus on a child to make up for their lost dreams and lost relationship, the overlay of unresolved loss becomes a burden for the next generation. Children may be bound into a special role to carry out missions left incomplete by the loss, or they may be constrained by the parents' inability to commit themselves to new relationships for fear of repeating the pain of loss.

THE FREUD FAMILY

The Freud family provides a number of interesting pattern repetitions, which appear to have been a legacy of loss (Figure 6.2). Sigmund, the oldest of his mother's eight children, was born in 1856 in Freiburg, Moravia. In addition to being the oldest, he was also the only son for many years. We know that he held a very special position in his family. He had an intense relationship with his mother, who always referred to him as her "Golden Sigi." By all accounts, he was the center of the household. He was followed by a brother who died, then five sisters, and finally by a brother 10 years younger.

Sigmund's specialness for his father was probably intensified by the death of his paternal grandfather three months before his birth. This grandfather, Schlomo, was a rabbi, and Sigmund, as a professor and leader of what many saw as the new "religion" of psychoanalysis, was following in his own way in his grandfather's footsteps. Sigmund's father, Jacob, had also lost two children in his first marriage, though we know no details about them. Such losses tend to intensify the meaning of children who come after, particularly the next in line, which in this case would have been Sigmund.

Sigmund's brother, Julius, born when he was 17 months old, lived for only 7 months. The child nearest in age, especially a child of the same sex, often becomes a replacement for a lost child. In Sigmund's case, his closeness to his mother may have become even more important after the death of her second son. The loss of this infant would itself have been intensified by the fact that exactly one month before his death, Amalia's youngest brother, also named Julius, died at age 20 from pulmonary tuberculosis (Krüll, 1986). Probably she knew already that her brother was dying when she named her son for him seven months earlier, since it is not generally the Jewish custom to name a child for a living family member. In later life Sigmund said that he had welcomed this brother with "ill wishes and real infantile jealousy, and his death left the germ of guilt in me" (Krüll, 1986). In addition, at this time Sigmund's nursemaid was dismissed from the household and the family moved twice, apparently because of financial difficulties. His nephew, John, and both half-brothers emigrated to England

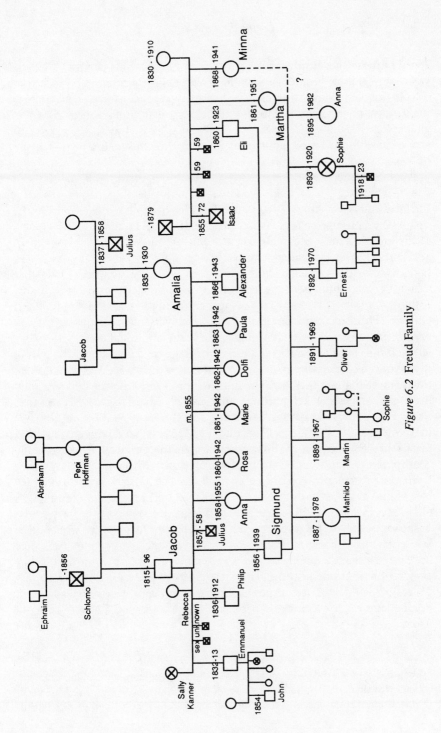

Figure 6.2 Freud Family

113

shortly afterwards. Furthermore, he soon had to share his parents' affection with a new sibling, Anna, with whom he was never to get along.

It is thus important to track family history carefully for loss in order to make sense of the relationships that develop. Freud's sense of his own specialness and religious fervor about his beliefs, as well as the relationships that evolved in the Freud family, were undoubtedly influenced by this pileup of losses surrounding his birth.

Another critical period in Freud's life was that surrounding his father's death, which happened when Freud was 40. This death occurred just after the birth of his last child, Anna, named not for his resented sister but for the daughter of his high school Hebrew teacher, Samuel Hammerschlag (Jones, 1953-1957, I; Krüll, 1986; Gay, 1988, 1990). At this time also, his sister-in-law Minna moved permanently into the household. Perhaps it is not surprising, given the power of the emotional legacy around a significant loss, that this last child, Anna, born the year Freud's father died, became his favorite, his primary follower, and by far the most emotionally linked to him of all his children. He also became emotionally involved with his sister-in-law, Minna, and for many years she was his intellectual and emotional companion. In a letter to his then closest friend, Wilhelm Fleiss, he describes Minna during these years as "otherwise my closest confidante" (Masson, 1985, p. 73). He often traveled alone with her, while his wife was left with the children, and there is strong evidence that he became sexually involved with her (Swales, 1982, 1986, 1987), a pattern that is not uncommon in families following a loss. We can often find, as Paul and Paul (1989) have pointed out, that affairs are precipitated by loss, even though the connection between the death and the sexual and emotional attachment remains out of awareness. Even more fascinating is that we have evidence of a repetition of this pattern of a sexual affair with a sister-in-law in the next generation between Freud's oldest son, Martin, and his wife's sister (Freud, 1988).

Jacob Freud, like his son Sigmund, had been 40 when his own father died. While this, like Charlotte Brontë's death at the same age as her mother, may be no more than coincidence, we have been impressed many times in our exploration of family histories with the emotional patterning of such coincidences, which may reflect a special identification with the parent, as indeed Freud seems to have had with his father. When his father died in 1896, Freud wrote:

> By one of those obscure paths behind official consciousness the death of the old man has affected me profoundly. I valued him highly, understood him very well, and with that combination of deep wisdom and romantic lightheartedness peculiar to him he had meant a great deal to me. His life had been over a long time

before he died, but his death seems to have aroused in me memories of all the early days. I now feel quite uprooted. (Masson, 1985, p. 202)

Sigmund, now 40, at this time experienced a major life crisis. He showed symptoms of depression and "pseudo" cardiac problems. He complained of lethargy, migraines, and various other somatic and emotional concerns. He was clearly in a great deal of distress. He began his famous self-analysis, and constructed the edifice of a new theory, which led to the publication of perhaps his most famous book, *The Interpretation of Dreams*. It was at this time also that he formulated his seduction theory, which he recanted soon after. Many have viewed this recanting as a response to a sense of guilt over the thought that his theory could apply to his father.

The death of Freud's father was certainly a key experience in his life, as the death of a a parent is for most people. Being confronted with significant death can lead to an intensification of emotion, which can be very productive in many ways and lead to creativity, as it obviously did for Freud. But whatever issues have been left unresolved in the relationships with survivors may then become fixed in time and lead to an emotional overlay in other relationships, binding them and others in their network and constricting them in their relationships. One might speculate on the role that emotional process in the Freud family played in the fact that neither Minna Bernays nor Anna Freud ever married and both seemed to have an enormous amount of emotional energy bound up with Freud throughout their lives.

Some deaths have more impact on a family than others. Particularly traumatic are untimely deaths such as the early death of Sigmund's brother Julius. A similar example two generations later was the death of Sigmund's four-year-old grandson, who had been orphaned as an infant by the death of Freud's daughter Sophie. This child was apparently extraordinarily intelligent.

He was indeed an enchanting little fellow, and I myself was aware of never having loved a human being, certainly never a child, so much. . . . I find this loss very hard to bear. I don't think I have ever experienced such grief; perhaps my own sickness contributes to the shock. I work out of sheer necessity; fundamentally everything has lost its meaning for me. (Freud, 1975, p. 344)

A month later he wrote that he was suffering from the first depression in his life. For more than three years he was unable to enjoy life and he appeared to go into a depression. His strong reaction seems to be due partly to its coinciding with his own diagnosis of eventually fatal cancer. He wrote to the child's father three years later:

I have spent some of the blackest days of my life in sorrowing about the child. At last I have taken hold of myself and can think of him quietly and talk of him without tears. But the comforts of reason have done nothing to help; the only consolation for me is that at my age I would not have seen much of him. (quoted in Clark, 1980, p. 441)

Contrast this with his reaction to the death of his mother at the age of 95 in 1930. He did not even attend her funeral, sending his daughter, Anna, as the family representative. Sigmund wrote:

I will not disguise the fact that my reaction to this event has, because of special circumstances, been a curious one. Assuredly, there is no saying, what effects such an experience may produce in deeper layers, but on the surface I can detect only two things: an increase in personal freedom, since it was always a terrifying thought that she might come to hear of my death; and secondly, the satisfaction that at last she has achieved the deliverance for which she had earned a right after such a long life. No grief otherwise, such as my ten years younger brother is painfully experiencing. . . . No pain, no grief, which is probably to be explained by the circumstances, the great age and the end of the pity we had felt at her helplessness. With that a feeling of liberation, of release, which I think I can understand. I was not allowed to die as long as she was alive, and now I may. Somehow the values of life have notably changed in the deeper layers. (Jones, 1953-1957, III, p. 152)

KENNEDYS DON'T CRY: WE'VE GOT TO CARRY ON

No American who was alive in 1963 can forget the image of John-John Kennedy saluting his father's casket on that cold clear November day. The little boy without a father, three years old, born on Thanksgiving day two weeks after his father's election to the presidency, reminded us all of the fragility of our lives. We have images of other Kennedy deaths as well: the Mozart requiem playing at St. Patrick's Cathedral for Robert Kennedy—his ten children all in mourning, Ethel still pregnant with the last, Ted's voice cracking in eulogy for yet another brother. John Kennedy himself had been a stand-in for his older brother Joe, after his death in World War II. A year after the mantel of leadership was passed to Ted, we recall his confused coverup about his role in the death of Mary Jo Kopechne at Chappaquidick. In the next generation there followed the terrible inglorious death of David Kennedy, whose drug overdose seemed so much the fallout of previous losses.

Some families seem marked by loss—they become almost tragic families. The multigenerational history of tragic losses in the Kennedy family goes back a long way and carries on far into the future, repeating over and over again the pain of untimely loss (Figure 6.3). Losses ripple down through families, often sending shock waves from generation to generation. We are fairly familiar with the losses of the Kennedys in our lifetime, just as we tend to be familiar with the losses in our own families within our lifetime. Usually we know less about the losses that have gone before — losses that have very much shaped family myths and attitudes. In fact, the Kennedys' history of tragic loss goes back way beyond the children and grandchildren of Joe and Rose.

Joe Kennedy's father, Patrick Joseph (P. J.), had been the only surviving male in his family. An older brother, John, had died at one year of age, and the father, Patrick, died when P. J. was six months old. These losses must have left P. J.'s mother with special feelings for her only son, and a heightened sense of the fragility of life — especially male life. Having come up the hard way — with no father and serving as a replacement for his dead brother — P. J. became a hardworking but cautious man. He "married up" to a clever woman, Mary Hickey, from a successful family. He too was clever, but his insecurities made it hard for him to say no to anyone. He started a liquor business, and like so many of the Irish of his time, moved into politics. He was always a caretaker for the families in his ward, serving eight terms in the state legislature. Mary resented his commitment to helping others as the boss of his district, because it intruded upon his own family's success. Yet he must have felt the need to do for others because he identified with them, having been raised as a fatherless child in desperate need himself.

The first child of P. J. and Mary was Joseph P. Kennedy, who again became the only surviving son of his parents. His already privileged position of oldest son was strengthened when his younger brother Francis died of diphtheria at the age of two. A granddaughter later said, "The death of the baby was so unexpected and so senseless that (Joe's mother's) only way of coping was to pour even more love onto Joe." Though he had two surviving younger sisters, Joe became the focus of attention for the whole family. Perhaps it is this legacy of specialness of the male survivor, intensifying the general cultural bias toward sons, that led Joe to focus his expectations so strongly on his own sons.

Joe grew up to emulate his mother, who believed in putting their family first, and saw his father's support for others as weakness. In the end, P. J. was defeated by the machine politics of Boston (very likely he was double-crossed by his son's future father-in-law, Honey Fitz himself!). Though he accepted his defeat with gentle dignity, underneath he grieved like a child who had been unjustly punished. The lesson his son Joe took from this was that political loyalty and generosity were merely commodities. The decision he then made was to trust no one but himself. Thus he developed a will of steel and a calculating, manipulative approach to dealing with others.

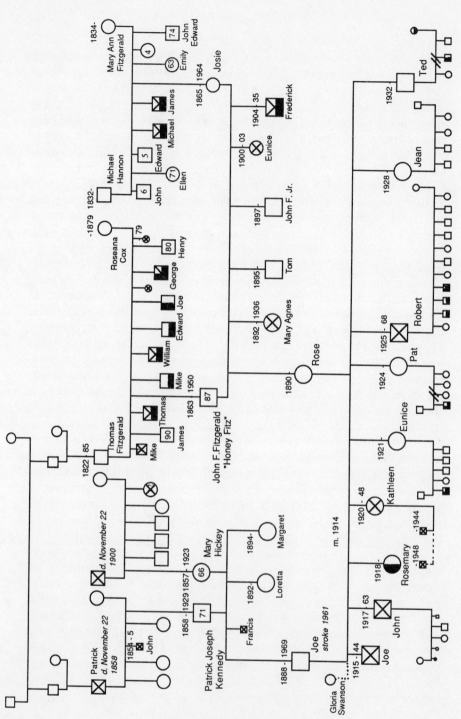

Figure 6.3 Kennedy Family

118

It would seem that Joe felt strong pressure to escape the embarrassing identification with his softhearted father, whose kindness, which seems to have been based on identifying with others who had experienced loss, was repaid with exploitation and rejection. A clue to Joe's relationship with his father is that, when P. J. died in 1928, Joe did not attend the funeral, but remained in California with his paramour, Gloria Swanson. As much as P. J. longed for a close relationship with his son, he did not succeed in achieving it. Just as P. J., having no father at all, had gravitated to his mother, Joe's special closeness was to his mother.

Rose Fitzgerald Kennedy's family also experienced overwhelming traumatic losses at critical times in their history. Her father, John Francis, called "Honey Fitz," was the fourth of twelve children. The only two daughters both died in infancy, as did the oldest son. Three others had lives totally wasted by their alcoholism. Two more, Michael and Edward, had severe alcohol problems as well. The ninth brother, Joseph, had brain damage from malaria and barely functioned. Thus, of the twelve children born in this family, only three, including Honey Fitz, survived in good health. Honey Fitz became the favorite son. After his mother's death, when he was 16, his father developed a special ambition for him to become a doctor, since illness had caused their family such painful losses. However, after one year at Harvard Medical School, the father died and John switched his ambitions to politics, which offered an immediate reward and an opportunity to provide jobs for his brothers. When he became mayor of Boston, many said that the whole brotherhood of Fitzgeralds actually ran the government. He considered it his responsibility to provide for his brothers, and he did. Later his grandsons would, of course, do the same.

John met his future wife, Josie Hannon, his painfully shy second cousin, only a few months before the death of his mother. Many said that his attraction and bond to her was based on their mutual losses. Josie was the fifth of nine children, only four of whom survived. One brother, age six, died of fever while her mother was pregnant with Josie, another died of inflammation of the lung four years earlier. Two other sons died early of alcoholism. The only surviving son had his leg crushed by a train at age 13. But the family's most tragic loss was the littlest sister, who died in a drowning accident with her best friend, while Josie was supposed to be caring for them. The devastating loss any family naturally feels with the death of a child was compounded here by a complex web of guilt of self-reproach — that the family and Josie, in particular, had contributed to the death by failing to protect the child adequately. The family never recovered. Those who knew the three surviving sisters said that sorrow and withdrawal hung over them for the rest of their lives (Kearns Goodwin, 1987).

It is easy to understand what attracted Josie to the confident, forceful, adventuresome and enthusiastic Honey Fitz, whose very name reflected his ability to charm others with his words. Honey Fitz's long courtship of Josie was indeed an effort to bring her out of herself with his humor, his magnetism, and his sociability. Like so many generations of his family that followed him, he dealt with loss by mobilizing into frantic activity and trying not to look back. Perhaps he chose her in the hope that, if he could "bring her back to life," he would symbolically make up for the loss of his mother and his two infant sisters. Perhaps he chose her because he saw expressed in her a reflection of the sadness that he felt himself, but could never dare to reveal. Women often seem to be the overt bearers of the emotional pain of loss for men in families. Men avoid, while women grieve for everyone. We know also that many people are drawn to mates who express for them a side of themselves that they shrink from at a conscious level. Most of the time you could hardly notice in Honey Fitz' jovial sociability the pain he buried from the losses of his mother, his sisters, his dreams of education or the burden of his dysfunctional brothers. Perhaps the effect of these losses was seen most clearly in his self-centered calculations of his own interest and in his willingness to sacrifice any relationship to his own needs, no matter what the betrayal entailed. (His son-in-law, Joseph Kennedy, had very similar personality traits.)

The coldness in Honey Fitz was probably deeply rooted in his childhood awareness that he had no one to turn to. His wife Josie's lifelong depression was similarly influenced by the early and repeated losses her sad family experienced. Once the challenge of Honey Fitz winning Josie was complete, the difference in their natures was overwhelmingly apparent. Or perhaps the very sadness in Josie, which had drawn him to her, now became toxic and he fled from it. As the years went by Honey Fitz expanded outward, while Josie turned further inward. It was his beloved firstborn daughter, Rose, who really seemed to replace his mother and his sisters. She grew up as his companion in the exciting political arena of his colorful life—she went everywhere with him.

She led a charmed life until adolescence, when suddenly it all changed. Her father's main character flaw: A self-centered manipulative ambition, the reflection of his early losses, led him to betray her. He sacrificed her dreams to his personal political aims. Perhaps there was also some compulsion to repeat his experience at 16, when he had had to give up his plans for medical school. She had an ardent nature, an untamed spirit. A brilliant student, her dream was to go to Wellesley where she had been accepted at 16; but Honey Fitz was in trouble. His political wheeling and dealing led to charges of fraud and to his being ousted as mayor of Boston. He made a deal with the leaders of the Catholic church that required her to go instead to a Catholic school. Rose was sent abruptly to a convent school abroad.

She was totally cut off from her family and her exciting social life and put in a rigid environment, which demanded silence and denied all spontaneous attachments. Typical of the repression of parochial schools of the era, the school even had a rule against the girls' forming "particular friendships." Rose's response was one she would manifest again and again in her long life: she smothered her feelings of resistance, bowed to her father's will, and forced herself to channel her energies through the rigid adherence to prayer, which was the only avenue open to her. A kind of detachment from human relationships was forged in that transition, which was to characterize all her later life. What she lost was a belief in her special relationship with her father, as well as the sense of power to determine her own life. She had to bend to the will of a stronger male. Religion helped her swallow that pill and the many other bitter pills to follow.

We are most familiar with the losses of Rose and Joe Kennedy's children by death, but their first loss was not a death. The first loss occurred when Rosemary, their oldest daughter underwent a lobotomy in 1941 at the age of 23. She has remained institutionalized far from the family and cut off from them (except for Eunice, the only family member to visit her regularly) for the past 47 years. Rosemary appears to have been retarded, in itself a serious loss for any family: Such a child represents a loss of dreams, an embarrassment, and a pain that does not go away. Wishing to keep her within the family, they kept her problems a secret for many years and made every effort to maintain her in as normal a fashion as possible.

By the time Rosemary was in her early twenties she had developed severe behavior problems. At a certain point Joe decided, while Rose was away and without consulting her, that Rosemary should have a lobotomy. The operation, which was kept totally secret, worsened her condition considerably. Apparently, Joe then had her sent to an institution in the midwest. He never told his wife—not then or afterwards—about the lobotomy. Rose was just told that it would be better if she didn't visit for some time. According to friends and relatives, it was only 20 years later, after Joe's stroke in 1961, that Rose began to piece the story together for herself (Kearns Goodwin, 1987). Why didn't she insist on visiting this daughter to whom she had devoted herself for so many years? How could she never ask? How could it be that others never asked or questioned the disappearance of one of their members? Did Joe blame himself for what had happened? Did others blame him or themselves for ignoring her for so many years? We don't know. We do know that in her memoirs, written 33 years after the operation, Rose still maintained that she had participated in the decision for the lobotomy and failed to mention that she had not visited or asked about Rosemary for 20 years.

The Kennedy family never talked about Rosemary's retardation within the

family; the first public mention of it wasn't until 1960. We do have a suggestion of the long-range impact of the family's inability to deal openly with
this "ghost" in an incident described about David Kennedy, the grandson
who eventually died of a drug overdose. One day, in the midst of his troubles, he found a magazine story about lobotomies that included a picture of
his aunt Rosemary. He is quoted as saying:

> She had a new pair of white shoes on and she was smiling. The thought crossed
> my mind that if my grandfather was alive the same thing could have happened to
> me that happened to her. She was an embarrassment; I am an embarrassment.
> She was a hindrance; I am a hindrance. As I looked at this picture, I began to hate
> my grandfather and all of them for having done the thing they had done to her
> and for the thing they were doing to me. (Collier & Horowitz, 1984, p. 441)

The shame and guilt leading to the secrecy and mystification that surrounded Rosemary's disability, lobotomy, and disappearance give this loss a
lingering power. Other family members are left with the feeling, "If she
could disappear, I could disappear." And their fantasies fill in the rest of the
story with whatever meanings they attach to the pieces of the story they do
know.

The ambiguity of Rosemary's loss must have been particularly distressing
because it could not be mourned like a death. She remained alive, but not
physically or mentally present. Rose said in her memoirs that Rosemary
remained pleased to see them and recognized them, but that she was "perfectly happy in her environment and would be confused and disturbed to be
anywhere else" (Kennedy, 1974, p. 308). Yet surely other family members,
like David, must have wondered whether this was true and questioned her
extrusion from the family.

Unfortunately, Rosemary was only the first of many children lost by the
Kennedy family. In each instance there was a similar tendency toward secrecy about any facts that did not fit with a positive image. Joe Jr., the "Golden
Boy," programmed by his father to become president, was shot down in an
unnecessarily reckless flying mission in June 1944. Only his heroism was
mentioned, not his exaggerated risk-taking or the fact that he had received a
warning that day from his electronics officer that his plane could not possibly make it (Davis, 1984; McTaggart, 1983). The Kennedys also never mentioned that he was living with a married woman, Pat Wilson, at the time of
his death. When Wilson wrote a letter of sympathy to Rose, the bereaved
mother did not respond.

It is hard to escape the sense that there is a repeated mingling of tragedy,
accident and tempting the fates in the Kennedy family. Joe Kennedy Jr. had
been repeatedly carrying out hazardous bombing missions where he was told

his chances of survival were less than 50%. He had already completed his tour of duty, but was looking for a mission from which he would return a hero, perhaps because his younger brother, John, had just received a military medal for his performance in the Pacific. (In that instance John had initially been reported missing in action, and a funeral had been held by the surviving crew members. Joe Sr. was told this news but kept it from his wife and children for a week, after which he learned that John had, in fact, survived.)

In this incident and others to follow, there are numerous examples of how the Kennedys dealt with loss. When Joe Jr. died, his father announced the fact to the children, warned them to be "particularly good to your mother," and then retreated to his room, while Rose retreated to her separate room. Neither at that time nor at any of their later tragic losses were they able to share their grief with each other. Rose said that she and her husband "wept inwardly, silently." At the time Joe said, "We've got to carry on. We must take care of the living. There is a lot of work to be done" (Kennedy, 1974, p. 453). She turned to religion, repeating the rosary over and over, leaving it up to her husband to handle arrangements and respond to correspondence. She was initially consumed by her grief, while he immediately mobilized into action—the usual response of the Kennedy men to loss and consonant with our culture's gender rules.

The second daughter, Kathleen, who had been cut off by her mother for marrying a British Protestant Peer in May of 1944, lost her husband in the war that September. When the news of his death came, she was in the United States with her family because of her brother Joe's death shortly before. She was out shopping and her sister Eunice went to meet her. Eunice, in typical Kennedy form, complimented her on her purchases and said nothing until they were finished shopping, at which point she suggested Kathleen call their father before they went to lunch. Joe then gave her the news of her husband's death. That night the family was solicitous of Kathleen, while diligently avoiding any mention of her husband's death! A friend who came to stay with her at the time was appalled by the family's frenetic need to carry on as if nothing had happened (McTaggart, 1983).

Kathleen once told another friend that she had been taught that "Kennedys don't cry." When her brother Joe had died and his roommate called her to give condolences, she had broken into sobs. Later she wrote him a letter of apology saying, "I'm sorry I broke down tonight. It never makes things easier" (Kearns Goodwin, 1987, p. 690). Following her husband's death, she left her parents' home and returned to England, where she did allow herself to go through months of overt mourning, staying in the home of her parents-in-law for comfort and support.

Four years later Kathleen fell in love with another Protestant, this time a married British Peer, Peter Fitzwilliam, who had a reputation for high living, gambling, and affairs. Rose Kennedy said that if Kathleen married, she would not only disown Kathleen but also see that Joe cut off her allowance. Rose vowed she would leave Joe if he refused. Kathleen decided she could not break off the relationship in spite of her mother's threat. In hopes of appealing to her father, she arranged to meet him while on a weekend trip with Fitzwilliam on the Riviera. In an eerily familiar scenario, Fitzwilliam insisted on flying in a small plane, although weather reports were so bad that all commercial flights had been cancelled and his pilot strongly urged a delay. Their plane crashed in the storm and both Kathleen and Fitzwilliam were killed.

The family could never admit the truth of what had happened in public or to each other. Joe, who had gone to identify the body, said Kathleen looked beautiful and as if asleep, though she had actually been horribly disfigured by the crash. The circumstances of her death with Fitzwilliam were concealed and she was buried as the widow of the first husband. Her father was the only family member to attend her funeral. Even then he took no role in the funeral arrangements, which were handled by her former mother-in-law, who even wrote her epitaph: "Joy she gave, Joy she has found." The Kennedys and the Fitzwilliams joined in a conspiracy of silence about the circumstances of the death.

Friends were appalled that Rose Kennedy sent a Mass card with a prayer for those who had not gone to heaven. Her brothers John and Bobby visited Kathleen's housekeeper, drew out all her recollections and then said, "We will not mention her again." They seem to have kept their word, though Bobby named his oldest daughter for her. Twenty-four years later Rose wrote in her memoirs:

> In 1948 (Kathleen) had taken a spring holiday on the Riviera and was flying in a private plane with a few friends to Paris, where her father was waiting to meet her. On the way—a route threading the edges of the French Alps—the weather went bad, navigation equipment was not adequate, and the plane crashed into a mountainside, killing all on board. Joe was notified and hurried to the scene. He watched as the body of his daughter was brought down the mountainside. We lost our beloved Kathleen on May 13, 1948. (Kennedy, 1974, p. 358)

All reference to the fiancé were eliminated, as if he never existed, along with all reference to the fact that Rose had disowned her daughter.

Since then the Kennedys have sustained many other losses and near losses. Three times John Kennedy was given up for dead and was administered the last rites. Twice Ted almost died, a year after John's death when he broke his back in a plane crash, and a year after Robert's death when he almost drowned (and his companion Mary Jo Kopechne did drown at Chappaquidick). Was it just coincidence that his near-fatal accidents followed so closely the tragic deaths of his brothers, or is this an example of something that has been documented repeatedly in the research of stress: that such experiences increase our vulnerability to illness, accidents, and emotional upset (Holmes & Rahe, 1967).

In the next generation of the Kennedy family, David Kennedy has died of a drug overdose and Joe was responsible for a car accident which injured David and left David's girlfriend Pam Kelley permanently paralyzed. There is also a report that Rose Kennedy injured a young woman in a serious car accident (Saunders, 1982). At least six of the Kennedy grandchildren have had drug problems or psychiatric hospitalizations (Robert Shriver, Chris Lawford, Joe, Bobby, David, and Kara Kennedy.) What leads a family into such reckless and self-destructive behavior? Many people have seen the reckless risk-taking behavior of Kathleen and Joe Jr, the promiscuous sexual behavior of Joseph and John Kennedy, and the politically dangerous liaisons of several of the Kennedys (Joe and John in particular) as a response to their fear of death — living on the edge and, as it were, "tempting fate" to prove to themselves that they were still alive.

Rose Kennedy's way of handling death was very different. She said in discussing her reaction to her son John's death:

> I had trained myself through the years not to become too visibly upset at bad news, even very bad news, because I had a strong notion that if I broke down, everybody else in the household would. (Kennedy, 1974, p. 484)

When the news came that John Kennedy had been shot, Rose decided to operate on a principal that she and Joe had adopted years before: bad news should only be given in the morning, not late in the day, because it would then upset your sleep. She therefore arranged for a "conspiracy of kindness" to keep Joe, who had by then suffered a stroke, from learning about the death until the next day. All TV's were unplugged, different stories were told about the relatives and friends who began to appear, and everyone kept up a charade of conversation with him for the whole afternoon and evening. He was told the next morning.

Rose believed that Jackie's composure at the time of John Kennedy's death was an example for the whole world of how to behave. The following week, Rose says, the family "had the Thanksgiving celebration, with everyone of us hiding the grief that gnawed at us and doing our best to make it a day of peace, optimism, and thanks for the blessings that were still left to us" (Kennedy, 1974, p. 485). Rose quotes Jackie's praise for how the Kennedy family deals with tragedy:

You can be sitting down to dinner with them and so many sad things have
happened to each, and — God — maybe even some sad thing has happened that
day, and you can see that each one is aware of the other's suffering. And so they
can sit down at the table in a rather sad frame of mind. Then each one will begin
to start to make this conscious effort to be gay or funny or to lift each other's
spirits, and you find that it's infectious, that everybody's doing it. They all bounce
off each other. They all have a humor. . . . It's a little bit irrelevant, a little bit
self-mocking, a little sense of the ridiculous, and in times of sadness of wildly
wicked humor of irreverence. . . . But to make a real effort to use the light touch
when everybody's sad. . . . My natural tendency is to be rather introverted and
solitary and to retreat into myself and brood too much. But they bring out the
best. No one sits and wallows in self pity. (Kennedy, 1974, p. 485)

Commenting on the death of her third son, Robert, five years after Jack's,
Rose said that the grim reality of the second assassination was so incredible,
it would seem beyond fiction to imagine. She says others commented on her
composure, her bravery, and her self-possession at the funeral, but also that
her waving a greeting to others was somehow "inappropriate." Rose responded:

As for my being composed — I had to be. If I had broken down in grief, I would
only have added to the misery of the others and possibly could have set off a
chain reaction of tearfulness. But, in fact, it was not just I who set an example of
fortitude. They all set it for one another. (Kennedy, 1974, p. 517)

Grief is a very personal matter. We should not be too quick to judge how
others mourn — whether they should be more expressive or less so. Every
family must find its own ways. The Kennedys reflect many Irish characteristics for responding to loss (see Chapter 10; McGoldrick, 1982, 1990;
McGoldrick, Preto, Hines, & Lee, 1988). They showed many strengths in
their handling of an incredible series of tragedies, and they also showed
glaring vulnerabilities, particularly in facing up to losses that were embarrassing and not heroic. The remarkable thing about this family is their
ability to persevere even after the most devastating losses.
   Families like the Kennedys that have experienced so many traumatic,
untimely deaths may develop a feeling of being "cursed" and unable to rise
above the experience, or they may come to see themselves as survivors, who
can be struck down but never beaten. After the death of her husband, which
followed closely on the death of her favorite brother Joe Jr., Kathleen Kennedy wrote to a friend:

One thing you can be sure of, life holds no fears for someone who has faced love,
marriage, and death before the age of 25. . . . Luckily I am a Kennedy. I have a

very strong feeling that that makes a big difference about how to take things. I saw Daddy and Mother about Joe and I know that we've all got the ability to not be got down. (Kearns Goodwin, p. 697)

Kathleen obviously felt empowered somehow by what she experienced as her parents' strength. Of course, this may also have been in part a show, to convince others and herself that she could and should "not be got down." The Kennedy bravado left its legacy in their dangerous risk-taking and defiance of death. In her case her risk-taking ultimately cost her her life. Yet, for all their difficulties in handling feelings, the Kennedys have shown an amazing life force and courage in overcoming tragedies. It is almost as if their sense of the family mission carries them through, in spite of their individual losses. Rose's statement of her own way of handling grieving sums up the Kennedy attitude well:

My reaction to grief takes in part the form of nervous activity. I have to keep moving, walking, pulling away at things, praying to myself while I move and making up my mind that I am not going to be defeated by tragedy. Because there are the living still to work for, while mourning for the dead. (Kennedy, 1974, p. 481)

CONCLUSION

Death always leaves a legacy, whether of empowerment or of trauma, which closes a system down and distorts survivors' relationships. Certain factors make the negative legacy of loss more powerful, as the examples of Queen Victoria, the Brontës, the Freuds, and the Kennedys illustrate. When death occurs off-time or in the context of conflictual family relationships, when there is a pileup of losses, or when death is stigmatized and surrounded by secrecy, the power of the legacy is intensified. When families are unable to mourn, to share acknowledgement of the loss and then reinvest in other relationships and life pursuits, recovery from loss is impaired and the legacy continues. To empower these families, we must help them examine the negative legacies and become active definers of their future, developing more open ways of responding to death.

REFERENCES

Becker, E. (1973). *The denial of death*. New York: The Free Press.
Bowen, M. (1978). *Family therapy in clinical practice*. New York: Jason Aronson.
Holmes, T., & Rahe, R. H. (1967). The social adjustment rating scale. *Journal of Psychosomatic Research, 11*, 213–218.
McGoldrick, M. (1982). Irish families. In M. McGoldrick, J. K. Pearce, & J. Giordano (Eds.), *Ethnicity and family therapy*. New York: Guilford.

McGoldrick, M. (1990). Irish mothers. *Journal of Feminist Family Therapy*, 2/1.
McGoldrick, M., Preto, N. G., Hines, P. M., & Lee, E. (1988). Ethnicity and women. In M. McGoldrick, C. Anderson, & F. Walsh (Eds.), *Women in families*. New York: Norton.
Paul, N., & Paul B. (1989). *A martial puzzle*. Boston: Allyn & Bacon.
Witchel, A. (1989, November 12). Laughter, tears. *New York Times Magazine*.

Brontë Sources

Bentley, P. (1969). *The Brontës and their world*. New York: Viking.
Cannon, J. (1980). *The road to Haworth: The story of the Brontës' Irish ancestry*. London: Weidenfeld and Nicholson.
Chadwick, E. H. (1914). *In the footsteps of the Brontës*. London: Sir Issac Pitman & Sons.
Chitham, E., & Winnifrith, T. (1983). *Brontë facts and Brontë problems*. London: Macmillan.
Fraser, R. (1988). *The Brontës: Charlotte Brontë and her family*. New York: Crown.
Gaskell, E. (1975). *The life of Charlotte Brontë*. London: Penguin.
Gerin, W. (1971). *Emily Brontë: A biography*. London: Oxford University Press.
Gerin, W. (1961). *Branwell Brontë*. London: Thomas Nelson & Sons.
Hanson, L., & Hanson, E. (1967). *The four Brontës*. New York: Archon Press.
Hinkley, L. L. (1945). *The Brontës: Charlotte and Emily*. New York: Hastings House.
Hopkins, A. B. (1958). *The father of the Brontës*. Baltimore: Johns Hopkins Press.
Hardwick, E. (1975). The Brontës. In E. Hardwick, *Seduction and betrayal: Women and literature*. New York: Vintage.
Lane, M. (1969). *The Brontë story*. London: Fontana.
Lock, J., & Dixon, W. T. (1965). *A man of sorrow: The life, letters, and times of Reverend Patrick Brontë*. Westport, CT: Meckler Books.
Mackay, A. M. (1897). *The Brontës: Fact and fiction*. New York: Dodd, Mead.
Maurat, C. (1970). *The Brontës' secret*. (M. Meldrum, Trans.) New York: Barnes & Noble.
Moglen, H. (1984). *Charlotte Brontë: The self conceived*. Madison: University of Wisconsin Press.
Peters, M. (1974). *An enigma of Brontës*. New York: St. Martins.
Peters, M. (1975). *Unquiet soul: A biography of Charlotte Brontë*. New York: Atheneum.
Ratchford, F. W. (1964). *The Brontës' web of childhood*. New York: Russell & Russell.
White, W. B. (1939). *The miracle of Haworth: A Brontë story*. New York: Dutton.
Wilks, B. (1986). *The Brontës: An illustrated biography*. New York: Peter Bedrick Books.
Winnifith, T. Z. (1977). *The Brontës and their background: Romance and reality*. New York: Collier.
Wright, W. (1893). *The Brontës in Ireland*. New York: D. Appleton & Co.

Freud Sources

Anzieu, D. (1986). *Freud's self analysis*. Madison, CT: International Universities Press.
Clark, R. W. (1980). *Freud: The man and the cause*. New York: Random House.
Eissler, K. R. (1978). *Sigmund Freud: His life in pictures and words*. New York: Harcourt, Brace, Jovanovich.
Freeman, L., & Strean, H. S. (1981). *Freud and women*. New York: Frederick Ungar Pub.
Freud, E. (Ed.). (1975). *The letters of Sigmund Freud*. New York: Basic.
Freud, S. (1988). *My three mothers and other passions*. New York: New York University Press.
Gerson, R., & McGoldrick, M. (1986). Constructing and interpreting genograms: The example of Sigmund Freud's family. In P. Keller & L. Ritt (Eds.), *Innovations in clinical practice: A source book* (Vol. 5). Sarasota, FL: Professional Resource.
Gay, P. (1988). *Freud: A life for our time*. New York: Norton.
Gay, P. (1990). *Reading Freud*. New Haven, CT: Yale University Press.
Glicklhorn, R. (1979). The Freiberg period of the Freud family. *Journal of the History of Medicine, 24*, 37–43.

Jones, E. (1953-1957). *The life and work of Sigmund Freud* (Vols. 1-3). New York: Basic.

Krüll, M. (1986). *Freud and his father*. New York: Norton.

Mannoni, O. (1974). *Freud*. New York: Vintage.

Masson, J. (Ed.). (1985). *The complete letters of Sigmund Freud to Wilhelm Fleiss: 1887-1904*. Cambridge, MA: Belnap Press.

McGoldrick, M., & Gerson, R. (1985). *Genograms in family assessment*. New York: Norton.

McGoldrick, M., & Gerson, R. (1988). Geograms and the family life cycle. In B. Carter & M. McGoldrick (Eds.), *The changing family life cycle*. Boston: Allyn & Bacon.

Nelken, M. (in press). *Freud's heroic struggle with his mother*.

Swales, P. (1982). Freud, Minna Bernays, and the conquest of Rome: New light on the origins of psychoanalysis. *The New American Review, 1, 2/3*: 1-23.

Swales, P. (1986, November 15). Freud, his origins and family history. UMDNJ-Robert Wood Johnson Medical School.

Swales, P. (1987, May 15). What Freud didn't say. UMDNJ-Robert Wood Johnson Medical School.

Kennedy Sources

Collier, P., & Horowitz, D. (1984). *The Kennedys*. New York: Summit.

Davis, J. (1984). *The Kennedys: Dynasty [disaster*. New York: McGraw-Hill.

Kearns Goodwin, D. (1987). *The Fitzgeralds and The Kennedys*. New York: Simon & Schuster.

Kennedy, R. (1974). *Times to remember*. New York: Bantam.

McTaggart, L. (1983). *Kathleen Kennedy: Her life and times*. New York: Dial Press.

Rachlin, H. (1986). *The Kennedys: A chronological history: 1823-present*. New York: World Almanac.

Rainie, H., & Quinn, J. (1983). *Growing up Kennedy: The third wave comes of age*. New York: Putnam.

Saunders, F. (1982). *Torn lace curtain: Life with the Kennedys*. New York: Pinnade Books.

Wills, G. (1981). *The Kennedy imprisonment: A mediation on power*. New York: Little, Brown.

Queen Victoria Sources

Auchincloss, L. (1979). *Persons of consequence: Queen Victoria and her circle*. New York: Random House.

Benson, E. F. (1987). *Queen Victoria*. London: Chatto & Windus.

Hibbert, C. (1985). *Queen Victoria in her letters and journals*. London: Penguin.

James, R. R. (1984). *Prince Albert*. New York: Knopf.

Strachey, L. (1921). *Queen Victoria*. New York: Harcourt, Brace, Jovanovich.

Weintraub, S. (1987). *Victoria*. New York: Dutton.

Woodham-Smith, C. (1972). *Queen Victoria*. New York: Donald Fine.

7

Family Scripts and Loss

JOHN BYNG-HALL

A FAMILY THERAPIST can help a family cope with a bereavement so that no long-term emotional damage results. That is important in itself, but it raises important questions. If we can influence the course of bereavement can we also — in the process — rewrite the family script and so strengthen the family? Further, can we influence the way in which the family conducts grieving in the future? If so, this makes bereavement a particularly privileged therapeutic moment. It carries the potential for long-term preventive mental health, with implications for future generations.

Although scripts come from the past and are enacted in the present, they are, above all, for the future. They inform one, from experience, what to do next, and the ensuing interaction provides a model for how to behave when similar circumstances occur in the future. Script theory, although originally popularized by the transactional analysts, has been elaborated on by other workers such as cognitive scientists (Schank & Abelson, 1977), developmental psychologists, psychoanalysts, and sex therapists. This theorizing has largely focused on individuals, but it has been extended to include the family system (Byng-Hall, 1985, 1988). The concept of family script is used to explain the mechanism that enables families to repeat particular family scenarios when similar contexts are encountered. The scenarios are encoded in scripts and may inform the family how to interact in particular contexts, including everyday events, such as mealtimes; transgenerational events, such as leaving home; or particular events that can happen at any time, such as a death in the family. Characteristic family roles and family inter-action patterns that are found across all contexts are encoded in "the family script."

A family death teaches individuals not only how to mourn but also how to die. In one family, the aged mother became extremely cantankerous as she died. The "saintly" daughter who had to suffer this changed her own person-ality completely when later she herself developed cancer, becoming just as difficult as her mother had been.

Family members inherit from previous bereavement experiences their rules about what should be repeated and what should be avoided. Scripts tend either to repeat past patterns—replicative scripts—or to prescribe behavior that avoids past painful experiences—corrective scripts. The "saintly" daughter might have followed a corrective script when facing her own im-pending death by being exceedingly uncomplaining; as it was, she adopted a replicative script and followed her mother's example.

The rules for dying and grieving are also encoded in family mythology and family legends about deaths in the family. The extended family often fills in the details of the scripts. As deaths, hopefully, are not frequent occurrences in any one family, cultural rituals and traditions are also impor-tant in guiding the family in what to do.

At a more immediate, and arguably more fundamental, level the way that the members of the family normally manage all their separations and losses determines the way that the distress of grieving is handled. Attachment theory (Bowlby, 1980) explores the issue of loss. Secure attachments provide caring relationships that can be relied upon to be available when needed, whereas insecure attachments cannot be relied upon either because availabil-ity is unpredictable, which often leads to clinging behavior, or because of repeated rejections, which lead to avoidance of closeness. Secure attach-ments provide a safe base for exploring the implications of a situation, especially frightening or upsetting ones, such as bereavement (Bowlby, 1988); insecure attachments do not.

Normally, repeated reviewing of the events surrounding a death allows for an exploration of what the death means. This can be done either in the imagination or in discussion, preferably with a secure relationship. If the main attachment figure is now dead, someone else has to stand in for him or her. The family therapist can act as a temporary attachment figure, but must use the role to establish a secure set of attachments within a family so that members can do their own mourning (Byng-Hall, in press).

At first, the full emotional implications of the death, either witnessed or imagined, may be overwhelming and the bereaved members of the family often cushion the impact by altering the script in a number of ways includ-ing:

(a) A temporary disconnecting of some or all the affect from aspects of the cognitive images: this is most marked at the point of numbed shock and can lead to someone behaving and talking as if he or she is merely a member of an audience looking in, rather than a member of the family.

(b) Denial of the loss, when the dead person is felt to be still present (e.g., is recognized in the street); or the death is accepted but the separation is not, so that the bereaved person feels him or herself to be in spiritual or telepathic communication. The relationship is thus felt to continue despite the death.

(c) The whole family selects a replacement who will fulfill the dead person's role and assume his or her identity. The dead person remains "alive," and the loss is cushioned. For example, on return from my father's deathbed, I suddenly realized that I was sitting in my father's chair at dinner. The place had been set for me, and I sat in it.

(d) Identification with only one of the roles when reliving the death scenario in the imagination. For instance, identifying with the nurse may help to anesthetize the pain of empathizing with other roles, say that of the dying person.

As the grieving process typically progresses, the implications of the death are accepted, however painful they may be, and members of the family can then act in the full knowledge of the real situation facing them. As Parkes (1972) puts it, their "assumptive world" changes from one in which it is assumed that the dead person will go on taking certain roles in an unfolding life script, to one where it is accepted that those situations in which the dead person would have been involved will now never happen or will be significantly altered.

The mechanism for cushioning the immediate impact of death may persist and so block the mourning process. Restriction of affect and denial may become permanent. The replacement of the dead person by another member of the family can be useful in maintaining the family roles, but unhelpful if he or she is assumed to have the same attributes as the dead person. A child conceived as a replacement soon after a death may become haunted by these expectations. An identification with one of the roles in the death scenario may become fixed in an attempt to ward off other identifications.

In reviewing what happened or might have happened a person may identify with four different roles: the dying person; good caregivers who attempt to help or, in the imagination, may even manage to prevent death; failed caregivers who are often held responsible for deaths; or killers who take an active role in promoting the death. Normally all members of the family may fleetingly, and at varying levels of awareness, imagine themselves, or other members, in these roles. This redramatization in the mind is one of the ways of entering into, and reviewing, the script.

Identifying with the victim can reduce the guilt of being to blame either for causing the death or for failing to accept the realities of the separation. Being the dead person in the imagination, if it becomes permanent, may lead to replicative scripts that are potentially dangerous or damaging. Bereaved people may put themselves in dangerous situations or become "dead" inside. One corrective script might involve becoming excessively active — "alive and kicking"; another might mean avoiding all contexts similar to that in which the death occurred, which may be cripplingly restrictive.

Identifying with the would-be rescuer can allow for undoing the lethal act in the imagination, an act of denial which can block grieving. When, however, the reality of the death finally has to be faced this leads to acute guilt at not having prevented the death — an identification with the failed caregiver. Psychotherapists are all too familiar with those who are racked with guilt about what they did or did not do. The guilt may act as a spur to the corrective script of becoming a compulsive caregiver. A replicative script would be to become a failed rescuer, trying to help those who cannot be helped.

Identification with the person held responsible for the death might protect against the terror of accepting that death cannot be controlled. Identification with an aggressor protects against the terrifying image of being killed. Replicative scripts can lead to putting other people in danger; corrective scripts can lead to a serious inhibition of aggression. Several scripts can, of course, coexist so that a normally passive individual may suddenly be triggered into violence by a context reminiscent of certain aspects of the death scenario (e.g., one in which he or she feels trapped).

The roles adopted will be influenced by the family script for illness that existed before the death, such as the "nurse" of the family, the "invalid," or the hardy individual who ridicules illness. This may affect the pattern of identification both accepted by and attributed to others. For instance, if someone is already identified as a person who does not take illness seriously, then both he or she and the rest of the family may easily come to blame that person for not getting help early enough.

CASE ILLUSTRATION

The clinical implications of this way of thinking are illustrated by the B. family. Family members show how their response to a traumatic death was influenced by past scripts, and how some family therapy altered the family grieving script. They responded differently to the next family death.

The B. family lived in a converted windmill in a village outside London, where they ran the local flower shop. Jenny, aged 14, was referred to me late one evening by a priest. She had just witnessed the hanging death of her 17-year-old boyfriend, Fred. The priest said that it seemed to have been an experiment that went tragically wrong.

In the first family session, Jenny seemed very composed. She sat in the middle of the couch, while her mother, Almena, sat down in a seat away to one side, and her stepfather, Stanley, in a seat on the other side. It was not possible for the three members of the family to be farther away from each other.

Jenny told the following story in a flat droning monotone—detached from any emotion—like a reporter giving an eyewitness account of some event. "I was in the loft, you know—the room at the top of the mill—with Fred. My parents were out. We were talking about all sorts of things, life and death and that sort of thing. Fred asked whether I thought it would hurt if you hanged. I said I thought not, it just broke your neck so you could not feel anything. He went over to a rope which was hanging from the ceiling and tied a noose in it. He used to mess about a lot with pranks, so I said he would never dare. He stood up on a box and put his head through the noose. I told him to stop messing about and to get down. He took no notice. Suddenly, he kicked the box away. I ran to him and tried to lift him back onto the box but he was too heavy. I tried to undo the knot but it would not budge. I kept shouting at him to stand on the box and stop being silly. His face went blue and his tongue started to stick out. I shouted for help but there was no one there so I ran out into the street and stopped people to ask for help. No one believed me; they thought I was just a silly kid. I rang for the police. I was panicking. I ran back to Fred. His face was a horrid black color. I finally found a knife and cut the rope. I just held him. I started to cry. It was ages before the ambulance came and took him off to the hospital. The police took me to the station. I waited for three hours while they looked for my parents. I kept on asking if Fred was OK. They said he would be fine. I imagined taking him flowers in the hospital. When my Mum arrived, she told me he was dead."

As a therapist, I needed to do two things: One was to reconnect the emotion to the image; the other was to connect Jenny to her parents. The therapist is most helpful if he or she enables the family to hold and comfort the grieving person so that the grieving can then continue, as it should, at home. This was achieved by asking a few questions about Fred and how long their relationship lasted. Jenny finally burst into tears when she described meeting him at a party a year before. I then asked her mother to go and sit next to her to comfort her, and a little later I also asked her stepfather to do the same. By the end of the session she was crying, sitting between her parents who had their arms around her. The change between the distance at the beginning of the session and the hugging at the end exemplified the work with this family. The writing of a new script had begun.

Engaging the Family

There had been considerable work done in order to get the family together. My immediate response to the priest's telephone call had been to offer to see the whole family the next evening. Of course, that was too soon; they were neither ready emotionally or organizationally to see me. It was nevertheless useful because it communicated to them that I was prepared to make myself available quickly. I then offered another appointment for the following week. On that occasion only the stepfather, Stanley, came. The other two were not yet ready. As it happened, this was very fruitful.

Stanley told me about the family background. Jenny and her mother had lived on their own since Jenny was two, when her father had left. Stanley had joined the family five years ago but had never been allowed to be a father to Jenny. Almena, Jenny's mother, had prevented him from taking disciplinary roles. On Stanley's arrival in the family, Jenny broke her very close relationship with her mother and replaced it with a close relationship with a friend of her own age, Samantha, and spent most of her time at Samantha's home. Indeed, since the hanging, Jenny had moved into her friend's home altogether.

Stanley and Almena had two children of their own, aged three-and-a-half and two. Stanley was able to be a full father to them. He felt upset, however, about his almost nonexistent relationship with Jenny. One of the advantages of grieving work is that the intensity and urgency of the emotions that are generated can be used to get people together and to alter the family structure. I gave Stanley the task of getting Jenny back home. This he did with considerable authority. He went and demanded her return. This not only embedded Jenny back in the family but began to establish a relationship between stepfather and stepdaughter in which Stanley had some authority.

At the beginning of the second family meeting, Jenny again sat on the couch but this time her parents sat in the chairs nearest to her rather than those farthest from her. Jenny told me that she had been fainting, which she called "passing out." I explored when these fainting attacks occurred and discovered that they happened just when she recalled Fred dropping off the box and being strangled. I suggested that she had put herself in Fred's shoes and imagined what it had been like for him and passed out when she visualized him dying. She told me that she had also felt faint when she imagined what she should have done to prevent the hanging. Putting these two together, I said, "Perhaps you feel so guilty about what happened that you think it should have been you, not Fred, who died, so you put your own head in the noose when you think about it, and pass out." It is important, when reviewing the death scenario, to talk openly about the most gruesome aspects. Otherwise these go untouched in the debriefing work and may reappear, in quite specific detail, in a reenactment at a later date.

During this period, I was aware that I was doing some individual work with Jenny while her parents looked on. This work was important because an identification with a suicidal act can be very dangerous. Yet, it created two problems. First, it de-skilled the parents, and second, the distress of the scenario may have gone beyond the parents' emotional threshold so that they would not be able to support Jenny in further exploration of this issue. There was some evidence of the first problem as the mother was heard to say, regretfully, that Jenny was telling me more than she ever told her.

I then asked what the parents were imagining during this discussion. I acknowledged that, although Jenny had been exposed to the worst experience, the parents also needed help to face what happened. This helped them to feel sufficiently held so that they did not have to sabotage any further uncovering of horrifying images.

Soon after this, the mother told me that Jenny had talked about suicide just after the funeral. I needed to assess just how suicidal Jenny was now. She admitted to feeling that she would rather be with Fred than be in this hell on earth. She was then thoughtful and said that she would never want her family, naming each one in turn—including Stanley—to suffer in the way that Fred's parents had. I felt relieved because Jenny's attachments to her family appeared to be powerful enough to hold her back. I knew that I could evoke sufficient caring within the family by touching their pain.

I asked if she had been able to cry again. Only on her own at night, she said. I then asked whose shoulder she would like to be able to cry on. There was an awkward silence. Mother broke it by saying it would be Samantha's mother, with whom she had been living. She said it in a way that told me that she was trying to preempt Jenny from saying so, as that would have been too painful for her to bear. During this conversation, I noticed that both Jenny and her mother had started to point their toes toward each other. I realized that each was longing to get together and that, if I could help Jenny to cry now, it might help this process. I asked about memories of Fred. This, as in the first session, helped her to cry. Her mother moved over to sit next to her, and put her arm around her shoulder. Jenny became quiet and thoughtful. I asked her where she had gone in her imagination, and she said that she was thinking about what I had said about "passing out." I asked her whether it had made sense. She said that it had. This is a good example of how exploring ideas is facilitated by being held in a way that is typical of a secure attachment. Jenny had been unable to think fully about what I had said before this.

I became aware of Stanley sitting awkwardly to one side and feeling left out. Clearly, there was a danger of recreating an overtight bond between mother and daughter and excluding Stanley. I asked Stanley to move his chair closer to Jenny so that he could comfort her as well. He moved over and put his hand on her shoulder. Now, as in the first session, each parent was actively comforting Jenny, this time, however, with less active intervention by me. For a grieving script that has been initiated by the therapist to become established, it has to be taken over by the family.

Almena said, "One knows what it is like to worry about hurting one's family if one's thinking about suicide." I said, "It sounds as if you know what it is like." She now told a story about how as a teenager, on her 14th birthday (Jenny's age), her boyfriend had jilted her, so she took one of her mother's belts, tied a noose in it, put it over her head, threaded it over a beam and pulled on it until she passed out. When she came around again she had, of course, let go of the belt. She described this scenario in a flat, unemotional way reminiscent of how Jenny first told her story. Jenny said, rather reproachfully, that her mother had never told her that story. Almena said, "Oh yes I did, I told you many times, I know I did."

The story threw new light on what might have been happening in the interaction that just preceded the hanging. Jenny may have been more active in creating a scenario in which part of her mother's experience was reenacted in a similar way at the same age. We learned later that Almena had used Jenny as a companion after her father left the family. She had been very depressed. She may well have been talking about suicide as a response to her husband's departure. It is also highly likely that she had recounted this hanging story to Jenny when she was very young. Small children may take in the concrete details of a story and forget the story itself. Family stories and legends provide ways in which scripts for future action may be laid down (Byng-Hall, 1988).

It transpired that Fred's father had also threatened, and attempted, suicide many times over the last few years. He had been taught a suicide script. This illustrates the point that both partners to a reenactment of a script must have the potential to fulfill the roles involved. The form of the final suicide, however, may well have been set by Jenny — via her mother.

Jenny then told me that she had just had a frightening and puzzling fight with her friend, Samantha. She had visited Samantha one afternoon and Samantha had wanted her to stay the night, but Jenny insisted on going home. Samantha barred the way, and Jenny attacked her. Samantha's father, who was just outside the door of their room, came rushing in to stop the fight. I noticed that while telling this story Jenny held her hand around her throat. I asked what form the fighting took and Jenny said that she had gone for Samantha's throat. After the two had been separated Jenny became very worried about her friend and, with Samantha's father, took her to the open window for a breath of fresh air. It was clear that Samantha had never been in serious danger—first, because Jenny knew full well that Samantha's father was just outside, ready to come to the rescue, and second, because she had fully recovered her breath before she was taken to the window. It was nevertheless a potentially dangerous attack that had scared Jenny.

I asked Jenny why she had gone for Samantha's throat. She thought a bit and said because Fred had been strangled. I said that I thought that Jenny had to find a way in which she could rely on adults again. With Fred, she had failed to get an adult to help someone who was suffocating. This failure to get help or be believed had shattered her trust in the world.

Whenever a crisis occurs between sessions I try to see if something has been redramatized. I assume that clients and families are trying to redramatize some script in order to see if they can master it, by creating a new, less terrifying ending to the feared drama. It is often possible, as in this attack, to see how this is done.

I added that in this fight she had also been able to get angry—something that always happens when someone dies—and that since it is difficult to get cross with the person who has died, it sometimes comes out in anger with someone else or with oneself. Jenny said that she was angry with Fred for leaving her like that. This aspect of grieving work is crucial. It is important that the whole family becomes aware of this problem and helps to reconnect the anger to its original source. It also acknowledged Jenny's identification with the aggressive part of this self-killing.

At the end of the second family session, I labeled the event as suicide. I no longer accepted it as an unfortunate prank that went wrong. If I had colluded with this, the true implications of potentially dangerous self-destructive acts in the future might have been denied.

Perhaps the most important piece of work in these two sessions was the development of a new grieving script in which, instead of turning away from each other, they came together and supported one another. This represented a shift from an avoidant family attachment script toward a more secure one.

Reducing the Sway of Old Grieving Scripts

Another approach to rewriting grieving scripts is to explore the family history with the focus on how mourning has been conducted in the past, and comparing this with what is being done now.

In the third session, I drew a family tree (genogram). Stanley had not experienced any deaths in his immediate family, so I turned to Almena. She had left home at age 17 to get away from her mother with whom she fought, and who made life a misery for her father, "but going was like leaving my father to the wolves." Her father died of a heart attack when she was 19. She had been very close to him, indeed she described having telepathic contact with him from the time that she left home. She had had premonitions of his death. When he died, she was completely shattered. She could not believe that it had actually happened. She could not cry.

ALMENA   I felt that if I had been there somehow I could have saved him — or if I had encouraged him to live with me — but I didn't.

THERAPIST   It is interesting, Jenny, that your Mum also struggled with that issue. She too felt that she could have saved somebody's life if she had done something different.

Almena described how these questions had started to go around and around in her head until she suddenly could not think at all. Language stopped being comprehensible to her.

ALMENA   I no longer understood what anyone said to me — I needed to be right out of contact with everybody.

She told me that she withdrew from people, and went around the world, living in 20 different countries. She described herself as having a break-down, but she never saw a psychiatrist because "they" would have locked her up.

THERAPIST   So you had a travelling breakdown. (laughter)

ALMENA   I never felt at home anywhere.

THERAPIST   (to Stanley) Are you finding it difficult to settle her at home?

All agreed that she had now turned her wanderlust into going on holidays and she said that she now felt at home. Returning to the topic of the breakdown:

ALMENA   I was just completely numb — too numb even to be scared. Yet I have never felt better.

THERAPIST   And at that time if your father had been there, do you think you could have talked to him — or did you go on keeping in touch [telepathy] with him?

ALMENA   No — it was too chaotic.

The "breakdown" lasted 10 years, until she joined a meditation group "and the parts of me that were not completely shattered came back."

She started to get "in touch" with her father again. I needed to explore the nature of this phenomenon, having in mind how Jenny might use the same mechanism to avoid grieving, especially as she had said, at one point, that Fred was still present.

THERAPIST   Tell me how you get in touch with your father. What happens?

ALMENA   I would be going through something difficult in some way. Suddenly, there would be something—and I would get some intelligent question such as "What is actually wrong? What do you want to do?" which would provoke me into thinking about it much more rationally. And then there would be this conversation dream in which I could work it out a bit better.

THERAPIST   So, it is as if your father . . .

ALMENA (interrupts)   In my head. I do not have to speak out loud.

JENNY   Conversations with your father in your head, or conversations with just you?

ALMENA   A very good question. I hear his voice or I hear talking (looking up toward the ceiling).

JENNY   So, it's between you and him. It's not just you and him just arguing with yourself in your head.

ALMENA   It certainly appears to be between us.

THERAPIST   What do you think of Jenny's question? Is this your memory of him speaking to him? Or is it your imagination?

ALMENA   How much can you recreate a person in your head? I have no idea.

THERAPIST   For you it is an important experience having the memory of him or the image of him in your head, helping you to work things out for yourself.

I now found out Almena still had these experiences occasionally. It was important, however, that Jenny established in her own mind what the nature of the telepathy was and why it occurred. Almena accepted that it had enabled her to feel that she had not totally lost her father. She went on to talk about her guilt about failing to save him, but finally concluded that there was nothing she could have done.

THERAPIST   So you finally came to terms with the fact that you did not kill your Dad. Jenny, maybe Mum can help you with the guilt you have. She can help you not to take 10 years to mourn.

It was now important to relabel Almena's "breakdown."

THERAPIST   Could I put it down (writing it down on the family tree in a formal fashion) that you failed to mourn? Would you accept that as a diagnosis—that you failed to complete the mourning?

ALMENA   Well, I don't know. It did get sort of prolonged anyway.

After a bit more discussion she accepted this view. She looked relieved. This was the first time that she had talked to a professional in the mental health field about these frightening experiences. It was extremely important that the family bore witness to such a relabeling. It was then possible to define what was needed for normal grieving and hence to write a new family mourning script. For instance, some time was spent in the therapy discussing how keeping in touch with Fred by telepathy would be one way in which Jenny could avoid facing the reality of his death. The implication was that she should avoid that mechanism to complete a normal grieving. I commented on how similar the start of Jenny's mourning had been to her mother's grief; each had left home and avoided contact with surviving parents. The aim of therapy was then defined as finding a way of reversing this tendency to disengage in a crisis.

Much of the remaining therapy, which lasted nine months and included 11 sessions, was aimed at consolidating the structural changes started when Stanley returned Jenny to the family. Some work was done with the younger children, Annie and Chester. Their parents were finding it hard to control them. Helping the parents to regain control freed time for them to be with Jenny. For a time, Jenny visited a sick friend in the hospital, taking her flowers every single day—an identification with the good caregiver. She was helped to see that this overzealous care represented her wish to make reparation for Fred's death. We recalled her image of taking Fred flowers in the hospital just before she was told that he was dead. The grieving became a less prominent part of the work. Jenny then became more relaxed and started to go out with other boys. At this point, I discharged the family.

Evidence of a New Grieving Script

Eighteen months after discharge Stanley called me to ask for an appointment. Almena had died the previous week from ovarian cancer. The mourning seemed to be going along as expected, but he wanted to consult me to make sure they were doing the right things.

Stanley and Jenny came to the first session. Both were tearful, and fully in touch with their feelings. I took them through all the details and did some more grieving work. Two weeks before the death, Stanley and Almena were married in a very moving ceremony in the hospital ward. All the children were present. They had felt that it was a fitting confirmation of their relationship, which they had always intended to formalize through marriage at some point.

Their report of the death scene was particularly poignant. Almena had died in the hospital in the middle of the night. The whole family was by the bedside, including Almena's sister who had flown from Australia, but excluding the small children. They had done a great deal of mutual hugging. When she died they refrained from telling the nursing staff because they knew that this would interrupt the grieving by bringing doctors in and so on. Instead, they remained in a long hug for an hour or so, remaining together, and with the body, until they were ready to say goodbye. They were all deeply moved and upset but felt very close to one another. The reality of the death was embraced. I remembered how the family, when they first came to see me, sat hugging on my couch at the end of the session.

When I discussed the funeral, Jenny said she had felt very cold when she saw her mother being buried. I reminded her of feeling faint after Fred's hanging. She recalled thinking that it must be cold in her mother's coffin. She could see that she was putting herself in her mother's place. I explored whether she had used telepathy to avoid parting with her mother. She had not.

This time the grieving process went much more normally. I saw the whole family, including the small children, now aged five-and-a-half and four, and Stanley's parents, who had taken on much of the parenting when Almena fell sick. I helped make a story of what happened that made sense to the children and was acceptable and accurate as far as the family was concerned. I always try to do this with young children because it establishes a shared version that can be elaborated upon as the children grow older and want to know more, without contradicting the simple story with which they started. This, coupled with their experiences that death brought the family together, will, it is hoped, write a healthy grieving script for them.

We must now return to the original question: Can we rewrite the family script, and if so, which parts of it? There is some evidence that the grieving script changed in this family from that of Almena's failure to grieve her father to that of her family being able to grieve her. The main change was that members of the family came together to help each other face the reality of what had happened and to enable one another to face the pain. What about aspects of the script that go beyond the grieving? My impression was that this had spread to their attachment behavior, having moved from being a disengaged family to one with the capacity for closeness.

Therapists must not be omnipotent however. I had not done work on how the individuals managed the ending of their relationships. I heard a year later that Jenny, now aged 17, had become depressed after the breakup of a relationship and had sought psychotherapy. When compared with her mother's flight from therapists, this can be seen as progress.

References

Bowlby, J. (1980). *Attachment and loss: vol. 3 loss. Sadness and depression*. London: Hogarth and New York.

Bowlby, J. (1988). *A secure base: Clinical applications of attachment theory*. Routledge: London.

Byng-Hall, J. (1985). The family script: A useful bridge between theory and practice. *Journal of Family Therapy, 7*, 301–305.

Byng-Hall, J. (1986). Family scripts: A concept which can bridge child psychotherapy and family therapy thinking. *Journal of Child Psychotherapy, 12:2*, 3–13.

Byng-Hall, J. (1988). Scripts and legends in families and family therapy. *Family Process, 27:2*, 167–180.

Byng-Hall, J. (in press). The application of attachment theory to understanding and treatment in family therapy. In C. M. Parkes and J. Stevenson-Hinde (Eds.), *Attachment across the life cycle*.

Parkes, C. M. (1972). *Bereavement: Studies of grief in adult life*. London: Tavistock.

Schank, R. C., & Abelson, R. P. (1977). *Scripts, plans, goals, and understanding*. Hillsdale, NJ: Erlbaum.

8

Helping Families With Anticipatory Loss

JOHN S. ROLLAND

THE ANTICIPATION OF loss in physical illness can be as challenging and painful for families as the actual death of a family member. There has been relatively little attention paid to the process of families' anticipating *future* loss and how their experience with protracted threatened loss evolves with illness, individual, and family development. Most literature on loss has focused on bereavement in terminal illness, when loss is imminent and certain. Overlooked are the enormous challenges to families living with uncertainty in the face of tragedy while needing to sustain hope. A myriad of feelings and transactions associated with anticipatory loss complicate all dimensions of family life over time. This chapter will offer a clinical framework to address the interweaving of family efforts simultaneously to sustain hope, cope with varying degrees of uncertainty, and prepare for loss over the course of an illness.

Lindemann (1944) first described the phenomenon of "anticipatory grief" in his study of spousal adaptation to wartime separation, noting the essential signs of "true" grief experienced in preparation for bereavement. Subsequent research has focused on the effects of anticipatory grief on parents with terminally ill children and on key survivors (e.g., spouses) of

A revised version of this paper appears in *Family Process, 29*, 229-244.

I wish to acknowledge the special contribution of Peter Lynch, M.S.W., of New Haven, Connecticut, in helping prepare the section on terminal illness and hospice.

terminally ill adults (Clayton et al., 1973; Friedman et al., 1963; Futterman et al., 1972; Gerber et al., 1975; Glick et al., 1974; Natterson & Knudson, 1960; Parkes, 1976; Parkes & Weiss, 1983; Rando, 1983; Schoenberg et al., 1974). Research has yielded inconsistent and often contradictory findings about both the value of time to anticipate loss and the kinds of coping strategies that are most helpful to long-term adaptation (Fulton & Gottesman, 1980).

In the family systems literature, the scant attention to loss has focused on the impact of prior unresolved losses on later family life (Bowen, Chapter 4; Coleman, Chapter 14; Coleman & Stanton, 1978; Herz, 1989; Paul & Grosser, Chapter 5; Walsh & McGoldrick, 1988). Future loss touches more closely on the existential fact of our own mortality as an anticipated event we may need to deny (Becker, 1973).

This chapter offers a systemic, interactional definition of anticipatory loss over the entire course of an illness, including the mutual influence of family dynamics with: (1) family members' threatened loss of the ill member; (2) the ill member's anticipation of losing his/her family; and (3) the ill member's expectation of disability and/or death. The threat of loss needs to encompass the "person," family relationships with the ill member, and the intact family unit.

The experience of anticipatory loss involves a range of intensified emotional responses that may include separation anxiety, existential aloneness, denial, sadness, disappointment, anger, resentment, guilt, exhaustion, and desperation. Emotional expression often fluctuates between these more difficult feelings and others, such as a heightened sense of being alive, life's preciousness, intimacy, appreciation for "routine" daily events, and hope. There may be intense ambivalence toward the ill member, vacillating wishes for closeness and distance, and fantasies of escape from an unbearable situation. Especially with chronic illnesses involving long-term threatened loss, families often become hypervigilant and overprotective. They may repeatedly rehearse the process of loss and imagined scenarios of family suffering and hardship. These complex emotions can powerfully influence families' dynamics as they try to adapt to threatened loss.

A systems oriented model that views the experience of anticipatory loss within a developmental framework clarifies how the meaning of possible loss evolves over time with changing life cycle demands (Rolland, 1987a, 1987b, 1988a,1989). Also, the salience of anticipatory loss varies depending on members' transgenerational experience with actual and threatened loss. A family's experience of threatened loss varies with the kind of illness, its psychosocial demands over time, and the degree of uncertainty about prognosis. Because the quality and degree of anticipatory loss vary with the developmental phases of illness (Rolland, 1984), it is essential to differentiate between family members' expectation of *inevitable* loss in the terminal stage of an illness and their awareness of the *possibility* at an earlier point. It is also crucial to assess anxieties about *disability* and *suffering* as distinct from *death*, since patients and families often express their greatest fears about helplessness in the face of uncontrollable suffering. As distinct from families in acute grief, such families are faced with seemingly incompatible psychosocial tasks earlier on. They try to sustain vital membership for a person who is expected to become disabled or die, simultaneously with efforts to maintain family integration by reallocating the ill member's role functions. These critical distinctions are easily overlooked, particularly at the time of diagnosis.

Finally, belief systems powerfully shape how families view and respond to life-threatening situations. The meanings ascribed to disability and death, as well as a sense of competence to influence the outcome of events, will affect how they act in the face of threatened loss. Unresolved issues of blame, shame, and guilt can strongly affect their view of the cause of an illness and the meanings attached to anticipated loss, seriously impeding adaptation (Rolland & Walsh, 1988b).

Recent studies by Wortman and Silver (1989) indicate that traditional assumptions about healthy mourning are largely myth. Their research strongly suggests a much broader range of nonpathological grief reactions and casts doubt on stage theories of loss (Kübler-Ross, 1975). Likewise, this discussion is based on the awareness that there are many effective coping strategies to deal with threatened loss. The aim of this chapter is to provide a framework for clinical assessment and research that will improve decision-making and effective intervention for a range of situations faced by families dealing with anticipatory loss.

FAMILY SYSTEMS–ILLNESS MODEL

The Family Systems–Illness model developed by the author (Rolland, 1984, 1987a, 1988a, 1989, in preparation) provides a useful framework for understanding the family experience of anticipatory loss. The model distinguishes three separate dimensions: (1) "psychosocial types" of illnesses; (2) major phases in their natural history; and (3) key family systems variables. On the first dimension, illness patterning can vary in terms of *onset* (acute vs. gradual), *course* (progressive vs. constant vs. relapsing), *outcome* (fatal vs. shortened life span or possible sudden death vs. no effect on longevity), and *incapacitation* (none vs. mild vs. moderate vs. severe). To identify the core psychosocial themes in the unfolding of chronic disorders, the second dimension delineates three major phases—(1) *initial crisis*, (2) *chronic*, and (3) *terminal*—each linked by critical transitions. A family systems assessment, as the third dimension, highlights the importance of various components of family life (e.g., development, belief systems, cohesion, adaptability, communication) in relation to specific types of disorders at a specific phase of the "illness life cycle." The Family System–Illness model enables clinicians to characterize any illness in terms of its practical and emotional demands and in relation to family interactional patterns.

Illness Timeline and Threatened Loss

The psychosocial types and phases of illness provide a timeline of potential nodal points of loss, including disability and death. Families begin to develop their own timelines at initial diagnosis. Discussions with health providers about the nature of the disorder, its prognosis, and prescriptions for management constitute a "framing event" for family members. Generally, this is a highly emotional and vulnerable period. Families face loss of "normal" life as it was before a diagnosis as they face threatened further loss through disability and/or death. This hypervigilant, anxious, trancelike state makes families highly receptive to intended and unintended messages about how to navigate the uncertainties that confront them. What is actually said, unstated, or left unclear about the prognosis by clinicians is critical. Who is included and excluded from these conversations influences how the family frames the experience. One family, accustomed to open, frank discussion, described how the physician came to the mother's hospital room and took the family to a separate room to inform them that the mother had cancer and to discuss the diagnosis. At this vulnerable moment, family members felt they were being instructed implicitly to exclude the mother in any discussion of her cancer.

Further, different families may hear the same discussion through very different historical/ethnic/cultural filters that can lead to conflictual and dysfunctional patterns later. Beliefs about the likelihood and timing of further disability and death strongly influence the relationship rules established in the face of threatened loss. In one family, the husband had a benign skin cancer removed and was reassured by the dermatologist that he need have no further worry about the growth. His wife's father had died from malignant melanoma a year after reassurance by his physician that he had removed a "benign" tumor. Her traumatic experience, unknown to the physician, led her to distrust the prognosis and live in terrified anticipation of her husband's demise. Therefore, it is extremely useful to ask each family member to discuss expectations about the anticipated course and outcome.

Progressive diseases, such as Alzheimer's disease (Boss et al., 1988) or multiple sclerosis, involve a number of losses. With Alzheimer's, although the timing of these losses is ambiguous, their inevitability is not. Family members anticipate and grieve each milestone as it is passed. With disabling conditions, at key illness transitions family functions may need modifications to shift to a new phase of adaptation. Clinicians should be sensitive to nodal points that may require discontinuous change for the family. For instance, one family tried at all costs to preserve the deteriorating father's role functions in order to maintain their strong belief in mastery. As disability increased, successful adaptation required acceptance of that which could not be changed.

Both the "if" and the "when" of death have enormous impact on the family. Most studies of anticipatory loss, by focusing on terminal illness, have not addressed the "if" aspect and have narrowed the "when" aspect to the last phase. At diagnosis most illnesses are uncertain on both counts. The only question is the *degree* of uncertainty and *when* anticipatory loss will become salient. For instance, when a family member's lung cancer is in remission, tremendous fear surrounds a possible recurrence. Every appointment with the physician, every ambiguous symptom bring apprehension. The loss of the first remission often shatters a family's hope for a cure and brings their worst fears to the surface. Medically, it means that the best treatment has failed to eliminate the possibility of early death and second attempts are even less likely to succeed. The ambiguous boundary between remission and cure stokes embers of anticipatory loss indefinitely. Even 20 years after treatment for cancer, a vague symptom can immediately rekindle fears in a family of recurrence and death.

Relapsing illnesses, like asthma or heart disease, can flare up or cause sudden death. Stable or low symptom periods alternate with periods of exacerbation, so that issues related to anticipatory loss hover between the front and back burner. Families are strained by both the frequency of transition between crisis and noncrisis and the ongoing uncertainty of when a life-threatening recurrence may strike. In the event of life-threatening crises (e.g., angina/heart attack, hemophilia), anticipated loss may preoccupy a family. Families fear most those crises that can arise suddenly, without warning, and require immediate help to avert catastrophe. One woman with longstanding diabetes abruptly and without warning signs developed severe episodes of hypoglycemia, resulting in loss of consciousness. She and her husband feared that an episode could endanger the safety of their small children, as well as end her life.

Frequently, family rules shift to protect against life-threatening situations. For instance, when a parent has had a heart attack, the family rule of open communication may shift to one of conflict avoidance to protect against a fatal recurrence. Because dangerous relapses can often be triggered by emotional upheaval, family members, particularly the well spouse, need explicit guidance about when recovery is sufficient to allow them to resume their normal disagreements, sexual life, and so on.

Relationship Between Psychological and Physical Loss

Illnesses vary in terms of the balance between expected physical and psychological disability. Psychological loss involves a range of cognitive deficits that impair participation in family life. For disorders like severe stroke, psychological death occurs long before physical death.

Psychological loss is especially painful for a family because it is associated with progressive loss of intimacy. With physical decline, intimacy can suffer if the family withdraws emotionally. Premature distancing can occur when family members are torn between their wishes to sustain intimacy and their need to "let go" emotionally of a member they expect to die. All relationships are predicated on the existential dilemma of choosing intimacy in the face of eventual separation/loss. Life-threatening illness heightens this universal form of anticipatory loss.

Boss and her colleagues (1984, 1988, Chapter 9) describe endpoint situations where an ill member becomes psychologically dead to the family but remains physically alive, as in Alzheimer's disease. She asserts that uncertainties about the illness trajectory push families either (1) to reorganize without the affected member or (2) to minimize the demands/existence of the illness and unrealistically expect the ill member to maintain usual family responsibilities. The timing of such a family decision depends both on the type, degree, and timing of anticipated loss, and on family stylistic variables such as cohesion and adaptability. For instance, a highly cohesive family may have less tolerance for ambiguity in the face of threatened loss. The need to maintain a cohesive family unit can lead to prematurely excluding the ill member or to tenacious denial. It is useful to inquire about the ill member's continued participation in family rituals (see Imber-Black, Chapter 11) and to note communication patterns that bypass the ill member.

Illness Phases and Developmental Tasks

Some family developmental tasks in the initial *crisis phase* facilitate family coping with long-term anticipatory loss. Families must grieve the loss of customary life as a family unit prior to the illness. In progressive and life-threatening disorders, families must accept expected hardship and the *possibility* of further disability or death. Family members must learn to live "in limbo" and grieve for the ambiguities they must endure over the long term. Efforts to resist acceptance of chronicity may express their wish to elude living with threatened loss or "death over their shoulder." Coping with threatened loss for an indeterminate period makes it much harder for a family to define present and future structural and emotional boundaries. Helping families establish functional patterns early on promotes later coping and adaptation to loss.

Facing loss can shatter a family's myth that life-threatening illnesses only happen to others. A family's loss of a sense of control can be an extremely debilitating experience, leading to frenetic or immobilized behavior. In this period of intense uncertainty, families desperately need to reestablish a belief (even illusory) that they have some control of the situation. Assisting families to prioritize tasks and take direct actions such as gathering information about the illness and community resources is especially useful in helping them reestablish a sense of mastery. Patient and family involvement in self-help groups for particular disorders should be encouraged. Educating families about significant versus minor physical symptoms, whenever possible, can avert unnecessary alarm. Helping them distinguish the expectable emotional roller coaster from their fears of craziness can lower reactivity at this stage.

The *chronic* or *"long haul" phase* presents different dilemmas for families. With caregiving demands, exhaustion and ambivalence are common as financial and emotional resources become depleted. The emotional tide of anticipation can shift from a fear of to a wish for death, fraught with enormous guilt and shame, which are seldom discussed. Clinicians need to distinguish normative ambivalence arising in the context of an extended ordeal from preexisting conflict in the relationship that has become heightened in the face of possible loss. In long-term disorders, customary patterns of couple intimacy become skewed over time by discrepancies between the ill member and well spouse/caretaker. Emotions often remain underground and contribute to "survivor guilt." As one young husband lamented about his wife's cancer, "It was hard enough two years ago to absorb that, even if Ann was cured, her radiation treatment would make pregnancy impossible. Now I find it unbearable that her continued slow, losing battle with cancer makes it impossible to go for our dreams like other couples our age." Psychoeducational family interventions that normalize emotions related to threatened loss can help prevent cycles of blame, shame, and guilt.

Medical care for life-threatening illnesses is often provided in specialty clinics, where patients and families dealing with similar disorders may develop significant relationships, even in the clinic waiting area. Progression, relapse, or death of another patient can trigger fears of "Will I (we) be next?" and deflate family morale. It is useful for clinicians to inquire about such contacts and offer family consultations.

The boundary between the chronic and *terminal phases*, when death is no longer an "if" but an inevitability, is often ambiguous. Once the ill family member enters the terminal phase, the only question that remains is the amount of time the family has to prepare. Medical technology and the imperative of a "leave no stone unturned" philosophy often reverse or delay these "natural" transitions. It is now possible to induce a third or fourth remission for cancer. Such persistent medical interventions designed to prolong life can be difficult to distinguish from caregiving attempts to comfort a dying patient. Also, medical training tends to promote ambiguous communication to families, leading doctors to be cautious about the prognosis or not to admit uncertainty. This "let's wait and see" attitude often generates heightened anxiety and ambiguity that confuses a family about the stage of the illness, as in the following case.

> Mr. and Mrs. L. were referred for consultation at rehospitalization for Mrs. L.'s lymphoma of ten years' duration because of their daughter's sudden refusal to visit her mother in the hospital. Three prior recurrences had been easily treated. This time a number of attempts had not worked. With a highly optimistic physician and a stable illness course, the family had never openly discussed the possibility of death. The daughter's behavior signaled a needed change. Mrs. L. continued to feel worse and thought she might be dying, but her physician maintained that she was "doing well" and proposed a number of as yet untried treatments (which the consultant recognized as long shots). Discussion with the oncologist revealed his steadfast belief in continued, aggressive treatment that would be undermined by any discussion of death with the family. The family's loyal belief in their physician blocked transition to a final stage of anticipatory grief. It was only 48 hours before her death, when she was in a coma, that the physician agreed to discuss with the family the fact that Mrs. L. was dying.

When families are coping with anticipatory loss in the final phase of an illness, the *quality* as much as the quantity of time becomes a priority. Clinicians need to explore a family's fears about the process of dying as well as the loss itself. The anticipation of a family member's increasing pain and suffering is often of even more concern than death. This is especially common in longstanding progressive disorders, where the anticipation of death has been rehearsed many times. Reassurance early on about effective means of pain control and informed discussion with the family as to the ill member's wishes about lifesaving heroics can alleviate a major source of anguish.

The needs of dying patients and their families have perhaps been best attended to through *hospice*, a professional caregiving system designed for the terminal phase of illness. Designed to be autonomous of mainstream health care, the hospice concept, simply stated, is that the patient-family is the unit of care with services available 24 hours a day, seven days a week for palliative and supportive care with emphasis on the biopsychosocial and spiritual needs of the patient-family.*

---

*Hospices, waystations for travellers and pilgrims in the Middle Ages, first served the dying in Dublin, Ireland in the 19th century. In the 1960s, St. Christopher's Hospice in London became a prototype for modern hospice care. There are now over 1,700 hospices in the U.S.

Within hospice, the patient, family, and professional caregivers become a tightly knit group, as together and separately they move through three distinct phases common to the terminal phase of anticipatory loss: (1) the arrival phase; (2) the here-for-now phase; and (3) the departure phase.

In the *arrival phase*, families typically arrive depleted from their protracted efforts to save a member's life. Clinicians need to help the patient and family accept that having hospice come into the home or entering a hospice facility acknowledges the ultimate hopelessness of the situation and the transition from curative to palliative care. This transition is fraught with possibilities for blame, shame, and guilt. The family may blame the medical team for failing to provide a cure, especially if physicians had earlier given an overly optimistic prognosis. The patient and family members may blame themselves or one another for having lost their battle with threatened loss. This is particularly true for families guided by a strong sense of personal responsibility and control, as in the following case.

Jeff, 30, had metastatic cancer for two years and was now terminally ill. Fiercely independent and professionally successful, he had vowed to cure himself, unlike his father, a "failure" who, divorced by his mother, later committed suicide. When Jeff developed brain metasteses and became demented and unmanageable at home, his wife was left with no alternative but to place her husband in hospice. She was burdened by intense guilt in assuming responsibility for his failed cure and the fact that he would die in an "institution," a sign of weakness like his father's. Couples therapy focused on these issues to unlink their sense of failure from the inevitability of death.

Clinicians can function as a guide for families, helping them gently relinquish their prior hopes for cure, initiate a humane plan for palliative care, and instill hope in developing a pathway for the experience of death. Their task is to join with the family at a time when members are preoccupied with thoughts of a final separation. In an inpatient facility, like hospice, clinicians need to sensitively orient the patient/family dealing with impending loss to a new, unfamiliar "home."

The *here-for-now phase* is a period of waiting when the anticipation of the "when" of loss is narrowed to a day-to-day experience. Families may need assistance redefining hope as present-focused rather than future-oriented. The patient and family need mutual understanding of unpredictable mood swings and the courage and strength to "live in the moment." The patient hopes for compassion for unpredictable responses to pain and its relief, and not to be abandoned while still alive. Exhausted family members may need reassurance that the dying member's effort to detach from the struggles of daily life is not rejection of the family or a rebuke for not having done enough. Clinicians now play a critical role in bridging the ever widening gap between the patient and family. They can help the family to stay involved with the patient while pacing themselves for the final separation. Once death's imminence has been accepted by patients and families, clinicians can deal more openly with practical arrangements, such as funeral, will, and unfinished relationship issues. The family's dilemma is, in certain respects, isomorphic with the role of the hospice/clinician involved in a time-limited form of therapy. Both need to set immediate objectives and plan termination; they learn to both expect and not need another visit to accomplish goals.

In the final *departure phase*, the patient lives in a world of diminishing concerns that center on control of pain and suffering and hopes for having meaningful people with them in their fading hours. The family's task is to share final moments and then to experience being left behind. There may be shame owing to a sense of abandonment or relief at the termination of a burden or complicated relationship. There is tremendous variation among families and cultures as to tolerance and experience with saying goodbye. Clinicians need to be mindful of the wide range of normative responses in helping families through this process. Moreover, seasoned clinicians learn to let go without losing themselves at each departure.

THE FAMILY LIFE CYCLE

A family's experience of threatened loss can be understood through a life cycle perspective, particularly transgenerational encounters with threatened/ actual loss and timing of life-threatening illness within the individual and family life cycles (Rolland, 1987a, 1989).

The Past: Transgenerational Issues

Genogram information related to prior family encounters with death, disability, threatened loss, and living with ambiguity are particularly important (Herz, 1989; McGoldrick & Gerson, 1985; Rolland, 1987a; Walsh & McGoldrick, 1988). It is useful to track patterns of coping in prior situations of anticipated loss. In addition to illness events, family experiences with other forms of uncertainty or loss, such as poverty, divorce, violence, abandonment, or dangerous occupations (e.g., military, law enforcement), provide valuable information about family hardiness in the face of adversity. Historical inquiry can clarify family members' learned differences, areas of knowledge and inexperience, and expected sense of competence or helplessness in the present encounter with anticipated loss. A history of unresolved, traumatic, or unexpected loss may generate catastrophic fear for a person confronted with threatened loss. This may be expressed in overprotectiveness towards the ill member or other family members or in distancing and cutoff. One man who had lost his first wife to breast cancer started an affair and filed for divorce from his second wife within weeks of her diagnosis of and surgery for breast cancer, despite the good prognosis in her case. The risks of "unfinished business" have been emphasized for *sudden* loss; yet having been a caregiver in a protracted illness can leave fears that one could never again endure the *process* of such an ordeal.

Present and Future Timing with the Life Cycle

Anticipatory loss poses different complications depending upon its fit with current or future family development imperatives. The impact will vary with a family system's oscillation between centripetal periods of high family cohesion, as in early child-rearing, and centrifugal periods of more family separateness, as in families with adolescents or young adults (Beavers, 1982; Combrinck-Graham, 1985). For instance, a family launching a 20-year-old daughter when she develops a disabling brain tumor that may prove fatal must shift gears to pull together.

ON-TIME VERSUS OFF-TIME.   The onset of serious illness is expected in late adulthood, when the quest for meaning, the integration and acceptance of one's own personal and family life, and the anticipation of death are normative universal tasks (Herz, 1989; Levinson, 1978, 1986; Neugarten, 1976; Rolland, 1987a; Walsh & McGoldrick, 1988). When a disabling or life-threatening disorder occurs earlier, it is "out of phase" in both chronological and social time. When the illness is off-time, spouse and family lack the psychosocial preparation and rehearsal that occur later, as peers are experiencing similar losses. The ill member and family are likely to feel robbed of their expectation of a normal life span. In the case of young couples, the threat of loss is out of phase in that it occurs simultaneously with hopes of child-rearing and career development. Although a serious illness breaks through denial of death and the promise of a full life span for both young and older couples, for well spouses of young couples, preparation for disability and death is not normally on the horizon. The hard fact is that, with the ill spouse, the family life cycle will be severely altered and possibly abbreviated. As one young woman whose husband had metastatic cancer confided, "As long as Jim has cancer we have no future." Suffering is compounded for couples when peers distance themselves because they want to avoid facing the possibility of loss of their spouse or child. These issues heighten discrepancies between the well and ill spouse and isolate the family.

LIFE CYCLE TRANSITION PERIODS.   In all life cycle models (Carter & McGoldrick, 1989; Duvall, 1977; Levinson, 1978), developmental transitions involve beginnings and endings (e.g., births, young adults launching, retirement, divorce, and death). Commonly, preoccupations about death, life's limits, and anticipation of separation and loss surface at such times. The diagnosis of a serious illness superimposes the illness life cycle onto that of the individual and family. One of the family's primary developmental tasks is to accommodate to the anticipation of further disability and possibly untimely death (Rolland, 1987a). Families in life cycle transitions may be more vulnerable to the emotional upheaval generated by anticipatory loss associated with illness. For example, suppose a family is in the stage of launching a young adult when the father has a serious heart attack. The threat of the father's death may heavily influence young adult members in transition leading them to alter their life decisions in ways that compromise their own independent strivings.

With long-term threatened loss, as families move through normative life cycle transitions, there may be a resurgence of prior feelings of anticipatory loss families thought were "worked through." Also, at times of transition, developmental tasks of the next life stage may need to be altered, delayed, or given up where they are unrealistic or impossible to achieve. At each transition, intense grieving can occur over opportunities and experiences that may have been anticipated but must now be relinquished in a more final way. Family members often need to grieve the loss of future hopes and dreams. For instance, when a mother learns of her daughter's diagnosis with a terminal form of cancer, she must grieve the loss of anticipated experiences ranging from school graduations and the daughter's wedding to her own grandparenthood. Clinicians should inquire about losses related to future life stages and explore options for alternative positive experiences.

Issues Related to Childhood- versus Adult-Onset Illness

Threatened loss will affect families in new ways as they encounter developmental tasks at each stage of the life cycle. Such differences can be illustrated by examining timing issues in childhood- versus adult-onset disorders as they affect the marital life cycle.

CHILDHOOD-ONSET, CONGENITAL, AND INHERITED DISORDERS. With such disorders, a child's socialization and belief system are shaped by continual interplay of developmental milestones with limitations and future risks of the illness. With many inherited disorders, family beliefs about mastery and the rules for social interaction are shaped over generations to be in sync with anticipatory loss (Rolland, 1987b). For example, with hemophilia, life-threatening bleeding episodes can be triggered by trauma, intense affect, or extended periods of stress. Because sudden death is ever present, parents often teach affected children a finely tuned form of mastery over their bodies that is juxtaposed with fear of social interaction. Emotions are carefully monitored in the interest of self-preservation. Anticipation of loss guides this interweaving of belief system and developmental processes.

The individual with a hereditary or childhood-onset disorder brings the developmental experience with threatened loss to adult relationships. Couples develop their relationship with the factor of possible loss overtly acknowledged or covertly overshadowing their commitment. It is important for clinicians to promote communication about the impact of possible disability and premature death on such areas as child-rearing, career, and division of labor, so that the couple can develop the flexibility necessary to adapt to the added strains of a life-threatening illness.

In long-term illnesses, such as diabetes and hemophilia, concerns about future loss become embedded in life cycle planning in more subtle and covert ways, as illustrated in the following case.

> Greg, a 45-year-old man with lifelong hemophilia, was referred for severe depression. Extensive disability required his using crutches to walk. He had been divorced three years earlier, and his only daughter had just left home for college.
>
> Evaluation revealed that his mother's family had a 200-year history of hemophilia, involving scores of cases. A brother had died in childhood after a traumatic injury, and only one member with hemophilia had lived beyond age 50. When asked about how he had conceived his life from childhood, he stated that he had felt that, if he could survive the higher risks of trauma in childhood (his brother being a vivid reminder), he had enough time to marry and raise children, but, given statistics and his lengthy family history, life beyond 45 seemed unlikely. After 40, he began to view his life as "pre-dead." He had no vision or plans for life beyond 50 except in anticipation of death.

This case demonstrates how someone can structure his entire life cycle to conform to an expectation of disability and death at a particular life phase. The timing of Greg's divorce coincided with a vaguely conscious plan to spare his wife from having to deal with his becoming a burden and dying, and gave him control over the end of the relationship. His daughter's launching left him alone with his depression, suicidal thoughts, and hopeless outlook. The case highlights both the potential danger of anticipatory loss becoming a runaway process and the need for a preventive clinical framework. Greg had a version of anticipatory loss that was inevitable and timed, rather than possible and of uncertain timing. Also, the runaway process accelerated at his most vulnerable point in the life cycle. An earlier intervention, which would have taken stock of how his transgenerational experience influenced his personal illness timeline, could have predicted the time of highest risk. That would have enabled him to plan for life after forty in a way that acknowledged the possibility of disability and early death but did not preclude meaningful life goals and relationships within a context of heightened uncertainty.

ADULT-ONSET ILLNESS.   Serious illness that occurs early in a couple's relationship is particularly stressful because the partners are still forming the foundation of their long-term relationship. For well-functioning couples, if disease onset occurs later in the family life cycle, strains are counterbalanced by a firmer relationship base. If dysfunctional patterns exist prior to the illness, then the threat of loss will more likely drive the couple farther apart.

The type of illness and time frame of anticipated loss influence how the spouses respond to threats to their life plans. With an illness such as diabetes, the possibility of disability or a shortened life span frequently remains distant. Often the person with diabetes accommodates to uncertain negative outcomes through denial and minimization. As the spouses form an intimate relationship, the well partner will need to be educated about diabetes. The ability of the partner with diabetes to inform the well spouse can be blocked by fears about deterioration, abandonment, and death, which are sensitive, loaded subjects for both partners. Often issues related to anticipatory loss become obscured in such pronouncements as, "It's my illness and I'll handle it myself."

Another common nodal point occurs with a couple's decision about having children. The couple must consider risks of pregnancy complications for both an ill mother and the unborn child. Other fears include those of: (1) genetic transmission to offspring who will carry the burdens of anticipatory loss; (2) anticipation of loss of a "dream child" who may contract the illness at some point; (3) anticipation of illness complications that would interfere with effective parenting; (4) fears that the ill spouse might not survive to rear children to adulthood; and (5) associated financial and psychosocial burdens for the surviving or well spouse.

BELIEF SYSTEMS

In the face of possible loss, creating a meaning for an illness that preserves a sense of competency is a primary task for a family. In this regard, a family's beliefs about what and who can influence the course of events is fundamental. Whether a family views the locus of control over health/illness as internal, in the hands of powerful others, or a matter of chance will affect how they interpret illness events, their health-seeking behaviors, and their involvements in caregiving (Lefcourt, 1982; Rolland, 1987b; Wallston & Wallston, 1978).

Clinicians should evaluate family members' ideas about what caused an illness and beliefs about what might influence the course or outcome. Beliefs that invoke blame, shame, or guilt block a normalizing process for the family. They are sufficiently toxic that, unless resolved, they almost invariably preclude establishing a functional family illness system. In the context of a life-threatening illness, the blamed family member is implicitly held accountable for negligence or even potential murder if the patient dies. Decisions about treatment can become filled with tension when every new stage of loss escalates the cycle of blame or guilt. For instance, a mother who feels blamed by her husband for their son's leukemia may be less able to stop low-probability experimental treatment than the angry, blaming husband.

Ambiguities blur for a family what behaviors can affect the odds of a tragic outcome, increasing the likelihood of blaming attributions whenever disease progression can be linked to errors of omission or commission. It is crucial for clinicians to help families obtain clear medical prognoses and management guidelines. In situations of threatened loss, women are more prone than men to attributions involving blame, shame, or guilt, because of societal role expectations of primary caretaker responsibilities for their children, husband, aging parents, and extended family.

For childhood disorders, parents and siblings (especially those close in age to the ill child and where rivalry is strong) are at heightened risk of guilt. They may feel guilty for being spared their own physical suffering and threatened death. Parents may ruminate about possible negligence as a causal factor. For some members, especially siblings, this feeling can be expressed as a general somatic preoccupation or catastrophic fear of suffering the same fate. When there has been a child whose apparent influenza turned out to be leukemia, the mildest respiratory symptoms in another family member can trigger panic. Family members may become overprotective of all their children. In other cases, guilt can surface in self-destructive behaviors (e.g., alcoholism, recklessness).

In my clinical experience, families with the strongest, at times extreme, beliefs about personal responsibility and those with the most severely dysfunctional patterns tend to overemphasize psychosocial factors in the cause or outcome of an illness. For high internal locus-of-control families, a belief in personal responsibility guides all facets of life, including "high stake" situations of threatened loss. A relative lack of acknowledgment of "outrageous fortune" as a factor in an illness can create a powerful nidus for blame, shame, and guilt. For such a family, disability or death implies a failure of will or effort. Anticipatory loss becomes loaded with a second life-versus-death struggle: that of willpower, and possibly, the family's belief system. This sort of family will tend to hold on tenaciously to an ill member. Families guided by an externally oriented belief system, centered around "fate," risk premature extrusion and grieving for the ill member.

Making peace with self, family, and world is a fundamental task in coping with threatened loss, especially in the terminal phase. Several kinds of beliefs complicate this normative process. Foremost, unresolved issues of blame, shame, or guilt seriously compromise movement towards closure and acceptance. Second, some families' beliefs about mastery are rigidly defined as an ability to control the biological unfolding and outcome of an illness. A more flexible definition of competence involves active participation in the overall process. To sustain a family value of personal control during a progressive or terminal phase of an illness, participation in a successful process of letting go needs to replace mastery over biology. When a family is experiencing a loss the difference between a legacy of competence versus defeat is connected to this kind of flexibility in the belief system. Clinicians need to be mindful that families with the strongest and most rigid beliefs about personal responsibility may function very well during earlier stages of threatened loss but are extremely vulnerable if an illness progresses. An attitude that conveys "We understand the risks, and we're going to try and beat this thing" needs to be distinguished from "We *have* to beat this thing."

Larger System Values

Historically, male, middle-class values emphasizing individual achievement and mastery have prevailed in America. We live in an era that promotes personal responsibility and effort as the road out of adversity. From national policy-making to popular psychology (Siegal, 1986; Simonton et. al, 1978), there is a tendency to internalize and localize problems in the individual or family. This societal value can interact powerfully with belief systems in a family facing threatened loss. The consequences of "losing" the battle with disability and death can become infused with a profound sense of public shame and failure. This negatively interpreted experience can alter a family's paradigm for generations. Clinicians need to guard against advocating too strongly a philosophy that the loss could be prevented if only the family took enough responsibility for the illness.

SOCIETAL STIGMA: THE EXAMPLE OF AIDS.   AIDS dramatically illustrates how the process of family coping with anticipatory loss and bereavement is severely compromised by societal stigma. The beliefs/metaphors attached to AIDS (Sontag, 1988) suggest that a restoration of health can only occur after a "moral cleansing" and proper atonement for immorality. Thus, larger system attitudes that victimize families can rival unresolved family problems as a potential cause of interminable grief linked to family guilt or shame. Threatened loss is too often experienced in a context of secrecy, which fosters isolation in the face of an ignominious death. Clinicians can help to remove such blocks, to promote positive rituals, and to facilitate community support for patients and their families.

AIDS is unique in several other ways. Because it is an epidemic, families and caregivers often experience multiple losses and are dealing simultaneously with a number of friends or family who are at various stages of AIDS, and therefore, different stages of anticipatory loss. Clinicians need to be sensitive to the continual immersion in waves of impending death and bereavement surrounding families in high-risk communities. People with AIDS must cope with their own fears of death, while at the same time they may be intimately involved with the threatened loss of their partner or another member of their family or community. One or both parents of a child with AIDS often are confronted with their own diagnosis at the same time as they learn about their infant's. When there are other children in the family, clinicians need to build extended family supports for the nurturance of the children and for planning a future which may not include their parents.

DISCUSSION

Overemphasis on anticipatory loss can itself become emotionally disabling if not counterbalanced by ways to harness that experience to improve the quality of life. In this regard, clinicians can be extremely helpful in assisting families to achieve a healthy balance. For illnesses with long-range risks, families can maintain mastery in the face of uncertainty by (1) acknowledging the possibility of loss, (2) sustaining hope, and (3) building flexibility into family life cycle planning that conserves and adjusts major goals (e.g., child-rearing) and circumvents the forces of uncertainty. Clinicians can help families agree about the conditions under which further family discussion would be useful, and who would be appropriate to include.

In situations of anticipatory loss, we must be cautious about judging the relative usefulness of positive illusions or minimization versus direct confrontation with and acceptance of painful realities. In many clinical situations, both are needed, and the skilled clinician must thread the needle supporting both the usefulness of exaggerated hope and the need for treatment to control the illness or a new complication. From a life cycle perspective, illness, individual, or family transitions are critical times to examine issues of threatened loss and weigh them in light of other developmental considerations. Open discussion and shared decision-making at these junctures will help prevent later blame-guilt cycles if loss occurs. A young adult whose father has cancer in remission may have difficulty leaving home, partly out of fear of never seeing the ill parent again. Promoting frank discussion of feelings between the parent(s) and young adult can be useful. Furthermore, there is greater incentive and importance for a family to confront denial of an illness when there is hope that preventive action or medical treatment can affect the outcome.

On the other hand, most of us cannot tolerate an unrelenting encounter with loss. There is a need for mental and physical respite. Taylor (1989) has described the normal, healthy need for positive illusions, and their importance in successful coping and adaptation. The healthy use of minimization or selective focus on the positive, as well as timely doses of humor, should be distinguished from denial, which is regarded as pathological.

A brush with death provides an opportunity to confront catastrophic fears about loss. This can lead to family members' developing a better appreciation of and perspective on life that results in clearer priorities. Active creation of opportunities can replace procrastination and passive waiting for the "right moment." Threatened loss, by emphasizing life's fragility and preciousness, provides families with an opportunity to heal unresolved issues and develop more immediate, caring relationships. For illnesses in a more advanced stage, clinicians should help families emphasize quality of life by defining goals that are readily attainable and that enrich their everyday lives.

Recent writings (Imber-Black et al., 1988) in the family therapy field have underscored the lack of rituals in many families dealing with loss. Threatened loss often heightens awareness that each family gathering and ritual may be the last together. Clinicians can help families dealing with threatened loss by promoting the timely creation and use of rituals of celebration and inclusion. A family reunion can invigorate a family and serve to coalesce its healing energies to support the ill member and key caretakers. In the context of threatened loss, traditional celebrations offer an opportunity to affirm and improve *all* family relationships. Emotionally distant and cutoff members can be reconnected to family life.

Finally, clinicians working with these families need to consider their own experiences and feelings about loss. Such factors as our transgenerational and family history with threatened or actual loss, our health beliefs, and our current life cycle stage will influence our ability to work effectively with families facing loss.

Fears about our own vulnerability are easily triggered when working with families coping with off-time illnesses. This is especially likely if the patient and family are at the same stage of the life cycle as the therapist. Self-awareness is particularly important if one has the same disorder or is at high risk of illnesses involving loss (e.g., strong family history of cancer or heart disease). Because these situations are so compelling, clinicians who work with a family for an extended period tend to shape their hopes and beliefs with those of the family. This can lead to excessive optimism and forgetting that loss is really possible. Finally, our own unresolved issues related to actual or threatened losses and fears about our own mortality can lead to maintaining excessive emotional distance, avoiding important, often painful discussions related to threatened loss, or becoming overinvolved with a particular family. As we come to accept the limits of our ability to control the uncontrollable and work through unresolved personal losses, we can work more sensitively with the excruciating dilemmas of these families.

REFERENCES

Beavers, W. R. (1982). Healthy, midrange, and severely dysfunctional families. In F. Walsh (Ed.), *Normal family processes*. New York: Guilford.

Becker, E. (1973). *The denial of death*. New York: Free Press.

Boss, P., & Greenberg, J. (1984). Family boundary ambiguity: A new variable in family stress theory. *Family Process, 23*, 535-546.

Boss, P., Caron, W., & Horbal, J. (1988). Alzheimer's disease and ambiguous loss. In C. Chilman, E. Nunnally, & F. Cox (Eds.), *Chronic illness and disability: Families in trouble series* (Vol. 2). Beverly Hills: Sage Publications.

Bowen, M. (1978). Family reaction to death. In *Family therapy in clinical practice*. New York: Jason Aronson Inc.

Carter, B., & McGoldrick, M. (Eds.) (1989). *The changing family life cycle: A framework for family therapy* (2nd ed.). Boston: Allyn & Bacon.

Clayton, P. J., Halikas, J. K., Maurice, W. L., & Robins, E. (1973). Anticipatory grief and widowhood. *British Journal of Psychiatry, 122*, 47-51.

Coleman, S. B., & Stanton, D. M. (1978). The role of death in the addict family. *Journal of Marriage and Family Counselling, 4*, 79-91.

Combrinck-Graham, L. (1985). A developmental model for family systems. *Family Process, 24*, 139-150.

Duvall, E. (1977). *Marriage and family development* (5th ed.). Philadelphia: Lippincott.

Friedman, S. B., Chodoff, P., Mason, J. W., & Hamburg, D. B. (1963). Behavioral observations on parents anticipating the death of a child. *Pediatrics, 32*, 610-622.

Fulton, R., & Gottesman, D. J. (1980). Anticipatory grief: A psychosocial concept reconsidered. *British Journal of Psychiatry, 137*, 45-54.

Futterman, E. H., Hoffman, I., & Sabshin, M. (1972). Parental anticipatory mourning. In B. Schoenberg, A. Carr, A. Kutscher, D. Peretz, & I. Goldberg (Eds.), *Psychosocial aspects of terminal care*. New York: Columbia University Press.

Gerber, I., Rusalem, R., Hannon, N., Battin, D., & Arkin, A. (1975). Anticipatory grief and aged widows and widowers. *Journal of Gerontology, 30(2)*, 225-229.

Glick, I. O., Weiss, R. S., & Parkes, C. M. (1974). *The first year of bereavement*. New York: John Wiley & Sons.

Herz, F. (1989). The impact of death and serious illness on the family life cycle. In B. Carter & M. McGoldrick (Eds.), *The changing family life cycle: A framework for family therapy*. Boston: Allyn & Bacon.

Imber-Black, E., Roberts, J., & Whiting, R. (Eds.) (1988). *Rituals in families and family therapy*. New York: W. W. Norton.

Lefcourt, H. M. (1982). *Locus of control* (2nd ed.). Hillsdale, N.J.: Lawrence Erlbaum Association.

Levinson, D. J. (1978). *The seasons of a man's life*. New York: Knopf.

Levinson, D. J. (1986). A conception of adult development. *American Psychologist, 41:1*, 3-13.

Lindemann, E. (1944). The symptomatology and management of acute grief. *The American Journal of Psychiatry, 101*, 141–148.

McGoldrick, M., & Gerson, R. (1985). *Genograms in family assessment.* New York: Norton Press.

Natterson, J. M., & Knudson, A. G., Jr. (1960). Observations concerning fear of death in fatally ill children and their mothers. *Psychosomatic Medicine, 22*, 465.

Neugarten, B. (1970). Dynamics of transition of middle age to old age: Adaptation and the life cycle. *Journal of Geriatric Psychiatry 4*, 71–87.

Neugarten, B. (1976). Adaptation and the life cycle. *The Counselling Psychologist, 6(1)*, 16–20.

Paul, N., & Grosser, G. (1965). Operational mourning and its role in conjoint family therapy. *Community Mental Health Journal, 1*, 339–345.

Parkes, C. M. (1976). Determinants of outcome following bereavement. *Omega, 6*, 303–323.

Parkes, C. M., & Weiss, R. S. (1983). *Recovery from bereavement.* New York: Basic Books.

Rando, T. (1983). An investigation of grief and adaptation in parents whose children have died from cancer. *Journal of Pediatric Psychology, 8(1)*, 3–20.

Rolland, J. S. (1984). Toward a psychosocial typology of chronic and life-threatening illness. *Family Systems Medicine, 2:3*, 245–263.

Rolland, J. S. (1987a). Chronic illness and the life cycle: A conceptual framework. *Family Process, 26*, 203–221.

Rolland, J. S. (1987b). Family illness paradigms: Evolution and significance. *Family Systems Medicine, 5*, 467–486.

Rolland, J. S. (1989). Chronic illness and the life cycle. In B. Carter & M. McGoldrick (Eds.), *The changing family life cycle: A framework for family therapy* (2nd ed.). Boston: Allyn & Bacon.

Rolland, J. S. (1988a). A conceptual model of chronic and life-threatening illness and its impact on the family. In C. Chilman, E. Nunnally, & F. Cox (Eds.), *Chronic illness and disability.* Beverly Hills: Sage Publications.

Rolland, J. S., & Walsh, F. W. (1988b). Blame, shame and guilt: Family belief systems in chronic and life-threatening disorders. Paper presented at 46th Annual Conference American Association for Marriage and Family Therapy.

Rolland, J. S. (in preparation). *Helping families with chronic and life-threatening disorders.* New York: Basic Books.

Schoenberg, B., Carr, A., Kutscher, A., Peretz, D., & Goldberg, I. (Eds.) (1974). *Anticipatory grief.* New York: Columbia University Press.

Siegel, B. S. (1986). *Love, medicine, and miracles.* New York: Harper & Row.

Simonton, C. O., Mathews-Simonton, S., & Creighton, J. (1978). *Getting well again.* Los Angeles: J. P. Tarcher, Inc.

Sontag, S. (1988). *AIDS and its metaphors.* New York: Farrar, Straus, & Giroux.

Taylor, S. (1989). *Positive illusions: Creative self-deception and the healthy mind.* New York: Basic Books.

Walsh, F., & McGoldrick, M. (1988). Loss and the family life cycle. In C. Falicov (Ed.), *Family transitions.* New York: Guilford.

Wallston, K. A., & Wallston, B. S. (1978). Development of the Multidimensional Health Locus of Control (MHLC) scales. *Health Education Monographs, 6(2)*, 160–170.

Wortman, C., & Silver, R. (1989). The myths of coping with loss. *Journal of Consulting and Clinical Psychology, 57(3)*, 349–357.

9

Ambiguous Loss

PAULINE BOSS

A UNIVERSAL TASK of all families, regardless of cultural diversity, is to resolve loss. For the most part, the larger community helps families to do this through rituals at which friends and family gather. But there are also losses that are not given such public validation. The loss is never officially documented or ritualized. A family member may simply be missing, as are hostages, missing children, and the men still missing-in-action in Southeast Asia. But loved ones can be missing in a family even while they are physically present. For example, they may be psychologically absent because of dementia, being in a coma, or being addicted to drugs, alcohol, or even work. They are physically present but emotionally gone. While the family appears intact, there is still a major void.

Elsewhere I have labeled this phenomenon *boundary ambiguity*, a situation in the family resulting from ambiguous loss. Lack of clarity about the loss of a family member generates confusion and conflict about who is in and who is out of the system. In this chapter, I explain what ambiguous loss is, why it matters, and what can be done to help families to overcome such

This Chapter reviews research presently supported by the National Institute on Aging (Project #IP50-MH40317-01) and the University of Minnesota Agricultural Experiment Station (Project #MIN-52048). Earlier research was done in cooperation with the Naval Health Research Institute, San Diego.

situations. The idea that boundary ambiguity is stressful for families was developed in 1973.*

Boundary ambiguity, a phenomenon in families resulting from the stress of ambiguous loss, is defined as the family's not knowing who is in and who is out of the system. The family may perceive a physically absent member as psychologically present or a physically present member as psychologically absent. In either case, the family boundary is ambiguous. This review is presented to clarify the meaning of boundary ambiguity and to explore its scope and application in research and clinical practice.

A major certainty in families is that over time there will be losses and separations. I posit that focusing on the degree of family boundary ambiguity rather than on specific coping resources may better explain why a family does or does not cope with loss. If a family cannot clarify who is in and who is out of the family system (as in the case of ambiguous loss and separation), it cannot reorganize; the process of morphogenic restructuring in the system is blocked; the system is in limbo.

The first theoretical and research papers on boundary ambiguity focused on ambiguous losses in families of military men declared missing-in-action (MIA) in Vietnam (Boss, 1975, 1977, 1980a). My thinking was influenced by systems theorist Walter Buckley (1967), family sociologist Reuben Hill (1971a, 1971b), and symbolic interactionist Erving Goffman (1974). The construct of boundary ambiguity was presented as a major stress variable with roots in three disciplines: (1) social psychology (symbolic interactionism); (2) sociology (boundary maintenance); and (3) symbolic experiential family therapy (a family's perceptual construction of who is in and who is out of the family system) (see also Boss & Greenberg, 1984).

Based on the family's own perception of the loss rather than quantification of family membership in traditional forms, this work provided a new way to assess and alleviate family crisis after loss. It is especially useful theoretically because the idea allows us to begin to answer the question of why some families are resilient whereas others become immobilized by loss and never recover.

To better understand the theoretical premise about ambiguous loss and the stress it causes families, I first summarize my general assumptions about families and change (Boss, 1988):

1. Families are systems and must maintain their boundaries in spite of internal changes if they are to survive and not collapse under pressure.
2. Family boundaries cannot be maintained by outsiders; they must be

---

*For details about the original research and theory development since then, the reader is referred to summaries and references in Boss, 1987, 1988, 1990, and Boss & Greenberg, 1984.

maintained from the inside, by the family itself. Clear and healthy family boundaries facilitate the management of stressful family life events and enable the family to manage inevitable, normative loss and change. Clear boundaries enable a family to resolve developmental changes in its members as well as to manage unexpected events or situations.

3. In order for a family system to maintain its boundaries, family members must know who is in and who is out of the family. This is determined by asking all family members to give both their *individual* and *collective* perceptions of who is in the family. Family boundaries are also determined by asking who is present at times of family celebrations and rituals.

4. A significant barrier to family stress management, then, is the ambiguity surrounding a loss experience when we do not know if the person is in or out of the family system.

5. Some degree of ambiguity is normal in any family, but long-term ambiguity is a severe stressor and will make vulnerable even the strongest families.

6. Although the idea of boundary ambiguity as dysfunctional grew out of the MIA family research, it appears to have relevance for other family events of loss, such as chronic illness and death.

7. When an event of loss cannot be changed, change is still possible in the family's *perception* of that event.

The degree of boundary ambiguity is critical to understanding families encountering the stress of change. Boundary ambiguity in families develops in either of two ways. First, the loss can present itself as ambiguous, that is, facts surrounding the event are lacking or unclear; there is no certainty about what is happening or how it will end. Such ambiguous losses for a family would occur, for example, if a loved one were taken hostage or declared missing-in-action. The family does not know where the missing person is or whether he or she is dead or alive. Another example of ambiguity in the event of loss is chronic illness, such as dementia or being in a coma. Family members know their loved one is going to die but they do not know when. Without a clear-cut diagnosis there is no clear solution. Such lingering situations of ambiguity are extremely hard on families.

There are also times when the event is clear, when a diagnosis is clear, and when the community of friends and relatives can clearly see the loss but family members ignore the facts and close their eyes to reality. Their construction of reality is based on an unreadiness to accept the loss. The facts are in but their collective perception makes the loss ambiguous. Such families keep physically absent persons psychologically present long after they are clearly dead and buried, or they close out physically present family members long before they are dead. In other words, some families construe a reality that artificially clarifies the family boundary because they cannot tolerate a sudden death or a lingering illness.

Whether the ambiguity begins in the event itself or stems primarily from the family's perception of reality, it is through this family perceptual window that therapists can enter. Only through the family members' reframing of how they see the situation can change take place. We must therefore see the loss *through their eyes* before we can know how to support and guide their resolution of it.

Based on these assumptions about families and loss, research has been conducted with various samples over the years. The following propositions have been updated from the original list (see Boss & Greenberg, 1984) but remain basically the same:

1. The higher the boundary ambiguity in the family system, the greater the helplessness (low mastery) and the greater the likelihood of individual and family dysfunction (depression and conflict). Boundary ambiguity can result from the outside world not giving the family enough information about the event of loss, *or* it can arise inside the family from its own denial of the loss. In either case, the ultimate indicators of who is in and who is out of the family are based on the family's collective perception, as well as individual perceptions, and most important, on the congruence among family members' individual perceptions.

2. In the short run, family boundary ambiguity may not be dysfunctional. That is, in the period immediately following an unexpected loss or separation, a period of boundary ambiguity may give the family time cognitively to accept the information that the status quo has been broken and that the loss is real. Family members may use this early period to deny the loss or to construe other meanings about what has happened to them. Over time, however, a resilient family system will begin to accept new information about what is lost, so that coping processes and reorganization can begin. Through collective and individual cognitive restructuring of the meaning of the loss, the boundaries of the system are clarified and more realistically maintained.

3. If a high degree of family boundary ambiguity persists over time, the family system is at risk for becoming highly stressed and subsequently dysfunctional. Holding a system in an ambiguously bounded state blocks cognition as well as the emotional and behavioral responses that begin the restructuring processes. For example, because of the persistence of ambiguous loss, families with a chronically ill member

may deny either the person's illness or the ill person's presence in the system, even while he or she is still physically present. Chronic illnesses, especially those which are in themselves uncertain in their progress and outcome (such as Alzheimer's disease), are more likely to result in a high degree of family boundary ambiguity than illnesses that are more predictable and treatable (see Rolland, Chapter 8). Although family members know the ill member is going to die, they do not know when (or, as in the case of remission, they are never quite sure whether the person is dying), so their stress will be extremely high. They are immobilized.

4. Families in varying cultural contexts differ in how they perceive their family boundaries — even after similar events of loss or separation. For example, the family's community or cultural context will influence how readily the system can accept information about events of loss or change. This holds true for a normative loss, such as the death of a grandparent, as well as for unexpected and catastrophic loss, such as the death of a baby, or prolonged deteriorating illnesses, such as Alzheimer's disease, which can pose great financial as well as personal loss. Other losses viewed differently in varying contexts are stillbirths, abortions, and miscarriages. These too are real losses for many couples, but, as with all these examples, it is the individual and collective perceptions that should guide our intervention and support.

General Strategies for Support and Clinical Intervention

What can we do about ambiguous loss? Our therapeutic goal is to help people to cope with a difficult and persistent situation in a more resilient way, one that allows them to be as masterful over their own destiny as possible, even while the family lives with the reality of a situation that lacks clarity and closure.

Our research indicates that, rather than limiting our focus to specific stressor events or coping strategies, it is crucial to assess the family's degree of boundary ambiguity after loss, since ambiguity, on top of the loss itself, generates family and individual immobilization and subsequent dysfunction. The following strategies are recommended for therapists who work with all types of ambiguous losses in families. They may range from severe to mild, short-term to long-lasting, normative to catastrophic, but in all cases the basic criterion is that family members are unclear about the absence or presence of a family member.

First, label the ambiguity as a major stressor for family members. Families report that just having the situation labeled by a professional as ambiguous and hearing empathy for that dilemma helps them to withstand a lack of clarity. Putting a label of ambiguity on the situation helps families to cope with it.

Second, provide a setting and structure for family meetings so that family members of several generations can sit together and hear one another's perceptions of the situation and what meaning they are making of it. Where teamwork toward problem solving is blocked, help family members to collaborate and support one another's efforts more effectively. If perceptions continue to differ, help family members tolerate one another's views. Insisting that all family members view the loss in an identical way will only impede the resolution of it.

Third, provide as much information as possible about their situation — technical as well as psychosocial. Families can often solve their own problems if given enough information to make decisions and change behavior. We can empower them to find the information they need about their loved one's situation and prognosis. Coach them on gathering pieces of information to clarify a loss situation. In some situations more active advocacy may be needed to press medical experts or other authorities for more information than has been forthcoming. In cases of life-threatening illness, psychoeducational interventions, especially management guidelines, are most helpful.

Fourth, provide families with sources and choices of support for their situation — peer as well as professional. Provide them with phone numbers, addresses, and names of people and groups that match their particular loss. Professionally led groups and self-help groups of families confronting similar loss situations can be valuable. Social contact and interaction, rather than isolation, are needed to stimulate change and adaptation to ambiguous loss.

Finally, and perhaps most important, families must be encouraged and provided a format within which they can work to find some meaning in their loss. Primarily, this means we must provide them with a format where they can talk together about how they construe what is happening to them. My experience has been that individual family members express different attributions over time so it is important that all family members hear each other's constructions of reality even as they change. Congruence of family perceptions will not happen without process and interaction. Also, it is important that blame and self-blame be minimized. The therapist may be most helpful in providing a format by which other family members can voice less incriminating attributions for the family dilemma. This is important for change because blame and guilt can become a major block against recovery in an already difficult situation of loss. Also, if the situation is interpreted as punishment from God or punishment from a spouse or parent, then resolution of an ambiguous loss is also much more difficult. Whenever family members feel blamed, by one another or an outside force, activated defenses tend to prevent the acceptance of new information and options. Attributions and meanings of unclear losses of loved ones are most effectively discussed in groups — family or peer — rather than in individual sessions.

SPECIFIC STRATEGIES:
PHYSICAL PRESENCE WITH PSYCHOLOGICAL ABSENCE

For families in which the person is emotionally missing but physically present, strategies and supports must aim at clarifying on what basis the absent person is still in and on what basis he or she is out. For example, an Alzheimer's patient who was once an expert carpenter may now only use hammer and nails to play with wood. If family members do not change their perception of the role the psychologically absent person can realistically play, they will continue to be frustrated and disappointed; they may even be in danger. A person who did all the driving, all the money management, or all the cooking must relinquish valued functions and be helped to allow others to take them over. In addition to the loss of part of one's identity and role performance, a parent or a mate must now be viewed as a dependent who needs care and supervision. This requires reassessment at regular intervals over progressive stages of the illness (see Rolland, Chapter 8). The person may get better or become even more helpless and child-like.

It is important to help the family to find new or different areas of functioning that can maximize the individual's participation in family life. Outsiders may be useful in helping close family members to make regular assessments, since caregivers may adapt before realizing major changes are in order. Extended family members can help; so can friends, neighbors, and clergy. Our major task as therapists is to widen the circle of support and intervention to include the community and kin networks when there is ambiguous loss. We alone do not have the power to bring about the major changes necessary in roles, rules, or rituals in such families. Two- and three-generational family meetings (even via speaker phone) are useful and powerful. They help the overwhelmed and sometimes guilty caregiver to see reality and brave necessary changes. Or if the caregiver sees the daily situation and other family members do not, the caregiver may receive support from some other family member to convince those reluctant that things will never again be the same and that change is necessary.

Spouses of Alzheimer patients frequently say that when they and the family are able to change their perceptions of the patient to become more realistic, then they can set boundaries, reassign roles, and take charge in new ways. A wife becomes the manager of the family finances and driver of the family car; a husband becomes the family cook. The therapist can help families to negotiate a reallocation of roles and responsibilities that fits within their belief system and with the needs and abilities of each generation of family members. Even if the players do not change, stress levels in the family go down when necessary tasks of daily life are performed.

STRATEGIES: PHYSICAL ABSENCE WITH PSYCHOLOGICAL PRESENCE

For families in which a person is physically missing, other strategies are in order. First, if there is a chance that the missing person will be found or will return alive and the family wants to take that gamble, therapists should encourage the family to keep the absent person present by continued inclusion in rituals and celebrations. Family members might buy holiday and birthday gifts for the missing person and store them for an anticipated return; they might write letters or create audio and videotapes of missed holidays and celebrations so the missing person can catch up after returning. Finally, we encourage family members to ask the community to reinforce their hope with visible symbols, such as the yellow ribbons used for hostages even today, or with annual vigils and candle light ceremonies used by the families of men still missing-in-action or families of missing children. Frequent family meetings are necessary so that checks can be made on the congruence among family members' perceptions of hope or hopelessness for their loved one's return. And if realistic chances for recovery fade, therapists need to help the family brace for disappointment and loss of hope. Over time, disagreements may arise in families about differing perceptions of reality. It is useful to make explicit such disagreements among family members about the absent person lest they become family secrets. (It is, in fact, conflict about differing perceptions that stimulates change.) This is precisely the reason resolving ambiguous loss is slower, if not impossible, when working with only one person as opposed to working with several generations of family members.

If and when the family comes to the agreement that the situation is hopeless and the person is not coming back, then a ritual is in order. The therapist can suggest guidelines, but in the end it is the family that should create this ritual. It should involve not only immediate family members but the community as well. Although it may be more difficult than organizing traditional wakes, funerals, or sitting shivah, some ritual needs to be created to "put to rest" the loss of a missing person. This can be done with memorial services and such symbols as photographs or other representations of the lost person. In this way, family members can at least symbolically gain some sense of closure about their loss, in spite of its ambiguity, as the community around them helps validate and memorialize what has happened.

Helping Families to Tolerate Ambiguous Losses

Ideally, the inevitable losses of family members over the life span will be clearcut. Such losses from death are not easy to bear, nor does one ever completely get over missing the absent person. However, there is less preoccupation than we find when losses are ambiguous. Grieving can be resolved more easily; the family can change and move on. Family members miss their loved one but they are not driven by or immobilized by loss because the situation is clear; the facts are in. After a period of grieving, they can more easily make decisions, choices, and changes. There is congruence in how family, friends, and community see the loss; they even gather together to grieve as a public validation of that loss. Things are sad but clear. There is little ambiguity about what to do next. Change is easier because the loss is clearer.

But often this is not the case. There are many chronic illnesses, events, or situations in which family members are physically present but emotionally gone. Sometimes recovery is possible — as with addiction to drugs, chemicals, or work. But when there is no recovery in sight (as with Alzheimer's disease), or even when there is remission yet the chance that the illness will return, families must learn to live with ambiguity. The question then becomes one of how to increase a family's tolerance for ambiguous loss. How can we live functionally with uncertainty? How can the boundaries of a family be maintained when it is not clear who is in and who is out of the system? Based on research and clinical observations, this is a summary of what such families have found helpful:

1. The parents (or siblings, if the parents are too elderly) of an emotionally absent offspring must take charge as a team. If it is a spouse who is affected, the remaining spouse must take charge. Everyone must increase mastery skills. For siblings, this may mean everyone getting involved in caretaking tasks and responsibilities, not just the women or the one who happens to live nearby. For traditionally socialized older women, this may mean taking charge of money management, driving, and all decision making — even if her husband is still alive. Younger women in the family may be helpful in teaching an older woman, especially one who has been a fulltime homemaker, how to gather information from financial consultants, community agencies, and medical centers to enable her to become more adept at making decisions in the world outside the home. Older males can also learn from the younger men in the family how to cook and do laundry.

2. The spouse, couple, and family must become flexible to enable them to reassign traditionally designated gender roles. It is necessary for a

husband to cook and do housework if his wife is ill; it's necessary for a wife to drive and manage money if her husband is ill. It is necessary for all siblings, regardless of gender, to participate in the caretaking of ambiguous losses in their family. Gender should not excuse or entrap anyone in the role of caregiver and nurturer. Younger family members should be encouraged in family meetings to teach and model flexibility in roles for their more traditionally socialized elders. Overall, women more than men have been designated as nurturers and emotional care-takers when family members are ambiguously lost to families. This is too heavy a burden for wives, daughters, and daughters-in-law; men and boys must also be encouraged to participate in nurturant care-taking.

3. The family should be encouraged to continue its usual rituals and celebrations. Do not skip birthdays or anniversaries just because someone is ill, but adapt these celebrations to include the ill person. Evening celebrations may be moved to afternoons. Restaurants may be foregone for home celebrations, but the celebration should take place nevertheless. For those rituals that involve individual participation — such as attending church or synagogue, or even shopping — the healthy spouse must be encouraged to continue participation. In addition, the special events and rituals of siblings should not be ignored just because the status of one child is ambiguous. Children who are fully present have needs also; parents must attend to them and not be totally preoc-cupied with the ambiguously lost child.

4. For families in which the ambiguity of the loss cannot be clarified, encourage regular use of respite care as well as community and extend-ed family support. Respite and connections with other people will minimize feelings of entrapment and helplessness for those living with ambiguous loss. Since nothing can be done to fix the situation or make it go away, family members must take care of themselves by taking a time-out several times a week, if not daily. Ideally, a network meeting of family and community people should take place to decide how to make time-outs possible for those who are routinely responsible for the emotionally absent person.

RESEARCH FINDINGS AND FUTURE DIRECTIONS

We have found that caregivers of Alzheimer's patients have more depression when they are less mastery-oriented and that they are less mastery-oriented when they perceive a high degree of boundary ambiguity in their family system. That is, when the caregiver perceives a mate as emotionally absent, mastery and problem-solving are blocked for the caregiver who is, thus, more depressed (Boss, Caron, Horbal, 1988; Boss, Caron, Horbal, & Mortimer, 1990). This research supports the therapeutic goal of removing as much ambiguity as possible so caregivers in families are not blocked in the mastery of the situation. Where some ambiguities cannot be clarified or resolved, families must learn to live with uncertainty. Paradoxically ambiguity is reduced when there is a clear expectation that the course or outcome is uncertain.

CONCLUSION

While there are many theories of loss and separation, heretofore there has been no theory about how to work with families when they are not certain if the family member is lost or not. When first working with families of the men who were missing-in-action in Vietnam and Cambodia, I thought this phenomenon was unique and rarely found in everyday family life. Over the years, however, I have come to realize that ambiguous loss is a common situation that, to some degree, occurs to all of us at times throughout the life cycle. Letting go yet staying connected to children and to parents; breaking up significant relationships, divorce and remarriage — all are common events in which family boundaries become grey, and often remain so throughout the inevitable transitions of life.

Therapists more often see the less than normative cases. We see families in which children are ill, elderly are frail, mates are missing, or loved ones are in a coma or demented. Our task is to guide families in the development of tolerance for losses that remain ambiguous. In this process of labeling, we help them to identify their sources of stress and immobilization — the ambiguity as much as the event itself. Once labeled, the situation can be managed. In this way, we help the families to help themselves. We guide them toward clarifying what is lost and what is still present — thus minimizing the ambiguity that blocks grieving and resolution of loss. We guide them as they gradually learn to tolerate shades of grey.

Most families can cope with most losses if they know what is happening, what the facts are, and where the lost person is in body and in mind. When we work with families who do not have the answers to these questions and cannot get them even with concerted effort, we may find the ideas about role and boundary ambiguity helpful. This is not a disease model; it is a family stress model. It is preventive as much as therapeutic. When there is ambiguous loss families are troubled and stressed. Care is taken not to attribute blame to the family by implying that family pathology necessarily caused their difficulties with loss.

The family stress management approach to loss is relatively new in the field of family therapy. We believe the approach provides a theoretical base for work with families on the task of resolving losses. Surviving an ambiguous loss is difficult for even the strongest of families. Whatever we can do to provide clarity for easing their stress will be useful in building resiliency and in reconstruction of family life.

REFERENCES

Boss, P. (1975). Psychological father presence in the missing-in-action (MIA) family: Its effects on family functioning. *Proceedings: Third annual joint medical meeting concerning POW/MIA matters*, pp. 61–65. Center for Prisoner of War Studies, Naval Health Research Center, San Diego, CA.

Boss, P. (1977). A clarification of the concept of psychological father presence in families experiencing ambiguity of boundary. *Journal of Marriage and the Family 39(1)*, 141–151.

Boss, P. (1980a). The relationship of psychological father presence, wife's personal qualities, and wife/family dysfunction in families of missing fathers. *Journal of Marriage and the Family 42(3)*, 541–549.

Boss, P. (1980b). Normative family stress: Family boundary changes across the lifespan. *Family Relations 29(4)*, 445–450.

Boss, P. (1987). Family stress: Perception and context. In M. Sussman & S. Steinmetz (Eds.), *Handbook on marriage and the family* (pp. 695–723). New York: Plenum.

Boss, P. (1988). *Family stress management*. Newbury Park, CA: Sage.

Boss, P. (1990). The influence of child development and social psychology training on research and therapy for families stressed with ambiguous loss. In F. Kaslow (Ed.), *Voices in family psychology*. Newbury Park, CA: Sage.

Boss, P., Caron, W., & Horbal, J. (1988). Alzheimer's disease and ambiguous loss. In C. Chilman, F. Cox & A. Nunnally (Eds.), *Families in trouble*. Newbury Park, CA: Sage.

Boss, P., Caron, W., Horbal, J., & Mortimer, J. (1990). Predictors of depression in caregivers of dementia patients: Boundary ambiguity and mastery. *Family Process, 29*, 245–254.

Boss, P., & Greenberg, J. (1984). Family boundary ambiguity: A new variable in family stress theory. *Family Process, 23(4)*, 535–546.

Buckley, W. (1967). *Sociology and modern systems theory*. Englewood Cliffs, NJ: Prentice-Hall.

Goffman, E. (1974). *Frame analysis: An essay on the organization of experience*. New York: Harper & Row.

Hill, R. (1971a). *Families under stress*. Westport, CT: Greenwood. (Reprint of 1949 ed.).

Hill, R. (1971b). Modern systems theory and the family: A confrontation. *Social Science Information 3*, 7–26.

10

Mourning in Different Cultures

MONICA MCGOLDRICK   RHEA ALMEIDA
PAULETTE MOORE HINES   ELLIOTT ROSEN
NYDIA GARCIA-PRETO   EVELYN LEE

A story is told of a Chinese servant who wanted time off to go to the funeral of his cousin. His grudging employer asked him how soon he thought his uncle would eat the bowl of rice he planned to leave at the graveside. His answer: About the same time that your aunt who died last week smells the flowers you placed on her grave.

—Schiff, 1977, p. 9

EVERY CULTURE THROUGHOUT history has had its own ways of mourning. Over time and through immigration and contact between different groups in the U.S., mourning patterns of groups have changed and continue to change all the time. Yet values and practices regarding bereavement still vary in profound ways, so that clinicians should be careful about definitions of "normality" in assessing families' responses to death (McGoldrick, 1989; McGoldrick, Hines, Garcia-Preto, & Lee, 1986; McGoldrick, Pearce, & Giordano, 1982).

Like everyone else, clinicians have their own notions of what is healthy mourning, concerning both emotional expression and the time it should last. We must never be too sure we know what is best or most appropriate for others in dealing with their grief. Others' negative judgment of how much mourning is enough and how much is too much may compound the difficulties of grieving for family members. The dominant American norm is that a certain, moderate level of emotional expression, and even depression, is "required," but that this should last only for a "reasonable" period of time — perhaps a year or two for the death of a close relative (Wortman & Silver, 1989).

It has been said that Jackie Kennedy, with her magnificent public stoicism at the nationally televised funeral of her husband, "set mourning back a hundred years" (Schiff, 1977, p. 16). Others might say, on the contrary, that Jackie Kennedy provided a remarkable model of courage and fortitude under excruciatingly trying circumstances. Wortman and Silver (1989), in their recent review of the research on response to loss, concluded that a substantial proportion of the population tends not to express excessive distress or depression either in the short run or the long run after a loss, while others express major distress in both the short and long run. They conclude that we have a lot more to learn about people's differing reactions to a loss before making gross generalizations about how much grieving is necessary to prevent long-term dysfunctions of "unresolved mourning." They also raise serious questions about the widespread clinical assumptions about the need to mourn and "get it out" in the period right after a loss. They question equally the unfounded assumption that anyone who has not "completed" mourning within a couple of years is somehow abnormal.

The manner of, as well as the length of time assumed normal for, mourning differs greatly from culture to culture. In certain Mediterranean countries, such as Greece and Italy, for example, women traditionally have worn black for the rest of their lives after a husband's death. The Empress of Austria, whose husband died on April 1, 1922, wore black for 67 years, until she died on March 15, 1989, and even then her burial was held up two weeks until the anniversary of his death, when he was reinterred with her. In Italy it is not at all uncommon for family members to jump into the grave when the coffin is lowered. In India, even into the 20th century, widows were expected to throw themselves onto the funeral pyre, a sacrifice for their husbands' life after death.

At the opposite extreme, Americans of British ancestry tend to value a "no muss, no fuss," rational way of experiencing the loss of family members. Among such groups, funerals are carried out in the most pragmatic, practical way. As one friend put it when explaining why he had not attended the funeral of his twin sister, "What would have been the point of spending money on the airfare to get there? She was already dead."

WASPs tend to prefer to die in hospitals where they are not an inconvenience to their family and where their dependence doesn't force them to incur any emotional obligations. In hospitals, care is provided on the "rational" basis of fee for service. For other ethnic groups, however, a death outside the family's emotional and physical environment is experienced as a double tragedy. Groups that value human interdependence, like Italians, Greeks, Puerto Ricans, and East Indians, consider it an unnatural deprivation not to care for a family member in such time of need.

Cultures even differ in major ways about public versus private expressions of grief. In Puerto Rican culture, women in particular "are expected to express their sorrow dramatically through displays of seizure-like attacks and uncontrollable emotions" (Osterweis, Solomon, & Green, 1984). But in Southeast Asian societies, although both men and women participate in public displays of emotion, in private they are expected to be composed and stoical about their feelings.

American culture has been moving increasingly toward the dominant WASP model of minimizing all expression and rituals for dealing with death. Through legislation, custom, and public health and work regulations considerable social control is exercised over the process. Funeral rituals have been taken over and commercialized by the funeral industry. The allowable leave for bereavement in the workplace (usually one to three days) severely limits performance of traditional practices of various cultural groups toward death and mourning.

In all the cultures of which we are aware, expectations for men and women in dealing with death differ dramatically (McGoldrick, Garcia-Preto, Hines, & Lee, 1989). In many cultures women are the chief mourners, or there are hired mourners. On the other hand, in some cultures women are excused from funerals because they are considered to be "too upset" to handle the death. In the United States women typically assume the major role in handling the social and emotional tasks of bereavement, from the expression of grief and caretaking of the terminally ill to meeting the needs of surviving family members, while men arrange for the funeral, choose the coffin, pay the fees, and in general handle the "administrative" tasks of death.

It is important for therapists to appreciate an ethnic group's particular attitudes about mourning and to find out from a family what its members believe about the nature of death, the rituals that should surround it, and the expectations of afterlife. Often a failure to carry out death rituals contributes to a family's experience of unresolved loss. In fact, because of our culture's tendency to minimize the need for rituals and the dominance of professional helpers in the death process, family members often ignore the personal meaning of death for them. They may regard lingering emotional reactions as a sign of weakness or as being "uncultivated" or superstitious.

Helping family members deal with a loss often means showing respect for their particular cultural heritage and encouraging them actively to determine how they will commemorate the death of a loved relative. While it is generally better to encourage families toward openness about death, it is also crucial to respect their cultural values and timing for dealing with the emotional aftermath of a loss. It is especially important to ask several questions about a particular cultural group's traditions:

1. What are the prescribed rituals for handling dying, the dead body, the disposal of the body, rituals to commemorate the loss?
2. What are the group's beliefs about what happens after death?
3. What do they believe about appropriate emotional expression and integration of a loss experience?
4. What are the gender rules for handling the death?
5. Are certain deaths particularly stigmatized (e.g., suicide) or traumatic for the group (e.g., the death of a child in Puerto Rican culture)?

In the following discussion we will consider six different cultural patterns for dealing with death and the implications for family intervention with each.

IRISH FAMILIES
by Monica McGoldrick

For Irish families, death is generally considered the most significant life cycle transition (McGoldrick, 1982) and family members will go to great lengths to give the dead person "a good send-off" to the life beyond death. They make it a point to attend all wakes and funerals of family members and friends, sparing no expense for drink and other arrangements, even if they have very little money. According to a familiar Irish joke, the way an Irishman asks a woman to marry him is to say, "How'd you like to be buried with my people?" The Irish think about their own funerals, often encouraging others to plan for a good celebration. And they often refer to their presence even after death: "Be sure to have a drink for me at my wake," or as my own Aunt Mamie used to say, "Make sure they carry me out from Casey's (funeral home) and be sure they put my glasses on, because I want to see who's there!"

The Irish, like American Blacks, traditionally delayed a funeral for days so that all family members could get there. Such customs undoubtedly relate to their belief that life in this world is generally full of suffering, so that death brings a release to a better world in the afterlife. (Actually they believe that all except the saints will have to spend a period of time in Purgatory, atoning for their sins, on their way to Heaven, but all except the worst sinners will finally make it.) As Shannon (1966) has described it:

Every Irishman was prepared to shake hands with Doom, since that gentleman had been so frequent a visitor in the past. He had no difficulty believing Christianity's doctrines of evil and original sin. These were the most congenial truths of his religion, for they were pertinent in organizing his own experience. It could not be otherwise in a captive, overcrowded society living on the economic ragged edge on an island where the forces of nature met few human barriers. This was life on the land, hard and lonely. Melancholy in these circumstances was a common cast of mind, death familiar and even looked forward to, and opportunities for social gathering the more dearly prized. Irish social customs accommodated and reflected these needs. The Irish wake, that national institution, expressed death's integral role. (p. 8)

Unlike Black families, who openly grieve at their funerals, the Irish are much more likely to get drunk, tell stories and jokes, and relate to the wake as a kind of party, with little or no overt expression of grief. Traditionally, wakes were often far merrier than weddings (Evans, 1957; Suilleabhain, 1967). There is an old Irish saying, "Sing a song at a wake, and shed a tear when a child is born." In the past, the Irish generally practiced wake amusements, "those bizarre forms of jolliness with which the Irish celebrated death — [which] involved kissing, mock marriages, and gross phallic symbolism, as well as 'playing tricks on the corpse'" (Greeley, 1972, p. 55). Humor has for centuries been one of the main Irish mechanisms for survival. It has even been speculated that a central element in the grotesque humor of Irish comedy is the result of the Irish preoccupation with ridiculing death — not infrequently by life-affirming sexual activity (Greeley, 1981).

The tradition was to have an all-night vigil with the corpse, which was not to be left alone until burial. Often this became an excuse for drinking, joking, and storytelling (Delaney, 1973). Perhaps, if the corpse was a male, he would be included in the card game, toasted, or maybe a drink would even be put in his hand. He might even be gotten out for a dance (Suilleabhain, 1967). At wakes in general, drink would be served and clay pipes smoked. While the clay pipes are now gone, the drinking generally remains, along with the jokes and storytelling. The last thing you would want is to have a "boring" funeral, and the best thing one can say about a "successful" Irish wake is that the deceased would have really enjoyed it. "Wouldn't Pat have loved it! Too bad he can't be here to enjoy it with us." Since humor is universally appreciated among the Irish, jokes and stories would also be seen as a fitting way to celebrate the death of a senior woman in the family, though these practices would, of course, be more common with males of a certain age (Evans, 1957) and would seldom occur with young adults or children or where the death was very traumatic for the family.

The Irish believed that it was important to have the window open at the moment of death so that the spirit could escape. They would place salt or tobacco on the body. They made it a point as well to send two people out to tell all the neighbors, and also the livestock and the bees, of the death. The Irish have a long history of beliefs in all sorts of spirits: leprechauns, banshees, pookahs, faeries. The banshee was a spirit particularly connected with death, a beautiful, pale, thin woman wearing white, whose appearance and "keening" (wailing or moaning) were a sure omen of imminent death. While most educated Irish would deny any belief in ghosts, there still may be a certain part of their minds where such beliefs persist. Joking may occur about whether the corpse is really dead, and there may be superstitions about what caused the death and what else must be done so that the "soul of the departed will rest in peace." It was after all, the Irish, who invented Halloween, a night when the dead walk the earth and play tricks on the living. They often do believe that the dead can see us and that, unless certain things go right, their spirits are restless or disapproving. They may be very reluctant to discuss such beliefs, maybe even to admit them to themselves, and it requires considerable patience and sensitivity to sit with the Irish until they are ready to trust that they can talk about what they are feeling. Such discussion does not come easily to them.

Clinically, the greatest difficulty is that family members are often quite unable to share their pain about the loss at all. Once the funeral is over, things are supposed to return to normal. Even before impending death, the Irish tend to suffer alone and in silence, their laughter often being a way to cover their hurt. Unlike groups who prefer to gather family members around at the moment of death, the Irish are often extremely uncomfortable with such situations, preferring to suffer alone (Zborowski, 1968).

The therapist may find it easier to explore unresolved mourning with a single individual or at most two members of a family rather than gathering the entire family together. It may also help to encourage private experiencing of the mourning, through individual visits to the grave, or letters written to or about the deceased. Where some family members prefer directness and are disturbed by the other family members' tendency toward mystification about a death, the differences in their reactions may be extremely upsetting for both. The person who wants to discuss a death may be seen as morbid and even labeled as crazy. One Irish immigrant, who had been unable to return to Ireland when both of his parents died, said, "Well, you can't just go around feeling sorry for yourself, can you?" For ten years he had not mentioned the deaths to anyone, not even his wife.

It is important in therapy to protect family members who want to deal with their feelings of loss so that they do not intensify the anxiety of, or precipitate rejection by, others in the family. Among the Irish, negative feelings toward the deceased are especially difficult to deal with. One young man, whose mother had died when he was 14, was troubled by her being treated as a saint by his father and older sisters. His own memories of his mother were of someone who was rather cold and distant. When he finally got up the courage to talk to his father about these memories, the father's response was, "God and your mother will forgive you for what you are saying." Therapeutically, it was important to allow the son room for his feelings at the same time that it was necessary to be empathic with the father's need to idealize his wife. Interestingly, two weeks after the son brought up the idea that perhaps his mother was not a saint, the father began dating for the first time since the wife's death five years earlier.

HINDU INDIAN FAMILIES
by Rhea Almeida

In Hindu culture* death is just another phase of the life cycle, bringing about a rebirth of being.

> He who is born begins to die. He who dies begins to live. Birth and death are merely doors of entry and exit on the stage of this world. In reality no one comes, no one goes. Brahma or the eternal alone exists. (Shivanand, 1979, p. 19)

Hindus believe that life begins before birth and continues after death. They see our lives on this earth as merely passages in time and believe that we are destined to our fate and have no power to alter it. They believe that at the moment of death the soul leaves the body and enters another being to being to continue the evolution of its karma, until finally it evolves, often through multiple incarnations of the person through cycles of birth, life, and re-death, to a final passage into "nirvana." This is the ultimate spiritual life to which Indians aspire. All of life is structured around sacrifices and rituals, the most important of which occur at the time of death. Hindus believe it is important that the dying person has completed all his or her worldly responsibilities, such as marrying all daughters and granddaughters; paying off any debts, since credit is not an Indian custom; saying goodbye to friends

---

*India has 800,000 million people of varying racial characteristics and religions. Hindus, who make up about 80% of the population (*The Europa Year Book*, 1989), are mainly in the south and west, Muslims and Sikhs are concentrated in the north, and Christians on the southwestern coasts, along with a tiny ancient community of Jews. Despite this diversity, the Hindu ideas regarding caste and karma are pervasive. In the U.S., since the 1965 immigration law eliminated national quotas, the Indian population has risen to about 200,000, largely around New York City and in California (Jensen, 1980). Most earlier Indian immigrants were professionals, from the upper castes. Now, however, the primary immigrant group are untouchables, who, in spite of the long Hindu tradition of passivity and accepting one's fate, have moved toward other values and are seeking a better life.

and family members; and reciting the name of God so that when death comes the passage onward will be handled smoothly.

When a person dies there are many rituals to be carried out. The body of the dying person is placed as close to the ground as possible to allow for an absorption of the spirit by the earth. Readings from the Bhagavad Gita (Hindu bible) are offered by Brahmin priests or elder members of the upper caste community. A close friend or relative usually bathes the body with soap and curd to symbolize life, and then dresses it. The body faces north with feet directed south to prepare for rebirth. To symbolize loss, it is wrapped in a white cloth measuring one-quarter less than the length of the coffin. No food or drink is offered from the house of the deceased for 10 to 12 days, after which family life is resumed, although women over 25 are expected to remain in mourning for life. The structure of this process is vital to the beliefs of pollutants and purity about rebirth and the final transmigration (Radhakrishnan, 1977).

The lower one's position in the caste system* the more death rituals are required to assist in the process of rebirth and death, which will ultimately lead the person to the tranquility of life after death: the afterlife (Toynbee, 1968). It is crucial that the death rites be performed as prescribed. Otherwise there is great fear that the person will be reborn to the same karma or life fate, and will not progress toward the desired spiritual afterlife.

The Indian belief in karma and transmigration of the soul provide a means of justifying one's experience, no matter how deprived or painful life on this earth may be (Bardhan, 1974). Karma is the belief that one's current life is fate, unchangeable. However, one can influence one's later destiny through this life's actions. Transmigration is the process of successive sacrificial offerings through death and rebirth by which one evolves into nirvana. Sacrifice** is essential to detach from pollution and obtain purity of being if the final state of nirvana is to be attained (Baechler, 1975). Hindu beliefs embody and glorify passivity and sacrifice (Smith, 1989).

Indians' concept of time is different from that of Americans. They are

---

*The caste system of India is an ancient system of stratification, based on Hindu beliefs about purity and pollution. Purity relates to the ability to lead a totally spiritual life and abstain from bodily "decadences." Pollution is the religious belief about groups of people who exist at the lower end of a rigidly stratified system that explains their current life dilemma as an attribution of fate (karma). Within this hierarchy of purity and pollution, the Brahmins have a superior position to the Untouchables, who are just below the lowest caste (Kamaraju & Ramana, 1984).

**Suffering and sacrifice in this life are self-disciplines toward a higher, more spiritual essence of being. Thus the Hindu yogi, whose position in society is even higher than that of the priest, fasts for long periods, eschews sex and sustenance from human relationships, and concentrates all energy on spiritual enlightenment in preparation for nirvana. Interested readers are referred to the "Vedas" (560 B.C.), original sacred writings of the Brahmins, to understand the different philosophical reconstructions of karma and rebirth between Hinduism and Buddhism (Kane, 1941).

past and future (nirvana) oriented. Present events and experiences are explained only as they relate to past actions (karma) or future life (transmigration). One's fate in life can be explained through previous life actions and may be altered in the afterlife by present actions. Life on this earth is part of a much larger context of life and death (Stevenson, 1920).

Women have historically experienced the same lack of status and rights as the lower castes (Altekar, 1959; Bardhan, 1982; Krishnaswamy, 1984). The death or illness of female babies is not considered as much of a loss as that of male babies, especially in the lower castes, where economics play a vital role in survival (Bumiller, 1990; Lynch, 1969). Very young widows, in both Hindu and Muslim traditions, are usually required to remarry either the brother of the deceased groom or another available bachelor. Widows with children are prohibited from remarrying due to considerations of property as well as religious and moral sanctions (Gore, 1965). Although women whose husbands die are expected to perform many rituals of sacrifice glorifying the family,* no similar rites are imposed on husbands or other family members (Stephens, 1963). Men, on the other hand, frequently somaticize their grief and become more dependent on their mother or other family members (Teja, Narang, & Aggarwal, 1971).

The family system, a network of relationships built through the male lineage,** plays a major role in cushioning the grief surrounding a death. In India the large network of extended family absorbs much of the anxiety about illness and death, a factor shown to be of major significance in the healing aspect of illness and death (Blotcky, 1981). The absence of this network among Indian families in the United States creates additional stress at times of illness or death.

In India bodies are generally cremated after death, except for children under the age of five who are typically buried, as it is believed that they will certainly return to earthly life for a fuller experience. This is quite contrary to the Christian belief that children are innocent and that, consequently, early death automatically affords them heavenly status. According to Hindu tradition, extensive prescribed rites have to be performed prior to a cremation or burial. In India burial grounds for different castes are usually sepa-

---

*Until recently, Hindu widows practiced a funeral rite known as suttee in which they burned themselves alive on their husbands' funeral pyre as a sacrifice for their husbands and themselves in the afterlife. Women were "raised to view self-immolation as their only escape from miserable marriages — or, worse, as an act of courage and religious inspiration" (Bumiller, 1990, p. 46).

**Typically all the sons in an Indian family bring their wives into a conjoint home that physically and economically supports the male siblings and their families, unmarried sisters, and aunts from the father's side, as well as the parents. This family system makes joint decisions about how money is made, spent, or invested. Education and travel abroad are communal decisions, and all marriages are arranged through the contacts of this extended family system.

rate and sacrificial rites performed at cremation sites vary for different castes. The freedom from caste burial practices in the United States is positive for lower caste Indians but may be problematic for others.

In the United States, health laws, hospital regulations, and routines of funeral homes may interfere with Hindu traditions for assisting the dying and the soul of the dead. When rituals must be performed in a funeral home, family members are likely to be embarrassed at not having the privacy of their own home and may feel that the body is being "tampered with" when strangers touch it. Consequently, there is great concern about the "ghost" or soul hanging around beyond the customary 10–12 days.

In India itself, the tradition is to die in the holy city of Benares, if at all possible, or at least to have one's ashes dispersed in the River Ganges (Shivanand, 1979). When the process of dispersing ashes in a flowing river and other rites are not completed, the soul is at an impasse between this world and the next. This creates a tremendous sense of burden, especially for the wife or mother of the deceased, as well as dishonor over the pollutants of the soul not having left peacefully, or what Hindus refer to as "a good death."

When someone dies in India, it is not considered appropriate to talk about one's reactions. The caste system sanctioned by the Hindu scriptures, with its emphasis on passivity and sacrifice, paradoxically brings honor to those who keep their emotions separate from current events (Kakar, 1978). Mourners wear white clothing and no jewelry. Typical symptoms shown at times of mourning include social isolation, not eating, somatization, or hysterical preoccupation with some aspect of the dead person.

When addressing loss, information regarding traditional customs and mourning rituals must be elicited (Tseng & McDermott, 1985). Enabling the process of these rituals within the constraints of hospital practices, health regulations, and funeral homes is necessary. Many of the customs can be adapted and still meet with cultural acceptance. Because of the traditional expectations that women will sacrifice themselves for their husbands or children, they are at greater risk for suicide after a death. This is a practice that should be challenged therapeutically, while understanding the premise of sacrifice and nirvana. Men are less prone to carry emotional burdens, mostly due to the higher value placed on male life, and the glorification of women through sacrifice in the Hindu scriptures. Women who commit suicide bring either relief or honor to their families, while men who commit suicide usually bring pain and dishonor. This Indian pattern of "splitting" events from emotions or social consciousness must be confronted within the cultural tradition of tolerance and passivity. Since sacrifice and family glorification are important tasks of completion around a death, rituals constructed in the way of offerings of food, money, prayers, fasting and chanting, or visiting the temple in groups to pray are helpful in moving the soul onwards and bringing the family honor.

DEATH AND AFRICAN-AMERICAN CULTURE
by Paulette Moore Hines

Death is no stranger to the average African-American, regardless of age. For example, in 1983, in my own family, there were five deaths in a three-month period: my grandfather, who died of cancer at age 66; two uncles, both under 60, who died of strokes related to stress and hypertension; a cousin, aged 32, who died of kidney disease; and my 17-year-old niece, who probably died of hospital negligence during her treatment for lupus. My family's experience is not rare among African-Americans, though the large number of deaths in a short time might seem extraordinary. Death has been an ongoing daily reality from the time that Africans were taken from their native homelands in chains. Many were victims of starvation, suffocation, drowning, suicide, disease, whippings, mutilations, direct killings, and a loss of will to live. The slavery experience which followed was no less gruesome. Lynchings, shootings, and death due to the conditions of enslavement were common.

Since slavery, the death rate among African-Americans has continued to exceed that of other ethnic and racial groups. In 1986, the infant mortality death rate for Blacks (18.0 per 1,000) was more than twice the rate for whites (8.9 per 1,000). For those who survive birth, estimations of the average life expectancy are 65.4 and 73.8 for African-American males and females (compared to 72.1 and 78.8 for white males and females). The leading causes of death among African-Americans, according to 1986 data, are: heart disease, cancer, stroke, accidents, homicide and legal intervention, and diabetes (U.S. Bureau of the Census, 1989). In fact, African-Americans have the highest rate of death from injuries and nondisease causes of any group. From 1970 to 1986 Black males were almost seven times more likely to die of homicide than were white males. However, suicide, in the traditional sense, is not a phenomenon of major numbers among African-Americans, although the incidence is rising. There are also a disproportionate number of African-Americans (25.2%) among AIDS- related deaths, given their representation in the overall population (11.2%); 52.8% of children who died from AIDS were Black and 54.5% of all females who have died from AIDS were Black (U.S. Bureau of the Census, 1989). These health and morbidity inequities have been perpetuated by a combination of physiological, cultural, and societal factors, including poor health care, inadequate health information, nutritional deficits, hazardous employment, poverty, and racial discrimination.

Needless to say, families often have had to deal with the sudden and traumatic loss of relatives without the benefit of anticipatory mourning. The fact that, for many people, the extended family is the primary source of support and insulation from the negative evaluation of a society that still rejects people of color intensifies the usual ramifications of death. There are numerous kin whose death may represent a critical loss of emotional support. In poor families, in particular, everyday survival may be threatened by a loss of concrete assistance with finances, childcare, housing, etc.

Present-day beliefs about death are clearly linked to the combined influence of African philosophy and Christianity. Wiredu (1980) and Opoku (1989) underscore the African belief that death is not the end but the inauguration of life in another form. Death is not viewed as an intrusion and does not rob life of meaning but is a progression. A "good death" is one in which a person dies of causes related to old age; a "bad death" is one caused by violence or an "unclean disease" (Opoku, 1989). Death not only may result from physical causes but may be willed by an individual; the two are not necessarily mutually exclusive. African-Americans commonly believe that deaths occur in conjunction with births and that people often resist death until anticipated significant events (e.g., birthdays, holidays) have passed, even though most are unaware of the basis of these beliefs in African (Asante) myth.

Christianity reinforced various traditional African beliefs. Even when death is by tragic means, it is looked upon as God's will and a necessary step to achieve a new life—free of pain, suffering, and sorrow. Death is not to be feared; problems and joys in life are not without meaning but relate to our next existence. Thus, it is believed that we should live our lives in preparation for death. For some, this translates into strict adherence to biblical commandments.

Themes about pain, suffering, and death are pervasive in African-American literature, poetry, and music. The words of one African-American spiritual, "Before I'd be a slave, I'd be buried in my grave, and go home to my lord and be free," convey the widespread attitude that "a life not worth dying for is not worth living."

Rituals and Traditions

African-Americans, like the Irish, place great importance on "going out in style" regardless of cost. The expense for the burial clothes and other accountrements for a funeral may be the final opportunity the family has to let the dead person have some dignity or status, so often denied to African-

Americans in life (Harrington, 1963). The importance of providing "the best" for a deceased relative is evidenced by the fact that the funeral industry is one of the largest in African–American communities. In contrast to the Jewish population, African-Americans place greater emphasis on attending a funeral than perhaps on any other family gathering. Since attendance symbolizes respect for the deceased and his/her family, there is likely to be much discussion about the turnout at a funeral and upset for years afterwards with absent family and friends. Failure to be present is seen as dismissing the importance of "sticking together" and opens absent relatives to the accusation of forgetting their roots.

The community may be apprised of a death by the placing of a wreath on the door of the deceased person's home. Largely for economic reasons, which may make it difficult for family members to take off from work and make travel arrangements, funerals typically take place three to seven days following death. Cremations are not forbidden but are very seldom performed. In the northeast, wakes are commonly conducted at a church or funeral parlor on the evening preceding the funeral. In the south, the prevailing ritual of "sitting up" involves family and friends bringing food or money and visiting the family from the time of death until the funeral. It is a time of mixed emotions as family members who have moved away return and reconnect. Unlike the Irish, African-Americans do not openly serve alcohol; a party atmosphere would be unthinkable.

Traditional African-American practices stand in direct contrast to the highly ritualized prescriptions of Jewish and Hindu cultures and the "no fuss," nonemotional WASP tradition. There are no prohibitions about the public expression of grief, particularly by women and children. Children are not excluded from the rituals surrounding death unless they prefer not to attend. At the funeral, the eulogy and music are typically designed to provoke the release of emotions. Moving spirituals are sung about the pain and suffering of this life, and the joy of reuniting with deceased relatives and achieving final peace. The practice of opening the casket during the funeral for a final viewing heightens the emotional intensity of the experience.

Therapeutic Considerations

It is unlikely that the average African-American family will show up in a family therapist's office of its own accord with a presenting concern directly tied to an impending or actual death. The cultural value is "to be strong," which often translates into handling adversity without tears or diminished performance of daily activities. However, when a death occurs, crying and open expression of grief are encouraged and considered helpful, if not essential, in order to overcome the potential debilitating effects of grief. At the same time, prolonged reactions of sadness beyond the funeral are not easily tolerated. It is expected that you will continue to grieve your loss but that you also will resume your usual functions at home and work within a few weeks of the funeral. The value placed on open emotional expression, traditional cultural attitudes about death, the immediate display of family and community support, and strong spirituality facilitate grief resolution.

Perhaps in the face of omnipresent suffering and death, one learns to cherish life in order to survive, to anticipate and accept death, and yet, necessarily, to cling to dreams of a better life. An excerpt from a session with a 32-year-old, terminally ill cancer patient illustrates the resourcefulness and resilience that has been characteristic of so many African-Americans in the face of tragedy:

THERAPIST   How do you talk to your mother about it?

CLIENT   "Well, I have Hodgkin's. What are we going to do about it?" My mother is very positive that I can live a fairly normal life or get well, but then there is always the possibility — we're both aware that I might die. That's not kept hush-hush or pushed under the carpet.

THERAPIST   What if it works out you do die? What does she say?

CLIENT   Well, she keeps telling me that she wouldn't be the only mother that has lost a child. She would continue to live. It would be the hardest thing that she's ever had to deal with . . . but that's life . . . and I go to her and say, "If I should die, you know I don't want my casket open." When we first found out, she looked at me and she was trying to keep from crying. She was being strong and we went home and we decided, "Okay, what is this? What are we going to do about it?" I told her, "You have 24 hours to cry and scream and feel sorry for me and everything else. After that we get down to business." And we cried a little bit more.

THERAPIST   What was "getting down to business"? What did you do?

CLIENT   Started with the doctor — the chemotherapy. There were more rough moments. My religion is real helpful. The dying process is not scary. It's the suffering, the hospital, wasting away, and all that. I think often about my daughter. My prayer is to see her grown.

Some, however, do have difficulty coping in the aftermath of a death. The belief that one must be strong sometimes translates into premature blocking of feelings for fear of being overwhelmed and unable to function. Family members may encourage constraint rather than release of pent-up feelings. This was the situation with a client who came to see me two weeks after her husband's death. Her adult children were alarmed whenever she cried openly and thought that she should be able to pursue her usual activities. "They don't really understand what it's like and are not accustomed to seeing me cry and not handle things." She felt angry and alone and was unwilling to accept the efforts her children made to support her. I chose to have her children clarify their concerns and suggested to the family that the client was being quite strong in dealing with her loss, rather than running away from it. Coaching them to give the client permission to recharge herself physically and emotionally, by allowing her to pull back temporarily, was a simple but valuable intervention. Once the mother was able to see that her children were trying to protect her and that they shared her sense of loss, she stopped avoiding them, felt less alone in dealing with her grief, and made better use of her peer network as well.

The death of a pivotal person in the nuclear or extended family may require reorganization of the family structure. One of the strengths of African-American families is their ability to exercise great flexibility in roles and to exchange emotional and concrete support (Hines & Boyd-Franklin, 1982). Adaptation to a death may require a move from one household to another so that responsibilities for child or elderly care can be assumed or any financial burden created by the death can be decreased.

There may be significant variability in the resources and lifestyles of family members within the extended family network. Those who tend to be overfunctioners and those who have achieved middle income status are most likely to feel obligated and overstressed when someone dies who was of great emotional and practical significance to the functioning of the family. One of the most useful interventions that a family therapist can make is to assist such persons in actively factoring their own personal needs into decisions regarding how to fill the vacuum created by a death. This may be more easily accomplished if a therapist verbalizes genuine appreciation of the value placed on "helping family" and encourages those who have a pattern of overfunctioning to weigh the long-term consequences for significant others if they are denied opportunities to develop the strength and creativity of their forebears. In some instances, this may mean that a client assumes less or different responsibilities rather than refuses any responsibility, as the resources of other family members may prevent them from helping in the ideal manner. It may also be useful to provide coaching on how to set limits, without cutting off and losing the benefits of family affiliation.

In instances of untimely and avoidable deaths, families are just as likely to struggle with feelings of anger, anxiety, and powerlessness as with depression. This situation is underscored in the following case illustration.

A couple sought consultation about their 15-year-old daughter, Marie, who was described as irresponsible at home and unwilling to apply herself consistently at school. Nine months earlier, Marie's older brother, Michael, a superachiever both in academics and sports, had shot and killed himself. The months prior to his death had been a time of terrible turmoil for the family, as Michael's drug habit had grown beyond his ability to manage it.

Michael's mother claimed that the family had "accepted his death from the moment it happened. It wasn't that he wanted to die — he just didn't want to live. Michael was not the kind of kid who could hurt other people and sleep at night. At least, we know he is at peace." Marie noted her belief that "Michael died a long time before he pulled the trigger."

One treatment goal in this case was to help the family understand how Michael's death had heightened his parents' anxieties about raising their only remaining child in an increasing unsafe environment. Whenever Marie wanted to go out, her parents would impose unreasonably strict limits and lecture endlessly until Marie would angrily storm out. Eventually Marie became openly defiant about doing her household chores.

I hypothesized that Marie's refusal to carry out her responsibilities at home was her way of reducing her parents' anxiety by forcing them to restrict her to the house as a punishment. These restrictions eased her fears about succumbing to pressures from her peers. I reframed Marie's defiance at home as her unique and misguided way of being responsible and caring, a way of remaining part of her crowd and, at the same time, maintaining her loyalty to her parents. This redefinition allowed the parents to discuss their many anxieties and how these had begun to color life in their family. I did not attempt to convince the parents that their fears were unwarranted, but rather, helped them to begin to think through alternative ways of responding to the dangers that their son's death had so indelibly highlighted.

There are several other issues to keep in mind when working with African-American families around issues of death and mourning. One cannot make assumptions about the meaning of a death simply on the basis of immediacy of the relationship; a relationship with a member of the extended family may hold as great or greater significance for an individual than a relationship with a member of the nuclear family. Second, it is more likely that family members are left to struggle with unresolved relationship conflicts in instances when death has not been anticipated than when it is expected. Families may benefit from open discussion of unresolved issues in spite of their inability to change their history with the deceased individual. Open communication between family members can be particularly helpful when "secrets" (e.g., parentage, substance abuse) revealed at the time of a death evoke confusion or conflict among surviving family members (Boyd-Franklin, 1989). Therapists can also be helpful by creating a forum for family members to vent their feelings about the circumstances surrounding a death and to find appropriate ways of channeling their anger without displacing it inappropriately and destructively on one another, self, or others.

PUERTO RICAN FAMILIES
by Nydia Garcia-Preto

Hispanics view death as part of life, an unavoidable event. Their preference, which is, perhaps, universal, is to die at a ripe old age, at home, surrounded by friends and family, after they have watched their children and grandchildren grow. Any other death, such as a sudden or traumatic death or one that takes place at an untimely stage in the life cycle, is much harder for them to accept. The heightened value placed on children makes the death of an infant particularly difficult for Hispanics to integrate. To help them deal with this most tragic loss, Puerto Ricans used to dress the baby in white, paint its face to look like an angel, and place flowers inside and outside the coffin. Music was played and songs were sung to hail the infant into heaven.

It is also extremely painful when parents die young, leaving children who still need care. In most cases, Puerto Rican extended families assume childrearing responsibility, especially when the mother dies. Since Hispanic males are not trained to be caretakers, the children usually stay with relatives until the father remarries, sometimes never returning to live with him. When it is the father who dies, the mother also depends on relatives to help with childcare and often has to go outside the home to work.

Because of the emphasis that Hispanics place on interdependence, the loss of a family member is experienced as an especially profound threat to the family's future and often touches off reactions of extreme anxiety. Perhaps that is one of the reasons why illnesses are so greatly feared within Hispanic cultures. Puerto Ricans, for instance, wait until they can no longer function before they seek professional advice, partly because they fear hospitals, where they expect to be diagnosed as terminally ill. Instead of seeking medical care, both men and women complain of pain, and many prefer to visit folk healers or ask the advice of family and friends.

Usually the ill are cared for at home, typically by the women, and they are hospitalized only when there is no alternative. This reinforces the belief that you only go to a hospital as a last resort — to die. When that happens, family members are likely to set up camp at the hospital. They pray, bring food, and ask a priest or minister to visit when the situation becomes critical. If death is expected, relatives are urgently summoned, especially when they are far away. Hispanics place great value on seeing a dying relative, resolving whatever conflict may exist, and saying a final goodbye. At the time of death, during the viewing, and at the funeral, both men and women are expected to express emotion intensely; women, in particular, sometimes lose control and display hysterics diagnosed as "ataques." But after the burial, the expectation is that one must accept the death and try to be strong.

Most Hispanics are Roman Catholic and believe in an afterlife. They maintain that the spirit of the dead person needs reassurance from the living before it can find peace in the afterlife. Puerto Ricans, for example, tend to perceive the afterlife as a place where loved ones go to rest and from where they can look after us. For many it is also defined as a spirit world, a level of existence that some people can experience while still alive and one that influences our everyday life. This is reinforced by a widespread belief that spirits go through an evolution beginning at a level of ignorance and moving towards a state of moral perfection. To attain this higher level of "light and understanding," spirits must be able to detach from earth, which may be difficult, particularly when a person dies prematurely, without resolving family conflicts or paying old debts.

Following a death, friends are expected to visit and bring food to the deceased person's family where they pray for the spirit of the dead to find rest, and light candles to brighten the way to eternal peace. Puerto Rican Catholics gather for at least seven nights to say the rosary. Visits to the grave and masses in church during the year following the death are also times when family members gather to console one another and to pray for the deceased person's spirit. Within this culture, communication with the dead is not perceived as impossible. Many Puerto Ricans visit spiritists or mediums when they want to resolve issues with the dead. This is especially true when they have dreams about the dead person returning to say farewell or deliver a special message. This is usually perceived as a sign that the spirit is restless and must communicate before leaving the material world.

Not being able to be present during the illness or death of someone close to them makes the loss more difficult for some people to accept and prolongs the mourning process. This is a common experience for Hispanics in the U.S., particularly when the death takes place in their country of origin. They may be unable to go home for political or financial reasons, or may arrive late, simply because of the distance to be traveled. I have found unresolved loss to be a common underlying theme for Hispanics in therapy regardless of the problems they present. The following case is an example of how the client's inability to say goodbye to her mother at the time of death, as well as her decision to control her emotions at the funeral, contributed to the depression for which she sought therapy. The interventions took into consideration cultural patterns and utilized rituals to help unlock the emotions and move the mourning process forward.

A 25-year-old Puerto Rican woman was referred to me by one of her professors in graduate school. She was depressed and having difficulty concentrating. She told me that her mother had died suddenly and unexpectedly three months earlier. A month later she herself had been diagnosed as having rheumatoid arthritis. She felt as if her whole world was falling apart.

She had first heard of her mother's illness when her brother called to say her mother was in the hospital. During the four-hour drive to the hospital she had hoped and prayed to see her mother alive. Upon arrival she found that her mother had, in fact, died of heart failure prior to the call, but because her siblings were afraid of her emotional reaction they waited to tell her in person. She was furious, feeling excluded and infantilized by her siblings' decision to handle things this way. She was also angry about not having had a chance to say goodbye to her mother; at the same time she felt guilty for not having been there. At the funeral, she had kept her emotions under control in an effort to show her family that she could handle herself.

In therapy, I asked her to bring pictures of her mother and other family members and to describe how she heard of her mother's death and what the funeral was like. All this precipitated very strong emotions. I also asked her to write a letter to her mother telling her everything she wanted to say, and then to visit the grave and read it aloud. She described this experience as emotional and very helpful. Later, a session with her sister and one of her brothers was very useful in promoting emotional support among them. They talked about their loss and my client's struggles with her own illness. Feeling more at peace with herself, she made plans to move closer to her family but to live independently. In this way she expressed the importance of her family and cultural connectedness, while at the same time she made efforts to help her siblings modify their culturally based view of her as fragile and needing to be "handled" and protected.

JEWISH FAMILIES
by Elliott Rosen

In Jewish families there are four primary patterns of belief and behavior at the core of functioning that can help us to understand the ways in which these families respond to sickness, death, and loss. These are: (1) the family as the central source of support and emotional connectedness; (2) suffering as a shared family and community value; (3) the prominence of intellectual achievement and financial success; and (4) the premium placed on the verbal expression of feelings (Herz & Rosen, 1982).

While Jews, like many other ethnic groups, have joined the mainstream of homogenized American society over the past three generations, it is clear that these beliefs and patterns of behavior have persisted, despite intermarriage and the pull toward assimilation. These patterns, rooted in the parochial and protected life of the 19th-century Eastern European ghetto and reinforced by the immigrant experience of the early 20th century, persist in subtle, and often more sophisticated, forms in contemporary Jewish-American life. In some

ways these patterns—particularly those of success and the expression of feelings—have also become integrated into mainstream American culture, especially on the two coasts, but they can still be identified as fundamentally
Jewish and maintain their powerful hold on the Jewish family.

Centrality of the Family

For Jews, family emotional connectedness is cherished and respected (Zuk,
1978). This value extends beyond the nuclear family to include extended
family members as well as previous generations. Ashkenazic Jews of Eastern
European descent, who make up the majority of American Jews, name their
children after deceased relatives. Most Jewish families, regardless of their
level of religious commitment, observe a yearly memorial day for those who
have died and, among the more affluent, consider it a great mark of respect
to make substantial monetary contributions to honor the memory of the
dead. To a great extent, Jewish institutions, both in the United States and
throughout the world, survive because of the philanthropic largess of Jews
who honor their deceased relatives. This notion of family extends even
further to include, both literally and symbolically, the entire Jewish community. The slogan of the largest philanthropic organization in the American
Jewish community, United Jewish Appeal, has long been "We Are One," and
most Jews understand the meaning of this phrase. While grieving, of course,
can take place within the privacy of the family, formal mourning can only be
conducted within the community, in the presence of a *minyan*, or full worship community of ten adults. In more traditional Jewish communities, the
minyan consists of ten men.

For Jews, the religious calendar and ritual observances are tied more to
the home than to the synagogue. Although communal worship and various
other activities may take place in the synagogue, the most important religious rites are actually conducted in the home and are intrinsically linked to
the life of the family and demand its participation. The weekly observance
of the Sabbath; the celebration of Hanukkah (for which there is no special
synagogue service); and the Passover *seder* (which is the premier family
gathering of the religious year) are examples.

For Jewish families, there are more important life cycle events than a
funeral. One's attendance at the funeral is not *de rigueur*, although it is
expected that family members and members of the community will pay a
shiva (i.e., condolence) call on the mourning family, preferably at a time
when the community gathers in the home for a service that honors the
deceased. But events such as ritual circumcisions (a *brit* or *bris*), Bar/Bat
Mitzvah, and weddings are considered more significant passages in the life
of the family than funerals and attendance at those times is more highly

valued. This, of course, is congruent with the child-focused nature of the Jewish family; life cycle events that celebrate the passage into adulthood are highly regarded and the failure of family members to participate in these events is seldom forgotten.

The fact that a strong belief in an afterlife is absent in most contemporary Jewish families may provide an additional explanation for why funerals are not considered central ritual events.

Suffering as a Shared Value

Among the more common Yiddish expressions brought to this country by Eastern European immigrants was "shver zu zeiner Yid," or "It's tough to be a Jew." In contemporary American-Jewish society the maxim has fallen into desuetude, but the underlying belief remains operant. Suffering is a fundamental dimension of life and serves a powerful social function, but unlike the Irish, Jews do not see the world as a cruel place but rather as morally neutral. The Biblical story of the Garden of Eden, which forms the core of Christian belief about the nature of humanity as tainted by sin, is interpreted in Jewish philosophy as the source of free will and moral responsibility. But the notion of fate ("beshert" in Yiddish) has always been a shared Jewish value. The good things that happen to us can be beshert and so can the bad things, and thus life is seen as capricious and unpredictable, but not inherently evil. A generation ago it was not unusual for a Jewish mother to warn her children that they ought not sing in the morning because they'd be crying at night.

But for Jews, life's pain is not to be borne stoically. Railing against the unfairness of the world — and even against God himself — is a part of Jewish folklore — acceptable, even expected. Thus, enjoying life for its own sake may be difficult, and having fun together is not something that comes all that easily to Jewish families. Suffering is traditionally a phenomenon that has drawn Jews together and given them a sense of emotional connectedness; the notion that one suffers for one's sins, a prevalent belief in many other cultures, is not common in Jewish families. Rather, one suffers because the world is not a perfect place, and while life may often be difficult, "the worst life is better than the best death." Unlike many other cultures, among Jews questions of what happens after death are not of central concern. It would be unusual nowadays to hear a eulogy that more than obliquely alluded to a world beyond, or one which promised a reunion with those loved ones who have died. The present life is the focus of concern. This may partly account for the propensity Jews have toward depression, somaticizing, and hypochondriasis (Zborowski, 1969; Zborowski & Herzog, 1952). These symptoms are frequently seen in reaction to illness or loss in the family.

History, of course, cannot be ignored as a major source of why Jews see suffering as an integral part of life. From the slaughter of Jewish sons in the Bible to the Nazi program of genocide during the Holocaust, Jews have suffered persecution throughout history and in all parts of the world. Survival has thus become an important value for the Jewish family and community. This may partially explain why the celebratory rituals of the life cycle take on a more powerful role in the life of the Jewish family than do those associated with deaths. A discussion of the place of suffering in Jewish experience would not be complete without consideration of the Holocaust. The destruction of whole families and entire communities is part of the legacy of loss in many Jewish families and is also an important dimension of contemporary Jewish communal ethos (Epstein, 1979; Moskovitz, 1983). Many Jews are descended from survivors of concentration camps who experienced the brutal death and disappearance of other family members. This has had profound multigenerational consequences, both in terms of survival as a central concern, and in how loss and death are experienced. While many of the clinical implications of the Holocaust experience are beyond the scope of this discussion, therapists who work with Jewish families around loss and death would do well to acquaint themselves with the ever-growing literature on this subject.

Intellectual Achievement and Financial Success

In many cultures, the notion of giving the deceased a "good send-off" is a prominent theme. This may include spending large amounts of money for an impressive casket, a custom that runs counter to Jewish tradition. Because the notion of a better life beyond the one we know is alien to Jews, the funeral is perceived as a reflection of life's achievements and as a comfort to the living, but not as an opportunity to demonstrate wealth or social station. This stands in interesting contrast to the often costly and ostentatious displays at Bar Mitzvahs and weddings, and undoubtedly reflects the fact that death rituals are rooted in ancient Jewish traditions—to which people are more likely to turn at these times—while many other life cycle events are a creation of the modern-day diaspora Jewish community. More important than the appearance of the funeral ceremony itself is who, and how many attended, and how the deceased was eulogized. Funerals are an opportunity to review the deceased person's life successes, as well as those of the family. A large crowd and a eulogy that brings tears to everyone's eyes are highly cherished. Unlike the Irish, Jews would find lightheartedness or a party-like atmosphere unacceptable. However, as mentioned above, coming to the home during the mourning period to comfort the bereaved remains more important than actually attending the funeral or the burial, reflecting the centrality of the family.

In Jewish families, the high value placed upon intellectual achievement and financial success often creates intergenerational conflict. This conflict is often exacerbated when families face life-threatening illness or death. In addition, the relative positions of men and women in traditional Jewish culture persists in contemporary families and frequently supersedes the value of success. A son perceived as professionally successful is often implicitly excused from "being there" for the family — both during times of illness and after a death — since his work is "important" and brings honor to the family. A daughter, however, regardless of her professional standing, would be expected to be present as a caretaker for her family, both during illness and after death. If the deceased has been the family breadwinner, how financially secure he has left the family will be carefully scrutinized by the extended family, as well as the entire community, and his value may be judged accordingly. In traditional families, the learned scholar who sat and studied and was financially nonproductive was theoretically accorded respect and honor, but in reality his having not provided adequately for his family made him an object of contempt.

Verbal Expression of Feelings

The ability to express oneself is highly valued in Jewish families and may be particularly evident in situations of life-threatening illness. As mentioned above, the expression of anger and other volatile emotions is not unusual and in many Jewish families serves as a visible indicator of the closeness between people. While children in a Polish family, for example, know that respect for their elders includes not talking back or using foul language, Jewish children are less likely to feel such constraints. Endless arguments and continuing, loud disagreements among family members are often conducted in the presence of the sick, and a funeral, burial, or presence in the house of mourning is not in itself enough to discourage one from expressing feelings. However, the expression of love and loyalty to the fatally ill or deceased is equally appropriate and fully expected. The stoic mien of a Jackie Kennedy, for example, is foreign to traditional Jewish values and, as one woman commented incredulously while viewing the Kennedy funeral, "Any self-respecting Jewish woman would have thrown herself in the grave."

Jewish Death Rituals

The rituals that surround death reflect traditional Jewish attitudes toward loss. During the period of terminal illness one's family is expected to be present and provide constant care. Upon death, this notion is expanded to include the community and a specially trained burial society (known as the *hevra kadisha*) takes the responsibility for preparing the body for burial; this includes washing the body, wrapping it in a shroud, attending the body constantly, and reciting Psalms. The burial shroud is made of simple cloth and any adornment is forbidden; likewise, the casket is constructed of simple pine and even steel nails are forbidden. Both of these restrictions emphasize the notion that in death there is no distinction permitted between rich and poor. Ecclesiastes best reflects the ancient notion of death as the great equalizer in its discussion of the accumulation of goods, which ends with the famous statement, "All is vanity."

Most modern Jews are usually far removed from these roots of traditional Judaism. With the diaspora, Jews assimilated into the dominant culture of various countries where they settled. At the time of death, families are more likely to desire a deeper connectedness with the ancient religious traditions. The funeral takes place at the earliest moment, which is considered most respectful of the corpse, and in the most religiously observant communities, as early as the same day. There is much respect accorded the body as having been a vessel for life, but embalming or otherwise preserving the corpse from natural decay is forbidden. In Jewish law, cremation is proscribed, an issue that is likely to cause some contention in families where individuals desire cremation for themselves or other family members. Such difficulties arise as commonly in nonobservant families as in Orthodox ones, since feelings about cremation may be highly toxic. From the time of death until the burial has taken place, mourners are exempt from the requirement of observing the ritual law, which reflects the notion that the powerful emotions set in motion by death prevent one's wholehearted participation in honoring God.

The funeral service and burial are simple, and family members are expected, when possible, to accompany the deceased person's body to the grave. At the burial, the family and friends participate by filling the grave. This is both cathartic as well as a symbolic way of laying the dead to rest. After the burial the family returns home and begins a mourning period (*shiva*, or "seven," signifying the number of days) during which family members are to be visited and comforted, primarily by sharing their recollections of the deceased. The family is not expected to host this shiva period and thus all food is cooked by friends, and all arrangements are handled by others. During the shiva period, when one is forbidden to leave home and must refrain from work, one is expected to sit on a low stool, rend a garment to signify the ripping away of a life (nowadays this is commonly symbolized by a mourning ribbon), and generally refrain from normal daily activities. After shiva, there commences a second stage of formal mourning (called *sheloshim*, or "thirty," once again the number of days), during which mourners begin to return to the mainstream but continue to wear their sign of mourning. Formal mourning continues for a year; the completion of this final stage is marked by the unveiling of the headstone. Each year, the anniversary of the death is marked by the lighting of a memorial candle, the giving of charity, and the presence of the survivors in the synagogue to publicly recite a memorial prayer.

It goes without saying that these rituals reflect the traditional pattern of Jewish practice. Today, most Jewish families do not consider themselves particularly observant and may opt for carrying out very few of these rituals. However, the therapist might do well to explore with families the decisions they have made regarding how they will mark the death of a family member and the subsequent mourning period. The incorporation of traditional rituals may prove palliative, while the refusal to perform any of them may provide clues to the family's functioning.

MOURNING RITUALS IN CHINESE CULTURE
by Evelyn Lee

Mourning rituals in Chinese culture are influenced by Confucianism, Taoism, and Buddhism. Death is traditionally considered the most significant life cycle transition. Over the past five thousand years, many rituals have evolved to help family members deal with their loss. Confucianism taught the virtues of filial piety and righteousness. "When your parents are alive, treat them with respect. When they are dead, bury them with pomp and honor them with proper rites" (*The Confucian Analects*). The rules of funeral rites are spelled out in one of the five classics of Confucian literature, *Li Chi* (*The Book of Rites*). These rules, and many customs added since the time of Confucius, have been loyally followed and practiced by many Chinese.

Like a wedding, a funeral is usually a community affair; its degree of elaborateness reflects the social status of the family. The concept of immortality of the soul has a great impact on mourning rituals. In order to give the deceased a good "send-off" and to ensure he or she will not live in poverty, paper money, paper houses, and other material goods are often burned. So as not to leave the dead hungry, many foods are offered, such as rice, wine, fowl, fruits, and buns. To demonstrate family members' sorrow and grief, professional mourners are occasionally hired. At the funeral procession, the male heirs usually lead, accompanied by other family members and funeral musicians. Afterwards, a funeral dinner is usually held for family and friends. Guests are expected to comfort family members and to say "good words" about the deceased. No jokes or happy music are allowed. Red envelopes with money and candy are given to the guests to get rid of the bad luck associated with going to a funeral.

In order to prevent the deceased from going to hell, many families hire Taoist monks or chanters to pray for the spirit. During the wake and funeral, the spouse and the children of the deceased are expected to cry uninhibitedly. However, they are expected to be in control of their emotions after the funeral. When a person dies, his/her body will be buried underground. Usually, a traditional geomancer will be consulted about the placement and architecture of the grave, especially when the deceased is an important figure in the extended family. It is believed that the grave placement will determine the fate and welfare of the deceased's descendants. After the funeral, the word "death" and its synonyms are not mentioned and are strictly forbidden on happy occasions such as birthdays or weddings.

Buddhists, however, do not believe in many of the above practices. They believe in karma and reincarnation and in predetermination of one's present life by good or bad deeds in the present life and past lives. Before a Buddhist dies, friends and/or monks will gather and assist the dying process by chanting Buddhist sutra. Display of uncontrollable emotions is not encouraged. Meat is not served during the funeral meals because Buddhists do not believe in killing animals. Cremation is the most acceptable form of burial.

Traditionally, the prescribed mourning period within Chinese families is 49 days (it was seven years in ancient China). On the seventh day after the funeral, the family will celebrate a special ceremony for the dead, which is repeated every seven days for seven consecutive weeks. During this 49-day mourning period, family members are expected to wear black cloth, strips, or armbands. Women are also expected to wear simple floral arrangements made of wool in their hair. No festive activities such as weddings are permitted during this time. The anniversary of the death and two special memorial days (one in March and the other in September) each year are set aside for surviving family members to pay their respects at the gravesites.

Continuity of family relations after death is very important. The ancient practice of ancestor worship is still followed in most Chinese households. Each day, prayers are said in front of a portrait of the parents or grandparents placed prominently in the living room. It is believed that the spirits of one's ancestors can be communicated with directly and, if honored appropriately, will confer their blessings and protect their progeny from harm. Many Buddhists do not practice ancestor worship; family members honor the deceased by placing a memorial plate in the temple for continued chanting purposes.

Many traditional Chinese make a very important distinction between a "good" death, in which all the prescribed rituals are expected to be followed, and a "bad" death, in which they are not. In a "good" death, the deceased dies peacefully in old age and is blessed with many children, especially sons. The last sight a dying person sees is all the relatives gathered around the bed to say goodbye. At the moment of death itself, care is taken to close the deceased's eyelids. A "bad" death means untimely death. Murder and suicide are particularly stigmatized. When a child dies, parents and grandparents are not expected to go to the funeral. The absence of discussion of such deaths is a socially acceptable form of avoidance to deal with "bad" deaths. Due to years of war, starvation in China, and the high mortality rate of women in childbirth, many Chinese have experienced untimely deaths and have not "completed" their mourning.

The mourning rituals previously mentioned have been dramatically curtailed in the past 40 years. Political, social, and economic forces have shaped the current mourning practices of Chinese in different countries. Under the Communist government in China, cremation is mandatory for everyone. Religious ceremonies have not been allowed until recently. Chinese in Hong Kong manage to maintain many of the traditions. However, due to overcrowded conditions, family members are expected to retrieve the bones of the dead after seven to ten years. Wealthy Chinese in the Philippines probably practice the most elaborate funerals. Very often, the tomb is constructed like a fancy house. The mourning rituals of Chinese in America depend a great deal on the degree of acculturation of the family members and the community where they live. Today, instead of a Chinese funeral being a communal affair, it is likely to be dictated by the procedures followed by the funeral home involved. The 49-day mourning period has been drastically reduced, typically to a bereavement leave of a week or less. And the religious ceremony at a funeral is now typically conducted by a minister or priest, instead of a Buddhist or Taoist monk.

Nevertheless, in large Chinatowns in cities like San Francisco and New York, the Chinese stubbornly adhere to tradition and attempt to integrate Chinese and American funeral practices. For instance, funerals in these cities often include paper money burning, funeral marches around the community, and a funeral dinner for relatives and friends. Typically, Chinese men assume the role of making major decisions such as the type and size of the funerals and financial arrangements, and Chinese women handle the social and emotional tasks of bereavement.

There are many clinical implications in helping Chinese to deal better with the emotional strains of the experience of loss. For example, the shame and cultural taboo against discussing the loss of someone who has suffered a violent or untimely death can exert a powerful force in Chinese families. One 60-year-old Chinese woman was referred for treatment after she discovered the dead body of an old man who had taken a room in her house. This experience triggered an intense reaction in the woman, so that she was unable to speak for several weeks. Slowly, over a period of many months, she was finally able to openly grieve over a lifetime of sudden losses in her family, including the death of her son at age five. Within her cultural framework, the loss of her son, who had died of a high fever many years before, had been a "bad" death and a shameful experience for the family. There had not even been a burial ceremony for the boy. In addition, her mother-in-law was murdered. She and her husband had not been able to grieve.

In working with Chinese families, the therapist needed to bear several things in mind. The Chinese typically do not make connections between past experience and their present behavior. Often the therapist needs to adopt the stance of a teacher instructing a client about the relationship between symptoms and past events. It is also important to recognize the extended length of time necessary to establish a trusting therapeutic bond that can bear the intensity of a client's grief reactions. Furthermore, the therapist must respect the cultural framework through which the client perceives family losses. In doing this, the following guidelines may be helpful:

1. Explore how the client perceives the cause of death: A discussion may reveal that, while the client seems to attribute a relative's death to a physical cause like a heart attack or cancer, he actually believes the cause was spiritual. In the above case, the woman was convinced her five-year-old son had died because of the transgressions of one of her ancestors.
2. Discuss how the client followed the burial and mourning ritual at the time of a death: The failure to follow traditional practices can lead to lingering guilt feelings. In some cases, accompanying clients to gravesites to have them complete burial rituals for long deceased relatives may be necessary.
3. Examine the client's beliefs about life after death: Chinese traditions dwell on the horrors of hell and have much less to say about the possibilities of heaven. Some extreme reactions to a death are best understood in light of departed relatives' fate in the afterlife and its implications for survivors in the family.
4. Look at communication with the dead person: The spirits of the dead are very much alive for many Chinese. In some cases, encouragement of prayers and chanting may be helpful, and sometimes even consultations with spiritual healers to help clients complete business with the dead is necessary.
5. Explore family changes that followed a death: Great importance is attached to fulfilling family obligations in Chinese culture. Failure to

do so can lead to intense feelings of guilt and shame, which are difficult to verbalize. It is always important with Chinese clients to understand how they perceive changes in their family obligations following a death and whether or not they believe that they have carried them out.

CONCLUSION

While it is impossible to develop prescriptions for intervention with families of different backgrounds in dealing with loss, the six ethnic descriptions presented here should make it clear that there are many important ways in which cultures differ in their handling of death. Be sure that in working with families to understand their losses you ascertain their beliefs about (a) handling the dying and the dead; (b) what happens after death; (c) appropriate emotional expression of mourning and integration of the loss experience; (d) typical roles and expected behavior for men and women; (e) which deaths are stigmatized or especially traumatic; and (f) how to minimize the negative impact of this trauma on the family's adaptation after the death.

Focusing questioning around these areas will allow you to learn from each family about its values and beliefs. Once you understand the family's values, you must raise delicate philosophical and clinical questions about how and when to encourage its members to modify maladaptive, but culturally sanctioned, practices (e.g., that suicide is acceptable — as for Indian widows or Japanese who have "lost face" — or that men handle the administrative aspects of death and women do the overt mourning for the family). There are no absolutes in this matter, but we urge clinicians to be clear about their own cultural values and to take responsibility for their own cultural perspective when they propose alterative responses to a family.

REFERENCES

General

McGoldrick, M., Pearce, J. K., & Giordano, J. (1982). *Ethnicity and family therapy.* New York: Guilford.

Osterweis, M., Solomon, F., & Green, M. (Eds.). (1984). *Bereavement: Reactions, consequences, and care.* Washington, DC: National Academy Press.

McGoldrick, M., Hines, P. M., Garcia-Preto, N., & Lee, E., (1986). Mourning rituals. *The Family Therapy Networker, Nov-Dec,* 28–36.

Schiff, H. S. (1977). *The bereaved parent.* New York: Crown Publishers.

Wortman, C., & Silver, R. C. (1989). The myths of coping with loss. *Journal of Consulting [Clinical Psychology, 57,* 349–357.

African-American

Boyd-Franklin, N. (1989). *Black families in therapy: A multisystems approach*. New York: Guilford.

Harrington, M. (1963). *The other America: Poverty in the U.S.* Baltimore: Penguin.

Hines, P., & Boyd-Franklin, N. (1982). Black families. In M. McGoldrick, J. Pearce, & J. Giordano (Eds.), *Ethnicity and family therapy*. New York: Guilford.

Opoku, A. (1989). African perspectives on death and dying. In A. Berger, P. Badham, A. H. Kutscher, J. Berger, M. Perry, & J. Beloff (Eds.), *Perspectives on death and dying: Cross culture and multi-disciplinary views*. Philadelphia: Charles Press.

U.S. Bureau of the Census. (1989). *Statistical abstract of the United States* (109th ed.). Washington, DC.

Wiredu, K. (1989). Death and the afterlife in Africa culture. In A. Berger, P. Badham, A. H. Kutscher, J. Berger, M. Perry, & J. Beloff (Eds.), *Perspectives on death and dying: Cross culture and multi-disciplinary views*. Philadelphia: Charles Press.

Irish

Delaney, M. M. (1973). *Of Irish ways*. New York: Harper & Row.

Evans, E. E. (1957). *Irish folk ways*. London: Routledge & Kegan Paul.

Greeley, A. (1972). *The most distressful nation*. Garden City, NY: Doubleday.

Greeley, A. (1981). *The Irish Americans*. New York: Harper & Row.

McGoldrick, M. (1982). Irish families. In M. McGoldrick, J. K. Pearce, & J. Giordano (Eds.), *Ethnicity and family therapy*. New York: Guilford.

McGoldrick, M. (1989). Ethnicity and the family life cycle. In B. Carter & M. McGoldrick (Eds.), *The changing family life cycle* (2nd ed.). Boston: Allyn & Bacon.

McGoldrick, M., Garcia-Preto, N., Hines, P. M., & Lee, E. (1989). Ethnicity and women. In M. McGoldrick, C. Anderson, & F. Walsh (Eds.), *Women in families*. New York: Norton.

Shannon, W. (1966). *The American Irish*. New York: Macmillan.

Suilleabhain, S. O. (1967). *Irish wake amusements*. Dublin: Mercier.

Zoborowski, M. (1969). *People in pain*. San Francisco: Jossey Bass.

Indian

Altekar, A. S. (1959). *The status of women in Hindu civilization*. Delhi: Motilal Banarsidas.

Blotcky, A. (1981). Family functioning and physical health: An exploratory study with practical implications. *Family Therapy, 8* (3).

Baechler, J. (1975). *Suicides*. New York: Basic.

Bardhan, P. (1974). On life and death questions [Special Issue]. *Economic and Political Weekly*, 1293–1304.

Bardhan, P. (1982, September 4). Little girls and death in India. *Economic and Political Weekly*. 4: 1448–1450.

Bumiller, E. (1990). *May you be the mother of a hundred sons: A journey among the women of India*. New York: Random House.

Gore, M. S. (1965). The traditional Indian family. In M. F. Nimkoff (Ed.), *Comparative family systems*. Boston: Houghton Mifflin.

Jensen, J. M. (1980). East Indians. In S. Thernstrom (Ed.), *Harvard encyclopedia of American ethnic groups*. Cambridge, MA: University Press. 296–301.

Kakar, S. (1978). *The inner world: A psychoanalytic study childhood and society in India*. Delhi: Oxford University Press.

Kane, P. V. (1941). *The history of Dharmashastra*. (Vol. 4). Poona: Bhandarkar Oriental Research Institute.

Krishnaswamy, S. (1984, October). A note on female infanticide: An anthropological inquiry. *The Indian Journal of Social Work.* Vol. *XLV*, No. 3. 361–369.

Lynch, O. (1969). *The politics of untouchability: Social mobility and social change in a city in India.* New York: Columbia University Press.

Radhakrishnan, S. (1977). *Commentary on the Bhagvat Gita* (6th ed.). Bombay: Blackie and Sons.

Shivanand, Swami. (1979). *What becomes of the soul after death.* Theri Garwhal, U.P. India: The Divine Life Society.

Smith, B. K. (1989). *Reflections, resemblance, ritual and religion.* NY: Oxford University Press.

Stephens, W. N. (1963). *The family in cross-cultural perspective.* NY: Holt, Rinehart & Winston.

Stevenson, S. (1920). *Rites of the twice born.* London: Oxford University Press.

Europa Publications. (1989). *The Europa world yearbook* (Vol 1, A-J). London: Europa Publications. 1296–1310.

Toynbee, A. (1968). Various ways in which human beings have sought to reconcile themselves to the fact of death. In A. Toynbee, A. K. Mant, N. Smart, J. Hinton, C. Yudkin, E. Rhode, R. Heywood, & H. H. Price (Eds.), *Man's concern with death.* London: McGraw-Hill.

Tseng, W., & McDermott, J. F. (1985). *Culture, Mind, and Therapy: An introduction to cultural psychiatry.* NY: Brunner/Mazel.

Teja, J. S., Narang, R. L., & Aggarwal, A. K. (1971). Depression across cultures. *British Journal of Psychiatry, 119*: 253–260.

Jewish

Epstein, H. (1979). *Children of the Holocaust.* New York: G. P. Putnam.

Herz, F., & Rosen, E. (1982). Jewish families. In M. McGoldrick, J. K. Pearce, & J. Giordano (Eds.), *Ethnicity and family therapy.* New York: Guilford.

Moskovitz, S. (1983). *Love despite hate: Child survivors of the Holocaust and their adult lives.* New York: Shocken Books.

Zborowski, M. (1969). *People in pain.* San Francisco: Jossey Bass.

Zborowski, M., & Herzog, E. (1952). *Life is with people.* New York: International Universities Press.

Zuk, G. H. (1978). A therapist's perspective on Jewish family values. *Journal of Marriage and Family Counseling, 4*, 103–110.

Puerto Rican

Garcia-Preto, N. (1982). Puerto Ricans. In M. McGoldrick, J. K. Pearce, & J. Giordano (Eds.), *Ethnicity and family therapy.* New York: Guilford.

11

Rituals and the Healing Process

EVAN IMBER-BLACK

EVERY CULTURE HAS elaborated rituals to address the complex process of mourning. Such rituals, composed of metaphors, symbols, and actions in a highly condensed dramatic form, serve many functions. They mark the loss of a member, affirm the life lived by the person who has died, facilitate the expression of grief in ways that are consonant with the culture's values, speak symbolically of the meanings of death and ongoing life, and point to a direction for making sense of the loss while enabling continuity for the living.

A cross-cultural examination of mourning rituals reveals differences that express a given culture's beliefs, while also showing similarities, in that all such rituals are time-bounded and space-bounded, providing a sense of psychological safety for participants. Mourning rituals occur in specific places, such as parts of the home, the church or synagogue, the cemetery, and for specific time periods, such as the wake or the shiva. Many cultures have yearlong periods of mourning with particular rituals designed to mark the passage of time and the reentry into normal living for the survivors. Scheff (1979) points to the ways in which rituals enable the support and containment of strong emotions. Thus, in mourning rituals, people come together to grieve in a time-limited manner that is mutually supportive and allows for the initial expression of pain and loss in a context designed to promote interpersonal connectedness. Such rituals often require shared meals and visiting the bereaved for a prescribed time period in order to prevent dysfunctional isolation during the period of immediate loss and grief (Van Gennep, 1960).

Many cultural and religious groups have rituals that occur subsequent to a death in prescribed time sequences, enabling the living to remember and honor the dead and deal with the loss over time. Such rituals as the Catholic anniversary mass or the reciting of the Kaddish on the anniversary of the death in Judaism speak to the reality of mourning as a process that occurs over time and that requires familiar structures to enable healing.

The capacity of rituals to express powerful contradictions simultaneously makes them especially relevant to the mourning process. Roberts (1988) describes an Ashanti funeral dance ritual whose movements capture the exquisite pain of each individual's loss, while at the same time connecting each person with the larger community in an affirmation of life. Culturally agreed upon mourning rituals contain elements of familiarity and repetition grounded in past traditions that paradoxically enable the shaping of future life and relationships.

Mourning rituals may operate at multiple levels, facilitating the expression of individual grief, marking relationship change, affirming a family's loss and enabling an entire community to heal. An example may be seen in the Vietnam war memorial in Washington, D.C., which functions as an ongoing mourning and healing ritual. Family members and friends who lost men and women in the war come to the memorial in trips that are referred to as pilgrimages, find their person's name on the wall, and often make rubbings to carry back home in a manner that symbolizes their own personal loss while connecting with a larger community of mourners.

THE DISJUNCTURE OF AUTHENTIC MOURNING RITUALS AND CONTEMPORARY LIFE

While mourning rituals do exist, the connection of these rituals in a meaningful way with the needs of a particular person or family may be missing. Rituals remain vital and authentic for people when they are both embedded in past traditions and can be created anew according to present needs. Customary mourning rituals may occur in ways that are hollow or rigid, leaving the living disconnected from any sense of genuine healing. Since most people now die in hospitals, rather than at home, often surrounded by complex technology instead of familiar symbols, the proximity of death and loss as a part of the human life cycle connected to caring rituals has all but disappeared. Frequently a eulogy may be given as part of a funeral ritual by a clergy person who barely knew the deceased and who conducts a cliché-ridden service that does little to facilitate healing the bereaved (Rule, 1990). Increasingly, our culture has allowed the funeral industry to shape mourning rituals, such that they express more about capitalism and the denial of death than about authentic healing. The most recent example of this may be seen in the newly established practice of "drive-through" visitation, where a mourner drives a car up to a video screen, punches in the name of the deceased on a computer, views the remains, notes the visit via the computer and drives away. The lack of authentic mourning rituals in contemporary life frequently impedes the required healing process following a death. Relationships that need to undergo the changes demanded by a death rigidify and symptoms emerge which are metaphoric expressions of incomplete mourning and unhealed loss. When this occurs, a family's subsequent ritual life is often affected in deleterious ways, that may, simultaneously, be the path to healing, especially when attended to in therapy.

RITUALS, LOSS, AND THE THERAPEUTIC PROCESS

A family's ritual life may serve as a powerful lens with which to examine and understand the family's ways of dealing with prior and current losses. This ritual life includes its daily rituals, such as meals; its traditions, such as birthdays, anniversaries, vacations, and unique practices; its holiday celebrations, such as Thanksgiving or religious holidays; and its life cycle rituals, such as weddings, the birth of children, and rites of passage. These rituals, which occur in the life of every family, also provide the path for needed mourning, healing, and commemoration.

Case Example – "Death Touches All Rituals"

A family consisting of a divorced mother, Cathy Colby, age 56, her ex-husband, Eric Colby, 57, his new wife, Susan Colby, 38, and the original couple's daughter, Ellen, 27, were seen in a consulting interview following the suicide six months earlier of the son, Brian, who was 28 at the time of his death. Hearing of my interest in rituals, the family had expressed a wish to talk to me, as they approached the upcoming Christmas holiday season with trepidation.

As the interview unfolded, the family spoke poignantly of many rituals. In describing his acute sense of grief and loss, the father began by telling me about a daily breakfast he and his son had shared, "Every day I would drive by his apartment, pick him up and go out for breakfast before we each went to work. This started my day, and we would talk about our previous day and our plans. Now, every morning, I wake up, my feet hit the carpet and I know I won't be seeing him for breakfast and I can barely start the day." Others in the family had not shared this daily ritual that had been part of the father's life for several years. As we spoke, the father located his most profound sense of loss in the time and space of his daily ritual, saying, "Even if I manage to function during the day and evening, the pain begins anew each morning and I have to climb out of it all over again."

For the mother, daughter, and stepmother, the upcoming Thanksgiving and Christmas were filled with a sense of dread. The mother spoke for the family, "I'd like to go away for the holidays, go someplace else, cancel Thanksgiving, cancel Christmas—then maybe it won't hurt so much. I just can't imagine having the holidays without him." In the face of profound loss, they were contemplating a ritual path that would lead them away from subsequent celebrations and which would have cost them the family support inherent in these.

Ellen talked of starting her Christmas shopping and discovering she had bought things for Brian before realizing what she had done. For the women, the enormity of their loss was focused on these family gatherings, for which they were primarily responsible. As we talked of Brian's place in their previous holiday patterns, an open sharing of family stories about Brian and his relationships, so crucial to the mourning process, was facilitated. Here, remembering the holiday rituals together opened a door to shared grieving and began to alleviate this extended family's fears of being together for this year's holidays.

Finally, the father and daughter wanted to speak about Brian's birthday, which would be several months hence. The father, who had been mostly silent during the discussion of Christmas, now began to weep. He described the yearly birthday tradition to me, which, in fact, was a metaphor for all of Brian's unhappiness in life, his previously unmentioned substance abuse, and the father's and sister's frantic attempts to help him. Here, the family heard the father's enormous guilt, which he had before been unable to express so articulately. As the father spoke of Brian's last birthday, the mother wept, recalling his birth.

For each family member, different rituals held powerful emotions and relationship connections which were evoked by Brian's suicide. For the father, the daily breakfast ritual and Brian's birthday were most important, while for the women, the impending holidays were the most crucial. This joint discussion of family rituals enabled shared grieving, mutual support, and differentiated expressions of loss as symbolized in the very different rituals that were most important to each person. I ended this session with a suggestion to both family and therapist that the family work with their therapist on a ritual connected to the upcoming holidays that would allow a time-bounded sharing of stories, symbols, and memories of Brian and previous holidays. This ritual would be designed to affirm their loss and honor Brian, while simultaneously facilitating their ongoing development as individuals and as a family. Such an intervention enables families to use the holidays in a conscious way to examine their loss and begin the healing process.

LOSS AND PATTERNS OF RITUAL PRACTICE

In a typology of ritual practice, Roberts (1988a) describes *underritualized* families who neither celebrate or mark family changes with rituals nor participate in larger social rituals, *rigidly ritualized* families who must always perform their rituals in exactly the same way, with no variation, improvisation, or evolution, and *interrupted ritual* families who are unable to fully experience a ritual due to sudden changes or trauma. In talking with families whose ritual patterns fit these categories, one frequently finds unresolved loss metaphorically expressed through the family's current rituals.

A trainee's description of a yearly Thanksgiving ritual in her family illustrates her own dawning recognition of the delicate relationship of loss, healing, and subsequent rituals, especially rituals of celebration:

"Elaborate beautiful tables filled with feast food and of course the mandatory turkey made for Thanksgivings that were beautiful enough to be photographed for any magazine cover; and yet did not distract anyone sufficiently from the pervading mood of gloom, tension, and insufficiently disguised sadness, as each year, each person was left to privately re-experience the discrepancy between form and feeling. Everything looked right, and yet there was no connection, no shared meaning. It was an attempt to recreate somebody else's ritual, and each year it left its participants lonely in the midst of many, waiting for it to be over. . . .

My parents, aunts, and uncles experienced a world torn apart, relatives and friends murdered, community and culture destroyed (in the Holocaust). . . . this tremendous loss was not openly mourned, not ritualized . . . but rather it was denied, made private, and hidden. At first this was because there was too much to do, survival came first . . . and later when there was time and physical safety enough to allow for some expression of grief, it was already too buried, too frightening, too mystified. So my family did not mourn its losses, did not create rituals around these terrible and terribly important transitions. Without the mourning of deaths, can there be a real celebration of births? With the denial of the meaning of major transitions, can a family with meaning mark other transitions, or do these rituals of transition then need to be carefully contained so that they do not lead too dangerously close to thoughts and feelings of other times of change, to those who are not here, and to feelings that have not been allowed?" (Roberts, 1988b, p. 388)

Through examining a family's entire ritual life, one may see the family's valiant attempts to make sense of their loss in ways that often ferociously and silently reinforce and amplify that very loss with which they are struggling. As I have sat with families and, with the stance of the anthropologist, inquired about their ritual life, I have been deeply moved by the ways in which rituals contain profound metaphors for the family's own healing path following tragic loss. The seemingly commonsensical and protective solutions adopted by family members emerge as ritual patterns that operate paradoxically to prevent the very healing for which members yearn.

Families may abandon all familiar rituals, placing a moratorium on celebration, and exist in a permanent state of joylessness and grief. One Hispanic single-parent family, for whom food had previously meant connection and caring and sharing, described that they no longer ate together. "Since when?" I asked. "Since daddy died and mommy began to eat alone in her room," came the reply. Healing began in this family through a therapy that focused simply on a gradual reinstitution of shared meals, working with the pain and grief that this evoked, juxtaposed with the simultaneous sense of support and love that the mother experienced in eating with her children.

Loss and Subsequent Holiday Celebrations

Celebration rituals are embedded in the external calendar of a culture or subculture. As such, they are celebrated simultaneously on a given date by a significant portion of the population and are quite impossible to ignore. Families who have experienced loss face a special challenge as they encounter subsequent celebrations. All around, people appear to be celebrating, sharpening one's own sense of loss and differentness.

In my own life, over the three years since the sudden death of my father, I have witnessed my mother as she struggled with the Jewish holiday rituals, which intensified her sense of loss. Her own gradual healing is visible through the prism of these rituals. The first year, she was unable to participate in Rosh Hashanah, the Jewish New Year. She sent no cards, which had been part of her ritual for 53 years with my father; she explained, "I can't sign just *my* name." She stayed away from the synagogue that had been at the center of their married life. Paradoxically, these seemingly reasonable attempts to protect herself intensified her pain and isolation. The second year, she sent no cards, and she went to an unfamiliar synagogue. She reported to me that she hated it and felt bereft not only of my father but also of his memory, which was so richly embedded in their synagogue. In the third year, I received a New Year's card from her, and she returned to her synagogue and sat in the seat that had been hers for 35 years. With keen understanding of the courage required to fully reenter familiar, but forever changed rituals in the midst of loss, she said to me, "I think it was very brave of me—it was hard, but I could feel your father's presence and that was good."

Differing from families who abandon their familiar celebration rituals in the face of overwhelming loss are those families who rigidly and stereotypically perform their rituals as if there were no loss. Such families establish an unspoken rule not to acknowledge the loss and to attempt the impossible by holding subsequent celebration rituals as if the person were not gone. Such a path prevents the family from speaking about the dead person and from telling stories about prior rituals in which the person participated. Frozen, sterile rituals come to symbolize the family's deep need for healing, which cannot be voiced. When families cannot affirm their loss, their rituals become carefully staged events, lest the spontaneity and unconstrained human interaction inherent in authentic rituals lead family members to the unspeakable and the unknowable.

Case Example — "What About Christmas?"

A family, consisting of two parents, Mr. and Mrs. Franco, 58 and 56, and their adult son, Alan, 33, came to the crisis unit of an inner-city hospital early in December. Alan lived at home and did not work or go out of the house. He had a long history of seeing therapists and of day hospital involvement with no change in his behavior or in his overall life, which he spent primarily in isolation. The current crisis involved Alan's behavior towards his mother, which had recently turned extremely angry, hostile, and threatening, while he begged his father not to go to work. Mr. Franco said this episode seemed familiar, occurring early every winter, but that this time it seemed much worse.

As the therapist attempted to talk with the family, Alan began to shout, "The story of Michael, the story of Michael, we have to discuss the story of Michael!" The parents looked very pained, and while the father said, "This is not about Michael," the mother quietly began to tell the therapist about their older son, Michael, who had died suddenly, 17 years earlier, at the age of 20, of a cerebral aneurysm. Michael was a star student and athlete, for whom this family had many hopes. He had married in early December, just before Christmas, and died in February, leaving a pregnant wife, who subsequently cut off from the Francos, refusing them access to their now 16-year-old grandson.

The therapist asked the Francos how they had grieved the loss of Michael. Each had grieved alone, separated from the other family members in a manner that Alan's current pattern of isolation seemed to represent. Mrs. Franco frequently went to church alone, and did all of her crying there, sitting in a pew by herself. When she returned home, she described "going through the motions" of daily life so that no one in the family would know of her intense grief. Mr. Franco went weekly to the cemetery, also by himself.

No one knew he made these pilgrimages to Michael's grave. Alan, at age 17, became extremely depressed, dropped out of high school just short of graduation, and was sent to individual therapy and ultimately to a day hospital. Without realizing it, the treatment system simply replicated the family's style of grieving separately, such that family healing was never addressed. Now Alan remained at home while his parents worked, seemingly a dropout from life. Since they were acutely sensitive to one another's grief, the painful subject of Michael's death was never discussed in the family. Rather, the family became distracted by Alan's increasingly bizarre behavior, which seemed to function to prevent mourning and to freeze the family in time, obviating individual and family development and change.

In the second session, as the parents began to complain of no change in Alan's threatening behavior, Alan again began to shout, yelling, "Christmas! Christmas! What about Christmas? We have to talk about Christmas!" While the parents insisted that Christmas was of little importance, the therapist chose to honor Alan's request, having learned previously that, while appearing and sounding odd, Alan was, indeed, the voice for the family's deepest pains.

The family's celebration of Christmas had remained identical for the last 17 years. Mrs. Franco decorated the house, in order to "pretend that we're happy, and that we're just like other families." She made a special dinner, which Alan always disrupted with angry shouting, preventing the family from inviting relatives or friends, and frightening the parents so they would not leave to go visiting. His meta-message seemed to be "we are certainly not happy—we are not like other families." Thus, locked in together, the specter of Michael's death permeated the holiday, but was not mentioned. "We try to make everything just as it would have been with Michael here," explained Mr. Franco. Mrs. Franco remarked that she always put out a crèche Michael had made when he was 12. At that moment, she grew silent, and then she said, "You know, that crèche isn't made very well—if he were alive, I think I would have stopped putting it out years ago. I don't think I'm going to put it out this year." She began to cry in front of her family for the first time. At this indication that this Christmas might somehow be different, and that the family might start the difficult and painful journey into the present, Alan quietly nodded and smiled at his mother with a warmth we had not seen.

I asked the therapist to raise the possibility of partaking in a mourning ritual that would enable the family's joint conversation about Michael and a new celebration of Christmas. She asked if each would be willing to bring a symbol of Michael to the next session, which was scheduled three days before Christmas. They agreed. The session was the first to begin without shouting from Alan. In response to the therapist's request, each shared his or her symbol. The father took out Michael's class ring from high school, which no one knew he had kept and carried for 17 years. The mother brought a poem about a mother's love for a child that she had discovered shortly after Michael's death. The poem was on wrinkled and yellowed newsprint, as she had kept it in her wallet for 17 years and had never read it to anyone. The therapist asked if she would read it to the family and she did. Alan brought a photograph of two handsome boys, portraying Michael with his arm around Alan. Quietly and gently, the therapist asked them to exchange their symbols with one another, tangibly connecting them through this action and altering their previously solitary and unchanging grief. She then asked each to relate a favorite story of Michael. Alan, who was frequently tangential and disruptive, sat respectfully and attentively while his parents spoke. They, in turn, listened to him with a new affirmation, anticipating and receiving clarity. This sharing of favorite stories led to a spontaneous sharing of formerly hidden and secret guilt and shame of each member regarding Michael's death. The family members cried together for the first time in 17 years, and we quietly cried with them.

Following this deeply moving and simple healing ritual, the Francos began to discuss their Christmas celebration. Alan agreed not to disrupt the family's holiday. He said he would eat dinner with his parents and that they should go visiting whether he joined them or not. He then began, for the first time, to discuss needs for his own future.

Following Christmas, they returned to say that they had, indeed, had Christmas dinner together and were able to talk openly about Michael. The impossible attempt to celebrate "as if Michael were still alive" had been replaced by a new Christmas ritual that both honored their loss and confirmed their present relationships.

This ritual, conducted within the safety of the therapy session and co-created by therapist and family, delicately combined the human needs for healing and celebration previously unavailable to the family. A way was provided for the Francos to share their profound loss of a son and brother openly, facilitating reconnection, open grieving, and celebration at Christmas for the first time in 17 years. This simple ritual offered a path that simultaneously honored the past, altered the present, and enabled a future (Imber-Black, 1988).

As the foregoing discussion of family celebration patterns illustrates, two tendencies predominate in the face of loss as a family struggles to re-enter celebration rituals in particular. In some families, an unspoken rule is established requiring no open discussion of the loss, supporting a pretense that the loss has not occurred and that the celebration can proceed as usual. In such families, tension becomes profound as the holiday draws near and symptoms often emerge in various members that frequently are not understood as relating to unacknowledged loss and approaching holiday celebrations. Families describe having to "get through the holidays"; their valiant attempts to avoid pain result in the avoidance of any genuine sense of connection and support, while also removing the family from the possibility of any new joy.

In other families, a moratorium is placed on holiday rituals. The family exists in an unchanging state of grief. Following the seemingly commonsensical route of "no celebrations," families discover that the context of celebration exists all around them, exacerbating their sense of pain with isolation, and cutting them off from the emotional support that lives within the fabric of familiar rituals.

As the therapist discovers the family's celebration ritual pattern in the face of loss, she has many therapeutic options. These include posing future-oriented questions regarding alternative modes of ritual practice that begin to incorporate the loss, story-telling in the session about previous holiday rituals and the place of the deceased person in these, and the co-creation of therapeutic rituals that will enable new ritual patterns to emerge while also facilitating healing. As one interviews the family regarding their rituals, it is important to find out if the person who had died was, in fact, the family's "ritual maker," the one who made sure that the ritual happened. If so, how has the family interacted in response to the loss of the ritual maker? The loss of the ritual maker in the family poses special issues. Some extended family celebrations disintegrate when, for instance, a grandmother who was the ritual maker dies. In other families, an intense struggle may ensue regarding who becomes the new ritual maker. Often this struggle represents larger relational issues over who will now lead the family in particular areas. In many families, the struggle goes underground, as one sibling simply announces that Thanksgiving, previously celebrated at a parent's home, will now occur in his home, prepared by his wife; the remaining siblings either come, full of unspoken resentment, or vote with their feet, providing various excuses for nonparticipation, none of which speaks to the actual shifts occurring in the family in response to the death of the ritual maker. Sensitively crafted family therapy sessions with grown siblings can address this issue openly, utilizing the family's rituals as an entry point into complicated family relationships.

Loss and Subsequent Family Tradition Rituals

Family traditions are embedded in the family's own internal calendar, and include such rituals as birthdays, anniversaries, and unique traditions a family may invent. There are no common paths for marking the birthday of a family member who has died or the wedding anniversary when a spouse has died, and yet those living are keenly aware of the approach of such a day. Families may need to examine the meanings of such a day and to create a ritual to capture both loving memories and the sense of loss.

Birthdays may pose special problems, as when an adult approaches the age at which a parent died. A person may go to therapy complaining of recent depression or anxiety, often coupled with a sudden wish to alter life circumstances drastically. Such symptoms begin to make a new kind of sense when they are connected with the coincidence of the age at which a parent died and the upcoming birthday (Walsh, 1983; see Walsh & McGoldrick, Chapter 2). Work in therapy may then proceed to uncouple the death and the birthday, cocreating rituals to address both. Similarly, a family member may die on another member's birthday, resulting in a permanent fusion of death with the passage and celebration of life usually marked by a birthday. When this occurs, the birthday may subsequently go unmarked and uncelebrated, and may only re-emerge with permission in a therapy focusing on the need to provide continuity in life, rather than stagnation. The tendency to only mark the death and not the birthday, or to try to ignore the death and pretend to celebrate can be countered with ritual, as ritual has the capacity to hold and express profound dualities and contradictions. Thus, a given ritual may contain symbols and symbolic actions, and utilize time and space in ways that enable both mourning and celebration.

Families may also need to create rituals to mark the anniversary of a death, especially if the death has been one that the family cannot discuss, such as a suicide, death that the family or the outside community associates with stigma, or ambiguous loss, as when a member disappears. Very often family members distance from one another in the face of such loss, preventing the healing that is needed by all. Roberts (1988a) describes a woman whose brother had committed suicide 20 years earlier. The family was one that marked all rituals together, but had been totally unable to talk about the brother's death or ritualize it in any way. Each year, the anniversary of his death came and went with family members unable to connect or share their grief. In a therapy that focused on rituals, the woman and her spouse were able to create a ritual to affirm the brother's death and her sense of loss. For several nights preceding the anniversary of his death and on the actual anniversary, they lit candles and talked about the dead brother, while also putting out pictures of him for the first time. The woman also described this ceremony to her mother, breaking the taboo surrounding her brother's death for the first time in 20 years.

LOSS AND SUBSEQUENT LIFE CYCLE RITUALS

Life cycle rituals, such as weddings, baby-naming ceremonies and christenings, rites of passage, such as bar mitzvah, confirmation or graduation, and funerals may all interact in powerful ways with prior losses. These life cycle rituals, which mark both individual and family development and change while simultaneously announcing family stability, sometimes bring new and unanticipated waves of grieving of a prior loss. At the same time, because such rituals are generally embedded in extended family and community participation, they may offer an opportunity to honor and connect the deceased to the family's present and future life. Since life cycle rituals incorporate a sense of family and group membership, while also expressing particular beliefs and ideologies, deceased members are acutely missed.

At the first life cycle ritual occurring after the death of a family member one may experience the finality of the loss. As one woman stated, "It was only at my graduation from college, three years after my father died, that I really began to face the enormity of my loss. Education was so important to him. When he died, I just studied harder, and didn't really cope with his death. He would have been so happy to be at my graduation. I missed him so much, and I couldn't pretend anymore. The graduation was full of confusion for me, sensing how proud he would have been, and yet feeling so much sadness myself. I felt guilty, too, for being pleased with myself. At my party, my mother did something that really helped me — she spoke about him, what this all meant to him, how he loved me and how proud he was of my accomplishments. She gave me permission to miss him openly *and* to keep going."

In her qualitative research on the bar mitzvah ritual, Davis (1988) describes spontaneous acts of healing prior losses occurring within the context of celebration. One father publicly gave his son his own deceased father's prayer shawl and prayer book in which five generations of bar mitzvahs had been recorded. Before the entire congregation, he told his son what the grandfather would have wished for him had he been alive: "Live your life to the fullest! Do what you think is right!" adding, "What my father gave me above all else was a feeling that I was always loved, that I was always good — and if I could give you anything it would be that." In this brief and simple passing of symbols from father to son, grandfather was honored, as were previous generations, and healing of loss merged with life cycle celebration in a powerful moment.

In those cultures and religions in which a new baby is named after a member of the family who has died, or in those families that simply choose to name a child in this way, the baby-naming ritual may evoke a sense of loss in the midst of the contradictory celebration of life. One mother described naming her son after a beloved cousin who had died a year earlier and witnessing her aunt, the cousin's mother, cry for the first time. The mother said she believed that the giving of his name marked the reality of his death for her aunt. The capacity of a ritual to hold the most powerful dualities of death and new life is evident here.

Frequently people come to therapy in advance of a particular life cycle ritual. Often they are initially unaware of the connection of the upcoming life cycle transition, and especially its public marking by a ritual, and the pain they are experiencing in life. As the therapy unfolds, both clients and therapist may discover the exquisite interplay of prior loss, life cycle passages, and rituals. Therapeutic work may need to be done regarding the loss, before an individual or the family is able to move on to the next life cycle phase, including whatever ritual may be attendant to this. Following such work, therapist and family members may be able to cocreate elements of the life cycle ritual that will affirm the loss in the midst of celebration.

Case Example – "How Can I Have a Wedding When I Love Two Men?"

A single young woman, Teresa, 25, came to therapy. In the initial session, she was anxious and distraught, and told me that she was extremely confused because there were two men in her life and she could not decide which one to marry. One man, Joey, 27, worked in the same business as her father, made a good living, and was very devoted to her. She had known him for many years, and she said he treated her "like gold." She believed he would make a good husband and a good father. He also was interested in her work. Her family liked him very much, and he was of her ethnic group, Italian, and her religion, Catholic. The other man, Kevin, 30, was somewhat unsure about his future, but knew that he loved her and wanted to marry her. She had met him a year and a half earlier. He was also Catholic, but he was Irish. Her family was not very fond of him, but Teresa told me that she was much more excited about him than she was about Joey. When I asked her why her family didn't like Kevin, she shrugged and said, "Oh, they think I spend too much time with him." Currently, she spent little time with Joey, but they did have frequent, long telephone conversations. She related that she vacillated several times a day regarding which man to choose. Of some curiosity was the fact that in her conversation with me, she talked much more about being unable to have a wedding than being unable to have a marriage, saying several times, "How can I have a wedding when I love two men?" At first glance, her predicament seemed to stem from being unready to marry anyone, and from possible conflicts with her family. When I asked how she had met each man, however, her struggle began to make a new kind of sense, embedded in profound and unmourned loss.

"I met Joey when I was a teenager. He was my brother Louie's best friend." At the mention of Louie, Teresa began to cry, and told me that Louie had died of cancer about a year ago. "Louie was my sweet, sweet brother. We were very close. If he were here, I would know what to do." We talked for a long while about Louie's illness and Teresa's role when he was sick. She had nursed him at home and had been the family member who stayed with him in the hospital towards the end of his life, as her parents were simply unable to, due to their own pain over his dying. She became the conduit between Louie and other family members and between the hospital and the family. She was also the main source of comfort and support to her parents. Little else went on in her life for many months. It was, however, at the hospital where she met Kevin. At the time, he was an orderly, and would spend time comforting Teresa. Her family considered him to be an intruder. She remarked that Joey also wanted to comfort her during Louie's illness, but she found him to be so distraught himself that she mostly stayed away from him. After Louie died, she started seeing both men fairly often, and her confusion grew. Towards the end of the session, she told me that her father was extremely depressed, and that she was worried about him. "I can't imagine having a wedding while my father is like this." Teresa's current "confusion" over which man to marry now seemed also to be her solution to her family's present inability to have any wedding at all, since as long as she remained confused there would be no wedding.

In the second session, Teresa told me more about Kevin and why her parents did not care for him. He had a drinking and drug problem, and had a lot of trouble holding a job. It seemed Teresa had gone from taking care of Louie to now taking care of Kevin. She allowed that this was so, and that taking care of Kevin helped her miss Louie less. I asked what she thought she would be doing if Louie had not died. Without hesitation, she said "Oh, I'd be planning my wedding to Joey and Louie would be the best man!" At this, she began to sob. Suddenly, it was clear that it was not only her father's inability to have a wedding, but her own as well.

Following this session, Teresa ended her relationship with Kevin. She also told Joey that she wanted to see him, but that she needed time to make any final decisions regarding marriage. She brought her parents to therapy, and we worked for several sessions with issues involving Louie's death. This was the first time that the family had sat together to talk about Louie, replacing a pattern in which Teresa and her mother would comfort each other, and both would tiptoe around the father, believing his pain was simply too great and would be made worse by conversation.

Over many months, Teresa made a decision to marry Joey. They came together for a few sessions, and we talked about their wedding plans. Teresa spoke again of being unable to imagine a wedding without Louie. Here, I introduced the idea that it would be important to plan an aspect of their wedding that would affirm Louie's memory, and I asked them to think about ways that they might do so.

When Teresa and Joey returned they described how they wanted to honor Louie within the context of their wedding. They decided it would be important to have a brief ceremony with their extended family the night before their wedding, in order to allow people openly to share their feelings of missing Louie, rather than have this go underground. They decided that they would tell family members about this plan ahead of time, and ask those who wished to speak about Louie's life to share what each thought Louie's hopes for their marriage would have been. For the day of the wedding, they asked Joey's brother, who was to be their best man, if he would mention Louie in his toast to them. Teresa said it was very important to her that people felt free to feel both their sadness and their happiness at her wedding, since she was feeling both and did not want to have to pretend on this most important day.

Teresa and Joey came in a month following their wedding. The ceremony on the night before their wedding had been very moving, and had indeed allowed people to experience the full range of emotions without pretense. A favorite aunt had brought a short home movie that showed Teresa, Louie, and Joey during adolescence. Others had brought photographs and mementos to frame their remarks. Teresa said, "What was most important was what people told us Louie would have wanted for us — it gave me permission from all of our family to go on with my life. Our wedding was beautiful — I missed Louie, but it was okay because I could feel that and say that and not be afraid. When our best man mentioned Louie in his toast, I responded with how much I was feeling Louie's love — I hadn't planned to do that — it just was the natural thing to do."

Sometimes a death will occur just at the juncture of a life cycle ritual, as, for instance, when a parent dies soon after a child's wedding, or a grandparent dies at the time when a child is born. Such a death may profoundly shape relationships, and a new ritual may be required many years later in order to free the relationship from the context of loss. One couple separated after 14 years of marriage. The wife's beloved father had died two days after her wedding. In her grief, she looked to her husband, although she felt he simply "could not measure up" to her father. He, in turn, managed to live down to her expectations, as they entered a cycle in which she was intensely disappointed with him and he kept disappointing her. The wife said that, even when things were going well between them, the approach of their anniversary each year would seem to set off a new round of fighting and despair. Our work in therapy involved helping her to mourn her father's death, separate his death from their marriage, and finally, when the couple was ready to reconcile, to make a new wedding ceremony, complete with a new anniversary date. The couple wrote new wedding vows, bought new rings, and the husband designed special glasses with their names and new anniversary date engraved upon them, freeing them from the memory of a wedding ritual that had, in fact, fused with her father's death.

DESIGNING RITUALS TO FACILITATE HEALING

As this chapter has made clear, the rituals in any family's life are the best entry point for facilitating healing. Familiar daily rituals, traditions, celebrations, and life cycle rituals all provide opportunities for dealing with profound loss and grief. At times, however, one may need to go beyond such normative rituals, and cocreate a special ritual to effect healing. Rituals' unique capacity to hold contradictions makes them especially relevant to the life task of grieving and moving on.

Designing such new rituals requires a search for the appropriate symbols and symbolic acts for a given individual, family, or community. These symbols and metaphorical action both connect the family with the familiar and provide a pathway to the unfamiliar. Symbols enable participants to develop multiple meanings in the ritual, and the actions provided move the participants beyond the verbal sphere.

As rituals involve the dimensions of time and space, care should be taken to utilize time in the ritual to draw particular distinctions, such as a distinction between time to mourn and time to reenter life's celebrations. Time may also be collapsed in a ritual to highlight simultaneous contradictions. The space where a ritual occurs may express particular beliefs, such as when a ritual occurs in a religious institution, or may hold special symbols, such as a cemetery, or may involve returning to a space that held unique meaning for the deceased or for one's relationship with the deceased, such as a house, a woods, a certain city.

Any newly designed ritual to address loss should be carefully cocreated and not imposed. Care should be taken to leave aspects of the ritual unplanned in order to enable authentic unfolding at the moment the ritual is enacted (Imber-Black, 1988; Whiting, 1988).

A powerful and newly designed contemporary healing ritual is the Names Project, also known as the AIDS Quilt. The Names Project is a national healing ritual embodied in a hand-sewn tribute to the thousands of men, women, and children who have died of AIDS. Thousands and thousands of three-by-six-foot panels have been designed and sewn into what has become the quilt. Each panel is lovingly made by people who have lost someone, and each contains expressions designed to capture an essential aspect of the person who has died of AIDS. Each showing of the quilt is accompanied by a ceremony in which all of the names are read aloud, affirming the unique life of each individual person while also capturing the overwhelming sense of collective loss. The choice of a quilt symbolizes the possibilities of warmth available through survivors' connections with one another, thus affirming life in the face of terrible death. For the individuals, stitching a quilt is an act of love, creativity, and continuity. For the community, the quilting bee has historically been an expression of solidarity, collaboration, hope, endurance, and joy. This painfully unfinished ritual functions on multiple levels to memorialize each person who has died, to connect a community that is grieving together, and to serve as a profound visual reminder to the broader community of the magnitude of the loss, while simultaneously celebrating life.

Working with clients in therapy to cocreate needed healing rituals at times shifts one's position from therapist to privileged witness, humble guide, or cotraveler on a precarious journey. The movement from loss to healing to reconnection with meaningful rituals in life is a spiral. Healing rituals do not provide simplistic or trivial closure, but rather enable transcendence, facilitating relationship reconciliation and reengagement with life.

REFERENCES

Davis, J. (1988). Mazel Tov: The bar mitzvah as a multigenerational ritual of change and continuity. In E. Imber-Black, J. Roberts, & R. Whiting (Eds.), *Rituals in families and family therapy*. New York: Norton.

Imber-Black, E. (1988). Ritual themes in families and family therapy. In E. Imber-Black, J. Roberts, & R. Whiting (Eds.), *Rituals in families and family therapy*. New York: Norton.

Imber-Black, E. (1989). Idiosyncratic life cycle transitions and therapeutic rituals. In B. Carter & M. McGoldrick (Eds.), *The changing family life cycle: A framework for family therapy* (2nd ed.). Boston: Allyn & Bacon.

Roberts, J. (1988a). Setting the frame: Definition, functions, and typology of rituals. In E. Imber-Black, J. Roberts, & R. Whiting (Eds.), *Rituals in families and family therapy*. New York: Norton.

Roberts, J. (1988b). Rituals and trainees. In E. Imber-Black, J. Roberts, & R. Whiting (Eds.), *Rituals in families and family therapy*. New York: Norton.

Rule, S. (1990). At the secular funeral, a tango may be tasteful. *New York Times*, January 10, A4.

Scheff, T. J. (1979). *Catharsis in healing, ritual and drama*. Berkeley and Los Angeles: University of California Press.

Van Gennep, A. (1960). *The rites of passage*. Chicago: University of Chicago Press.

Walsh, F. (1983). The timing of symptoms and critical events in the family life cycle. In H. Liddle (Ed.), *Clinical implications of the family life cycle*. Rockville, MD: Aspen Publications.

Whiting, R. (1988). Guidelines to designing therapeutic rituals. In E. Imber-Black, J. Roberts, & R. Whiting (Eds.), *Rituals in families and family therapy*. New York: Norton.

12

Strange and Novel Ways of Addressing Guilt

DAVID EPSTON

GUILT ASSOCIATED WITH the death or dying of others is well-known, but there has been little discussion of it apart from those conventions derived from the notion of "working through." It is almost as if, in the face of death and dying, the creativity many therapists bring to bear on their work is forsaken. The seriousness adopted can stymie any measures apart from attempting to talk the person out of feeling guilty. I am not arguing here that we should not take death and dying seriously; rather, I am advocating the deep play associated with creative endeavor. The stories that follow are written with the hope that others might be encouraged to play deeply in the face of death and dying, for in the stories of Billy, Hayden, and Martin and Sally, the therapist was required by urgency to have recourse to such an aptitude. In each case study, the person was experiencing guilt somewhere along the continuum of self-accusation/condemnation, self-punishment, self-starvation, self-torture, self-exile, and finally self-execution. For Billy, Hayden, and Martin, rapid and enduring relief was found by strange and novel ways.

BILLY GIVES GUBA THE SLIP

Billy, aged 12, was referred to a residential community because of his persistent truanting, running away from home, and more recently, abusing alcohol. Billy was the third of four sons from a fundamentalist family. His father worked long days in his small business but still had trouble making ends meet and the family's circumstances were impoverished. The mother had come from an "aristocratic" and highly successful family that had rejected her when she married her husband.

At the age of three, Billy had been struck down by a bicyclist, sustaining disfiguring facial injuries that had required corrective surgery. Although this surgery was very successful, from that day on, the family story went, Billy had "rejected" his parents. By their account Billy refused to accept their attempts to "cuddle" him and commenced wandering away from home. According to Billy, they blamed him for his "stupidity" for running into the path of the cyclist; Billy blamed them, in return, for not having watched over him adequately.

When Billy was seven, his father was diagnosed with cancer of the kidney. The father's condition deteriorated over the next three years. Finally, a last ditch attempt was made to save his life by surgery and, surprisingly, he went into remission for some time.

I was urgently requested to consult with Billy two years after his father's surgery and six weeks after his family insisted on his admission to residential care because of his failure to attend school and the danger posed by his running away. He had attended less than ten days of school in the previous six months. Billy's father's health had suddenly deteriorated drastically and his mother became emotionally paralyzed, refusing to talk to anyone. Because there were no other family members able to care for Billy, residential placement became a way to avoid the legal action that would make him a ward of the state. It would also maximize the possibility that Billy and his family could be reunited at some time in the future.

The family therapy team of the residential unit found Billy's family to be "devastated" and extremely difficult to reach. Meanwhile, the therapeutic community could not contain Billy by recourse to any conventional measures. He continued to run away by night, making his getaway on stolen bicycles. He had stolen 20 by the time I met him. At the same time, he had suffered numerous physical injuries, many of which he really couldn't explain. Both staff and fellow residents felt there was "something crazy about him," and none of them liked associating with him. What was most unnerving for Billy's therapist was the reckless way he rode his stolen bicycles, at times appearing to throw himself into the path of oncoming cars. At other times, he could be found sheltering in churches, perilously perched in the belfries, drunk on altar wine. Once he had broken into the home of a funeral director and stolen the keys to their hearse. These events so distressed the residential staff that the only option they could see to reduce the mayhem he was creating was to transfer him to a secure unit where he could be incarcerated. Instead, the therapist, in an attempt to bring Billy under some measure of control, commenced the ritual process that Michael White (1989) developed called "the ritual of inclusion." This ritual involves a phase of physical restraint but is reframed as a matter of getting in touch with others rather than punishment. Such a ritual process often triggers a crisis of intimacy in which the young person seeks out physical closeness and a sense of belonging.

In the intimacy that this intervention provoked, Billy told his therapist of his conviction that he had caused his father's cancer and was possessed by a devil. Attempts were made to convince him otherwise; when these failed Billy saw his family doctor, whose efforts fared no better. Everyone felt so desperate that someone proposed an exorcism, a practice that was consistent with the family's fundamentalist Christianity. Billy seized this opportunity, which was enacted under the appropriate ecclesiastical guidance. He experienced immediate relief, but, unfortunately, it only endured for 24 hours before he felt his "devil" had regained control over him. It was at this point that I was requested to consult to Billy and his therapist. His father's medical condition had recently deteriorated and his death was believed to be imminent. We speculated that Billy would expect his devil to demand his own death in retribution for his father's demise.

I was requested by the unit's family therapy team to do an emergency consult with Billy. One thing seemed strongly in my favor in meeting him: I am a cyclist and had ridden to the consultation on a racing cycle, wearing a cycling jersey under my shirt. How could two cyclists not joint together? When Billy entered the room, I was surprised how open, friendly, and unsuspicious he was. Still, I thought it would be prudent to show my credentials. I asked if he would like to check over my bicycle. He eagerly accepted. I revealed my cycling jersey. My first question, after our "cyclist's union," was, "Have you ever had a good day in your life?" He considered the question very seriously and came up with his answer: "That day in the church when I got exorcized . . . and the day I got my first bicycle." As the effects of the former experience were so short-lived, I decided to pursue the latter. I invited him to tell me about it in detail. To assist him in his description, I asked what his bicycle had been called. His answer was fortuitous: "Sidewinder!" I then inquired if he knew what a sidewinder was. "Yes," he said, "a deadly snake." I agreed with him: "You're quite right. No one in his right mind would mess with a sidewinder." From here on in, I took every opportunity to add the comments—"Cycles are good. . . . cycling is good . . . cyclists are good . . . and goodness drives out badness"—into our conversation. These comments located us in the same status: good cyclists opposed to badness. Billy's belief that he was possessed by the devil and consequently evil-doing had been immune to discrediting. I provided him with a counterproposition, one that no longer constrained him from his blindness to discrepancies between events in his father's life and events in his own.

I then requested that he show me his devil by drawing a picture of it. He did so without any reservation. His representation had horns, a trident, a forked tail, and a third eye in the middle of his forehead. Underneath was inscribed "Guba." I showed no fear but treated Guba's representation with the same degree of respect one would accord any worthy adversary. I placed the picture of Guba in one corner of the room and asked Billy and his therapist to bring their chairs and join me in the opposite corner. We huddled and spoke in confidential and hushed tones. I renamed Billy "Sidewinder." His therapist accepted the name of the "White Knight" and I took the name of the "Avenging Angel." Right there and then, we all agreed to join forces against Guba. Whenever an opportunity arose, I restated the counterproposition: "Cyclists are good; goodness drives out badness."

I then proceeded to tell Billy about the Molteni cycling jersey that had recently been returned to me by another client, who had had life-threatening asthma. It had been his talisman while he gained good control over his asthma and had became a competent cyclist. I also informed him that the most famous cyclist in the world, Eddie Mercyx, rode for the Molteni Spaghetti Company and won the Tour de France five times. I then went into some detail how "the Molteni" assisted me in cycling from England to France and said that, when I weakened, I always knew I could count on "the Molteni" to get me to my destination, no matter what. At the end of the session I gave "the Molteni" to Billy.

I started regularly telephoning Billy and would initiate contact as follows: "Come in, Sidewinder . . . come in. Can you read me? This is the Avenging Angel . . . can you read me?" After Billy would acknowledge our contact, I would inquire: "Any sign of the enemy today? Has Guba tried to bug you or take over your mind?" Billy usually told of some skirmishing and the tactics he was now employing, concluding with, "And I gave Guba the slip." I would check with him if he thought he had enough resources and he would reassure me that "the Molteni" was working. "I'll check back in a few days, Sidewinder. This is the Avenging Angel signing off. Over and out."

We met again two months later after my return from overseas. Billy, according to both himself and his therapist, had utterly repossessed himself. I found it hard to conceal my amazement. Within two weeks of our first meeting, he had stopped running away, stealing bicycles, and damaging himself, and had become more accessible to both his therapist and fellow residents. I asked his permission to ask him a number of questions so I could satisfy my curiosity as to how he had given Guba the slip. The following is the 'letter' format I used to validate Billy's new story by retelling it.

Dear Sidewinder:

This is a copy of our talk today. You can read it over when you want to. If you forget it, this will help you remember it. Billy, this is what you had to say:

The Molteni jersey made me believe that I could fight Guba. I think Guba didn't like it. He's ready to make another move. But he can be killed by goodness. I'm into goodness and Guba is into badness. My special name gave me strength because it stands for a very poisonous snake. My therapist, Tim, makes sure I'm good and not bad. Tim is on the side of goodness and strength. I didn't know I had so much strength of mind before today. I figured this out when Tim promoted me to a higher grade in the residence. If I keep going, I soon will be a senior. I am getting used to the fact that I have inside of me a personal strength and goodness. I have tons more goodness today than when I first met you. Your friend, Michael White, was right when he said that I would be all right because I could fight back against Guba and that I shouldn't be so impatient. He was right too when he said that everything that needed to be done had been done and that I would do the rest.*

I know that life is full of ups and downs and when I am down, I will be vulnerable to the tricks and sneakiness of Guba. It is easy to fight back, even when I am down and Guba tries to take over my mind again. I have a mind of my own now and it is a strong mind. I can call on the White Knight and the Avenging Angel if Guba tries to make a sneaky move on me. I have already fought back by using my mind strength to be good and not be tricked into doing bad. I just didn't listen to Guba anymore. I just told myself not to listen and that's all there was to it. Even if Guba shouted at me, I could shout even louder. I got my strength from within my own mind and I know now I always had it. The trouble was I didn't know I had it. Now I know.

I was really interested to learn of your anti-Guba tactics. Still, it might be a very good idea to practice fighting Guba with Tim. How you could do this is by pretending you are down and vulnerable and to spy on the ways Guba tries to ambush your mind and take it over with its garbage. Tim will help you here by helping you pretend and by helping spy on Guba's habits. If Guba is going to fight dirty, you are going to have to be on the look-out. Spying is the best thing to do while life is on the up for you. If the going gets tough, you will be ready for anything Guba tries on you to take over your mind. Guba is going to be awfully upset to find that you have strengthened your mind so much. He usually preys upon weak minds. You are no weakling — that's for sure. Keep this in a safe place.

Yours sincerely,
The Avenging Angel

---

*Billy knew of Michael White because his ritual of inclusion had been referred to as "Michael Whiting" in his residential community, so he was very keen to learn what Michael White thought of his predicament when he learned that I was visiting Michael in Australia.

Still, fearing for Billy's sanity in the event of his father's death, we thought it prudent to make provisions for this possibility, should our interventions fail. We arranged to meet with Billy's oldest brother, who had just returned from abroad, for a videotaped discussion. We suggested its purpose be the exculpation of Billy, but that we might have to save the video until Billy was ready to appreciate its contents. However, Billy was enthusiastic about viewing the video as the relationship with this brother was his strongest relationship in his family. During my discussion with Billy's brother, I proposed an explanation of the father's cancer to counter Billy's: "Your dad works so hard . . . it's almost as if he's working himself to death." Billy's brother agreed and we investigated this proposition at some length during our videotaped meeting. Although I had been informed that Billy's father denied that his life was in danger and had refused to discuss any plans for the family's future with either his wife or Billy's therapist, I wrote him a letter, seeking his cooperation in preparing a video.

Dear Mr. Brown:

I am putting my thoughts in writing because I cannot be there when you make the video with Tim [the therapist]. I regret that I am unable to do so. This next hour could be the most critical experience for your son's future. I am aware that this is dramatic, so allow me to explain myself. As you may know, Billy *mistakenly* believes that he, and he alone, is responsible for your cancer and any suffering you have undergone. Although you may be surprised by this and unwilling to accept his childish beliefs, he entertains these ideas despite your best intentions to dissuade him and our best attempts to talk him out of it. It seems to us that he formed these ideas some years ago when he was very young and from *his point of view*, everything that has happened since then supports his argument. He cannot yet see it from an adult point of view because to some extent he is stuck at an earlier level in his thinking. His love for you is so great that he is devastated by your illness. If he loved you less, his problem would be considerably smaller and we would not be so concerned. He believes unconsciously that he should be punished and tortured and that is exactly what he does to himself at times. These times are very dangerous for his well-being. There is also a grave risk that he will have a tortured life-style, in which his unconscious thoughts of guilt and blame for your suffering will dictate self-punishments to him. If we do not do something, it is possible he will serve a life sentence for something he did not do. He will pay with self-torture for a crime he did not or could not have committed. We know this; you know this; but Billy has a very different set of ideas to explain your misfortunes. He is a victim, like you and your family, but he views himself as your villain.

It is my opinion that you, and only you (as his father and the one who is suffering the most) can absolve him. And I am afraid to say that his suffering may persist until he has the adult understanding to believe your words and be fully aware of their meaning. I request for your son's sake (and your own) that you record and document your absolution of your son to keep him from torturing himself with guilt and blame for your illness. It is not likely that this will have an immediate impact but we promise you that we will hold it in trust and make it available to Billy when either he or we think he is ready to know the real truth. So no matter what happens to you or us, this tape will remain the property of your son and I believe that it may very likely mean the difference between a tortured life-style for Billy and a good future. Once again, it is my considered opinion that what you are about to do will have more influence over your son's life than anything else, aside from his conception and birth.

I am not there with you and Billy's therapist but I want you to know I am there in spirit. Good luck to you both and what you do now could change the course of Billy's life.

> Yours with respect and admiration,
> David

Billy's father decided against a videotaped meeting but instead chose to meet with Billy himself. Four months later, he died. Billy, along with his family, had been at his father's bedside throughout the last week of his life. Although his grief was profound, Billy was able, at all times, to act with personal dignity and integrity and support other family members. At his therapist's suggestion, Billy accompanied his father's body to the crematorium along with his therapist and the minister and once again participated in every way possible until all there was left for him to do was say farewell to his father.

Two years later, I learned that Billy had grown quite a bit and probably could fit into the Molteni. So we arranged to meet together. Billy recalled how Guba "got inside me and caused me to run away and get into bad things . . . it instructed my brain to just do things." When I asked how he accounted for his success, he proposed a number of possibilities:

BB   Firstly, I found out that people did care about me. Before I didn't think anyone cared about me; secondly, the Molteni. A good friend gave it to me . . . and that's you. I knew I would be able to trust it. Like God gave this to you or the person who gave it to you. It was like a powerful thing that would stop all my enemies. And I know that ever since I've had it, it stopped everything bad from happening to me. I really thank it. And thirdly, express your life to people that you know love you. . . . After I was talking to you, it sort of lost power like when you see electricity in a light and then you turn it off.

DE   Now tell me, before Guba was giving you the idea that you were to blame for your father. When your dad died, that would have been a time I would have thought that Guba would have tried to reassert itself in your mind. Did it not have any impact on you? None of these ideas got through to you?

BB No . . . no . . . I was believing for a while that I was the one to blame for my dad getting sick.

DE How did you get that idea?

BB Guba made a signal into my mind but I was the one to get out of it. I listened to my father when he talked to me. He told me to try to get better because he knew what was happening to me.

DE You got yourself out of that idea?

BB Yah!

DE If you didn't have the strength you had, what do you think Guba would have done to you in the end?

BB He probably would have turned me into a vegetable and sent me to a psycho hospital.

DE I'm glad that didn't happen.

BB So am I.

DE Because you strike me as a very fine person and if I had to describe you in one word, it would be courageous. It seems to me that you have lived through a pretty hard thing for a young person — your dad's death. And Tim gave me the impression that you were particularly helpful to your family and your father would have been very proud of you. Do you think so?

BB Yes.

After our discussion, Billy posed for a photograph wearing the Molteni. I then invited him for an inaugural ride on my bicycle. He returned 15 minutes later, having worked up a good sweat, but he and my bicycle were in one piece. Never I have known anyone to look so proud when he dismounted and returned my helmet. Since then, Billy has become a very popular young person both in the residence and at school, where he is regarded as "the most centered kid."

Considerable work has been done by the therapeutic team to assist Billy and his mother in reuniting, a very difficult proposition, because after the father died it was discovered that he had mortgaged all his life insurance and the mother had to sell their home to pay off their creditors. In this process a second son had to move in with friends. (At this point efforts are being made to shore up financial resources and extend family support for Billy's mother to enable the family to come together again. It seems likely that Billy will be able to return to his family in the near future.)*

---

*Most credit for this case goes to Billy's therapist, Tim, and the therapeutic team who worked with him with care and perseverance over many years.

Confession, Penance, and Absolution*

Sally, aged 26, made an appointment for her husband, Martin, aged 28, and herself because her husband was refusing to acknowledge her three-month-long pregnancy. When I met and talked with them, it was very easy to understand why. Sally and Martin had met at age 13 and 15 and had joined their lives together almost from then. They had always wanted children; however, first they traveled abroad so that Martin could advance in his accounting career. This was very important to him because his family had been very poor as a result of his father's unwise business decisions. He, by contrast, wished to insure the financial security of his family, including his mother, who had separated from his father, and his mother's mother. Sally became pregnant while they were living abroad and wished to return home. Martin urged that they stay on for another year to complete his contract. Because there was some indication of obstetric risk, near the end of her pregnancy Sally was to be admitted for a "trial of labor" to decide whether a caesarian section was indicated. The medical staff mistakenly proceeded with normal birthing. After 18 hours of labor, a young doctor unsuccessfully attempted a high forceps delivery, and Sally was then urgently transferred to the operating room. During the delay, the baby stopped breathing and had to be resuscitated. As a result, he was profoundly brain-damaged. Martin and Sally returned with their baby to New Zealand, and the baby spent nine months between hospital and home before he died. This was an extremely difficult time for all concerned and their distress and grief were almost unendurable.

During this time, Martin became preoccupied with his guilt. He blamed himself on two counts: first, if he hadn't wanted to remain in England this wouldn't have happened, and second, he should have been aware that the medical staff were mistaken and acted accordingly to set them right. Although Sally acknowledged that she had some grieving to do, she felt able "to look forward rather than backward" and had deeply hoped that the current pregnancy would have the same effect on Martin.

On the contrary, Martin was quite oblivious. Although he was still able to maintain his job, he became preoccupied with all the reasons he was to blame for their first child's demise. This was taking two to three hours of his time every day. In addition, he was preparing a legal action against the doctor in question. He was determined to pursue this course despite what he described as "a hell of a lot of conflict in my mind." To some extent, he didn't know whom to blame more—the doctor or himself.

---

*This story was written with the collaboration of Martin and Sally Lyttleton and I thank them for their counsel.

I listened for quite a while and then asked this question: "How many people have tried to talk you out of your guilt?" They assured me that their many friends and family had done just that without any success whatsoever. In fact, Martin now avoided all social occasions. He described feeling estranged and "not normal." In our discussion, I alternated the more self-referential term "self-torture" for guilt and then used it almost exclusively. I proposed that there was a well-established escape route from self-torture: confession, penance, and absolution. I inquired if they had ever heard of this. They laughed for the first time and assured me they had. I asked once again if they thought there was any chance of my convincing Martin that he oughtn't to feel so guilty, since "after all, it's not your fault." They insisted that this had been tried extensively without Martin's experiencing any relief whatsoever.

So we all agreed to start with Martin's confession. I invited him to employ the "seven deadly sins" as his moral reference points. He was very clear about the charges he had laid against himself:

> The reason we were in England was because of my drive. . . . I kept Sally there by a mixture of deceit and God knows what else. . . . On the day of the labor, I didn't grab anyone by the head. . . . I wish I hadn't been so concerned about Sally. I should have looked at what people were doing.

Sally and I convened and came up with the sins of dishonesty, greed, and ignorance. Martin found himself 100% to blame. Sally and I started to work out some appropriate penance, which we referred to as "torture" instead of "self-torture." We came up with ideas for "torture runs" and "torture jobs," all of which were particularly benevolent, since over the period of time since the baby's death Martin had gained 30 pounds and was extremely overweight. The mood changed dramatically and it would be fair to say that we were all laughing loudly, especially when we would concur with one of Martin's self-charges and also insist that he hadn't fully considered his "sinfulness."

The following letter was sent to them immediately after the session:

> Dear Martin and Sally:
>
> You made your confession yesterday, which probably was something of a relief to you. Now you are in a better position to take some affirmative action in the form of penance. This will take the place of self-torture. As you yourself noted, self-torture was a sentence without limit—a life sentence, in fact. There was the possibility that your mind would become your prison and your guilt would become your jailer.
>
> In your confession, you found yourself 100% to blame for the following self-charges:

1. In order to provide for your mother and grandmother and your own family in a manner different from that of your father, you traveled to England to secure a good income. You did this so that you would not experience the insecurities that you did as a child. You were driven because of these concerns to advance yourself in your career and you did everything in your power to convince Sally to stay on. For the above, you have accused yourself of the sins of dishonesty and greed and have found yourself guilty.

2. During the day of Sally's labor, "I didn't grab someone by the hand. I should have looked at what people were doing." Instead, you were guilty of spending all your time by Sally, comforting her and sharing her pain. You have found yourself guilty of ignorance. "I should have known what 'trial of labor' meant, should have gone to medical school and done a post-graduate Diploma of Obstetrics and Gynecology."

Instead, you advanced yourself in your accounting career and invested a lot of time and energy in it. And, in addition, you refused to work as an accountant for altruistic motives and insisted on payment for your services. With your payment, instead of giving all your money away to a worthy cause — Sally suggested the Society for the Prevention of Cruelty to Animals — you attempted to secure your life and Sally's along with the generation of your children and the generations of your mother and her mother.

You agreed that justice would only be done if you inflicted upon yourself some fair and just penance for the sins of greed, dishonesty, and ignorance. And I imagine there were a few other deadly sins that slipped your mind during your confession.

The tortures are as follows:

1. Every day, rain or shine — I hope it rains! — you are to rise at the unseemly hour of 6:30 a.m., don appropriate jogger's suit, and run for exactly 20 minutes. During this time, you are to say over and over to yourself a list of the ways you, Martin, can insult yourself. Sally will provide you with such a list and replenish it when required.

2. Sally will allow you to forget to put the rubbish out and then insist that you put it out late at night and do so barefoot.

3. Martin, you are to leave your clothes all over the place and Sally will hide them so you, Martin, will experience a sharp, short burst of torture finding them. Sally will claim that her pregnancy has made her forgetful and that she just can't help herself.

4. Martin, you are to paint the roof within one month's time. Randomly, Sally will phone you so you have to get down from the roof, being the kind of person who can't resist answering the telephone. Sally will inquire if you are torturing yourself to your satisfaction.

5. Once again, during tortures 2, 3, and 4, Martin, you are to recite to yourself your self-blaming jingles that Sally will compose for you.

I look forward to meeting you both in one month's time to see if you, Martin, are ready for absolution. Good luck!

Yours sincerely,
David

We met one month later and, as soon as we saw one another, we all cracked up laughing. Martin informed me that he had "slightly changed your torture" from running to swimming. He was doing between six and eight lengths of the pool per day. I commented, "Swimming is good because you are quite mindless. Did you fill your mind up with blaming?" He laughed and told me he just didn't have the energy for it. Good progress was being made on the roof too. Sally informed me that Martin had become more energetic, more "like your old self" and less depressed. When I asked when this occurred, she said: "Straightaway, really! You were better within 24 hours." Martin happily agreed, saying that he no longer felt "abnormal" and was 80% of his old self: "I'm getting so close that a lot of people wouldn't notice the difference."

DE   What do you think happened at this place that set the stage for your comeback?

ML   It acted like a turning point. Now, whether that turning point would have happened a bit further along, we don't know. But it couldn't have happened when he died. It was a couple of months after and it was a turning point. That's the only way you can describe it.

DE   How do you understand how that occurred? What do you think I did or said that allowed all of you to change course in a sense?

ML   You were sensible in what you said but the approach you took was slightly silly, bordering on the ridiculous. It was that approach. Underneath, I could see your motives and they were good. It was slightly ridiculous. It made everything I was feeling seem ridiculous.

SL   (bursting out laughing) And it was that thing you said that a lot of people have been telling you that it wasn't your fault. And that didn't work. If you're guilty, you've got to get it out of your system.

We then went on to discuss how they had grown apart by protecting each other by "going off into our little, separate corner." They felt that the wedge that had been driven between them was gone. They also talked about the friction that had arisen between them with Sally encouraging Martin "to become your old, confident self" and Martin feeling annoyed. Sally also expressed her relief that Martin was no longer indifferent to her pregnancy. She had feared that he would, in a manner of speaking, lose this child too. They agreed that this was all behind them, although they still had some grieving to do. Now they were determined to share their grief. Martin had taken up all the social activities he had abandoned. They had carefully selected "a good gynecologist" and were confident things would go well this time.

I don't think I ever looked forward to a six-month follow-up quite so much. Sally told me that she would be having a caesarian and couldn't wait to have her baby in her arms. Martin was somewhat apprehensive but doing well. She then laughed and told me that I might be interested to learn that Martin was now swimming a kilometer a day and had lost 30 pounds in weight. When I asked what was happening with their legal action, she replied: "You know, Martin hasn't mentioned it since the first time we saw you six months ago." I wished her well. Three weeks later, I received a card announcing the birth of a "beautiful and healthy baby girl." We met a year later for review and for me to meet their daughter. Martin informed me that he now considered that the death of his son had deepened him as a person, and for that he would be forever grateful. Their legal action was proceeding but Martin no longer had any interest in it and was considering withdrawing it.

Hayden Barlow Regains His Appetite*

Hayden, aged 11, had had a malignancy diagnosed when he was three and had had several rounds of surgery, radiotherapy, and chemotherapy. Recently there had been a recurrence involving further surgery. This was followed, over a period of several months, by a dramatic weight loss and complete loss of appetite, apparently unrelated to his disease process. I was asked to consult with him and see if I could find out what he thought the problem might be. Hayden pulled the brim of the baseball cap he customarily wore down over his face. All I could see were his tears trickling out from under it. He hated anyone to see him cry. He told me he couldn't eat. Every time he sat down to a meal, he would see a drip and feel nauseated, just like he did after chemotherapy. At night, he had nightmares of tombstones with drip bottles and infusion lines running into them. He was dying while doctors and nurses climbed out of the tombstones towards him saying, "We're going to get you! It's your fault!" Then he would turn to see a truck bearing down on him. Although Hayden seemed relieved to tell me of his fears, I knew this was insufficient for him to recommence his chemotherapy. Hayden requested that I tell his parents what was happening to him. He had been unable to reveal to them that his usual bravado was just a front. The family agreed to a referral for family therapy.

When I first met Cynthia and Roy Barlow, they appeared both confused and desperate. Hayden was buried beneath his baseball cap and within his father's logger jacket. They told me that Hayden was extremely independent and for some time had preferred to manage his hospital treatments on his

---

*A complete report of this story, written in cooperation with Hayden's mother, Cynthia Barlow, his physician, Dr. Louise Webster, his social worker, Lynn O'Flaherty, and Mike Murphy, has been published in Epston (1989, pp. 29–44).

own. However, he wasn't managing anymore and I surmised that they must be dreadfully concerned about his unaccountable weight loss, his having become "pale and miserable" over the past month, and his refusal to undergo any further treatments. Hayden's eyes were downcast but I noticed that, when I turned towards his parents, he would look up at me. After establishing the parents' concern and confusion, I turned quickly towards him, meeting his gaze for the first time, and said, "Do you think your parents can stand up to your strong feelings?" Hayden was caught off-guard and uttered a defensive "dunno." "Well, why don't you put them to the test? They look strong enough to me but you'll never know until you test them."

I turned to his parents: "Do you mind if Hayden tests you to see if you are strong enough to stand up to his worries?" Although uncertain as to the nature of the test, they wholeheartedly agreed to undergo it. It was agreed that his father would go first and that his test would last exactly 15 minutes; his mother would then join them for her test, which was also to last exactly 15 minutes.

The physician, Cynthia, and I retired to another room, leaving father and son sitting across from each other with a box of tissues placed midway between them. After exactly 15 minutes, Cynthia joined Ray and Hayden. The physician and I knocked on the door when Cynthia's test was up and were welcomed back into the room. The floor was littered with tissues so I guessed things had worked out as I had hoped. Everyone had composed themselves; Hayden looked somewhat relieved and was laughing for the first time. Hayden, with some pride, assured me that his parents could stand up to his strong feelings.

I then asked Hayden to give me a measure of his worries, as opposed to his fun, by holding his hands apart to indicate the "bigness" of each. I carefully took measurements with a tape measure: 50 cm. of worry and 15 cm. of fun. The physician reiterated that this month's chemotherapy would be deferred. Instead, I invited them to return the next day to meet together again.

The next day, the mood was lighter but Hayden and his parents still didn't know what to expect. I met with Hayden alone first and told him that his physician had informed me of his bad dreams. He told me he dreamt that a group of doctors surrounded him and pointed their fingers accusingly at him, shouting: "That's the one!" They then stood aside for him to see a truck bearing down on him. He would then awake from this nightmare. He went on to tell me that, as a young boy, he had been responsible for the supervision of his intellectually disabled uncle. They had been crossing a road together when the uncle walked in front of an oncoming truck. Hayden recalled: "He went to the hospital but before he died he had drips in him. I just about beat up the truck driver. I didn't think!" I elicited Hayden's feelings of guilt and self-accusation but did not challenge them in any way. I merely accepted his construction of events.

I then asked his parents to join us and requested their permission for me to hypnotize Hayden. They sat by my side, looking on with keen anticipation. I guided us all into a trance by inviting Hayden to close his eyes and then asked him if he could see a TV set in his mind and inquired: "Is it black and white or color? Is it a big one or a small one?" To further confirm the trance behavior for both Hayden and his parents, I had Hayden levitate his hand by proposing he imagined a balloon being linked to his wrist by a fine string. While his hand was levitated, I told the following story:

> A long time ago and at another faraway place, I was doing the job I'm doing now. A man came to see me. He told me he couldn't eat anymore, and that he used to really like his grub. "Why not?" I asked. He told me that it was a long story. I told him I had plenty of time and he could tell me the whole story if he wished. He said he had to. He had no choice. It had been bothering him for a long time and he had had enough of it. He told me he was a truck driver and had killed a man *accidentally*. And ever since then, he hadn't been able to eat properly. "How did it happen?" I asked. He told me that he had been driving along when a young boy crossed the road in front of him. Then a bee came from nowhere and stung him in the face. Then he temporarily lost control and ran over a man who had followed the boy. "Well," I said, "you can start eating again. It surely was not your fault. It was the bee's fault!" He replied: "I know that . . . I know that! That's not what I'm worried about. I'm worried sick about the boy." I became confused and asked him why. He said: "He'll blame himself even though it was the bee's fault. He was only a boy and surely won't understand." Now I knew I was getting somewhere. I told him: "Look, I've been doing this job for nine years and I know what I'm talking about. I want you to know that no boy would believe such a crazy idea." He immediately brightened up and asked me if I was sure. "Sure I'm sure," I said. And you know, he went home that day, regained his appetite and started eating again. He let me know later that his life improved in many other ways, although to this day he doesn't like bees much. But I guess that is easy to understand.

I continued with some "trance talk" and then asked Hayden what his favorite foods were. After some thought, he said they were Kentucky Fried Chicken and pizzas. I then mockingly warned him that if he didn't start to eat I would get some drips from the hospital and give them to his parents. They were then to put a pizza on one plate and some drips on another and he would have to choose between them. He said he would definitely choose pizzas over drips. I then said that his parents were to insist that he jump up and down on the drips, saying: "That isn't food. That's for the doctors and my getting better!" Before he was allowed to start on his pizza, he should throw the drips in the rubbish bin. He assured me that this would be no trouble for him. I said: "At the dinner table, there's only *one* thing you're going to have that's food." I gradually reoriented Hayden, who immediately grasped above his head for the imaginary balloon, much to his parents' amusement. We agreed to meet a day before his next treatment in a month's time.

I began the next session by asking Hayden if I could reassess his fun versus worry ratio. Everything about him and his family told me the result would be a good one. It was 120 cm. of fun versus 1 cm. of worry. When I asked him how this had happened, he told me that finding out that his mother and father "could stand up to my worries" had helped him cut down on his worrying. "I tell them my worries. I had tested them. They can take a lot." Both Roy and Cynthia told me that they had been unaware of the nature of his concerns and felt they had now convinced him that he didn't have to be "so strong." They said there had been big changes since our last meeting. Hayden was talking a lot, looking happy, not hiding within his father's logger jacket, and eating well. In fact, he had gained 4 kilograms. Now his plate was always piled up and he did not share my concern that he would become overweight. His nightmares had stopped and had been replaced "by good dreams of just nothing." He no longer saw drips so his parents didn't have to play "our joke" on him. The color had returned to his face and he was able to look at his hair growing back, whereas before he didn't dare to. Cynthia commented that Hayden was no longer frightened of his treatments. Two months later, these changes had been sustained.

I later discovered that Hayden was one of the worst reactors to his chemotherapy that the pediatric oncology unit had ever met. He would vomit approximately five times in anticipation of his treatment, after which he would persist in dry retching. He required medication and often had to remain overnight in the hospital to be rehydrated. We joined forces once again over two sessions. Hayden was able to train himself to substitute movies in his mind for the nausea associated with chemotherapy. Hayden was never to vomit again and endured the remaining treatments with equanimity. Things were certainly looking good for Hayden. He also applied for my assistance in relation to problems controlling his temper in the classroom and stealing. He informed me that he used his "self-hypnosis" on the problems with great success and then extended its use to studying and improved his marks and concentration. However, he refused to do the same on the sports field, as he thought it would give him an unfair advantage over others.

A year later, it was discovered that Hayden had another site for his disease. His family decided against further treatment as his prognosis was so poor. Several years later his mother wrote the following:

Hayden learnt to cope with many emotions. Adjusting to changes in his appearance was one of his greatest hurdles, along with trying to accept the fact that many things he longed to do would never be. Hayden had a collection of many things that filled his room. This included the many hats he wore wherever he went. Although Hayden's life was short, he accomplished a lot more than many others who live a lot longer. He made us realize that life is too short to worry about petty things; we should live life to the fullest. Hayden feared sleep but not death. When he died in his father's arms, we no longer feared death either. The most precious memories of Hayden we hold in our hearts are those two last years. Hayden was loved and admired by many. Anyone who took the time to sit and listen to him learned so much. Being a very unselfish and special boy, Hayden had many friends with whom he shared his thoughts and ideas. The hardest task for those close to him was not being able to relieve his pain; we could only help him cope with it. The pain and torment Hayden endured no one will ever know, but we can only assume. Hayden has left us with the gift of love, patience, how to endure suffering and understand each other. Through him, we learned the closeness and the importance of friends, neighbors and family. This closeness is a lifelong bond. Thank you, son.

CONCLUSION

These three stories have in common the experience of people devastated by guilt in relation to the demise of a loved person: a father, a newborn son, and a handicapped uncle. In each story, the person believed himself responsible and was moving inexorably towards his own personal tragedy. Grieving, either in anticipation or in the event of a loved one's death, was blocked. Once freed of their respective modes of self-punishment, all were able to take back control of their lives. The approach I took was highly individual but the results were identical—that is, the person's guilt and self-blame appeared to evaporate. Recently, I have been providing guilt-driven people with these same stories and they have had a similar effect on their lives. However, my more general purpose is to bring guilt/blame more fully into the grief/loss discourse, along with the creativity of deep play.

REFERENCES

Epston, D. (1989). *Collected papers.* Adelaide, South Australia: Dulwich Centre.
White, M. (1989). Ritual of inclusion: An approach to extreme uncontrolled behavior in young children and adolescents. In M. White, *Selected Papers* (pp. 77–84). Adelaide, South Australia: Dulwich Centre.

13

Adolescent Suicide: The Loss of Reconciliation

STEVEN E. GUTSTEIN

To MAKE THE decision to die, you must no longer believe that things can change, that they can somehow improve. The "suicide" has come to the conclusion, no matter how irrational the premise, that life is not worth living in the present, and that something has been lost or changed, making it certain that life will never be worth living.

When someone is psychotic, has a clear terminal illness, or is spiritually and physically imprisoned, we can understand the source of this degree of present despair and complete loss of hope for the future. However, when we refer to adolescents in good physical health, with "their whole life ahead of them," it is difficult, if not impossible, to understand the thoughts underlying such a final action. Why would a suicide follow on the heels of losing a boyfriend or girlfriend, not making the cheerleading squad, or failing an exam? Despite intensive study, adolescent suicide has remained a disturbing enigma.

My work with suicidal adolescents has focused on loss as one of the primary precursors to suicidal action. Recent theory on the impact of loss and grief (Felner, Farber, & Primavera, 1983; Hirsch, 1980; Parkes, 1971) has taken a constructivist viewpoint, punctuating the personal meaning of the loss on those affected by it, rather than the number or type of actual losses per se. It is quite evident that many adolescents endure severe and numerous crises and losses without resorting to taking their lives. I believe that it is the way losses are managed in the family and the "myths" about

loss that develop within the context of the family and larger kinship system
that determine whether suicidal action will be the response to perceived or
anticipated loss.

When my clinical research team began studying and treating suicidal
adolescents and their families in 1983, we were struck by the degree to which
the extreme solutions adopted by these teenagers were reflective of the drastic ways that their family members had dealt with crises for several generations. When taking multigenerational history, we were impressed with the
amount of self-destructive behavior, abuse, violence, divorce, abandonment, long lasting feuds, and emotional cutoffs that characterized family
relationships over generations. Equally striking was the extent to which
adolescents, their siblings, and their parents were isolated from current
relationships with extended family members and close family friends.

The "Ecology" of Personal Myths

When we repeatedly requested, and at times insisted, that families involve
their relatives, friends, and neighbors in crisis intervention meetings, we
were stymied by the reluctance of parents and children alike to seek out the
help of their kinship system. In defining the kinship system, we use Williams' (1970) definition of a "set of interpersonal social relationships involving strong interests and emotions . . . and many reciprocal bonds of dependence and support" (p. 47), including "blood" relatives as well as close
family friends who act as "honorary kin." Quite often, all contact with
relatives had been lost. Parents or adolescents would strongly veto any
communication with those who remained involved. They told stories that
vividly illustrated the toxicity of relationships with family members, who
were typically portrayed as totally incompetent, undergoing crises themselves, or acting in ways that would further polarize existing conflicts.

I became convinced that these poignant stories were a reflection of the
central "personal myths" developed by the suicidal adolescent. By personal
myths, I refer to core family fables that are interpreted to reinforce deep-
seated beliefs about the ways that one can successfully function in the
world. The power of the myth derives not from the story alone, but from the
bonding of the story with its "moral." The tragic and limited myths about
the worthlessness of family and about the danger of trusting and caring for
others, derived over several generations of crises, were a major precursor to
the adolescent's decision to act in a suicidal manner.

The maintenance of a wide, flexible range of personal myths rests upon a
foundation of such myths in a healthy kinship system. In a functioning
kinship system, various members both embody and share a variety of myths
without being excluded from the system. These myths exist in an open

"ecology" in which diverse and even contradictory beliefs about relationships and personal worth are illustrated and supported by actions and stories of different members. Myths that develop around critical events reinforce a wide range of ways of relating to others. Similarly, the same event may be "storied" by different participants or observers in ways that reinforce drastically different beliefs about self and others.

Children who grow up in this rich, subjective context are provided access to a full range of myths and thus develop their own diverse ecology of personal myths to choose from as circumstances warrant. For example, stories about how an uncle or aunt took on a parenting role following the death of a child's mother or father may exist alongside stories in which the loss of a crucial family member led to a long-lasting vacuum in family functioning. Stories may be recalled in which there was a special bond between a child and her grandmother, which remain balanced by other stories emphasizing the clear primacy of the parental relationship ("you only have one mother").

A major crisis that eliminates or challenges a particular personal myth such as the death of a parent (i.e., "No one will ever love you as much as your mother") may lead to grief and sadness. However, the child can gradually accept the loss of the myth and replace or modify it from his/her repertoire to adapt to the crisis ("No one will ever love me like my mother did, but Grandma and Grandpa will always love and take care of me"). The child is able to carry on a process that I term *reconciliation*.

The suicidal adolescent faced with a major crisis has a severely limited range of personal myths with which to manage. When these myths are rendered untenable, then the vulnerable adolescent has no means of adapting or replacing them. Bereft of any way of anticipating a future that might have a successful outcome, unable to achieve reconciliation, he or she sees suicide as a viable option.

THE RECONCILIATION PROCESS

Reconciliation is defined as both an internal and external process, a compromise carried out by family members in times of crisis to alter their personal myths about the types of relationships they require and the way they and others must act to meet their needs. The process of reconciliation can occur following the perception of an abrupt change in the nature of a crucially perceived relationship, such as the death of a parent or child, or following a loss that demands a major shift in personal identity, such as failing to meet an important career goal.

The family life cycle provides numerous occasions in which individuals must alter their most basic assumptions about themselves and the key persons in their lives (McGoldrick & Carter, 1982). A husband who looked to his wife to provide all of his intimacy and support must find alternative ways to meet these needs if he becomes a widower. An only child who had counted on being the center of the universe for his mother and father must adapt to sharing that universe with a new baby. The mother who believed that her main value derived from her parenting ability must find a new identity when her last child leaves home.

When faced with intense disruptions in basic assumptions, each of us must cope with the loss of personal myths that are experienced as crucial to ongoing well-being and success. We must be able to accept the loss of the myth, mourn the lost fantasy that the myth represented, and then modify or replace the lost myth with others that fill the niche that it once occupied. Reconciliation occurs with the experience that, though the new myth can never fully replace the old, it provides enough hope for present and future happiness to continue on. Reconciliation cannot occur when alternative myths are not available or acceptable, when one single way of establishing identity or one single crucial relationship is seen as the only means of existing.

Through the loss of relationships with an extended kinship system and the development of a limited range of extreme personal myths, the family of the suicidal adolescent loses the capacity for reconciliation. The goal of my research centered on understanding this loss and developing a method to intervene around the current suicidal crisis in a manner that might restore the adolescent's and family's capability for reconciliation. The first step was to try to understand what had happened to the kinship systems of these families and to speculate about the effects of the "fragmentation" of these systems on future generations.

KINSHIP SYSTEM FRAGMENTATION

Kinship systems become vulnerable when overloaded by numerous severe losses, or by drastic changes in cultural or environmental conditions. Members may come to believe that their survival is threatened and that the kinship system, as constituted, cannot protect them, that their kin are without the resources to meet the needs of all members, and that some must be sacrificed so that others can survive. An analogy would be that of survivors of a shipwreck, who find themselves in a lifeboat built for half their number, cast adrift in the midst of an ocean, with only several days' rations.

Given the high levels of perceived threat and sense of urgency, family members may feel compelled to take drastic, rapid solutions. Engaging in a process of reconciliation, which involves incorporating a range of differing personal myths, and inevitably entails struggle, negotiation, mourning, and acceptance, may appear too unwieldy in the face of imminent disaster. Rigid, extreme, "survival" solutions may begin to predominate, typically involving the cutting off of competing myths, either by leaving the field oneself, to escape from a "toxic" family, or by excluding others who are perceived as threatening to the continued existence of the larger unit. In this context of survival, the balance of myths is disrupted. Extreme solutions predominate, and myths develop about these solutions, which then reinforce extreme beliefs. Extreme myths tend to promote other extreme myths of either the same type or the opposite. For example, growing up in a context in which loyalty is viewed as all-important may lead one either to rigidly maintain this belief or to react by believing that any type of commitment to the family is intolerable. A similar process of extreme, rigid loyalty occurring with extreme cutoff has been described by Minuchin (1974) in his concept of enmeshment and by Bowen (1976) in his discussion of how children growing up in emotionally fused families resort to total emotional cutoff in breaking away from parents.

Over time, as leaving the field and excluding others become the predominant ways of dealing with crises, rigid myths about the necessity of extreme "survival solutions" to life transitions lead to the fragmentation of kinship systems. This becomes a circular "deviation amplifying process" as survival myths lead to extreme actions in times of crisis and these "lifeboat" solutions reinforce survival myths. The effects of this process on future generations can be catastrophic. As Boszormenyi-Nagy and Krasner (1986) have stated,

> [If] loss of reassuring, concerned relationships engenders serious misfortune for the offspring, recent history pictures an ominous course of each successive offspring's progressive bereavement of hope for security. The loss of stabilizing, supportive, if burdensome, ongoing family relationships places each subsequent generation into a more exposed, vulnerable condition. (p. 198)

Erickson (1984) has pointed out the drastic, multigenerational consequences of even a single extreme crisis resolution. For example, children of a man who has left home with a belief in the importance of escaping from a toxic family may never be able to access their father's relatives as part of their own system.

As this process continues, the number of members in a kinship system who remain emotionally available to each other progressively diminishes, as members who leave or are excluded remain unreplaced, and individuals who cut themselves off develop personal myths that preclude their joining or developing new kinship systems. As extended families fragment, isolated, highly dense family clusters develop, each emotionally distanced and/or polarized from others, each holding onto and tolerating only a few rigidly held, extreme personal myths.

PERSONAL MYTHS IN THE CULTURE OF SURVIVAL

As fragmentation continues and the family takes on a siege mentality, specific types of survival myths begin to predominate. Myths develop about the need for either *unquestioned loyalty* (e.g., the family always comes first no matter what the personal sacrifice) or *extreme independence* (e.g., every man for himself) in times of crisis. "Loyal" family members and "disloyal" outsiders are seen in dichotomous "in/out, either/or" ways. Alternatively, family members are seen as inevitably betraying and damaging those relatives with whom they remain emotionally connected.

Instead of learning that losses of significant others can be mourned and then healed, family members come to believe either in *irreplaceability*—that relationships once lost can never be replaced—or in *complete replaceability*—that relationships are interchangeable and that any loss can easily be supplanted, thus leading to the devaluation of kin and their substitution with highly transient, nonfamily relationships.

Family members come to believe that there is only a finite amount of love that anyone has to give, so that when it is given to one person then someone else must inevitably be deprived. This ultimately leads to the myth of *exclusivity*, in which developing new relationships outside the fragmenting system is seen as threatening remaining members and is responded to in extreme ways. The message is implicitly but clearly communicated that "your relationship with another cannot be separated from your relationship with me and has dire consequences for our relationship." The exclusive characteristic of relationships means that members who remain in the family do so at a forfeiture of intimacy with nonsanctioned members or outsiders, and those members who replace losses with new relationships are likely to be excluded from the family. Alternatively, family members may respond to fragmentation with a belief in *undifferentiated intimacy*, in which relationships are developed in disregard of any primary family loyalty and no discrimination is made between degrees of closeness.

THE LOSS OF RECONCILIATION

Reconciliation is rarely possible once relationships are based on this culture of survival. Because of rigid beliefs about the absence of relational alternatives and supports, the compromises and sacrifices inherent in reconciliation are perceived as untenable. The loss of reconciliation has dire implications for the social development of children in the isolated cluster, particularly in its impairment of a child's ability to form individuated intimate relationships. Without reconciliation, developmental changes in the child do not lead to a modified definition of the parent-child relationship. Once separated, a parent and child cannot be reunited. The loss of a parent cannot be replaced in even modified form. New additions to the family result in bitter conflict and triangulation or exclusion. Losses are not acknowledged and mourned. Temporary replacement relationships are typically not available to buffer the impact of the loss or separation. Even when available, such replacements are viewed as threatening and thus not tolerated by the child or the emotionally unavailable parent.

The child at risk in the isolated family learns that losses cannot be replaced and that separations, rather than being followed by reconciliation, lead to further isolation and alienation. This experience of *irreplaceability*, combined with the child's yearning for an exclusive, symbiotic relationship, and the family's rigid responses to developmental transitions, set the stage for the child's later suicidal response to the adolescent crisis.

THE CRISIS OF ADOLESCENCE IN THE ISOLATED CLUSTER

Adolescence constitutes a life-threatening crisis for the isolated family. As in past developmental transitions, the family is unable to accept the inevitable losses and changes inherent in a child's emergence into adolescence. As Richman (1981) has stated:

> The developmental demands of adolescence are a threat to some families. These families see the outside world as the enemy and set up barriers to shield themselves. Adolescence entails an acknowledgment of differentness, of being a separate other which in the "suicidiogenic" family is felt as a threat to symbiosis and the loss of the symbiotic partner. (p. 137)

The isolated family reacts in extreme, rigid ways to the adolescent's attempts at individuation. As the adolescent increases emphasis on relationships outside of the family, he/she is perceived as disloyal. Demands are placed upon the adolescent for exclusivity—e.g., "choose me (us) or her." A second reaction might be outright rejection. In some instances, the movement into adolescence engenders emotionally self-protective reactions in parents who anticipate the eventual rejection of the adolescent. For example, a single parent who had previously maintained an exclusive relationship with her child may pursue an equally exclusive and excluding relationship with a new boyfriend.

For their part, adolescents in isolated families tend to pursue outside relationships in extreme ways and seem to willing to sacrifice their loyalty to the family on a moment's notice. These children have learned that an exclusive symbiotic relationship is essential to survival. A single special relationship is all important, but they have lost any hopes for this relationship within their family. Adolescence offers the opportunity for the adolescent to replace family relationships perceived as empty with a new, exclusive relationship. The desire to form a symbiotic relationship may be transferred from a parent to a boyfriend or girlfriend. This relationship is then perceived as central to the youth's identity and irreplaceable if lost. Attempts at forming close peer relationships are made in a desperate manner, which is off-putting to many peers and leads to inevitable rejection. This reinforces the adolescent's beliefs about the impossibility of having nonexclusive relationships. An adolescent may succeed in forming a new symbiosis, but at best it is precarious. At worst the child has burned his bridges behind him.

The unavailability of cohesive kin relationships means that the cycle of rejection will not be interrupted. Extended family members are not accessible to act as mediators or to provide alternative solutions to the escalating conflicts. When the adolescent or parent perceives rejection, there are no temporary replacements, no places of refuge, to buffer the sense of loss. Powerful kinship system myths about abandonment and exclusion, along with the lack of historical precedent for conflict mediation and compromise, increase the belief in the necessity of extreme, self-protective actions.

The adolescent in an isolated family exists in a precarious situation, in which any actual or anticipated loss, be it through the birth of a new child, the loss of a peer relationship, or the involvement of a parent in a new intimacy, may lead to suicidal behavior. The adolescent has been unable to develop and unwilling to accept any individuated intimacy. The physical changes and biological imperatives of adolescence in themselves threaten the loss of the exclusive parental relationship, as parents emotionally and physically withdraw from the child in anticipation of their impending loss and abandonment. Even if the exclusive parental relationship is replaced by a peer, the nature of adolescent intimacy is such that it is tenuous at best and inevitably linked to future rejection.

For these adolescents, perceiving the need for exclusivity and believing in the irreplaceability of key others, the anticipated loss of an exclusive relationship is experienced as a disaster. The suicidal threat or attempt may be made in a desperate effort to forestall the impending loss. The behavior may be precipitated by a loved one's actual or anticipated severance of a relationship. Its purpose is to influence the other not to make a choice exclusive of oneself, or to reverse an exclusive choice one is being forced to make. When the adolescent believes that the loss has already occurred, then the act is no longer an attempt to change the other, but a more final and fatal decision.

THE SYSTEMIC CRISIS INTERVENTION PROGRAM

Based on a belief in the crucial role of multigenerational family myths in the suicidal process, our clinical team at the Houston Child Guidance Center developed the Systemic Crisis Intervention Program (SCIP). The goal of SCIP is to use the suicidal crisis as an opportunity to teach isolated families the possibility of accessing their kin in a way that can be an opportunity for the creation of a new, expanded system of myths. SCIP methods are more completely described by the author in a related paper (Gutstein, 1987).

In SCIP, we assemble family and friends to ritualize the suicidal crisis as a major developmental transition akin to birth, death, or marriage. We try to develop a ceremony of reconciliation in which family members can experience their strength and unity as well as the family's capacity to adapt to meet the unique needs of its members. We hope that the ceremony will take on significance in the future stories and myths that emanate from this crisis. The importance of reintroducing the suicidal adolescent to his or her kin and of parents' acknowledging that they cannot cope alone is seen firsthand. A powerful effect is witnessed as adolescents examine the extreme solutions that they, or their parents or grandparents, made in the past that resulted in isolation and polarization. Coming together in their mutual loss, family members have the opportunity to reunite through a sense of shared grief over the kind of family they dreamed of but never had.

We do not expect to repair every damaged or disconnected relationship. A crucial part of the reconciliation process is the acceptance of relationships that are lost or unsalvageable. We hope that family members will emerge from the current crisis with the belief that they belong or can belong to some network that can meet their needs for intimacy as well as for individuation. We work to retell family stories and create experiences from which will emerge new myths of family strength, tolerance for plurality, and network support.

Intervention is based on three beliefs regarding the effective treatment of suicidal children and adolescents:

1. *Using the opportunity of the crisis*: The shock of the suicidal crisis may be an opportunity, if used correctly, to "loosen up" previously rigid family behavior patterns, which have contributed to the current crisis, and to bring family members together who had previously become polarized and distanced. This temporary period of increased openness, so characteristic of crises, provides a brief window of opportunity for powerful intervention. Therefore, clinicians must be careful not to "buffer" the crisis by communicating to parents that their child is being totally taken care of by "experts." This message may lead to a premature termination of family members' sense

of crisis, and thus, a decrease in both their involvement and their motivation to seek change. The crisis clinician must walk a delicate tightrope, responding intensively enough to minimize danger and instill confidence, but not so intensively as to end the sense of crisis. We have found that family members, if suitably instructed and motivated, and if 24-hour backup is available, can often safely monitor their adolescent's behavior at home during periods of acute suicidal crisis. Hospitalization is used when the family is unwilling or unable to mobilize the necessary resources to maintain the child's safety, and then only for brief periods and for the specific purpose of maintaining the child in a safe environment while the family prepares to take on this responsibility.

2. *Gathering of kin around the crisis*: Family members, separated for years by conflicts and physical distance, can come together when faced with the possible loss of a child in their family, if the proper context is created for their gathering. In this regard, the suicidal crisis can be an opportunity to reverse the process of kinship fragmentation and create a ceremony of reconciliation.

For over twenty years, network therapists have demonstrated the importance of including extended family and social network members in treatment during a crisis (Rueveni, 1977; Schoenfeld et al., 1986; Speck & Attneave, 1973). Unlike network therapists, I do not believe that more is better and that a larger assembly of family and network will necessarily lead to a more effective outcome. Researchers on the effects of social support have been impressed with the power of well-intentioned family and friends to generate further disruption and negative outcomes (Wortman & Lehman, 1986). I have found it more effective to selectively assemble those network members who are necessary to carry out a process of reconciliation around the current crisis. This may include those members who are centrally involved in the crisis, those who play a central role in maintaining and creating family stories and myths, and those with potential to powerfully support reconciliation in the current crisis.

3. *Multiple advocacy*: Along with other clinicians working with suicidal youth, I have found that family members are often so polarized and in such conflict that a single therapist is unable to gain the trust of all members and adequately represent their needs. For example, Richman (1986) and Pfeffer (1986) have discussed the apparent loss of empathy that characterizes parent-child relationships in the families of suicidal adolescents. Family members have typically adopted extreme, "either/or, win/lose" survival myths in which compromise and negotiation appear untenable. The clinician attempting to remain neutral in family conflicts quickly finds that family members respond with a "you're either with me or against me" position.

To gain family members' trust and participation and to help them learn that their unique points of view can be tolerated and addressed by the family without resorting to extreme solutions, we have developed a multiple advocacy process, in which each family member who is centrally involved in the crisis receives his or her own advocate. The job of the clinician-advocate is to become completely convinced of the rightness of his or her client's position and be willing to defend that position against all others. However, unlike a courtroom advocate, the team advocate maintains an equal commitment to a process of reconciliation, in which all family members' needs are met and extreme solutions are avoided.

Methods of SCIP

Clinicians are contacted at the time of a suicidal crisis, through phone calls from a variety of referral sources. Team members conduct an immediate initial screening by phone. Plans are made for emergency response as necessitated on a case by case basis. Within 24 hours of the initial call, a three-hour evaluation is conducted by two crisis team staff. During this evaluation, the danger level of the current situation is assessed using five criteria: (1) any prior history of suicidal behavior or thinking; (2) the patient's and parent's current affective and mental status; (3) the lethality of the attempt; (4) the specificity of plans for future suicidal actions; and (5) the degree to which the suicidal behavior has elicited a sense of crisis for at least some family members. Throughout the SCIP process, the patient's risk level is monitored daily.

If the evaluation indicates that a safe emergency response can be established and key family and network members can be involved, then clinicians immediately begin to meet individually with family members to prepare them for upcoming family gatherings. Two critical tasks during these meetings are (1) working with family members to invite the patient's extended family and close friends to an upcoming gathering and (2) developing advocacy positions for the centrally involved family members.

We do not expect that family members will be excited about inviting their kin to large meetings. Part of our work is gradually developing a context in which it makes sense for each client to have family and friends present. It may be a positive context, such as the need for support, or a negative one, such as exposing duplicity of a supposedly loving family member. What is most important is that the request to invite significant others makes sense to the clients from their frame of reference.

We typically conduct two four-hour gatherings over the course of two to four weeks. These gatherings are usually attended by 12 to 20 members of the nuclear and extended family and three or four team members. The team members spend several hours planning the gatherings. They collect relevant stories to tell, plan enactments, and design rituals. During the gatherings,

the advocates sit with their clients, scattered among the family. One clinician, designated as a meta-advocate, takes responsibility for the process of
the gathering, making sure that there is a movement from one stage of the
process to another, that no advocacy position wins out, and that a safe
atmosphere prevails. We have divided the gathering into four stages, which
we believe are the essential components of the reconciliation process.

THE CREVANT FAMILY

Tammy, 15 years old, had taken a large overdose of painkillers two days
before we first saw her in the intensive care unit of a local hospital. She had
just broken up with her 23-year-old boyfriend. She believed that her mother
had rejected her over this most recent relationship and would never love her
again. She also believed that her mother was so preoccupied with her little
sister and her stepfather that she no longer had time for a teenage girl. Other
than this boyfriend, Tammy had no close friends.

Tammy's father, Lloyd, died in a boating accident two weeks before her
birth. After her husband's death, Tammy's mother, Colette, became severely
depressed, and for the first several years of Tammy's life, was unable to
perform adequately many of the normal tasks of mothering. At the time,
Colette lived close to her own parents so that Tammy grew up looking
toward her grandfather and grandmother as a father and mother. For a time,
Tammy felt some security in this family. Then several events shattered the
family she had known. When Tammy was five, her mother gave birth to an
illegitimate child. Suddenly, the attention shifted to the new baby and away
from her. One year later, Colette remarried and the family moved five hundred miles away from their home in Louisiana, to Houston. Within six
months of the move, Tammy's grandfather was dead. Tammy blamed her
mother for the death, believing that the move had broken his heart. Tammy's
grandmother also blamed her daughter for her husband's death. She had
refused to attend her daughter's wedding and, when her husband died, she
cut off all contact for three years.

Tammy grew up having never met her father or any of his family. Lloyd's
entire family blamed Colette for his death. The story was told that Lloyd
drank to escape from Colette's incessant demands. In-laws and other relatives cut off relationships with Colette and her children after the funeral.
Tammy's experience of her mother's family was of having kin around her
and then irrevocably losing them. With her mother's remarriage, their move
to Houston, and the death of her grandfather, Tammy lost the relationships
that had been most important to her. Feeling that her mother was preoccupied with the other family members, Tammy sought to replace the special
relationship she had lost with her grandmother by becoming involved with
older men. Each relationship left her feeling used and empty. Her persistent

violation of her mother's rules in dating these men left Tammy more and more isolated from her mother. Tammy had lost the one relationship she had counted on. Now she feared that she had burned her bridges behind her and would never be accepted back into the family.

Following their initial meeting with two members of the crisis team, Tammy's mother and stepfather, Ed, took time from their jobs and other responsibilities to share in a 24-hour suicide watch until the time of the first crisis gathering, eight days following the suicide attempt. During the interim, members of the crisis team met with key family members to build alliances, to learn the family stories of the events that had led to so much conflict and polarization, and to invite other family members to the gathering. Team members were successful in mobilizing members of Colette's family as well as Ed's brother and parents. The first gathering included members of Colette's family. A second gathering was conducted, several weeks following the first, with Ed's family present.

We begin such gatherings by celebrating the past unity and cohesiveness of the family. A sense of underlying unity is necessary to withstand the conflict and separateness that inevitably occurs later in the gathering. In this unity stage, family and team members are often called upon to tell stories that reflect the past heroism, love, and cohesiveness of the family. Grandparents and other members of older generations are particularly important here as they are often repositories of these stories and, by their very presence, symbolize the continuity of the family.

Present for the first Crevant family gathering were Tammy; her mother, Colette; her stepfather, Ed; her brother, Ernest (18); her sister, Cheryl (10); her stepbrother, Billy (8); Colette's two sisters, Thelma Jean and Marie; Thelma Jean's husband, Burt; and Colette's mother, Michelle. The gathering began with an opening "invocation" delivered by the meta-advocate;

> We're glad that you all could come today. We know you're here because you love and care very much. Everyone's hoping and praying that you can leave today with a feeling of being even stronger than when you walked in. Even more united than you're feeling now. My prayers are that we can walk out of this with a feeling of being united. Please join me in a moment to silently pray for us all.

After the invocation, the gathering moved to stories of past cohesiveness and sharing.

META-ADVOCATE   Some of the people on this team were telling me stories of the strength in this family and certainly there have been ways that you've been united before. Your family and honorary family have survived to get to this place.

ADVOCATE   Somebody was telling me about a camping trip when the sisters were young.

MICHELLE   The worst part was that one of the children was a bed wetter. We spent a lot of evenings in washaterias.

ADVOCATE   What about the story about the binky?

TAMMY   It was a pacifier. I called it a binky.

THELMA JEAN   It went flying out the car window and she said "oh shit." The more we laughed, the more upset she got, and she wanted to go back and find her binky.

MICHELLE   Remember that time at Mardi Gras? If Tuesday had been like the other days I'd have passed out. Remember the crowds on Bourbon Street?

MARIE   You couldn't have been on Bourbon Street, Mamma, not with five kids.

MICHELLE   Why not? In those days I'd take you kids anywhere and everywhere. You were like a part of me.

The meta-advocate gradually shifts the focus of the gathering from the unity of the past to the sense of separateness that has precipitated the present crisis. The stage of separateness is a time for family members to face their essential differences. For a plurality of myths to coexist, the kinship system must be a forum where individuals with very different beliefs and ways of acting can maintain their differences and yet still maintain their primary connection. The separateness stage illustrates the difficulties that the family experiences in reconciling the apparently irreconcilable differences that have led to the crisis. The primary enactment of this phase is the multiple advocacy process. Together, advocates and their clients present their position in a highly committed and determined way. Each family member's position is emphatically upheld to the exclusion of others. Friends and relatives are solicited to line up behind one of the positions. Advocacy looks like an old time, small-scale, political convention. Advocates walk over and huddle with different family members, playing the crowd, trying to get support for their positions. No one is allowed to sit back and watch. Everyone may be talking at once. The room seems chaotic. Several different heated conversations may be running simultaneously. Confrontations occur alongside small caucuses. Advocates and their clients interchange roles. Interruptions are frequent. The focus of conflict shifts back and forth among several issues and family members. The following dialogue illustrates the seemingly chaotic and intense nature of the advocacy process.

TAMMY'S (PATIENT) ADVOCATE   From talking to Tammy it's clear that she *couldn't* talk to her mother. That her mother *never* has taken her seriously right from the beginning.

COLETTE'S (MOTHER) ADVOCATE   At least Colette is still trying. Tammy gave up a long time ago.

ED'S (STEPFATHER) ADVOCATE   Ed feels like he gets stuck in the middle.

COLETTE'S ADVOCATE   It just seems like those times were very few when Ed was *anywhere*.

TAMMY'S ADVOCATE   She'd be amazed if you asked her to go to the movies or go shopping. Tammy *always* gets pushed aside.

COLETTE   There's lots of times when Tammy will ask me to do something and I have. My mind gets so cluttered I forget and I ask her to remind me.

TAMMY   Why can't you just remember?

THELMA JEAN (COLETTE'S SISTER)   There's more than one child.

ED'S ADVOCATE   Ed tries over and over to give support to both of them and gets pushed away.

MARIE (COLETTE'S SISTER)   He doesn't try hard enough.

ED   Don't you think working two jobs and getting four hours sleep a night is enough?

MARIE   Hey, Colette is working two jobs and taking care of these kids.

BURT (TAMMY'S UNCLE)   That family over there are six people living under a common roof. That's not a family over there. That is not a family unit, definitely not — it's a joke.

TAMMY'S ADVOCATE   It doesn't feel like a family at all for Tammy.

THELMA JEAN   It's six people living at the same address.

MARIE   I think that before the move to Houston there was some family. When they moved away they left their family. Especially leaving Paw Paw. Tammy needed Paw Paw.

TAMMY'S ADVOCATE   Maybe he wouldn't have died if they hadn't moved.

ERNEST (TAMMY'S OLDER BROTHER)   Tammy wasn't the only one who hurt.

MICHELLE (COLETTE'S MOTHER)   Paw Paw even had a house next door all ready for them to move into.

COLETTE   I didn't want to live my life according to my daughter's wishes. Goddamn it! I had to live my own life!

TAMMY'S ADVOCATE   Even if it kills Tammy?

The meta-advocate moves out of separateness when all present have come to realize that the positions presented are apparently irreconcilable, that no compromise will be worked out, and that no easy, satisfactory solution will be achieved. Utilizing the sense of despair that accompanies such an exhausting, frustrating experience, the team switches the focus of the gathering to a shared acceptance of the grief that all family members feel about the loss of a loving, safe family that they remember or once fantasized about. In the acceptance stage, team members relate stories of the many losses that their clients have shared with them. Family members are encouraged to share the very personal dreams they once had of a family that would fulfill all of their needs. A new unity is developed around everyone's shared sense of grief.

Acceptance with the Crevant family began by the sharing of collective dreams of what might have been if Lloyd (Tammy's father), Carol (Ed's first wife), and Paw Paw (Tammy's grandfather) had not died. Each family member talked of the tender moments they recalled best with each of their lost loved ones. Colette was seated right across from Tammy. The rest of the family was placed in a tight circle around them. The climax occurred as Colette, for the first time, shared her memories with Tammy of her courtship with Lloyd, of the feelings she had the day that Tammy was born, of the plans that she and Lloyd had made for the future, and of her feelings on the day that Lloyd died. The family became tearful and reunited, arm in arm. As Colette finished telling her story, Tammy, with the help of her advocate, talked of her dreams of what life with her father would have been like. As she continued her story, tears began streaming down her face, as she cried for the first time since her suicide attempt. Colette, coached by her advocate, took Tammy in her arms and rocked her, with her husband by her side, surrounded by her family. After a time, Colette asked Tammy if Ed could hold her for a time. For the first time in her life, Tammy agreed and Ed took her in his lap. She clung to him, and he grasped her tightly.

Utilizing this new unity, the team again shifted the focus to the present crisis. The goal of the final stage of reconciliation and commitment is to help the family to resolve the crisis in a way that accepts the different needs of family members while also promoting the strength and unity to be found in the family and kinship system. During this stage, we rely heavily on the construction of family rituals and physical enactments to symbolize the new unity. Examples of rituals might be a coming-of-age ceremony, a mourning ritual for a crucial family member who is no longer physically or emotionally available, planning a celebration of an upcoming holiday in a new way, or formally inducting friends as honorary kin to replace the losses of unavailable family members.

For the Crevants, the reconciliation and commitment stage entailed the planning by all present of a different type of Christmas ritual, one where the family could have the opportunity to forge its own identity with the support of kin.

META-ADVOCATE   It's been a long time since the children had a Christmas with family that they felt was their own. It would be nice for them to know about the family they've got. I'm thinking of this new family where Ed's the father and Colette's the mother. At the same time I don't want them to forget about their other kin.

THELMA JEAN   There will come a time when Ernest and Tammy will have their own families. That will break our family up as far as having Christmas together. When they move off to New York or California, they may not come home for Christmas.

META-ADVOCATE   People have to figure out how to stay together but they also have to figure out how to be their own family too. The Chazwick-Crevant family is a different family. It will be hard for Tammy and Colette to join this new family. The men may have to help them. Billy (Ed's son), as one of the men, suggested to them that they have a celebration here in Houston on their own and not go to Louisiana this year until New Year's. The Chazwick-Crevant family has the strength to be a family and celebrate Christmas on their own.

THE EFFECTIVENESS OF SCIP WITH SUICIDAL YOUTH

Suicidal adolescents treated with Systemic Crisis Intervention during a period from January 1984 through June 1985 were followed over an eighteen-month post-treatment period to test the effectiveness of SCIP. For a more complete discussion of research methodology and results see Gutstein et al. (1988) and Gutstein and Rudd (1990).

Of the 50 adolescents involved in this study, only two (4.3%) engaged in suicidal behavior during treatment or in the 18-month follow-up period. In both cases the behavior occurred within six months following treatment, and in neither case did it cause any physical harm. One attempt involved minor drug ingestion and the other superficial cuts on the wrist. Additionally, there were no reports of injury to either the identified patient or family members during the treatment phase or the follow-up periods.

The vast majority (over 87%) of parents rated their child's behavioral problems as "severe" or "catastrophic" at the outset of treatment. However, only a very small minority were rated as such following treatment. Ratings improved markedly three months following treatment, with only 27% indicating that the crisis had, for the most part, not been resolved. This trend continued over the six-month period and by the 12- to 18-month follow-up period, only 12% of parents (six cases) indicated that the problem remained severe ($F = 98.65, p < .0001$).

Although no comparison or control group was used in this study, a rough estimate of the comparative safety of SCIP can be obtained by comparing the results of SCIP with other treatment studies of suicidal youth. After a thorough review of the literature, we were unable to find any attempts to measure the effectiveness of a primarily outpatient-based treatment program. We located six studies evaluating psychiatric hospital-based treatment for suicidal children and adolescents (Barter, Swaback, & Todd, 1968; Cohen-Sandler, Berman, & King, 1982; Hawton et al., 1982; McIntire et al.,

1977; Stanley & Barter, 1970; White, 1974). In these studies, rates of suicidal behavior in periods averaging between 12 and 21 months following discharge ranged from 14 to 50%.

A major goal of SCIP is to develop a healthy mutual interdependency of extended family and social network members, rather than the institutional dependency that can sometimes occur after long periods of hospitalization (Kiesler, 1982). Some estimate of our success can be made with regard to this goal by using the families in our study as their own controls. Thus, we compared rates of institutional placement of our identified adolescents during the year prior to and following treatment with SCIP. Ten of 47 (21%) had been in an institutional setting at least once in the 12 months prior to SCIP. By comparison, only one (2%) required hospitalization or residential placement during the follow-up period.

DISCUSSION

Just as the isolated nuclear family represents the inevitable culmination of the progressive fragmentation of the kinship system, so the adolescent suicide attempt may be the inevitable end product of the isolation of the adolescent from the rich diversity of myths and connections available from his or her kin. If this is the case, then treatment methods aimed at decreasing the isolation of family members and fostering reconciliation with kin might prove essential in forestalling future adolescent suicidal crises.

Our outcome research lends preliminary support to the efficacy of mobilizing kin systems as a safe and successful intervention in adolescent suicidal crises. Although the SCIP approach requires intensive team effort, it is highly cost-effective when compared with the cost of a long hospital stay.

Although our research effort begins to demonstrate the usefulness of SCIP, it in no way portrays the extent to which we were impressed by the willingness and ability of the great majority of family members to assume a major role in the treatment process when strategically empowered by professionals. For example, many parents took off a week or more from work, with little advance notice, to ensure the safety of their child during the initial acute crisis period. Equally impressive was the response of close family and friends. Relatives who had been out of contact for years became active participants in the crisis and family members often traveled great distances to attend gatherings. Even when bitterness and betrayal prevail in present relationships, there remain alive memories of love and tenderness and the fantasies of belonging to a group that, when functioning, provides a degree of security and identity that no other system can provide. When strategically evoked, they exert a powerful force, long after we might expect them to have faded to nothing.

REFERENCES

Barter, J. T., Swaback, D. O., & Todd, D. (1968). Adolescent suicide attempts. *Archives of General Psychiatry, 19*, 523-527.

Boszormenyi-Nagy, I., & Krasner, B. R. (1986). *Between give & take: A clinical guide to contextual therapy*. New York: Brunner/Mazel.

Bowen, M. (1976). Theory in the practice of psychotherapy. In P. J. Guerin (Ed.), *Family therapy: Theory and practice*. New York: Gardner.

Cohen-Sandler, R., Berman, A. L., & King, R. A. (1982). A follow-up study of hospitalized suicidal children. *Journal of the American Academy of Child Psychiatry, 21*, 398-403.

Erickson, G. D. (1984). A framework and theories for social network intervention. *Family Process, 23*, 187-198.

Felner, R. D., Farber, S. S., & Primavera, J. (1983). Transitions and stressful life events: A model for primary prevention. In R. D. Felner, L. A. Jason, J. N. Moritsugu, & S. S. Farber (Eds.), *Preventive psychology: Theory, research and practice*. New York: Pergamon Press.

Gutstein, S. E. (1987). Family reconciliation as a response to adolescent crises. *Family Process, 26*, 475-491.

Gutstein, S. E., & Rudd, M. D. (1990). Systemic crisis intervention with suicidal youth: An outcome study. *Journal of Adolescence, 13*, 265-277.

Gutstein, S., Rudd, M., Graham, C., & Rayha, L. (1988). Systemic crisis intervention as a response to adolescent crises: An outcome study. *Family Process, 27*, 201-211.

Hawton, K., O'Grady, J., Osborn, M., & Cole, D. (1982). Adolescents who take overdoses: Their characteristics, problems and contacts with helping agencies. *British Journal of Psychiatry, 140*, 118-123.

Hirsch, B. J. (1980). Natural support systems and coping with major life changes. *American Journal of Community Psychology, 8*, 159-172.

Kiesler, C. A. (1982). Mental hospitals and alternative care. *American Psychologist, 37*, 349-360.

McGoldrick, M., & Carter, E. A. (1982). The family life cycle. In F. Walsh (Ed.), *Normal family processes*. New York: Guilford.

McIntire, M. S., Angle, C. R., Wikoff, R. L., & Schlicht, M. L. (1977). Recurrent adolescent suicidal behavior. *Pediatrics, 60*, 605-608.

Minuchin, S. (1974). *Families and family therapy*. Cambridge, MA: Harvard University Press.

Parkes, C. M. (1971). Psychosocial transitions: A field for study. *Social Science and Medicine, 5*, 101-115.

Pfeffer, C. R. (1986). *The suicidal child*. New York: Guilford.

Richman, J. (1981). Family treatment of suicidal children and adolescents. In C. F. Wells & I. R. Stuard (Eds.), *Self destructive behavior in children and adolescents*. New York: Van Nostrand Reinhold.

Richman, J. (1986). *Family therapy for suicidal people*. New York: Springer.

Rueveni, U. (1977). Family network intervention: Mobilizing support for families in crisis. *International Journal of Family Counseling, 5*, 77-83.

Schoenfeld, P., Halevy-Martini, J. H., Hemley-van der Velden, E., & Ruhf, L. (1986). Long-term outcome of network therapy. *Hospital and Community Psychiatry, 37*, 373-376.

Speck, R. V., & Attneave, C. L. (1973). *Family networks*. New York: Pantheon.

Stanley, E. J., & Barter, J. T. (1970). Adolescent suicidal behavior. *American Journal of Orthopsychiatry, 40*, 87-96.

White, H. C. (1974). Self-poisoning in adolescents. *British Journal of Psychiatry, 124,* 24-35.

Williams, R. M. (1970). *Kinship and the family in the United States in American society* (3rd ed.). New York: Alfred A. Knopf.

Wortman, C., & Lehman, D. (1986). Reactions to victims of life crises: Support that doesn't help. In I. G. Sarason & B. R. Sarason (Eds.), *Social support: Theory, research and application*. The Hague: Martinus Nijhof.

14

Intergenerational Patterns of Traumatic Loss: Death and Despair in Addict Families

SANDRA B. COLEMAN

As WE ENTER the final decade of the 20th century there is alarming evidence that many life-threatening problems are menacing our society and the environment that once nurtured it. It is thought by some that our planet itself is dying. Perhaps more than ever before, except during times of war, universal attention has been given to death and dying.

Most of us will probably not live to see if the earth and its inhabitants survive, but we are all witnessing the effects that some human dilemmas, such as AIDS and drugs, are having on society. Although such problems are personal in nature, they cannot be understood without considering the interpersonal context within which their often fatal outcomes take place. What is unusual about someone who dies from AIDS or from drug abuse is that he/she is often quite young. This creates a situation that differs significantly from that surrounding a person who dies in the latter stages of life and whose family and friends may have died before him/her. In the case of the young terminally ill person, family members and/or significant others are alive, often playing a major role in the dying process. Thus, it is important to understand the roles of the dying person and those involved with the dying process. Although this chapter focuses largely on the heroin addict, the material presented also applies to those who have contracted AIDS through intravenous drug use.

BACKGROUND

The degree to which a dying person assumes special status in the family was discussed almost 20 years ago by Kastenbaum and Aisenberg (1972), who suggested that the dying member often serves as a symbolic representation of *all* of the family's deceased ancestors. These authors paid particular attention to the social participation imposed by death, a view first expressed by Slater (1964), who was intrigued by the way people at funerals surround the corpse, giving it love and attention. Kastenbaum and Aisenberg further observed that a terminal condition may accelerate group interactional processes by offering the dying family member an opportunity to participate in his/her idiosyncratic death rituals. Thus, as Becker (1973) suggests, death is an integral and functional part of life, an event that all families face at varying points throughout their life cycle.

Consistent with Carter and McGoldrick's (1980) view of the life cycle in terms of "the meaningfulness of intergenerational connectedness in the family," death of a family member creates an experience that must be faced and dealt with, similar to many other life tasks. Carter and McGoldrick are particularly concerned about the intersection between contemporary, developmental, here and now events and historical family patterns, suggesting that family dysfunction is most apt to result when normal, developmental tension collides with transgenerational stress. Surely, one of the most traumatic events in the life of the family is the death of a significant member, particularly when that death is sudden or premature. As with other developmental traumas, there may be long-term effects. Whether or not the events subsequent to death are negative or positive depends on many intervening family variables. For example, Eisenstadt (1978) proposed a theory of the eminence of genius as a consequence of parental bereavement, stating that there is a creative mourning process that "is related to a sequence of events whereby the loss triggers off a crisis requiring mastery on the part of the bereaved individual." He elaborated, "If the crisis is worked through, that is, if the destructive elements and the depressive features of the experience of bereavement are neutralized, then a creative product or creatively integrated personality can result" (p. 220).

Eisenstadt suggests that a major intervening variable between the death of a parent and the desire for fame, eminence, and occupational excellence is the nature of the family unit prior to the disruptive period preceding the death. He offers support for his theory by reconstructing parental loss profiles of 699 eminent people who experienced early loss of one or both parents. Comparative orphanhood data from the general population, i.e., actuarial information, indicated that the eminent group had a considerably greater degree of parental loss. Comparisons with delinquent groups, however, showed that delinquents were orphaned at rates comparable to those found among the eminent group. Thus, Eisenstadt suggests that the critical issue is not necessarily loss itself, but the way it is mastered. The eminent group seemed to invest considerable energy in intellectual pursuits, which may represent a creative approach to coping with bereavement.

The important question arising from Eisenstadt's theory is, what happens when bereavement is not mastered? The delinquency data suggest that the inability to mourn creatively may well be a function of family characteristics that emerge at the time that a member dies. If this is the case, the important variable is not death but the family transactions and interrelationships that lead to the successful or unsuccessful resolution of death.

A Theory of Incomplete Mourning and Substance Abuse

Clinical Evidence

The basic tenets of my incomplete mourning theory were developed several years before Eisenstadt's work was published (Coleman, 1975), but the central concepts are remarkably similar. The early foundation for the theory lies in a pilot study of the prevalence of death among 25 recovering heroin addicts and their families (Coleman, 1975). At least one traumatic or untimely death in either the addict's family of origin or family of procreation was experienced in 72% (N = 18) of the families. The investigation was limited to those deaths that were premature, unexpected, and not a function of illness associated with the normal aging process. Thus, the majority of deaths reported took place during the addicts' or parents' developmental years. Further findings revealed that 68% (N = 17) of the families had an alcoholic parent or sibling in either of the two generations studied. It is interesting to note that, in addition to heroin addiction, death and alcoholism were common variables among these families.

The following case examples are representative of the families who served as subjects in the pilot study.

> After a heated argument with his wife, Mr. A. left her and his two young children to join friends on a scuba diving adventure from which he never returned. Several days later, his body was washed ashore. Investigation revealed that his air regulator had failed and he had presumably drowned at sea. Mrs. A.'s guilt about her role in the marital dispute was excessive.
>
> After an extremely traumatic funeral experience, Mrs. A. was visited frequently by the manager of the funeral parlor, who was estranged from his schizophrenic wife. Eventually, Mrs. A. married the undertaker (who ultimately had to leave the funeral industry due to intense anxiety attacks associated with the sight of cadavers).
>
> Several years later, when Mrs. A's children were adolescents, they became seriously involved with drugs and had to enter a therapeutic community for drug

rehabilitation. During this time, in a marital therapy session that was part of the program's family therapy component, Mrs. A. recalled an intense confrontation she had, during her own adolescence, at her mother's deathbed. This therapeutic "visit" helped her to say farewell to one of the ghosts that had long haunted the family system.*

Mrs. P. married her deceased husband's twin brother after being widowed due to an unexplained, strange, and sudden death. Both Mr. and Mrs. P. had several children from their former marriages, three of whom later became involved in drug abuse and alcoholism. The only child from their union (born prior to their marriage) also became heavily involved with drugs at the age of 13. One daughter from Mrs. P.'s first marriage was killed in a suicidal automobile accident after a violent argument with her mother. Mr. P.'s oldest son was hospitalized in a mental institution and was suspected of being involved in a homicide case while using drugs.

Mrs. F.'s alcoholic father deserted her mother when Mrs. F. was quite young. After her mother died, Mrs. F. was raised by her maternal grandmother, who died suddenly when Mrs. F. was in her early teens. She married an alcoholic and had five children, one of whom became seriously involved with drugs and alcohol. Another son, the eldest and most successful, was the innocent victim of a murder in a robbery-homicide in his college boarding house. Shortly thereafter, Mrs. F.'s only granddaughter died at the age of 11 months from an unusual congenital illness. It was not long before another daughter became involved with drugs.

In addition to these examples from the lives of families with substance-abusing members, clinical evidence for the significance of death and death-related issues among addict families was found in my weekly group therapy sessions with the siblings of recovering addicts (Coleman, 1978, 1979). This group was developed as a primary prevention project for preadolescents who were at high risk for future drug dependency. All of these youngsters came from families with repetitive intergenerational addictive patterns. It took these youngsters almost a year to settle down from their chaotic, acting-out behavior in group, but when they finally felt secure enough to sit quietly and share their emotions, fascinating material emerged.

Death — either symbolic or real — was the most familiar recurring theme. It always had a sobering effect on the members:

The first such group experience occurred when 13-year-old Rita's 23-year-old brother was the victim of a robbery-homicide. Ironically, this brother was the only member of Rita's family who was not addicted to drugs, alcohol, or food. Rita, her mother, and a married sister were all very obese; her father was an alcoholic who, as a result of family therapy, became sober for the first time in over a decade; another brother and sister were drug abusers. Rita and her family came for family therapy immediately following the murder.

---

*An excerpt from this therapy session appears in Coleman and Stanton (1978).

In the group Rita sobbingly said that, upon learning of her brother's death, she wanted to return to sibling group therapy, after having dropped out several weeks before. Almost all of the group members became tearful as she recounted the sad episode. Each member then shared a personal experience with death. Considering their youth, they had suffered a wide range of untimely losses, including that of one boy's four-year-old sister who had died of leukemia several years before. An interesting result of Rita's tragedy was that, in contrast to her previous peripheral position in the group, she became an integrated and accepted member.

Several months later, another 13-year-old broke into sobs. Her older brother, a diabetic since childhood, had started to use drugs again. In the past, the combination of his physical illness and the heroin abuse had so threatened his life that he was given last rites three times. Sue told the group that she feared this time his drug use would prove fatal. Again, the group members talked seriously about their past experiences with death. They suggested that Sue disclose her fears to her brother, which she subsequently did. Although she doubted that this would change his behavior, she felt considerable relief in having faced him so honestly.

One of the youngest members, Margo, dropped out of the group before the first spring, saying she could not tolerate the stress and acting-out of the others. In midsummer, when her pet dog was killed by an automobile, Margo quickly returned to group. She cried profusely and told everyone how angry she was toward the careless driver, an insensitive neighbor. Margo had considerable difficulty overcoming the loss, even though her parents bought her a new puppy. There was little change in her affect until it was suggested that the new dog be brought to group. Following the puppy's much approved visit, Margo's grief subsided.

Supportive Literature

Comprehensive reviews of the literature on death, separation, and loss appear in previously published literature and are not repeated here (Coleman, 1980a, 1980b; Coleman & Stanton, 1978; Stanton & Coleman, 1980; Stanton et al., 1978). However, in view of their conceptual significance, major research findings are presented.

A central issue in the lives of drug abusers is the inherent suicidal element in addict populations. A high proportion of addicts die at an early age; in addition, supporting data reveal a high incidence of early death of at least one of the addict's parents (Blum & associates, 1972; Ellinwood, Smith, & Vaillant, 1966; Harbin & Maziar, 1975; Klagsbrun & Davis, 1977; Miller, 1974). It is interesting to note that a study of treatment outcome (Harris & Linn, 1978) found that one of the few background characteristics that significantly differentiated heroin addicts from nonheroin drug users was that the heroin addicts were more likely to have experienced the death of their fathers before the age of 16.

The prevalence of death symbols further reflects the unique role that death plays in addict families. From observing the roles, communications, metacommunications, and interactions within 25 families, I (Coleman, 1975) distinguished three metaphoric, death-related phases on the addiction continuum: (1) the imminence of death (early drug use); (2) the funeral (removal from the house to a residential therapeutic community); and (3) the resurrection (family treatment). In this sense, addiction is analogous to a slow dying process. Coleman and Stanton (1978; Stanton & Coleman, 1980) suggest that addiction facilitates the family's death-related participatory behavior. By treating the drug abuser as if he/she were going through a slow, tedious death, the family members are able to perpetuate (vis-à-vis the addict) the premature and unresolved death of a former member. The addict thus becomes a substitute or "revenant" of the deceased. This is consistent with Stanton's (1977) view of the addict as the sacrificial member who martyrs him/herself in order to fulfill the family's need for a death. Stanton considers that the addict's role as "savior" allows the family to become mutually involved in a suicide conspiracy.

In addition to separation caused by death, any type of disengagement is particularly difficult for addict families. Stanton (1980), Stanton et al. (1978), and I (Coleman, 1978, 1979) have written extensively about the conflictual elements of separation, expressing doubt that it is mere coincidence that drug use becomes intensified during adolescence, when separation conflicts are at a peak. As Stanton et al. (1978) point out, drug abuse is a "paradoxical resolution" to growing up and leaving the family. The drug permits the user to leave as a means of establishing some independence, but it also facilitates the return to the hearth when it is time to "crash." This perpetuates the cyclical pattern of leaving and not leaving, keeping the addict straddled between home and the outside world of drugs. The profound conflict that separation presents for these families has been discussed extensively in other publications.

THE ROLE OF RELIGIOSITY* IN DRUG ADDICT FAMILIES

Akin to exploring the role of death in addict families is the investigation of the function of religion in family life. The family's religious beliefs or philosophical systems of thought are apt to be the major interface between death and the family's adaptive behavior. A sense of faith may either alleviate or

---

*Religiosity or religion, as used here, extends beyond formal doctrine and includes any system of philosophical belief that represents a specific view about the meaning of life. Thus, the term "religion" embraces a sociological view or Weltanschauung that includes the conceptualization of the purpose of one's existence. This is considered to be one of the motivating forces that guides purposive behavior—an internal determinant, to some extent, of one's life process.

exacerbate the sorrow, rage, and guilt that accompany or follow the loss of a loved one. Consequently, in order to understand how families respond to death and loss, it is necessary to explore their religious value system and practice as well as their philosophy of life.

Supportive Literature

There is some evidence for linking drug use with a lack of childhood exposure to religious training. For example, Blum and associates (1972) found that high-drug-risk families were inconsistent or ambiguous about their children's religious practices. In contrast, the low-drug-risk families instilled in their youngsters the foundations of religion and belief in God during early childhood and became more flexible about church attendance when the children reached adolescence. A relationship between religion and drug use is also suggested by Gorsuch and Butler (1976), who claim that those who practice abstinence may have learned that their basic needs could be met by traditional parental socialization factors, i.e., religion. This idea gains support when it is viewed in conjunction with Blum and associates (1972) findings that youngsters from traditional families, regardless of social class, race, or ethnicity, are least apt to engage in drug abuse.

In addition to exploring the relationship between formal doctrinal religion and drug use, it is necessary to consider the role that religion plays in the consequences of death. Feifel (1959) maintains that one's religious orientation, coping mechanisms, and personal reaction to death are all related. The major thesis underlying Frankl's (1963) logotherapeutic system is that man's primary life force is the search for meaning. Frankl suggests that the loss of meaning creates an "existential vacuum" in which one lacks a rationale for living, thus creating hopelessness and despair. He explains alcoholism as a function of the "existential vacuum" and further suggests that the frustrated will to meaning may be compensated for by the substitution of a will to pleasure. Could one then suppose, in view of such a theoretical premise, that drug addiction is also a means of coping with the spiritual void?

Although these findings are interesting, the nature of the interactions between child and parents is perhaps more important than specific religious practices. Kastenbaum (1965) relates object loss in the form of death to alienation from God, in that a significant loss tends to increase the fear of further loss. He also suggests that the loss or lack of a belief system, especially in conjunction with the loss of a love object, may produce intensified feelings of despair, helplessness, and a loss of power, reinforcing the depressive state. Thus, it is postulated that the belief in any system, whether deism, atheism, etc., is in itself a resolution and represents a philosophical-religious construct regarding life and its experiential meaning. The lack of such a system leads to a state of noncommitment which induces a feeling of helplessness, powerlessness, and frustration. If the loss of a significant family member takes place within the vacuum of an amorphous religious belief system, it is assumed that drug use may represent a search for meaning and a defense against one's own mortality.

Research Findings

Data from several large research studies suggest that death, loss, and separation are highly significant factors in the lives of intravenous drug abusers. In a national survey of family therapy and drug abuse, researchers found that separation from families, depression, and death and loss issues were frequently cited as major conflicts presented in family therapy (Coleman, 1976; Coleman & Davis, 1978). Among 16 possible variables affecting treatment families, only acting-out, additional addictions, and sexual problems ranked higher.

An investigation of loss and death issues across varying racial/ethnic groups and other minorities reveals interesting supportive material. Consistently, across all these populations, loss and separation conflicts prevail. Particularly common to drug abusers whose parents are first-generation immigrants is alienation from the country of origin. This creates a separation problem that extends across three generations. For example, a Hispanic family that settles in the southwestern United States becomes separated from its native country as well as from parents and extended family, who are usually of great importance to Hispanic family systems. As the children grow up, their American acculturation is in sharp contrast to the more highly visible ethnic characteristics of the parents, creating even more separation between the generations. This results in an enormous loss of family traditions and connections.

No population shows greater effects of this loss of tradition than Native Americans. Among the Navajo, I (Coleman, 1979) found that loss issues encompassed individual families as well as their entire nation, for, in addition to all the familial changes, the Navajo are beset with problems threatening their loss of religious rituals. The latter are often replaced by new revivalist religions, which have a seductive effect on the very needy Native American people. Disputes with the Hopi over territorial boundaries present continuous threats of the loss of land, with concomitant deprivation of large quantities of livestock. Navajo family counselors feel that the stripping of their people's cultural identity exacerbates and contributes to addiction. As one worker said, "Unless the Indian can keep his rituals he will most assuredly die."

These studies reinforce the theory of incomplete mourning and form the foundation for more extensive research directly investigating the role of heroin addiction in helping families cope with death, separation, and loss across the life cycle. This more recent research (Coleman et al., 1982; Coleman, Kaplan, & Downing, 1986) provides a systematic investigation of the role of death, loss, separation, and religiosity in the context of the family life cycle of a two-generation sample of heroin addicts, psychiatric outpatients, and normals. It was based on the theoretical premise that drug use serves to maintain family patterns that keep the drug-abusing member helpless and unable to leave the family. This process tends to unify the family and sustain its intactness. Within the complex set of feedback mechanisms involved in the drug-taking process lies an overall sense of family hopelessness and lack of purpose or meaning in life. Thus, there is a purposive role played by the ritual of heroin addiction.

The sample population in this study was given an extensive battery of tests, including an individual structured interview (*The Coleman Family Background Questionnaire*, "CFBQ," Coleman, Kaplan, & Downing, 1982) that includes questions on demographic factors, religion, meaning in life, experience with pain, attitudes toward death, addictive behaviors, relationships with parental figures, incest, living arrangements, and children. It also provides a retrospective overview of major life events, the subject's responses to those events, and his or her perception of family members' reactions. Questions about family composition over time lead to a "map" of the subjects' homes and of all those who have lived with the subjects. For every deceased family member or significant other, details are elicited as to the cause of death; age of subject and deceased; closeness of the relationship; emotional and practical impact of the death; extent of mourning by the subject, parents, and siblings; whether the subject attended the funeral; and the impact of the funeral. Each permanent and temporary separation from a family member is also explored to determine its timing, cause, and effect and whether the subject was reunited with this person.

Results of this research support the study's major premises. The total incidence of death varies strikingly across groups and differs significantly for the addicts whose family life cycle across two generations (1) is invaded by multiple death experiences that are often premature and bizarre in nature, (2) is laced with suicide and suicidal ideation, and (3) shows an extreme, obsessional fascination with death. In addition, addicts are more frequently separated from their entire families during childhood or adolescence; such separations, though often temporary, appear to be associated with traumatic events or to occur in a most distressing manner. Further, addicts, more than any other population, are apt to be permanently separated from their families of origin and grow up in homes that are not those of immediate family members. As a group, addicts tend to develop a distinct, repetitive, intergenerational pattern of separating from and returning to their families of origin. Finally, concerning the concept of religion, neither generation develops a clearly defined central meaning or purpose in life.

Perhaps most interesting is the placement of the findings in a developmental family life cycle framework, particularly when some of the qualitative results are included. During childhood, there is a greater tendency for an addict to have a prolonged separation from either the entire family or from the mother or mother surrogate. Also during childhood, the addict is more likely to have an older sibling leave home for reasons not associated with normal expected change, i.e., incarceration, running away. Even temporary separations occur in more than 50% of the addict population. Amid these disruptions, addicts are also more likely to have a grandfather die. Thus, childhood for an addict appears to hold a strong element of loss and separation.

Immediate consequences of these experiences are reflected in the work of Bowlby (1980), who 10 years ago reaffirmed his classic findings (Bowlby, 1951) that early childhood loss without resolution produces disturbed patterns of attachment behavior, eventually leading to chronic stress and severe depression. This is similar to Eisenstadt's (1978) view that early loss triggers a crisis that demands mastery or "creative bereavement," without which antisocial behavior may follow. Eisenstadt sees the family unit as the major intervening variable. Thus, the context within which the crisis occurs is perhaps more significant than the traumatic event itself.

During adolescence there are again more separations from the entire family for the addicts as compared with the psychiatric and normal subjects. As in the previous stage of development, in the midst of all this, a sibling may leave home unexpectedly. When one considers that the addicts are more apt to experience the death of an immediate family member at this time as well as that of a significant nonfamily member, the adolescent period emerges as highly disruptive and traumatic.

One of the relevant contextual issues is that the addict is more apt to have parents who during childhood lost family members who lived in their home. These death experiences may well infuse the parent with heightened anxiety regarding any kind of loss in the family of procreation. Thus, when a child prepares to leave home, even at an appropriate stage, this normal life cycle event becomes surrounded with conflict and ambivalence. This could explain the repetitive pattern of leaving home and returning, a pattern that is vastly different from that of either psychiatric inpatients or normals. This particular behavior suggests that the addict is not the "street person," as often described, but is actually very connected to home and family, even if this tie is associated with inordinate anxiety. These findings support much of the clinical data reviewed by Stanton (1982).

Another contextual issue is the addict family's resistance to talking about death and dying, a family communication function that is generally associated with psychologically healthy families (Lewis, Beavers, Gossett, & Phillips, 1976). Perhaps addict families' inability to confront the human issue of death directly is connected to the more conflictual environment in which they live, a fact supported by findings on the Moos Family Environment Scale. When coupled with heroin addicts' lack of formal religious involvement and their generalized purposelessness, the overall family environment seems to be bleak and grim.

Value systems also differ considerably for the addict group. Both addicts and their parents believe that what happens to you when you die is related to how you lived your life on earth. Both generations are less willing to die for someone than either normal subjects or parents of normal or inpatient subjects. This may reflect the addict parents' moderate degree of anxiety about death and dying. It may also be related to the lack of meaning or purpose in their lives, for surely giving one's life for a justifiable cause is indicative of some form of purposefulness.

Addicts appear to have a relatively concrete value system. They place high importance on money but are not particularly concerned with the more abstract values associated with making a contribution to society, being a community leader, or correcting social and economic inequalities — values much more frequently associated with the normal subjects. It is interesting to note, however, that the addict sample reported the greatest concern with having a good marriage and family life and wanted, more than the others, to give their children better opportunities than they had experienced. Although at a deep level they feel, and surely behave, as if life has little meaning, on a more cognitive plane they hope for something better. One might speculate that the latter is related to their own ties to family of origin. This self-reported information is likely to be a function of both the denial, which permeates the addict's life style, and his/her counterphobic behavior. This characterizes addicts' central, adolescent-like conflict. They are not yet ready to encompass society's goals and values, as they are still locked into the incomplete task of growing up and leaving home. Thus, addicts cling to the family even when hierarchically ordering their values and attitudes, which often reek of despair. To go beyond the family system to embrace the larger system is a step they are not ready to take.

This preoccupation with self is probably most obvious in the addicts' degree of bodily concern. Their high somatization scores suggest a very strong focus on their bodies, a fact that is certainly understandable in view of their heroin use. In a paradoxical fashion, these people are compulsively compelled to inject a powerful drug into their veins and then worry obsessively about the very bodies they are steadily abusing.

CONCLUSION

It is apparent, from both clinical and research material, that death and loss issues affect families in profound ways, intruding upon and influencing interactional patterns for generation after generation. It is likely that similar characteristics prevail in many families besides those with drug-dependent members, particularly families where there are other kinds of abusive or addictive behaviors. Examples are families with eating disorders, sex and love addictions, obsessive gambling, or workaholism.

In addition to the multigenerational familial context within which the addict develops, one must always consider the larger society and its interactive effects. Clearly our inner-city poor, our homeless, and our deprived populations are overwhelmingly fraught with death, loss and hopelessness. More than any others, these families are confronted with daily violence and fear, for which perhaps the only relief is that of a substance that chemically alters their suffering. The battlefield of crime and poverty is fertile ground for the very conditions that generate the previously described patterns.

With regard to the issue of AIDS, the increasing problem of this autoimmune deficiency disease among IV drug users may further reinforce the pattern described here. Surely the growing number of deaths caused by AIDS has a high probability of contributing to the sense of helplessness and overwhelming angst that permeates the drug world. If one accepts the theoretical premises and their implications as described here, attempts to put clean needles on the streets and in the shooting galleries are likely to do little to reduce the incidence of drug dependency and its relationship to the AIDS infection. Rather, one might expect that the risk of AIDS only enhances the sensation-seeking behavior of the IV drug user, making the drug experience that much more exhilarating. As for the family system, AIDS offers an opportunity for more ghosts to hover over future generations; if inadequately mourned, these may perpetuate the circular dance that accompanies the ceremony of addiction.

REFERENCES

Becker, E. (1973). *Denial of death*. New York: Free Press.

Blum, R., and associates. (1972). *Horatio Alger's children*. San Francisco: Jossey-Bass.

Bowlby, J. (1951). *Maternal care and mental health*. Geneva: World Health Organization.

Bowlby, J. (1980). *Attachment and loss* (volume 3). New York: Basic Books.

Carter, E., & McGoldrick, M. (Eds.). (1980). *The family life cycle*. New York: Gardner Press.

Coleman, S. B. (1975). Death as a social agent in addict families. Paper presented at the 83rd Annual Convention of the American Psychological Association. Chicago, Illinois.

Coleman, S. B. (1976). Final report: A national study of family therapy in the field of drug abuse. Prepared for the Behavioral & Social Science Branch: National Institute on Drug Abuse. Grant No. 3H81-DA-01478-0151.

Coleman, S. B. (1978). Sib group therapy: A prevention program for siblings from drug addict families. *International Journal of Addictions, 13*, (1), 115-127.

Coleman, S. B. (1979). Siblings in session. In E. Kaufman & P. Kaufman (Eds.), *Family therapy of drug and alcohol abuse*, (pp. 131–143). New York: Gardner Press.

Coleman, S. B. (1980a). Incomplete mourning and addict family transactions: A theory for understanding heroin abuse. In D. Lettieri (Ed.), *Theories on drug abuse* (pp. 83–89 & 315–318). National Institute on Drug Abuse, Research Monograph 30, DHHS Pub. No. (ADM) 80-967. Washington, DC: U.S. Government Printing Office.

Coleman, S. B. (1980b). The family trajectory: A circular journey to drug abuse. In B. Ellis (Ed.), *Drug abuse from the family perspective*. National Institute on Drug Abuse, Office of Program Development and Analysis, DHHS, Pub. No. (ADM) 80-910.

Coleman, S. B., & Davis, D. I. (1978). Family therapy and drug abuse: A national survey. *Family Process, 17*, (1), 21–29.

Coleman, S. B., Kaplan, J. D., Gallagher, P. R., Downing, R. W., & Caine, C. (1982). Heroin—A family coping strategy for death and loss: Final report 1979–1981, National Institute on Drug Abuse, Grant No. R01-DA-02332-02, Achievement Through Counseling and Treatment, Washington, DC.

Coleman, S. B., Kaplan, J. D., & Downing, R. W. (1986). Life cycle and loss—The spiritual vacuum of heroin addiction. *Family Process, 25*, (1), 5–23.

Coleman, S. B., Kaplan, J. D., & Downing, R. W. (1982). *Coleman Family Background Questionnaire*. Copyright Registration Number TXu 258-477.

Coleman, S. B., & Stanton, M. D. (1978). The role of death in the addict family. *Journal of Marital & Family Counseling, 4*, (1), 79–91.

Eisenstadt, J. M. (1978). Parental loss and genius. *American Psychologist, 33*, 211–223.

Ellinwood, E. H., Smith, W. G., & Vaillant, G. E. (1966). Narcotic addiction in males and females: A comparison. *International Journal of Addictions, 1*, 33–45.

Feifel, H. (1959). Attitudes toward death in some family and mentally ill populations. In H. Feifel (Ed.), *The meaning of death*. New York: McGraw-Hill.

Frankl, V. E. (1963). *Man's search for meaning*. New York: Beacon Press.

Gorsuch, R. L., & Butler, M. D. (1976). Initial drug abuse: A preview of predisposing social psychological factors. *Psychological Bulletin, 83*, 120–137.

Harbin, H. T., & Maziar, H. M. (1975). The families of drug abusers. A literature review. *Family Process, 14*, 411–431.

Harris, R., & Linn, M. W. (1978). Differential response of heroin and non-heroin abusers to inpatient treatment. *American Journal of Drug & Alcohol Abuse, 5(2)*, 179–190.

Kastenbaum, R. (1965). Engrossment and perspective in later life. In R. Kastenbaum (Ed.), *Contributions to the psychobiology of aging*. New York: Springer.

Kastenbaum, R., & Aisenberg, P. (1972). *The psychology of death*. New York: Springer.

Klagsbrun, M., & Davis, D. I. (1977). Substance abuse and family interaction. *Family Process, 16*, 149–173.

Lewis, J. M., Beavers, W. R., Gossett, J. T., & Phillips, V. A. (1976). *No single thread: Psychological health in family systems*. New York: Brunner/Mazel.

Miller, D. (1974). *Adolescence, psychology, psychopathology, and psychotherapy*. New York: Jason Aronson.

Slater, P. E. (1964). Prolegomena to a psychoanalytic theory of aging and death. In R. Kastenbaum & R. Aisenberg (Eds.), *The psychology of death*. New York: Springer, 1972.

Stanton, M. D. (1977). The addict as savior: Heroin, death and the family. *Family Process, 16*, 191–197.

Stanton, M. D. (1980). A family theory of drug abuse. In Lettieri, D. et al. (Eds.), *Theories on drug abuse*, National Institute on Drug Abuse. Research Monograph 30, PHHS Pub. No. (ADM) 80-967. Washington, DC, Supt. of Docs., U.S. Government Printing Office.

Stanton, M. D. (1982). *Family therapy of drug abuse and addiction*. New York: Guilford Press.

Stanton, M. D., & Coleman, S. B. (1980). The participatory aspects of self-destructive behavior: The addict as a family model. In N. Farberow & D. Lettieri (Eds.), *The many faces of suicide*. New York: McGraw-Hill.

Stanton, M. D., Todd, T. C., Heard, D. B., Kirschner, S., Kleiman, J. I., Mowatt, D. T., Riley, P., Scott, S. M., & Van Deusen, J. M. (1978). Heroin addiction as a family phenomenon: A new conceptual model. *American Journal of Drug and Alcohol Abuse, 5*, 125–150.

15

Death in the Therapist's Own Family

BETTY CARTER

I wrote the following paper in March, 1973 and read it at the Georgetown University Symposium on Family Psychotherapy in November, 1973. At that time I was just completing my training in family therapy. In the 17 years that have passed since then, I have continued my efforts to "practice what I preach," although in a less formal way. This work, which reconnected me permanently to my family of origin, is still the approach I use in my clinical practice when faced with the death or threatened death of a family member.

WHAT FOLLOWS IS A summary of my efforts to change my relationships with the members of my family of origin *in vivo* instead of in my head. Like many others, I had done the latter, concluded that my parents loved me and had done the best they could under their life circumstances, and that, of course, since things could never be "real" between either of them and me, I could at least be "understanding" of them and tolerate the "boredom" or "irritation" of such visits as duty required. My major emotional investment, in any case, was in my own nuclear family and I was prone to put my energies into making things work out with my husband and two young sons.

Three things led to my decision to try the "radical" course of going back to my family of origin: one was reading Murray Bowen and listening to him and others of his persuasion at professional conferences; the second was my growing feeling of discomfort in my work with families, as I saw the futility of trying to ignore or bypass their old family cutoffs, and found myself recommending to clients steps that I did not have the nerve to take in my own family; and third, in spite of our best efforts to cope with it, there was tension between my husband and me that was producing anxiety symptoms in both of us and conflict with or about our children.

I have divided this account of work that is still very much in progress into three parts: reentry into the family; my father's illness; and the anniversary party. The time period covered in this report is one year—from March 1972, when I started planning my reentry, to the writing of this paper in March 1973. I consulted periodically with a family therapist who was also supervising some of my work with families during this period.

REENTRY INTO THE FAMILY

In March 1972, I decided that when my parents returned from their winter stay in Florida, I was going to try to change my relationship with each of them. I spent the two months before their return to New York alternately thinking about the family and what I wanted to change about my position in it, and struggling with bouts of dread and anxiety beyond what I had expected. Although my insomnia, backaches, and assorted tics tempted me to abandon the idea before I began, they also seemed to indicate that the project was more important than I had realized. Drawing a genogram, making lists, trying to organize all kinds of data, and otherwise striving for some academic distance from the family were helpful both in reducing my anxiety and in producing some ideas about how to start moving.

My family is Irish Catholic on both sides. I knew a lot more about my mother's family than my father's, having grown up in the two-family house in Brooklyn where my parents still lived and where my mother had lived with her family before marrying. Aunt Clara, my mother's youngest sister, still lived upstairs and was in close daily contact with my parents. I had lots of data on my mother's family, had known her mother well, and remembered her father vaguely but warmly. On my father's side, I was unsure of the number (there were eight) and ages of his siblings, had never known his parents, who had both died before I was born, and could not remember his ever having spoken of either of them! I had vivid memories of most of my father's brothers and sisters from my childhood, but two had died suddenly in the 1940s, one had attempted suicide at about the same time and had been mostly estranged from the family since then, three I had never seen and seldom heard of, and the others I had lost touch with years ago. My father, the youngest of the six brothers, had had polio as a child and was lame throughout his life. In 1966, after a family party celebrating his birthday, he had fallen, breaking his weak leg, and since then he had depended on a walker. In August 1971, just before his 75th birthday, he had a malignant tumor removed from his throat and the family had been told that there were no further signs of the cancer.

My mother and father were married in 1928 and had five children; I was the oldest, and had a sister one-and-a-half years younger and a brother four years younger than I. Twin girls born prematurely died in infancy—one shortly after birth and one at 18 months (when I was 12 years old) of an overdose of sulfa prescribed for a strep throat. She died on my father's birthday, a few months after my mother had undergone a major operation for intestinal cancer from which she had been given rather slim chances of recovery.

As I surveyed the extended family system as a whole for the first time, it became apparent that it bore all the earmarks of a closed emotional system that popped at the seams periodically with sudden death, serious illness, accident, or breakdown. These events were handled by a series of tense, whispered conversations among the adults and somewhat more open grieving by the women at a wake and funeral. Then they were dropped from discussion or reference as family members went on with their lives in the Irish tradition of endurance and persistence in the face of "troubles." As I looked at my position in each of the major triangles in my original family, I saw myself "tuned into" but conflicted towards my mother, sister, and sister-in-law, and warmly disposed toward, but enormously distant from, my father, brother, and brother-in-law (all named Jack, incidentally). My sister and I had both left home immediately after college, she to get married and I to work in Europe. For the past 20 or so years, after a stormy adolescence, I had maintained polite, friendly, and superficial contact with my family, avoiding "controversial" emotional issues, which tended to be converted into political arguments or other abstract discussions. There had been one brief breaking through of this facade in 1959, when I created a family scandal and uproar by marrying a divorced Protestant outside of the Catholic church at a wedding attended by only my sister, brother, and a first cousin. After about a year of tension, this had been "accepted" and "forgotten" without discussion or further reference to it.

I decided that, in order to get to know the men in my family, I would have to feel friendlier toward the women, whom I perceived as standing between us. I planned my first "new" visit shortly after my parents' return from Florida on the occasion of my 43rd birthday. It also happened to be the day before Mother's Day and a week before my Aunt Clara's birthday. I brought with me the most uncharacteristic gifts I could think of—things handmade by me, who, it was well-known, had no talent or patience for handwork. My husband and children came with me (I had never visited home alone since my marriage 13 years earlier), and I further relieved my rising anxiety by taking the first tranquilizer of my life and by deciding that on this first reentry I would concentrate on staying out of old traps rather than doing anything in particular.

The "reentry" visit was a great success as a first move, although somewhat co-opted by the family's response to "the return of the prodigal daughter." I was able to respond with joking remarks to comments of theirs that I would previously have argued with or silently disapproved of. My new interest in family history was rewarded with information about my father's family (such questions to him being mostly answered by my mother), and the conversation was livelier and the visit several hours longer than usual. Their warm response to my new behavior and interest was the first of many occasions that caused me to wonder what percentage of the distance and superficiality was of my own making.

My Father's Illness

A telephone check-in with my mother in the week following my "reentry" visit found her in lively spirits in spite of the fact that both she and my father were suffering from bronchitis. A week later, on Memorial Day, my father was taken to the hospital with pneumonia and was tested for recurrence of the cancer that had been discovered the year before. On June 5, 1972, my mother phoned me to report that the doctors had diagnosed my father's cancer as terminal (lymphosarcoma). He was losing weight rapidly and the doctors planned cobalt treatments and chemotherapy to forestall a kidney operation that he might not be strong enough to undergo. Under the stress of this news, we both cried for a moment, but then my mother pulled herself together quickly and warned pointedly, "Of course, he's not to know. We'll all be brave and go on as usual."

The blow of this news and uncertainty about how much time there would be caused me to change my plans and priorities. I would have to move straight towards my father if I were going to establish any contact with him before he died. Although my emotions screamed for distance from this whole scene, I hoped that, if I could control my feelings and move in instead of out, I might find other family members more available than in periods of calm. I also anticipated that everyone's tension levels would be high and that my family system's automatic tendency to close down under stress would be in full operation, as heralded by my mother.

During the seven weeks of my father's hospitalization in June and July of 1972, I made frequent visits to the hospital alone, at times when I knew other family members would not be there. I made a list of subjects that I wanted to bring up with my father. His approaching death headed the list as most important and most difficult. I also wanted to bring up unspoken issues between us, including my wedding and my entry into the field of social work after years of hearing my father rail against the social workers who had interfered with his own work in rehabilitation of the physically handicapped. I wanted to break through the taboo against discussing with my father the circumstances surrounding his retirement 10 years ago after a pitched battle for control of the business with his cousin. I wanted to know something about his mother and father and what his early family life had been like for him. I wanted to feel free to mention if I felt like it that my husband and I sometimes have loud arguments and disagreements (in spite of the family rule against open conflict) and that raising a neurologically impaired child has been difficult for us (in spite of the family rule against complaining). I wanted to get to know something about him as a person, and I wanted him to know something about me as the adult I sometimes am outside the family.

Before each visit to the hospital, I chose one of these topics and planned elaborately "casual" ways of getting to the topic via some tangential and less loaded topic. Before each visit, I also carefully prepared some remarks that alluded to his illness and approaching death, such as "I know that cobalt is terrible stuff but everyone hopes it will give you more time," or "Well, you are certainly the coolest member of the family; the rest are up the walls worrying about your dying." I further structured my visits by deciding ahead of time on the length of each visit so that I would not chicken out (I worked up to two hours before the seven weeks were up). Although such precautions sound silly, I don't believe I could have done anything without them. As it was, I once walked in and out of the hospital lobby three times before I could force myself to get on the elevator, and I usually had to go into the bathroom in my father's room and lecture myself in the mirror before I could actually bring up any of the issues I had prepared myself for. I am laughing now, but the face looking back at me in that mirror was not laughing when I said to myself: "You are 43 years old and you are afraid to mention your wedding to your father. Are you prepared to live with that?"

For his part, my father's resistance to discussion of emotional issues was as great as my own. He would start worrying about my "safety in this neighborhood" and try to chase me out almost as soon as I got there. He would launch into long discussions of safe topics like the children's doings, or would suggest that I hurry along to get home in time for dinner. When I said jokingly that if I didn't know I was his favorite daughter I'd think he was trying to get rid of me, he laughed and had to cut some of it out. When I persisted and brought up my issue, the length of his response was in inverse proportion to the importance of the issue. Thus, he responded at some length and detail to some of the subjects, but limited his response to allusions to his death to something like, "Well, we've all got to go sometime."

While we were not exactly having long, easy flowing conversations on important emotional issues, it was clear that my father and I were beginning to make contact on other than a superficial level. He always looked brighter and perkier by the time I left, and his greetings to me took on a warmer and livelier quality. Although the visits never got easy, they got easier, and I felt delighted after them. During this period, I frequently drove to see my mother and aunt at their home after leaving the hospital and found that, without any particularly elaborate plans, my relationship with my mother was almost automatically changing. I referred constantly to my father's dying in conversations with my mother, and I questioned my aunt about how my mother was doing at every opportunity. I also kept up a barrage of talk about my father's dying and my mother's well-being with my brother and sister-in-law and found my relationship with each of them changing too.

With my sister, who has lived in Europe for almost 10 years, it was a different story. I had written asking her for any thoughts she had about my long emotional distance from the family. This, of course, tweaked at her own distant position, and she fired back a bristling lecture by return mail as to how I might go about becoming more responsible regarding the family instead of leaving everything to my brother. This got to me; caught in the system again, I was not able to do anything but chat superficially or avoid her during a brief visit she made to see my father in the summer of 1972, during which time she complained to a mutual friend that I was a nuisance who always wanted to know what went on inside people and tell them what I thought, instead of letting things be.

After my father's release from the hospital in July 1972, he seemed to recover for a while. He gained weight and felt better than he had in weeks. My brother and I planned a three-generation birthday party in August, at my brother's house, for my father's, brother's, and nephew's birthdays. During the party, my father appeared depressed and apathetic and horrified the family by asking if the brand name on one of the presents was the name of a funeral home. There was stunned silence. I made some crack about his black humor, and the conversation moved quickly and nervously on. Again, he appeared better during September and October, improved in spirits, and there was some talk of my parents' going to Florida for the winter. However, during this time there was also a swelling on my father's abdomen and his memory started to fail.

In early November 1972, my father landed back in the hospital to check out his abdominal swelling. Having found little opportunity to speak to him alone since his last hospitalization, I made the same kind of plans as before to continue trying to talk with him. This time it was easier and I was much looser with him than I had ever been. On my first visit, he told me that they were going to operate in a few days to remove his kidney. I started to cry and said I was afraid he was going to die. He took my hand, wiped a tear from his eye, and we went on to have several hours of the best talking we've ever done. My father did a kind of life review, focusing mainly on the great satisfaction he had gotten from work. We went on, with some real ease, to many family topics, some of them elaborations on issues I had gingerly raised during his previous hospitalization, and he listened and responded to me in a new way. As I was leaving that night, he smiled at me and said, "You've grown up," and he used a pet name he had not used with me for almost 30 years. I cried all the way home. We had two more visits like this before his operation. At the last he announced that he now felt ready for surgery, unlike the summer, when he had been sure it would kill him. "And I'm ready for that possibility, too," he said.

On the day the operation was scheduled, my mother, brother, and I spent about four hours with my father before learning that the operation was cancelled and rescheduled for the following day. The next day, he was already in the operating room when we arrived, and my mother, brother, and I spent several hours in his room awaiting the results. I introduced dozens of family topics into the conversation, gathering information as we waited. Whenever I felt anxious about my father or sensed that they were, I would talk about him and the operation, or mutter about the "damned doctors who don't even let you know whether he's dead or alive." The report of the immediate outcome came in the form of my father being wheeled back into the room, semiconscious and groaning. When he had been put back to bed, we gathered around him. He opened his eyes and said, jokingly, about his groaning, "Pardon the symphony. I hope I'm on key." The doctors then reported their amazement at his strength and condition. The kidney was not cancer-ridden, as expected, but was swollen as the result of a congenital condition independent of the cancer, which was apparently still in temporary remission.

After his operation, my father remained in the hospital for several weeks, gaining in strength and spirits. We continued our talking during my visits to the hospital, although we both pulled back somewhat after the removal of the immediate threat of his death. His memory continued to fail, although there was no more of the disorientation in the present that had overtaken him several times before the operation. I felt confident enough that I planned to show the pictures of my wedding to the gathered clan at Thanksgiving or Christmas, as well as childhood movies that had not been shown for years because so many family members in them were dead. But here, relaxing my vigil after the strain of my father's operation, I was not quick enough to outwit the system. At Thanksgiving, my father was still in the hospital and my mother and aunt begged off on grounds of exhaustion. At Christmas, although my father was at home and had been doing well, they similarly begged off my brother's invitation to celebrate together. I think now, in retrospect, that, without realizing it, I got caught in the family's thing about "getting through the holidays." In fact, it was not until I wrote this paper that I realized how many of the family catastrophes have occurred on holidays and birthdays, triggered partially, perhaps, by the enormous tension engendered by our attempts to deny or suppress all unpleasantness on such occasions under the guise of protecting "the others." At any rate, my brother's family and mine got together at both Thanksgiving and Christmas and I had long, warm, open talks on each occasion with both my brother and my sister-in-law.

On Christmas day, 1972, when we called my parents from my brother's house, my mother informed us that my father had been in severe pain all day. It was a sudden turn for the worse and continued to occur for some part of most days thereafter. Mother reported sadly that two doctors had confirmed her fears that "the bone pain has begun," and the anxiety level went up throughout the family. My father was, once again, apathetic and listless. The family party idea I was toying with, to celebrate my parents' 45th wedding anniversary in February, seemed like a crazy idea as I sat in their living room in January, watching my father tune out and fade before our eyes. He no longer read or commented on television news, but spent most of the day sleeping and taking his medication for pain, for the kidney condition, and so on.

The Anniversary Party

Somewhat to my surprise (because I was again half caught in the system's probable reaction to my idea of celebration at such a time as outrageous), my brother agreed readily to my proposal that we arrange a surprise party for my parents' anniversary in February 1973. He agreed that it would have to be a surprise because otherwise they would veto it, and that Aunt Clara should also be "surprised" or she would object to the plan on their behalf. We decided to have the party at my parents' home, since no ruse would get them to go anywhere with my father in his present condition. After this conversation, my brother, who is an airline pilot, flew off for several days, leaving the arrangements to his wife, Mary, and me. Mary and I had a wonderful time planning the party. The rather simple resolution to curb my natural bossiness with her, and not to pay attention to hers with me, had wrought a dramatic change in our relationship, and I could no longer understand why I used to feel irritated with her in the past. Although in some ways she had become very much a part of our family system in the 17 years of her marriage to my brother and, in some cases, knew better than I what different relatives' reactions to each other were, she was also outside of it enough to be able and willing to move around in some parts of the system more freely than I could, after years of cutoff from many in the family. First, we agreed on the menu and divided responsibility for bringing the food and champagne. Then we made a list of every living family member whom we knew about, in my parents' generation and in ours, including a housekeeper of my long-dead aunt who had stayed in touch with my mother, and the husband and new wife of my mother's dead cousin. There were a number of people to be invited whom I had never met, and others — cousins, aunts, and uncles — whom I had not seen in almost 20 years.

Of eight siblings in my father's family, only he, an older brother, Pat, and the youngest sister, Meg, were still alive. Pat and Meg and their spouses were in Florida. Meg, the one who had attempted suicide years ago and had been only sporadically in touch with the family since, had been "too depressed to come to the phone" during my mother's last contact with them at Christmas. Mary agreed to put Meg and her husband in charge of seeing that Pat and his wife got up here from Florida. Aunt Meg, when she finally agreed to come to the phone, loved the idea of the party and agreed to press Pat (who was 84 years old) and his wife to come. Meanwhile, I called my mother's oldest sister, Sarah, in the midwestern convent where she resides and teaches, and told her that, although some of the family were afraid she might report the surprise to my mother, I knew she wouldn't and could she get permission from the convent to come. She swore herself to secrecy and said that, although it would be hard to get permission to come home so soon after Christmas, she would give it a good try and would let me know. Since she was so responsive, I wondered if she had any thoughts about the refusal of my Aunt Ellen to come, because it was the anniversary of her own wedding to my dead Uncle Tim, Mother's favorite brother. She said she would write to Ellen that very day.

My brother phoned my sister in London, urging her to try to come. She said she'd try. And so on through the list: cousins who hadn't been in touch with anyone in 20 years and an old aunt and her three unmarried daughters, all of whom had been long estranged. Most of them responded with apparent delight and said they'd come. Actually, when a cold snap hit New York a few days before the party, the elderly Florida contingent backed out. My aunt, the nun, had gotten permission to come, but had come down with the flu, as had my sister in London. Aunt Ellen didn't come or phone in any further excuse. Those who actually came were from the New York, Staten Island, Long Island, and New Jersey area, and they numbered almost 30 people, including us. All who didn't come, except Aunt Ellen, phoned during the party.

The party was a total surprise to my parents. The bell just kept ringing and new people kept appearing. When enough unexpected guests had arrived to make it impossible to pretend coincidence, we led them to the dining room where we had quietly set up the party table. There was, however, one slipup. My brother greeted me at the door with the news, "You'll never believe this, but Aunt Clara is out at a party." Aunt Clara almost never goes out on weekends, and we hadn't expected this. I found out where she was, attending her school principal's retirement party in a nearby hotel, and called her there. She was furious at me for not telling her. I said I couldn't understand why she didn't appreciate being spared the burden of this secret and the arrangements for the party. I told her I'd do my best to watch out for mother until she could get to the house. She replied, huffily, that it would be quite a while before she would get home, and we hung up. I immediately went all around the party telling everyone that Aunt Clara was furious and what should we do when she got here? When she finally appeared, I watched my sister-in-law Mary do what I used to do—argue with her about the situation—while I jokingly complained to her about taking so long to get home, and repeated my bewilderment at her lack of appreciation for all we'd done without bothering her. My husband told her he'd tried to convince us to tell her, but we wouldn't listen.

Toward the end of the evening, Aunt Clara sat down beside me and started telling me how hurt she had been at Aunt Ellen's withdrawal from the family since Uncle Tim's death. When Mary commented that Bobby, one of our long lost cousins there today, hadn't even attended her wedding, I said loudly, "*Bobby* didn't attend your wedding? *No* one in the family attended mine!" My Aunt Clara, who had been most angry at the time of my marriage, said cheerfully, "Well, I'd come if it were today." Thereupon, I called out to my husband that we should consider remarrying, to give the family a second chance to give us wedding presents.

At the opening of the anniversary presents, I gave a joking toast to my parents that ticked through, in reversals, a list of their attributes that used to bug me, but no longer did, "The rumor about my parents' getting divorced," I announced, "is not true. Mom complains a lot, but she's trying to take better care of Dad; and Dad hates to be waited on, especially by women, but he's trying to let her do it," etc., etc., to the accompaniment of much laughter from the family. I ended with the announcement that my brother, Jack, would now make a long, boring speech. Jack, not to be outdone, began, "For some reason, words have always failed me in the presence of my oldest sister. . . . " We laughed at each other and a 40-year-old battle was understood and buried, as my husband joined in with, "Gee Jack, I thought I was the only one who had trouble with all her talking."

Throughout the party, I tried to bring out into the open, in some way, the issue of my father's impending death, which was on everyone's mind, with comments like, "Well, Dad, they would all have come to your funeral, so why not to your party?" or, "Anniversary parties are more fun than wakes, don't you think so?" My father laughed and replied, "Especially for the victim," and I said, "I thought you'd see it that way, Dad." Of the several people in earshot, only the new wife, making her first acquaintance with the family, had a comment, "She's right, you know. You raised her good."

At this writing, in March 1973, one month after the anniversary party, my father is mysteriously doing well again. He has started painting again (his favorite hobby), for the first time since he got sick last May. He reads again with interest, and fumes at the news on TV. He is eating well and takes no more pain medication or kidney pills. Mother reports that he hasn't had any pain at all "in about a month." Clara attributes his remarkable improvement to the new eyeglasses he got "about a month ago," which have enabled him to read more.

Throughout the family, acquaintance is being renewed. My favorite first cousin called me to rehash the party and to suggest plans for future family reunions. My mother sent thank you notes to all and has received numerous replies.

Throughout this year, there has been a steady reduction of tension between my husband and me, and between us and our children. Our impaired child is doing very well again, after setbacks earlier this year. My insomnia has disappeared, along with the backaches, and I'm really enjoying my work again. Aunt Clara has accompanied us for the first time on visits to our son's special school and wants to do so again soon. I am feeling less overburdened, and my husband and I are planning our first weeklong vacation without the children in 12 years. I know there's still a lot to do, especially with my sister, but it doesn't seem nearly as anxiety-provoking as it did. And of course, I suppose I should mention that, although I still find doing family therapy to be difficult work, lately I don't find it as difficult to avoid taking sides emotionally within families.

Six weeks after I presented this paper, my father died. Subsequently, with varying degrees of "success," I have continued my efforts to have an adult personal relationship with my mother (who died in 1981), with my brother and sister, and with my Aunt Clara, who has become a major presence and support in my life.

Index